Labor and Employment Law

in

Indian Country

2022 Edition

Kaighn Smith, Jr.

Joel West Williams
Executive Editor

Native American Rights Fund
Boulder, Colorado

Drummond Woodsum MacMahon
Portland, Maine

NATIVE AMERICAN RIGHTS FUND
1506 Broadway
Boulder, Colorado 80302
303-447-8760 • Fax 303-443-7776 • www.narf.org

DRUMMOND WOODSUM MACMAHON
84 Marginal Way
Portland, Maine 04101
207-772-1941 • Fax 207-772-3627 • www.dwmlaw.com

Copyright © 2022 by Drummond Woodsum MacMahon

All Rights Reserved. With the exception of short excerpts used in reviews, no part of this publication may be reproduced or transmitted in any form or by any means, electronic or mechanical, including photocopy, recording, or any information storage or retrieval system, without permission in writing from the publisher.

ISBN: 978-0-9794099-6-7

The feather appearing on the cover and in the chapter headings is reproduced with permission from the Native American Rights Fund.

Copyedited by Ann Chapman and Esther Labrado, Drummond Woodsum MacMahon, Portland, Maine.

Design and production by Nicole Ochsenbein, Drummond Woodsum MacMahon, Portland, Maine.

Printed and bound by The Copy Center, Winthrop, Maine. Print production assistance by Port Printing Solutions, Cape Elizabeth, Maine.

While the author and publishers have endeavored to provide accurate, up-todate analysis of the law, this book is not intended as legal advice, and it should not be relied upon as such. Anyone in need of legal advice should consult with competent legal counsel.

Additional books may be ordered at www.narf.org and at www.dwmlaw.com.

For
Kaighn Smith, M.D. and Rev. Ann Robb Smith
(1928-2021)

Contents

Foreward, By John E. Echohawk xi
Preface xiii
Acknowledgments xix

1 Introduction: Historical Framework 1
   A. Early Federal Indian Policy Failures: Removal, Reservation, and Allotment 2
   B. The Indian New Deal: Reorganizing Tribal Governments 4
   C. The Indian Bad Deal: Termination Backlash 7
   D. The "Modern Era": Tribal Self-Determination 8
   E. Looking Forward 14

PART I:
THE FUNDAMENTAL PRINCIPLES OF TRIBAL SOVEREIGNTY UNDERLYING LABOR AND EMPLOYMENT RELATIONS IN INDIAN COUNTRY 19

2 Affirmative Tribal Sovereignty: Legal Bases for Tribal Authority over Labor and Employment Relations 21

   A. Introduction 21
   B. The Established Attributes of Inherent Tribal Sovereignty 22
   C. Tribal Authority Over Labor and Employment Relations 27
      1. Regulatory Authority 29
      2. Adjudicatory Authority 36
   D. Conclusion 37

3 Defensive Tribal Sovereignty: Barriers to State and Federal Authority Over Labor and Employment Relations in Indian Country 39

   A. Introduction 39
   B. Barriers to State Authority: Infringement and Preemption Doctrines 40
      1. The Infringement Barrier 41
      2. The Preemption Barrier 43
      3. Application of the Barriers 45

v

		C.	Barriers to Federal Authority: Federal Infringement 48
			1. Supreme Court Decisions Affecting Federal Infringement 49
			2. Varying Approaches to the Application of General Federal Labor and Employment Laws to Tribes and Tribal Enterprises 52
			a. Ninth, Second, and Sixth Circuits: Federal Law Applies Absent Interference with Treaty or "Purely Intramural Matter" 52
			b. Tenth and Eighth Circuits: If the Application of Federal Law Will Undermine Tribal Sovereignty, The Law Will Not Apply Absent a Clear Congressional Directive 56
			c. Seventh Circuit: Uncertainty 59
			d. D.C. Circuit: Degree of Infringement Affects Outcome ... 61
		D.	Deference to Tribal Court Authority: The Exhaustion Doctrine... 64
			1. The Roots and Elements of the Tribal Court Exhaustion Doctrine 64
			2. The Exhaustion Doctrine and Labor and Employment Disputes in Indian Country 69
		E.	Conclusion 78
4	DEFENSIVE TRIBAL SOVEREIGNTY: SOVEREIGN IMMUNITY AND TRIBAL EMPLOYMENT DISPUTES 81
		A.	Introduction 81
		B.	Sovereign Immunity: Basic Principles 82
		C.	Sovereign Immunity: Individual Capacity and *Ex Parte Young* Lawsuits 85
			1. Individual Capacity Lawsuits 86
			2. The *Ex Parte Young* Doctrine 88
		D.	Sovereign Immunity: Tribal Enterprises 90
			1. Sovereign Immunity and "Arms of Tribes" 93
			2. Tribal Gaming Enterprises and Sovereign Immunity................ 96
		E.	Waivers of Sovereign Immunity 97
			1. The Effect of "Sue and Be Sued" Clauses 99
			2. Arbitration Clauses and Contractual Waivers 102
			3. Forum Selection Clauses 104
		F.	Conclusion 105

PART II:
FEDERAL AUTHORITY AND LABOR AND EMPLOYMENT RELATIONS IN INDIAN COUNTRY 107

5   CIVIL RIGHTS AND TRIBAL EMPLOYMENT 109

    A. Introduction 109
    B. The Indian Civil Rights Act of 1968 110
        1. Non-Enforcement of ICRA in Federal Court 111
          a. *Dry Creek* Exception 113
        2. Tribal Court Enforcement of ICRA 114
    C. Federal Civil Rights Laws and Tribal Employment 116
        1. Federal Civil Rights Acts 116
        2. Federal Employment Discrimination Laws 121
        3. Exemptions of "Indian Tribes" Under Title VII and the ADA 122
        4. The Age Discrimination in Employment Act of 1967 126
        5. Federal Employment Discrimination Laws Tied to Federal Funding 129
    D. Conclusion 132

6   FEDERAL LAWS GOVERNING EMPLOYMENT TERMS AND CONDITIONS AND TRIBAL EMPLOYMENT 135

    A. Introduction 135
    B. Occupational Safety and Health Act 136
    C. Fair Labor Standards Act 140
    D. Family Medical Leave Act 144
    E. Employee Retirement Income Security Act 145
        1. Application to Tribal Enterprises Before 2006 Amendment 147
        2. Application to Tribal Enterprises After 2006 Amendment 149
    F. Other Laws 154
    G. Conclusion 155

7   THE NATIONAL LABOR RELATIONS ACT AND TRIBAL EMPLOYMENT 157

    A. Introduction 157
    B. Early NLRB Concerns 161
        1. Determining Whether a Tribal Enterprise is Part of Government 162
        2. Determining Whether the Government Exemption Extends to Tribal Entities Off-Reservation 165
    C. The NLRB's Change of Course: Indian Gaming 167

    D. The D.C. Circuit's Decision in *San Manuel* 170
    E. Tribal Authority Over On-Reservation Labor Relations: The Tenth Circuit's Decision in *Pueblo of San Juan* and the Sixth Circuit's Decision in *Little River Band of Ottawa Indians* 172
    F. Other Cases 177
        1. *Soaring Eagle Casino v. NLRB* and the Sixth Circuit Split 177
        2. The Ninth Circuit's Doubling Down on the *Coeur d'Alene Tribal Farm* Framework 178
        3. *Chickasaw Nation d/b/a Winstar World Casino*: The "Treaty Rights Exception" 179
    G. Conclusion 180

PART III:
TOWARD TRIBAL LABOR AND EMPLOYMENT LAW 183

8   DEVELOPING TRIBAL LAW: CIVIL RIGHTS AND EMPLOYMENT DISCRIMINATION 187

    A. Introduction 187
    B. Civil Rights Protections for Employees Under Tribal Law 192
        1. Navajo Nation 194
            a. The Navajo Bill of Rights: Protections for Government Employees 194
                i.   The Navajo Sovereign Immunity Act: Waiver of Immunity for Money Damages 195
                ii. Sovereign Immunity: Civil Rights Claims Versus Employment Claims 197
            b. Navajo Nation Preference in Employment Act: "Just Cause" and Other Protections for Public and Private Sector Employees 200
        2. Mashantucket Pequot Tribal Nation 202
            a. Mashantucket Pequot Civil Rights Code: Protections for Government Employees 202
            b. Mashantucket Pequot Employee Review Code: "Just Cause" and Procedural Protections for Nation Employees 204
        3. Mohegan Tribe 209
            a. Protections for Mohegan Government Employees Under ICRA 209
            b. Mohegan Discriminatory Employment Practices Ordinance 209
        4. Little River Band of Ottawa Indians 213
            a. Protections for Tribal Government Employees Under the Constitution of the Little River Band of Ottawa Indians . 213

			b.	Fair Employment Practices Code of the Little River Band of Ottawa Indians 214
		5.		Squaxin Island Tribe 217
		6.		California Tribes with Employment Laws Required by Compact 220
	C.	Civil Rights in the Employment Setting: Selected Substantive Issues 222
		1.		Sovereign Immunity Issues and the Scope of Governmental Action Under Tribal Civil Rights Codes 222
		2.		Due Process and Government Employment 226
		3.		Freedom of Speech and Governmental Employment 230
		4.		Burden of Proof Issues in Discrimination Cases 234
	D.	Conclusion 238

9 DEVELOPING TRIBAL LAW: UNIONS AND COLLECTIVE BARGAINING 241

	A.	Introduction 241
	B.	Tribal Governance of Labor Relations: Public and Private Sectors 246
	C.	Tribal Laws Governing Unions and Collective Bargaining Before *San Manuel* 248
		1. Right-to-Work Laws 249
		2. The Tribal Labor Relations Ordinance in California 251
	D.	Tribal Laws Governing Unions and Collective Bargaining After *San Manuel* 255
		1. Mashantucket Pequot Tribal Nation 255
		2. Little River Band of Ottawa Indians 257
		3. Other Tribes 259
	E.	Significant Policy Issues in Tribal Labor Organization Laws 262
		1. Key Decisions Facing Tribes in Enacting Labor Relations Laws 262
		2. Union Solicitation 263
		3. Elections 265
		4. Employee Rights, Union and Employer Duties, Unfair Labor Practices, and Dispute Resolutions 266

			a.	Employee Rights 267
			b.	Union Duties, Violations of Which May Be Unfair Labor Practices 268
			c.	Employer Duties, Violations of Which May Be Unfair Labor Practices 268
		5.		Strikes and Lock-Outs 269
		6.		Collective Bargaining Impasse Procedures 271

	7. Picketing 272
	8. "Right to Work," "Free Riders," and "Fair Share" 274
	F. Conclusion 276

10　DEVELOPING TRIBAL LAW: NATIVE AMERICAN EMPLOYMENT PREFERENCES IN TRANSITION 279

    A. Introduction 279
    B. The Legal Basis for Indian Employment Preference Laws 280
        1. *Morton v. Mancari*: "An employment criterion reasonably designed to further the cause of Indian self-government" 280
        2. The Inherent Authority of Tribes to Enact Indian or Tribal Member Employment Preference Laws 283
    C. Tribal Member Preference *Versus* Indian Preference: Contradictions and Controversy 285
        1. Inconsistent Federal Statutes and Regulations 286
        2. Challenges to Tribal Member Preferences: Do They Constitute Unlawful Discrimination on the Basis of "National Origin"? 288
    D. Conclusion: Challenges Past and Present 297

11　CONCLUSION 301

Appendix A: Variables Affecting the Governance of Labor and Employment Relations in Indian Country 307

Appendix B: Federal Labor and Employment Laws of General Application 321

Appendix C: Labor and Employment Laws of Indian Tribes 325

Index 367

Foreword

For more than 50 years, the Native American Rights Fund has undertaken its work based on the premise that the best hope for the survival of Native Americans is the maintenance and development of tribal governments. The inherent sovereign powers to hold land, regulate activities on those lands, and command the respect of other governments are essential to the concept of nationhood. Much of the Native American Rights Fund's work has been about ensuring that this concept endures as a reality for Tribal Nations.

Labor and Employment Law in Indian Country represents a natural outgrowth of the work of the Tribal Supreme Court Project, a joint project of the Native American Rights Fund and the National Congress of American Indians. In recent decades, Indian tribes have faced a series of challenges to their sovereign authority and have suffered a number of critical losses in the United States Supreme Court. Recognizing that the interests of tribes generally rise and fall together, tribal leaders established the Tribal Supreme Court Project in 2001 to foster greater coordination among tribes in their legal advocacy. This included combining and coordinating the resources of NARF, NCAI, Indian law professors, Indian law attorneys, and Supreme Court practitioners to monitor cases that could affect the future of tribal sovereignty and undertaking a strategic effort to protect tribal interests in those cases.

In 2007, despite the best efforts of the Project, Indian tribes experienced a significant setback in *San Manuel v. NLRB,* when the U.S. Court of Appeals for the D.C. Circuit affirmed a decision by the National Labor Relations Board (NLRB) that reversed thirty years of solid precedent. Until *San Manuel,* the NLRB had treated Indian tribes like the states and the federal government, which are exempt from the National Labor Relations Act (NLRA). The D.C. Circuit held that a gaming enterprise, owned and operated by the San Manuel Band, was an "employer" within the scope of the National Labor Relations Act and therefore subject to union organizing and related coercive authority of the NLRB in accord with that Act.

San Manuel was a wake-up call. For the first time, the NLRB could apply the provisions of the NLRA — the federal law governing labor organizations and collective bargaining *in the private sector* — to a *tribal government's* on-reservation enterprise. Previously, the NLRB had treated Indian tribes and their enterprises in the same way that it treated other governments and their enterprises: as *public sector* entities, which were excluded from the Act. As a result of the *San Manuel* decision, we recognized that tribal governments were not exercising — or did not know they could fully exercise — their sovereign authority to enact tribal laws regulating labor and employment relations. And the law, like nature, abhors a vacuum. It was in this context that the seeds for *Labor and Employment Law in Indian Country* were sown and grew into a collaborative effort between NARF, the oldest and largest non-profit Indian law firm in the country, and Drummond Woodsum, a firm with a respected national Indian law practice.

As Executive Director of NARF, I am honored to bear witness to the publication of the second edition of Kaighn Smith, Jr.'s *Labor and Employment Law in Indian Country*. We at NARF have worked hard to develop tribal law, to provide legal references, and to supply information for tribes who are developing their own laws. One of the most important components of this book has been its comprehensive look at existing tribal labor and employment laws and its reference to tribal case law. The book provides important examples of how tribes are expanding their own labor and employment laws and adjudicating these issues in tribal courts. Additionally, an up-to-date Appendix offers a collection of tribal labor and employment laws and is an unparalleled resource for anyone practicing in this field.

Much of the practice of the law involves the balancing of precedent with the modern needs of the people — and, in Indian law, doing so while keeping tribal sovereignty intact. The importance of *Labor and Employment Law in Indian Country* is that it discusses labor and employment law from its historical perspective, explains the complex web of laws guiding the field, and leaves the reader with a fuller understanding of labor and employment in the tribal context. By setting the topic in this structure, the book truly is able to convey the depth of challenges tribal governments currently face in the labor and employment arena while keeping a keen eye on its future development.

John E. Echohawk

Preface

Eleven years after the first edition of this book, labor and employment law in Indian country remains a critical battleground for tribal sovereignty. This is particularly so with respect to the application of federal laws targeting a host of "employers" that are entirely silent about whether they apply to Indian tribes. Federal agencies continue efforts to enforce those laws against tribes, tribes continue to resist such intrusions on the grounds of tribal sovereignty (some pointing to their own laws covering the rights at issue and some not), the federal courts continue to be split on what rule governs the outcome (whether Congress's silence prevents the intrusion or not), and the Supreme Court has yet to resolve that split.

The most recent example of such a silent federal law is Congress's first law to address the historic COVID-19 pandemic, the Families First Coronavirus Response Act. Congress (once again) failed to mention Indian tribes. The Act requires "covered employers" to provide paid leave to employees who face specific hardships while granting offsetting tax credits to those employers. Certain "private entities" and "public agencies" fall within the Act's definition of "covered employer," but one struggles in vain to determine whether Indian tribes do so. And the Department of Labor provided no guidance.

Over the last decade, the Supreme Court's federal Indian law decisions signal cautious optimism for the future of tribal sovereignty. Even while the Supreme Court has issued important decisions supporting tribal sovereignty in recent years, its composition has also shifted significantly, raising the question of whether that trend will continue.

* * *

We have updated this book with a decade's worth of new developments, but have maintained its basic structure. This reflects the fact that the landscape of the law remains largely unchanged.

This edition, as with the first, is intended to serve as a resource for anyone concerned with labor and employment relations in Indian country. It is also a practical guide for anyone interested in how basic principles of federal Indian law operate in a specific field. It should be of use to elected officials of tribal governments; managers and officers of tribal enterprises; human resources staff; attorneys representing Indian tribes and their enterprises; attorneys representing non-Indian interests doing business in Indian country; students of Indian law; and judges in tribal, state, and federal courts.

A central theme and driving force in this area of the law is *competition for power*, particularly the emerging competition between tribal governments and federal agencies over the regulation of labor and employment in Indian country. This competition has been playing out in the lower federal courts for decades and, surprisingly, has yet to be addressed by the United States Supreme Court or clarified by Congress. At stake is the very operation of tribal sovereignty, not only as a means for regulating labor and employment relations in Indian country in accord with the unique values of sovereign Native nations, but as a defense to federal authorities seeking to impose federal law standards on Indian country employment relations without a clear mandate to do so.

Perceptions of a gap in the baseline protections for workers in Indian country puts enormous pressure on this dynamic. If tribal governments fail to provide legally enforceable rights to employees who suffer discrimination or unfair working conditions, federal authorities will continue to make the case that they must have power to fill that gap with federal law.

This book unabashedly argues that Indian tribes must affirmatively exercise authority over labor and employment relations in Indian country as a means to protect tribal self-determination. This is necessary on two levels: to provide fairness to employees and to stave off federal intrusions. Thus, this book is designed not only to be a tool for dealing with practical legal problems, but as a resource for tribal decision-makers to examine and shore up legal infrastructures for tribal self-government at a critical juncture in history.

The area of labor and employment law in Indian country lends itself particularly well to the application of root principles of tribal sovereignty. Controversies in this area invoke a wide spectrum of federal Indian common law doctrines, ranging from the inherent power of Indian tribes to regulate economic relations within their territories, to limitations on federal agency powers to impose authority from the outside, to questions of whether a particular tribal entity or officer may be immune from suit. This book, therefore, combines a study of fundamental principles of tribal sovereignty with a practical application of those principles to labor and employment relations.

A book dealing with issues of tribal sovereignty cannot do justice to the subject without providing the reader with a historical framework for the development of federal Indian law. After all, Indian law may best be viewed as the product of a difficult — sometimes tragic, sometimes heroic — history, and less a product of rational doctrinal development.[1] Thus, our introductory chapter (Chapter 1) seeks to provide the necessary historical context for understanding the conflicting policies that inhere in this area of the law.

In structuring the presentation of the second edition of *Labor and Employment Law in Indian Country,* we retain the three distinct parts of the book with substantial updating to account for new legal developments. Part I sets out the legal principles that provide the basis for Indian tribes to exercise authority over labor and employment relations within their territories. Chapter 2 examines the basis for tribes to exercise what may best be termed "affirmative sovereignty": the authority to regulate economic activity and to adjudicate labor and employment disputes arising in Indian country. Chapters 3 and 4 then examine the principles underlying what may be termed "defensive sovereignty": legal barriers used to defend against asserted authority. Chapter 3 addresses the barriers to assertions of authority by the state and federal governments over labor and employment relations in Indian country. Chapter 4 looks at the operation of tribal sovereign immunity as a barrier to the authority of courts to resolve labor and employment disputes.

In Part II, we turn to the continuing problem of the application of federal laws to labor and employment relations in Indian country. Chapter 5 addresses federal civil rights laws affecting employment relations, including the Indian Civil Rights Act, Title VII of the Civil Rights Act of 1964, the Americans with Disabilities Act, and the Age Discrimination in Employment Act. Chapter 6 looks at how a variety of federal labor and employment laws of general application have been applied to Indian tribes and their enterprises in Indian country: the

---

[1]*See generally,* Charles F. Wilkinson, American Indians, Time, and the Law: Native Societies in a Modern Constitutional Democracy (1987).

Occupational Safety and Health Act, the Fair Labor Standards Act, the Family Medical Leave Act, and the Employee Retirement Income Security Act. Chapter 7 then turns to the ongoing controversy over the application of the National Labor Relations Act to collective bargaining and labor organizations in Indian country after failed efforts at a legislative fix.

Part III changes gears to survey what tribes are doing with respect to the enactment, implementation, and judicial enforcement of their own labor and employment laws. Chapter 8 examines a variety of tribal laws that provide remedies for civil rights violations and employment discrimination. Chapter 9 looks at laws governing collective bargaining and unions. Finally, Chapter 10 addresses tribal employment preference laws and the clarity that recent federal court decisions have brought to tribal governmental authority in this sphere. The book concludes with broad observations about the course of the law and the Supreme Court's likely resolution of power struggles between federal agencies and tribes over the application of federal labor and employment laws in Indian country.

Appendix A presents, in summary fashion, the legal standards governing jurisdiction by Indian tribes, states, and federal agencies with respect to labor and employment relations in Indian country. These standards vary depending upon the parties involved and the location of the employment relationship. Appendix B is a summary of a variety of federal labor and employment laws of general application, what matters they regulate, the federal agencies that administer them, and the current status of their application to Indian tribes and tribal enterprises. Finally, Appendix C provides an updated comprehensive guide to the wide variety of existing tribal laws regulating labor and employment relations within Indian country. These include employment discrimination codes, tribal employee retirement income security acts, safety and health provisions, wages and overtime regulations, and many others.

*＊＊

This second edition of the book continues to be a call to action. It identifies an imperative for Indian tribes: "govern or be governed." Tribes have significant opportunities to enact and implement their own laws to govern labor and employment relations within their territories, consistent with their particular values and policy priorities.

Making those policy determinations is the essence of tribal sovereignty. The great irony in this field of law is that the failure of Indian tribes to exercise such sovereignty places their sovereignty at risk. For failure to act leaves the perceived "gap" for outsiders — in particular, federal agencies — to try to fill. If tribal self-determination is a worthy goal, this book is a tool for its preservation in the arena of labor and employment relations where it continues to be particularly vulnerable.

Acknowledgments

This second edition of *Labor and Employment Law in Indian Country* is the result of an ongoing unique collaborative effort by the author, the Executive Editor, and our colleagues at Drummond Woodsum and the Native American Rights Fund. We remain indebted to those we listed in the 2011 edition, but we are now the beneficiaries of the efforts of a host of other colleagues.

As was the case with the first edition, this project would not have been possible without the unwavering support of the president and managing director at Drummond Woodsum, this time, Ben Marcus (and his recent successor, Toby Dilworth), and the firm's Board of Directors. Their continued openness to "unconventional" endeavors by their colleagues — here, a significant commitment of time by the author — is extraordinary. Likewise, we commend NARF's Board of Directors for its commitment to the development of Indian law and its willingness to dedicate valuable attorney time and resources to this effort.

This book could not have been published without the invaluable assistance of staff and colleagues at Drummond and NARF. Those at Drummond include, Nicki Ochsenbein, who labored tirelessly to perfect the layout and design of the book; Ann Chapman, who took on the tedious task of line-editing the entire manuscript; and Esther Labrado, who provided invaluable editing for Chapter 9. We are also grateful to Drummond librarians, Louise Jensen and Alexandra Carpenter for updating voluminous authorities and to Chena Immel, Donna Swiderek, and Terri Wilber. Corey Hinton, Dan Rose, and Campbell Badger, the core of Drummond's Tribal Nations Employment Practice, also provided unwavering support at every turn.

We are equally indebted to NARF's law clerks and support staff, including Mauda Moran, Anne Lucke, Zachary Topkis, Logan Cooper and Liliana Elliot. In particular, we are grateful to Logan for his work on updating Appendix C, scouring additional sources for tribal laws governing labor and employment relations. Zachary and Liliana did additional legal research that was extraordinarily helpful in bringing this edition up-to-date.

A number of attorneys (you know who you are) were asked and volunteered their time to review different chapters of the book and their input greatly improved this work. One area of special contribution was the helpful comments from tribal attorneys to update the tribal laws discussed in Part III: Paul Spruhan (Navajo), Linda Acampora (Mohegan), Marietta Anderson (Mashantucket Pequot), and Rebecca Liebing (Little River Band of Ottawa Indians) all provided very helpful substantive comments and edits.

Of course, the mistakes are all ours.

                                      Kaighn Smith, Jr.
                                      Joel West Williams

1

INTRODUCTION: HISTORICAL FRAMEWORK

The law of labor and employment relations in Indian country is situated in the broader field of federal Indian law, a field that is deeply influenced by history. The themes of this book necessarily reflect that history. It is a history marked by the ever-shifting policies of a "dominant power," the United States, in dealing with the "Indian problem."[1] Federal Indian policies have, at times, sought to destroy tribal governments, while at other times worked to preserve them. Whether tribal sovereignty will prevail to control labor and employment relations in Indian country or be swept aside by federal authority has yet to play out. The outcome may reflect the "bright side" of the history of American Indian affairs, by shoring up tribal sovereignty, or its "dark side," by undermining that sovereignty. This book looks to the bright side but soberly situates its subject within a troubling historical context.[2]

---

[1] *See generally* ROBERT T. ANDERSON, SARAH KRAKOFF, AND BETHANY BURGER, AMERICAN INDIAN LAW, CASES AND COMMENTARY, 77 (2020); BROOKINGS INSTITUTION, THE PROBLEM OF INDIAN ADMINISTRATION (1928).

[2] The term "Indian tribe" will be used throughout this book to refer to federally recognized Indian tribes. Because this is a book about the law, and the governing law of the United States Supreme Court and Congress employs the term "Indian tribe," consistency of terms warrants the employment of that term throughout. This is not without recognition that the term "Native nation" or "Indigenous nation" may more accurately describe the sovereign Indigenous governments of the territory now known as the United States. For the same reason, the terms "Indian" or "Indians" are used throughout this book to refer to the enrolled members of federally recognized Indian tribes. This is not without recognition that it would be more accurate to refer to individuals who hold such status with specific reference to their tribal citizenship.

A. Early Federal Indian Policy Failures: Removal, Reservation, and Allotment

The early federal policies of removal, reservation, and allotment sought to minimize the power of Indian tribes — the power of *sovereignty*, recognized in some of the first Indian law decisions of the Supreme Court — first by expelling tribes from their lands, and then by attempting to assimilate them into American civilization. The removal policy reflected the country's initial effort to cause the disappearance of Indian tribes,[3] an "out-of-sight, out-of-mind" approach toward Indian people.[4] Implemented between 1817 and 1848, the removal policy "dealt with" the established Eastern tribes, in particular the so-called Five Civilized Tribes — the Cherokee, Creek, Seminole, Chickasaw, and Choctaw — by forcefully removing them to lands further west.[5]

Next, during the reservation period, from 1848 to 1886, the federal government concentrated tribes on reservations "where they could be groomed for civilization under the control of federal Indian agents."[6] It was during this policy era that Congress eliminated treaty-making, thereby ending any notion that the U.S. would deal with tribes as co-equal sovereigns.[7] Henceforth, Congress would address Indian tribes through enacting bicameral legislation.

---

[3]George Washington, like other "Founding Fathers," believed in the notion of the "disappearing Indian," writing:
> [I]t is like driving the Wild Beasts of the Forest which will return as soon as the pursuit is at an end and fall perhaps on those that are left there; when the gradual extension of our Settlements will as certainly cause the Savage as the Wolf to retire; both being beast of prey tho' they differ in shape.

Letter from George Washington to James Duane (September 7, 1783), in DOCUMENTS OF THE UNITED STATES INDIAN POLICY 1, 2 (Frances P. Prucha ed., 3d ed., 2000) (quoted in ANDERSON ET AL., *supra* note 1, at 48).

[4]*See generally* ANDERSON ET AL., *supra* note 1, at 49-51. For a fuller discussion of the removal policy and its impacts upon Indian tribes and Indian people, *see* F. COHEN, HANDBOOK OF FEDERAL INDIAN LAW § 1.03[4][a] (2005 ed.) (hereinafter COHEN).

[5]*See* ANDERSON ET AL., *supra* note 1, at 49-51.

[6]*See* ANDERSON ET AL., *supra* note 1, at 77.

[7]*See* ANDERSON ET AL., *supra* note 1, at 77. For a fuller discussion of the reservation system, *see* COHEN, *supra* note 4, at § 1.03[6][a].

Finally, with the General Allotment (Dawes) Act in 1887, Congress launched the allotment and assimilation era, when the government opened Indian lands to non-Indian settlement.[8] This policy was accompanied by a concerted effort to eliminate tribal governments and assimilate Indian people into the American mainstream by turning them into farmers and sending native children to boarding schools in an effort to destroy their cultural identities.[9]

The allotment and assimilation policy resulted in the impoverishment of Indian people, loss of their land base, and the destruction of their cultural identities. In 1928, the federal government abandoned the assimilation and allotment policy, and subsequently, in an about-face, embraced the continued existence of Indian tribes as governments pursuant to the sweeping Indian Reorganization Act of 1934.[10] As described below, apart from the relatively short-lived "termination era" of the 1950s, the fundamental policies of the IRA, built upon some of the earliest Supreme Court holdings recognizing the sovereign authority of Indian tribes, endure. But history shows that the legal ground upon which Indian tribes must relate to the "dominant power" has never been secure.

---

[8] 25 U.S.C. § 336, *repealed by* Indian Reorganization Act of 1934, 25 U.S.C. § 5101 (2018).

[9] Under the General Allotment Act, reservations were broken up into individual land holdings, many of which were sold off to non-Indians. Allotments reduced Indian land from 138 million acres to 48 million acres. Allotments also left many reservations in a "checkerboard" state with non-Indian and individual Indian landholdings interspersed with lands owned by the tribe or held in trust by the United States, all within the original reservation boundaries. ANDERSON ET AL., *supra* note 1, at 77, 88, 103-11. For a fuller discussion of the Allotment and Assimilation Era and its impacts upon Indian tribes and Indian people, *see* COHEN, *supra* note 4, at § 1.04.

[10] 25 U.S.C. § 5101 (2018). Congressional enactments in the early 1900s reflected a growing awareness that tribal self-determination could be worthy of protection. For instance, in 1908, Congress enacted the Buy Indian Act, requiring federal government providers of services to tribes to attempt to purchase Indian-produced goods and services in order to spur reservation economic development. Buy Indian Act, 25 U.S.C. § 47 (2018).

B. The Indian New Deal: Reorganizing Tribal Governments

In 1928, the Institute for Government Research, the predecessor to the modern day Brookings Institution, released the so-called *Meriam Report*, named after its editor, Lewis Meriam.[11] Sponsored and initiated by the federal government, Meriam's research examined contemporary life for tribal communities nationwide. It conveyed a particularly troubling portrait of the poverty, health risks, weak economic prospects, and lack of access to education in Indian country. The report roundly criticized long-entrenched "policies adopted by the government in dealing with the Indians . . . which, if long continued, would tend to pauperize any race."[12]

In response to the *Meriam Report*'s findings, Congress passed the Leavitt Act in 1932, authorizing the Secretary of the Interior to release tribes from any debts incurred from federal mismanagement of resources and construction projects on Indian lands.[13] Additionally, Congress passed the Johnson-O'Malley Act of 1934, which allocated funding to state and local governments that could better provide urgently needed educational and medical services to Indians.[14] After clearing past debts and establishing emergency services, Congress set about enacting legislation aimed at fostering tribal self-governance and lessening direct federal control over tribes.

The centerpiece of this effort was the Indian Reorganization Act of 1934 (IRA).[15] Aptly termed the "Indian New Deal," the IRA provided a congressionally-sanctioned vehicle for tribes to develop their own forms of government under constitutions approved by the Department of the Interior, and to manage their tribal resources to a de-

---

[11] LEWIS MERIAM ET AL., INSTITUTE FOR GOVERNMENT RESEARCH, THE PROBLEM OF INDIAN ADMINISTRATION (1928).

[12] *Id.* at 7.

[13] 25 U.S.C. §386(a) (2018).

[14] 25 U.S.C. § 5342 (2018).

[15] 25 U.S.C. § 5101 (2018).

gree previously unseen.[16] The IRA repealed the General Allotment Act,[17] thereby terminating programs and policies that the *Meriam Report* had determined were poisoning tribal societies.[18] The IRA refocused federal policy toward acknowledging tribal governments, cultural pluralism, and Indian self-determination in an effort to build Indian economies at a time when the country as a whole was suffering through the Great Depression.

Two laws in particular aimed to stimulate tribal economic development by integrating reservation markets with the larger economy: the Indian Arts and Crafts Act in 1935 (IACA)[19] and the Indian Mineral Leasing Act of 1938 (IMLA).[20] The IACA established the Indian Arts and Crafts Board, a division of the Interior Department, "to promote the economic welfare of Indian tribes and the Indian wards of the Government through the development [and marketing] of Indian arts and crafts."[21] The Board conducted market research, recommended loans to establish Native-run craft businesses, oversaw trademarks to ensure the authenticity of Native-made products, and negotiated contracts for their sale.[22] It also protected tribal businesses from attempts by non-Indians to market counterfeit crafts, purported to be Native American.[23] In short, the Board cultivated genuine market demand for Indian art and crafts, and assisted Indian people to produce and sell such goods on a larger scale than they had previously achieved.

---

[16]*Id.*

[17]*Id.*

[18]*See* LEWIS MERIAM ET AL., *supra* note 11.

[19]Pub. L. No. 74-355, 49 Stat. 891; 25 U.S.C. § 305 (2018); 18 U.S.C. §§ 1158-1159 (2018) (penalizes counterfeiting of the Indian Arts and Crafts Board's trademark).

[20]25 U.S.C. § 396(a) (2018).

[21]Pub. L. No. 74-355, 49 Stat. 891.

[22]*Id.*

[23]*Id.*

Similarly, with the passage of IMLA, the federal government assisted tribes in leveraging their natural resources for economic development.[24] The Act permitted tribal governments to enter into leasing agreements with large-scale oil, gas, and mining companies, subject to approval by the Secretary of the Interior.[25] Prior to IMLA's enactment, tribes had been precluded from executing such leases. While the Act has since been criticized for allowing mining corporations to derive huge profits at the expense of tribal governments (notwithstanding Interior Department oversight of the leases), policymakers at the time saw the Act as another positive step in the direction of tribal economic development through self-government.

It was during the Indian New Deal that Felix Cohen, serving as Assistant Solicitor at the Interior Department, wrote his seminal treatise on federal Indian law.[26] Cohen's treatise identified federal Indian law as a field, setting forth the foundational principles of tribal sovereignty, the federal government's trust responsibility to tribes, and the barriers to state authority as originally established by the Supreme Court.[27] Official acceptance of tribal sovereignty and self-determination advocated by Cohen and his Interior Department colleagues, however, was not without its dissenters. Indeed, Department of Justice lawyers at the time did not take kindly to Cohen's work when they learned, contrary to their assumptions, that it did not support their defense against land cases brought by tribes.[28] As a result, the Department of Justice fired Cohen from supervising staff involved in the treatise, and this forced the Interior Department alone to support and publish the treatise.[29]

---

[24] 25 U.S.C. § 396(a) (2018).

[25] *Id.*

[26] *See* COHEN, *supra* note 4, at xxvi.

[27] *See* ANDERSON ET AL., *supra* note 1, at 131.

[28] *See id.*

[29] *See id.*

C. The Indian Bad Deal: Termination Backlash

The short but infamous termination policy of the 1950s was largely shaped by one man, Dillon Myer. Myer served as the head of the War Relocation Authority during the 1940s. In that role, he gained recognition for defusing a politically charged and potentially embarrassing problem: the relocation of thousands of Japanese-Americans, who had been forcibly segregated at internment camps during World War II. Myer quietly initiated and executed a program to disperse interned persons across the major American cities.[30] President Truman took note of his success and appointed him to head the Interior Department's Bureau of Indian Affairs (BIA).[31]

Consistent with his approach to relocating the interned Japanese-Americans, Myer's BIA launched an urban relocation aimed at tribal members. Under this policy, over 100,000 tribal citizens were removed to urban centers and isolated from their communities, ostensibly to facilitate assimilation into the majority culture.[32] Myer's approach was compatible with undercurrents then taking charge of federal Indian policy. Indeed, just before he took office at the BIA in 1950, the Bureau had begun to selectively terminate the federal trust relationship with certain tribes in the name of federal cost-savings, but in flagrant violation of treaty provisions.[33]

In contrast to Felix Cohen and his Interior Department colleagues, Myer and his administration did not accept the view that the federal government had a trust responsibility to support Indian tribes and their self-determination. Rather, he saw this as a hindrance to the inevitable assimilation of segregated communities.[34] Myer outlined plans to rid the federal government of the oversight of most programs

---

[30] *See* ANDERSON ET AL., *supra* note 1, at 139; Jennie R. Roe, *Forced Relocation and Assimilation: Dillon Myer and the Native American*, 13 (2) AMERASIA J. 161, 162 (1986-87).

[31] *Id.*

[32] *Id.*

[33] *Id.* at 164.

[34] *Id.* at 163.

benefiting tribes by transferring them to states or to the tribes themselves.

These plans served as basis of the formal federal termination policy, set forth in House Concurrent Resolution 108, which was passed in 1953 and was implemented after Myer left office.[35] The policy resulted in the legislative termination of federal recognition of twelve Indian tribes between 1953 and 1962, and the administrative termination of countless other tribes. Many of these tribes fought, or are still fighting, long battles to reinstate federal recognition and restoration of their lands.[36]

D. The "Modern Era": Tribal Self-Determination

Ultimately, the programs of the termination era failed, just as the allotment and assimilation era policies had before them. These policies did nothing to improve the standard of living for Native Americans living on reservations or relocated to urban centers away from their homelands and tribal communities. Presidents Johnson and Nixon were forced to acknowledge these failures, and just as President Roosevelt's Indian New Deal cast aside the allotment era policies, President Nixon renounced the termination policy and called for Congress to begin a new era of tribal self-determination.[37] Congress worked to reverse the effects of Myer's termination and relocation programs, and rehabilitated the Indian New Deal efforts to foster tribal self-sufficiency through economic development programs and formal support for tribal sovereignty.

The era of tribal self-determination began somewhat indirectly through President Johnson's War on Poverty programs established in the early 1960s.[38] By far, the most important of these programs for Na-

---

[35]*Id.* at 164.

[36]*Id.*

[37]Lyndon B. Johnson, President, Special Message to Congress on the Problems of the American Indian: The Forgotten American (Mar. 6, 1968); Richard M. Nixon, President, Special Message to Congress on Indian Affairs (July 8, 1970).

[38]Lyndon B. Johnson, President, Special Message to Congress: Proposal for a Nationwide War on the Sources of Poverty (Mar. 16, 1964).

tive Americans was the Economic Opportunity Act of 1964, which provided funding to rebuild communities from within through the creation of legal services, Project Headstart, and the Community Action Program.[39] Anthropologist Phileo Nash, then head of the BIA, pressured the Johnson administration to make poverty funds directly available to Indian tribes.[40] Because of Nash's advocacy, tribes were able to bypass the BIA and apply directly for funding for housing, education, job training, and legal services programs. Moreover, direct funding allowed tribal governments the first opportunity in decades to oversee the administration of rehabilitation programs and to hire community members for reservation program implementation.

This opportunity, plus the support of a growing civil rights movement aimed at reclaiming fundamental principles of tribal sovereignty, cemented the change in government policy toward tribal self-determination. Grassroots movements for Native American nationalism further inspired the amendment of the Judicial Code in 1966,[41] giving tribes the right to sue in federal court if the U.S. Attorney failed to commence actions on their behalf. The Indian Civil Rights Act of 1968 (ICRA),[42] announced individual rights within Indian country similar to those secured under the Bill of Rights and the Fourteenth Amendment to the U.S. Constitution. The Supreme Court later clarified that, with the exception of habeas corpus relief, such rights would be within the exclusive authority of tribal forums to define and enforce.[43]

Tribal self-determination became formal policy for the federal government when President Nixon delivered a special message to Congress in July 1970, calling on legislators to "break decisively with the past and to create the conditions for a new era in which the Indian

---

[39] Pub. L. No. 88-452, 78 Stat. 508 (repealed 1981).

[40] LORETTA FOWLER, THE COLUMBIA GUIDE TO AMERICAN INDIANS OF THE GREAT PLAINS 130 (2003).

[41] Pub. L. No. 89-635, 80 Stat. 880; 28 U.S.C. § 1362 (2018).

[42] 25 U.S.C. §§ 1301-1303 (2018).

[43] *See Santa Clara Pueblo v. Martinez*, 436 U.S. 49, 55-56 (1978).

future is determined by Indian acts and Indian decisions."⁴⁴ President Nixon called the termination policies "clearly harmful" and called for the restoration of the "special relationship between Indians and the Federal government" grounded in the "solemn obligations which have been entered into by the United States Government," not by some "act of generosity toward a disadvantaged people that [the federal government] can discontinue . . . whenever it sees fit."⁴⁵ In his address, President Nixon reminded Congress that future Indian policy must take into consideration that "Indians have often surrendered claims to vast tracts of land and have accepted life on government reservations" in exchange for federal support promising to allow tribes to maintain their communities and enjoy "a standard of living comparable to that of other Americans."⁴⁶ In the decade following President Nixon's address, Congress responded by enacting the seminal pieces of self-determination legislation that continue to influence tribal economic development and self-government today.

Few laws since the IRA have been as sweeping in their impact as the Indian Self-Determination and Education Assistance Act of 1975 (ISDEAA).⁴⁷ The ISDEAA's goal is to promote tribal self-government by supporting tribal control of Indian education and economic development.⁴⁸

Title I of the ISDEAA substituted tribal governments for BIA agencies as the providers of direct social and educational services to tribal citizens in Indian country.⁴⁹ Under the new system, tribes became eligible for block grants from federal agencies to construct and administer basic social infrastructures, such as schools and hospitals.

---

⁴⁴Richard M. Nixon, President, Special Message to Congress on Indian Affairs (July 8, 1970).

⁴⁵*Id.*

⁴⁶*Id.*

⁴⁷Pub. L. No. 93-638, 88 Stat. 2203.

⁴⁸*Id.*

⁴⁹*Id.*

Title II of the ISDEAA stands in stark contrast to the reservation-era boarding school policies under which Indian children were sent away to boarding schools to be "cleansed" of their language and cultural ways.[50]

In addition to the ISDEAA, Congress passed other major legislation beginning in the early 1970s to establish special financing programs for tribal businesses and natural resource development.[51] One such statute, the Indian Financing Act of 1974 (IFA), granted the Secretary of the Interior the authority to insure and guarantee private loans made to Native American-owned small businesses.[52] The purpose of the IFA is to "provide capital . . . to help develop and utilize Indian resources, both physical and human, to a point where the Indians will fully exercise responsibility for the utilization and management of their own resources and where they will enjoy a standard of living from their own productive efforts comparable to that enjoyed by non-Indians in neighboring communities."[53] These legislative efforts revealed Congress's commitment to restore and support tribes as providers of governmental services to their citizens and thereby eliminate the wide disparity in economic conditions between Indian and non-Indian communities.

Beginning in the early 1980s, Congress implemented a new strategy to spur economic development in Indian country that continues today: using the tax and finance systems to integrate reservation economies into the national economy, and promoting manufacturing suitable to the isolated rural areas where the federal government established reservations. An early product of this strategy was the Indian Mineral Development Act of 1982 (IMDA),[54] which gave tribes far more au-

---

[50]*See generally* ANDERSON, ET AL., *supra* note 1, at 123-125 (discussing Indian boarding schools).

[51]43 U.S.C. §§ 1601-1642 (2018).

[52]Pub. L. No. 93-262, 88 Stat. 77; 25 U.S.C. §§ 1451-1453 (2018).

[53]25 U.S.C. § 1451 (2018).

[54]25 U.S.C. §§ 2101-2108 (2018).

tonomy in governing resource development in Indian country than its "New Deal" counterpart discussed above.[55]

Perhaps the most significant legislation affecting tribal self-determination in the "modern era" of federal Indian policy is the Indian Gaming Regulatory Act of 1988 (IGRA).[56] Congress passed IGRA in the wake of *California v. Cabazon Band of Mission Indians*, the Supreme Court decision confirming that tribes have inherent authority to raise governmental revenues through gaming operations within their reservations, and holding that California could not regulate gaming activity that was not prohibited as a matter of state criminal law or public policy.[57] Through IGRA, Congress preempted the field of gaming in Indian country in order to "promot[e] tribal economic development, self-sufficiency and strong tribal governments"[58] and established the National Indian Gaming Commission to regulate and enforce key parts of the law.

By 2018, thirty years after the passage of IGRA, 252 tribal governments operated 488 gaming facilities in 28 states.[59] Gross revenues from Indian gaming nationwide amounted to $33.8. billion in 2018, and related hotels, restaurants, and entertainment businesses generated

---

[55] While the New Deal-era IMLA had helped tribes develop their natural resource industries, tribes were placed in a subordinate status to the federal government. In the wake of independent studies in the 1970s showing that tribal mineral leases were severely mismanaged and undervalued by the federal government, tribal governments lobbied for autonomy in dealing with their mineral leases. *See* RICHARD KEITH YOUNG, THE UTE INDIANS OF COLORADO IN THE TWENTIETH CENTURY, 206 (1997). This effort was led by the Council of Energy Resource Tribes (CERT), an organization formed by tribal governments to bolster tribal control over natural resources management and development. *See id.* In 1982, Congress finally acted by passing the IMDA, which removed the federal paternalism of the IMLA, and confirmed the authority of tribes to negotiate and manage mineral exploitation within Indian country.

[56] 25 U.S.C. §§ 2701-2721 (2018).

[57] *California v. Cabazon Band of Mission Indians,* 480 U.S. 202 (1987).

[58] 25 U.S.C. § 2701(1) (2018).

[59] *2019 Annual Report*, NATIONAL INDIAN GAMING ASSOCIATION, 18 (July 1, 2019), https://online.flippingbook.com/view/317287/.

an additional $5.3 billion in gross revenues.[60] Indian gaming facilities employed 229,253 people, with an additional 75,423 employed in related hotels, restaurants, and other enterprises.[61]

Other "modern era" acts of Congress designed to support tribal self-government and economic development include:

- The Indian Tribal Government Tax Status Act of 1982, giving tribes the same tax-exempt status as state and local governments in their issuance of bonds;[62] and

- The Omnibus Reconciliation Act of 1993, providing a tax credit for businesses that hire Native Americans or their spouses on or near an Indian reservation;[63]

- The Community Renewal Tax Relief Act of 2000[64] and the Indian Reservation Economic Investment Act,[65] providing tax credits for investors and businesses participating in reservation economic development;

- The Community Development Banking and Financial Institutions Act of 1994, authorizing the federal government to provide financial incentives to small town banks in low-income communities (including tribes) engaged in community development financing programs;[66]

- The U.S. Department of Agriculture Reorganization Act of 1994, granting the Rural Utilities Service authority to provide 100percent guarantees for loans to qualified elec-

---

[60]*Id.*

[61]*Id* at 29.

[62]Pub. L. No. 97-473, 96 Stat. 2605.

[63]Pub. L. No. 103-66, 107 Stat. 312.

[64]Pub. L. No. 106-554, 114 Stat. 2763.

[65]S. 558, 107th Cong. § 2 (2001).

[66]Pub. L. No. 103-325, 180 Stat. 2163.

tric and telecommunications companies engaged in infrastructure projects in rural communities;[67]

- The Native American Housing and Self-Determination Act of 1996, improving the development and affordability of housing for Indian people through tribal government housing authorities;[68] and

- The HUBZone Act and the Taxpayer Relief Act of 1997, setting up geographic areas in which small businesses could qualify for preferences in federal contracting[69] and federal funds could support rural development.[70]

In sum, congressional action in the modern era has been marked by recognition of the benefits of sustaining and promoting strong tribal governments and economic development across Indian country. As President Nixon announced in 1970, this commitment is grounded in the federal government's legal obligation to deal fairly with tribes and to right the wrongs of the past.

E. Looking Forward

Given the federal government's inconsistent treatment of Indian tribes since the founding of the Republic, why would any observer of history put stock in the stability of the modern era of Indian self-determination? Although Congress and the Executive Branch have appeared firmly committed to tribal self-government and independence, uncertainties within the Supreme Court of the United States leave much in the air.

---

[67] Pub. L. No. 103-354, 108 Stat. 3178.

[68] 25 U.S.C. §§4101-4212 (2018).

[69] *See* HUBZone Act, Pub. L. No. 106-554, 111 Stat. 2592.

[70] *See* Taxpayer Relief Act, Pub. L. No. 105-34, 111 Stat. 788.

In *Kiowa Tribe of Oklahoma v. Manufacturing Technologies, Inc.*,⁷¹ for instance, a majority of the justices reluctantly upheld the doctrine of tribal sovereign immunity but signaled policy concerns to Congress:

> At one time, the doctrine of tribal immunity from suit might have been thought necessary to protect nascent tribal governments from encroachments by States. In our interdependent and mobile society, however, tribal immunity extends beyond what is needed to safeguard tribal self-governance. This is evident when tribes take part in the Nation's commerce. Tribal enterprises now include ski resorts, gambling, and sales of cigarettes to non-Indians. . . . In this economic context, immunity can harm those who are unaware that they are dealing with a tribe, who do not know of tribal immunity, or who have no choice in the matter, as in the case of tort victims.⁷²

This statement reflects a great irony: the very economic success of the modern era policies of tribal self-determination threaten to undermine its foundation of tribal sovereignty.

This irony is playing out in contemporary legal battles over the regulation of labor and employment relations in Indian country. Thanks in large part to IGRA, many tribes are successful participants in the nation's economy, generating hundreds of thousands of jobs for their tribal citizens and non-tribal citizens alike.⁷³ However, these very successes have generated increased scrutiny of tribes' labor and employment practices by outsiders. Long-assumed tribal freedoms from external intrusions into the regulation of reservation employment, grounded in the established law of tribal self-determination, are now

---

⁷¹*Kiowa Tribe of Oklahoma v. Manufacturing Technologies, Inc.*, 523 U.S. 751 (1998).

⁷²*Id.* at 758.

⁷³*2019 Annual Report*, NATIONAL INDIAN GAMING ASSOCIATION, 29 (July 1, 2019) (estimating that in 2018, Indian gaming facilities employed 229,353 people), https://online.flippingbook.com/view/317287/.

being called into question by federal agencies and lawmakers. In this environment, the Crow Nation Court of Appeals has observed, "If . . . tribe[s] do not take steps to enact appropriate waivers of sovereign immunity [for employment claims], we believe it is only a question of when Congress will do it for us."[74]

In 2004, the National Labor Relations Board (NLRB) sent shock waves across Indian country when it reversed thirty years of precedent and determined that enterprises owned and operated by tribal governments located on reservations are subject to labor organizing laws under the National Labor Relations Act, a law that expressly excludes all other governments.[75] A three-judge panel of the United States Court of Appeals for the District of Columbia Circuit unanimously affirmed the decision, stating that a tribe's gaming operations—the target of the union activity at issue—were not sufficiently at the core of tribal sovereignty to warrant protection from the requirements of the Act.[76] Two other courts later followed suit,[77] but not all courts are in sync; so the law remains in a state of flux calling for resolution by the Supreme Court.[78]

Thus, the era of tribal self-determination is vulnerable to the vagaries of judicial decisions. To many outsiders, Indian tribes appear well-assimilated on the American economic fast-track, with non-tribal citizens flocking to their reservations to take up employment.[79] Arguments are made that tribal sovereignty allows tribes to "get away

---

[74] *One Hundred and Eight Employees of the Crow Tribe of Indians v. Crow Tribe of Indians*, No. 89-320, ¶ 112, (Crow Ct. App. Nov. 21, 2001) available at: http://www.tribal-institute.org/opinions/2001.NACT.0000001.htm.

[75] *San Manuel Indian Bingo & Casino*, 341 N.L.R.B. 1055 (2004).

[76] *See San Manuel Indian Bingo & Casino v. NLRB*, 475 F.3d 1306, 1315 (D.C. Cir. 2007).

[77] *Pauma v. Nat'l Lab. Rels. Bd.*, 888 F.3d 1066 (9th Cir. 2018); *Soaring Eagle Casino & Resort v. N.L.R.B.*, 791 F.3d 648 (6th Cir. 2015); *Nat'l Lab. Rels. Bd. v. Little River Band of Ottawa Indians Tribal Gov't*, 788 F.3d 537 (6th Cir. 2015).

[78] *See* Chapter 7.

[79] *See Indian Casinos*, TIME MAGAZINE (Dec. 16, 2002).

with" violating workers' rights.[80] And federal agencies like the NLRB, responsible for enforcing federal labor and employment laws, are not shy about suing tribes or their enterprises for alleged violations of those laws.[81] Because a number of federal court decisions hold that tribes cannot claim sovereign immunity from suits brought by the federal government, these suits go forward.[82]

The paramount legal question then becomes whether Congress intended any given labor and employment law to apply to Indian tribes or their enterprises when it failed to indicate its intent, one way or the other, on the face of the law. Federal courts differ in their approaches to this question. Some look at whether application of the law would undermine a tribe's treaty right or governance of a "purely intramural matter."[83] Others suggest that, if application of the law would infringe on established attributes of tribal sovereignty, courts must presume that Congress intended not to apply the law to tribes.[84] It is surprising that the Supreme Court has yet to resolve this uncertainty.

As discussed in the next chapters, Indian tribes have ample support in established federal law to regulate labor and employment relations within Indian country. However, the outcome of unfolding power struggles over that regulatory authority, mostly between the federal regulatory agencies and tribes, will have a lasting effect upon

---

[80] *See, e.g.,* Joel Millman, *House Advantage: Indian Casinos Win By Partly Avoiding Costly Labor Rules, Sovereignty Helps Shield Them from Unions and Lawsuits, Can Limit Worker Benefits---Some Say It Beats Field Work*, WALL ST. J., May 7, 2002, at 1; Donna Leinwand, *Seminoles Fight Sexual Harassment Suit*, MIAMI HERALD, Feb. 12, 1996, at A1.

[81] *See, e.g., Menominee Tribal Enterprises v. Solis,* 601 F.3d 669 (7th Cir. 2010); *EEOC v. Karuk Tribe Hous. Auth.*, 260 F.3d 1071 (9th Cir. 2001); *EEOC v. Fond du Lac Heavy Equip. & Constr. Co.*, 986 F.2d 246 (8th Cir. 1993); *Reich v. Mashantucket Sand & Gravel*, 95 F.3d 174 (2d Cir. 1996); *Donovan v. Coeur d' Alene Tribal Farm*, 751 F.2d 1113 (9th Cir. 1985); *Donovan v. Navajo Forest Products*, 692 F.2d 709 (10th Cir. 1982).

[82] *See, e.g., Quileute Indian Tribe v. Babbitt*, 18 F.3d 1456, 1459-60 (9th Cir. 1994).

[83] *See, e.g., Reich v. Mashantucket Sand & Gravel*, 95 F.3d 174 (2d Cir. 1996); *Donovan v. Coeur d'Alene Tribal Farm*, 751 F.2d 1113 (9th Cir.1985).

[84] *See, e.g., EEOC v. Fond du Lac Heavy Equip. & Constr. Co.*, 986 F.2d 246 (8th Cir.1993); *Donovan v. Navajo Forest Products*, 692 F.2d 709 (10th Cir. 1982).

the law governing tribal sovereignty. In this setting, Indian tribes must proceed with care if they want the law to develop in a manner that strengthens, rather than weakens, their sovereign authority.

PART I

THE FUNDAMENTAL PRINCIPLES OF TRIBAL SOVEREIGNTY UNDERLYING LABOR AND EMPLOYMENT RELATIONS IN INDIAN COUNTRY

The exercise of tribal sovereignty may be "affirmative," in the sense that it provides the legal basis for Indian tribes to govern individuals and entities engaged in activities on Indian lands. It may also be used in a "defensive" manner; that is, to set up barriers to the imposition of external authority upon Indian tribes or their enterprises, or to prevent external authority from supplanting the regulatory authority of tribes. The law of labor and employment relations in Indian country involves all of these elements of tribal sovereignty.

The following three chapters set forth the fundamental principles of tribal sovereignty that guide the governance of labor and employment relations in Indian country. The starting foundation, the legal basis for Indian tribes to exercise affirmative sovereignty in this area, is provided in Chapter 2. Next, Chapter 3 examines the law that protects tribes from interference by state or federal authority. Finally, Chapter 4 explores the operation of tribal sovereign immunity as a barrier to lawsuits that might be brought under state, federal, and tribal laws to address labor and employment disputes.

2

AFFIRMATIVE TRIBAL SOVEREIGNTY: LEGAL BASES FOR TRIBAL AUTHORITY OVER LABOR AND EMPLOYMENT RELATIONS

A. Introduction

This chapter examines the law surrounding the sovereign authority of Indian tribes to regulate labor and employment relations within their lands.[1] For some tribes, this authority may be constrained by particular treaty provisions or federal statutes. The focus here is on the application of general principles of Indian law. The issue of tribal authority over nonmembers is explored in some detail.

---

[1] Throughout this book, the terms "Indian lands," "Indian territory," and the like refer to lands over which Indian tribes exercise governmental authority that are within the boundaries of any Indian reservation; land held in trust by the United States for the benefit of any Indian tribe or tribal citizen; and land held by an Indian tribe or tribal citizen subject to restrictions against alienation. This is consistent with Congress's definition of Indian lands under IGRA. *See* 25 U.S.C. §2703(4) (2018). Generically, all such lands are referred to as "Indian country," lands within which tribes exercise their inherent authority as tribal governments. *See Oklahoma Tax Comm'n v. Citizen Band Potawatomi Indian Tribe*, 498 U.S. 505, 511 (1991). As a result of the General Allotment Act of 1887, and the federal policy of assimilation during the same period (discussed in Chapter 1), most reservations that had been set aside for Indian tribes by treaty, statute, or executive order became so-called checkerboard in their land ownership configurations. Individual parcels within the exterior boundaries of any given reservation were variously owned in fee by non-tribal citizens or entities, individual tribal citizens, and Indian tribes, and other parcels were held in trust or restricted status by the United States for the benefit of individual tribal citizens or an Indian tribe.

B. The Established Attributes of Inherent Tribal Sovereignty

While the legal roots of tribal sovereignty in American law are to be found in some of the earliest decisions of the Supreme Court[2] and some of the first enactments of Congress,[3] the modern era of tribal sovereignty (one might even say the very field of federal Indian law) first took shape in the 1930s when the nation woke up to the colossal failures of the government to deal equitably with tribes. Much of the scholarship underlying the body of law that is now referred to as "Indian law" can be traced to Felix Cohen, who served in the Solicitor's Office at the Department of the Interior in the 1930s and 1940s.

In October 1934, shortly after the enactment of the Indian Reorganization Act (IRA), then Interior Solicitor Nathan Margold, under the guidance of Cohen, issued an opinion, entitled *Powers of Indian Tribes*, to describe the sovereign authority of tribes acknowledged by federal law. Margold looked at "the whole body of tribal powers which courts and Congress alike have recognized as properly wielded by Indian tribes, whether by virtue of specific statutory grants of power or by virtue of the original sovereignty of the tribe insofar as such sovereignty has not been curtailed by restrictive legislation or surrendered by treaties."[4] He wrote:

> Perhaps the most basic principle in all of Indian law . . . is the principle that *those powers which are lawfully vested in an Indian tribe are not, in general, delegated powers granted by express acts of Congress,*

---

[2]*See, e.g., Johnson v. McIntosh*, 21 U.S. 543 (1823); *Cherokee Nation v. Georgia*, 30 U.S. 1 (1831); *Worcester v. Georgia*, 31 U.S. 515 (1832).

[3]*See, e.g.*, Indian Trade and Non-Intercourse Act of 1790, Pub. L. No. 1-33, 1 Stat. 137-138, *codified as amended*, 25 U.S.C. § 177 (2018).

[4]*Powers of Indian Tribes,* 55 INTERIOR DEC. 14, 46 (1934). *See generally Arizona Public Service Co. v. Office of Navajo Labor Relations*, No. A-CV-08-87; 17 Indian L. Rptr. 6105; 6 Nav. R. 246 (Nav. Sup. Ct. 1990) (discussing Margold opinion in delineating inherent powers of Navajo Nation).

> *but rather inherent powers of a limited sovereignty which has never been extinguished.*[5]

Solicitor Margold went on to list the well-established attributes of the "inherent powers of a limited sovereignty," which he enumerated to include:

1. The power to adopt a form of government, to create various offices and to prescribe the duties thereof...

2. To define conditions of membership within the tribe...

3. To regulate the domestic relations of its members...

4. To prescribe rules of inheritance...

5. To levy dues, fees or taxes upon the members of the tribe and upon nonmembers residing or doing business of any sort within the reservation...

6. To remove or to exclude from the limits of the reservation nonmembers of the tribe... and to prescribe appropriate rules and regulations governing such removal and exclusion, and governing the conditions under which nonmembers of the tribe may come upon tribal land or have dealings with tribal members...

7. To regulate the use and disposition of all property within the jurisdiction of the tribe and to make public expenditures for the benefit of the tribe out of tribal funds...

8. To administer justice with respect to all disputes and offenses of or among the members of the tribe....[6]

---

[5] *Powers of Indian Tribes,* 55 INTERIOR DEC. 14, 19 (1934).

[6] *Id.* at 65-66.

In 1941, Felix Cohen published his famous *Handbook of Federal Indian Law*, incorporating *verbatim* these bedrock principles of tribal sovereignty.[7] Cohen's treatise, now in its fifth edition, is the most widely cited authority in the field.[8]

In 1978, eight years after President Nixon announced the "modern era" of Indian self-determination and with Congress fully committed to it,[9] the Supreme Court affirmed these principles of tribal sovereignty. In *United States v. Wheeler*,[10] the Court wrote:

> The powers of Indian tribes are, in general, *inherent powers of a limited sovereignty which has never been extinguished*....
>
> Indian tribes are, of course, no longer possessed of the full attributes of sovereignty. Their incorporation within the territory of the United States, and their acceptance of its protection, necessarily divested them of some aspects of the sovereignty which they had previously exercised. By specific treaty provision they yielded up other sovereign powers; by statute, in the exercise of its plenary control, Congress has removed still others.
>
> But our cases recognize that the Indian tribes have not given up their full sovereignty. [They] are a good deal more than private, voluntary

---

[7] *See* F. COHEN, HANDBOOK OF FEDERAL INDIAN LAW § 1.03[4][a] (2005 ed.).

[8] *See, e.g., Nevada v. Hicks*, 533 U.S. 353, 383-85 n.5 (2001) (citing the treatise); *Nat'l Farmers Union Ins. Cos. v. Crow Tribe of Indians*, 471 U.S. 845, 854 n.16 (1985) (same); *Iowa Mut. Ins. v. LaPlante*, 480 U.S. 9, 18 n.9 (1987) (same).

[9] *See* Chapter 1, Section D.

[10] *United States v. Wheeler*, 435 U.S. 313 (1978) (holding that prosecution of a Navajo tribal member defendant under Navajo criminal law after conviction under federal law would not violate the defendant's constitutional protection against double jeopardy because the prosecution under Navajo law involved action by a separate sovereign).

> organizations. The sovereignty that the Indian tribes retain is of a unique and limited character. It exists only at the sufferance of Congress and is subject to complete defeasance. But until Congress acts, the tribes retain their existing sovereign powers. In sum, Indian tribes still possess those aspects of sovereignty not withdrawn by treaty or statute, or by implication as a necessary result of their dependent status.[11]

The Supreme Court consistently reaffirms that the source of an Indian tribe's sovereignty lies in its historical status as a government, pre-existing the United States.[12]

How can Indian tribes lose their inherent sovereign powers? This is a question pervading the ability of tribes to exercise affirmative tribal sovereignty over labor and employment relations in Indian country. As the Court made clear in *Wheeler,* tribes retain all of their existing sovereign powers "not withdrawn by treaty or statute." The United States Constitution vests Congress with "plenary and exclusive" authority over Indian tribes.[13] That is why Congress has power to "withdraw" attributes of tribal sovereignty. But, in a separate case, the Court also said that tribal powers may be "withdrawn . . . by implication as a necessary result of [Indian tribes'] dependent status" – more specifically, when the exercise of tribal sovereignty would be incompatible with the "overriding interests of the National Government."[14]

---

[11]*Id.* at 322-23 (citations, quotations, and footnote omitted).

[12]*See, e.g., Michigan v. Bay Mills Indian Cmty.*, 572 U.S. 782, 788 (2014); *Puerto Rico v. Sanchez Valle,* 579 U.S. 59, 70 (2016). *See generally,* REST., LAW OF AMERICAN INDIANS (Tent. Draft No. 2, Mar. 13, 2018) §20.

[13]*United States v. Lara,* 541 U.S. 193, 200 (2004).

[14]*Washington v. Confederated Tribes of Colville Indian Reservation,* 447 U.S. 134, 153 (1980). *See also* REST., LAW OF AMERICAN INDIANS (Tent. Draft No. 2, Mar. 13, 2018) §34 ("Indian tribes retain authority to regulate the conduct of nonmembers on Indian lands, except when a federal statute divests an Indian tribe of that authority or when tribal authority conflicts with an overriding national interest"). The Court's recent pronouncements about the means by which tribes may lose their inherent sovereign powers do not include loss "by necessary implication of their dependent sta-

Given the Constitution's allocation of power over Indian affairs to Congress, not to the Court, it may be questioned whether the Court can divest tribes of their sovereign powers.[15] Against the backdrop of Congressional enactments leaving little doubt that Congress intended to eliminate any dueling exercise of tribal sovereignty,[16] the Court has found tribes to have lost the authority to: (1) engage in "direct commercial or governmental relations with foreign nations"; (2) arrest and prosecute non-Indians of the United States for crimes committed on the reservation; and (3) alienate tribal lands to non-Indians without federal oversight.[17] Congress can readily restore an attribute of tribal sovereignty rendered dormant by the Supreme Court in this manner.[18]

The Supreme Court has consistently held that the attributes of inherent tribal sovereignty are well-protected from diminishment.[19]

---

tus," only by express Congressional enactment. *See Puerto Rico v. Sanchez Valle*, 579 U.S. at 70 ("unless and until Congress withdraws a tribal power . . . the Indian community retains that authority in its earliest form"); *Michigan v. Bay Mills Indian Community*, 572 U.S. 782, 788-790 (2014) ("unless and until Congress acts, the tribes retain their historic sovereign authority").

[15]*See generally* Matthew L. M. Fletcher, *Statutory Divestiture of Tribal Sovereignty*, 64 FED. LAW. 38, 40-42 (April, 2017).

[16]*See, e.g., Window Rock Unified School District v. Reeves*, 861 F.3d 894, 900 n.6 (9th Cir. 2017) (observing that the Court's decision in *Oliphant v. Suquamish Indian Tribe*, 435 U.S. 191 (1978), holding that tribes' inherent authority to prosecute crimes against non-Indians arising within Indian country had been "implicitly divested," rested on the Court's conclusion "that relevant legislation and treaties at the time required this outcome.").

[17]*Wheeler*, 435 U.S. at 326; *accord Nat'l Farmers Union Ins. Cos. v. Crow Tribe of Indians*, 471 U.S. 845, 853 n.14 (1985) (quoting *Wheeler*, 435 U.S. 313).

[18]*See United States v. Lara*, 541 U.S. 193, 199-207 (2004).

[19]The doctrines protecting tribal sovereignty from diminishment without a clear Congressional directive have their roots in the Constitution's Indian Commerce Clause, U.S. CONST. art. I, § 8, cl. 3, and "the unique trust relationship between the United States and the Indians," which itself derives from the federal government's plenary power over Indian affairs. *County of Oneida v. Oneida Indian Nation*, 470 U.S. 226, 247 (1985). *See also Morton v. Mancari*, 417 U.S. 535, 551-53 (1974); *Penobscot Nation v. Fellencer*, 164 F.3d 706, 709 (1st Cir. 1999) (citations and quotations omitted).

First, apart from the rare instances in which the Court has found tribal sovereignty to be incompatible with Congress's enactments furthering "overriding national interests," the sovereign powers of tribes remain fully intact unless *clearly* divested by Congress.[20] Second, absent a clear directive from Congress, tribal powers are generally shielded from state intrusion.[21] Third, they remain intact even if not affirmatively exercised by a tribe.[22] Finally, any ambiguity about what Congress might intend with respect to the diminishment of an attribute of tribal sovereignty must be resolved by the courts to protect and uphold the tribal power in jeopardy.[23]

C. Tribal Authority Over Labor and Employment Relations

The authority of tribes to regulate labor and employment relations within Indian country derives from the specific attributes of their inherent sovereignty as enumerated by Solicitor Margold in 1934. The

---

[20]*Michigan v. Bay Mills Indian Cmty.*, 572 U.S. at 790; *Wheeler*, 435 U.S. at 322; *Merrion v. Jicarilla Apache Tribe*, 455 U.S. 130, 140 (1982).

[21]*See* Chapter 3, Section B.

[22]A tribe's "sovereign power, even when unexercised, is an enduring presence . . . and will remain intact unless surrendered in unmistakable terms."*Merrion v. Jicarilla Apache Tribe*, 455 U.S. 130, 148 (1982). *See also Segundo v. City of Rancho Mirage*, 813 F.2d 1387, 1393 (9th Cir. 1987) (failure of a tribe to legislate in an area of inherent sovereignty, such as land use regulation, "does not constitute a relinquishment of its authority to do so"); *Bottomly v. Passamaquoddy Tribe*, 599 F.2d 1061, 1065-66 (1st Cir. 1979) ("The mere passage of time with its erosion of the full exercise of sovereign powers of a tribal government cannot constitute an implicit divestiture").

[23]*See Bay Mills Indian Cmty.*, 572 U.S. at 2031-32; *White Mountain Apache Tribe v. Bracker*, 448 U.S. 136, 143-44 (1980); *California v. Cabazon Band of Mission Indians*, 480 U.S. 202, 217-20 (1987); *Three Affiliated Tribes of Fort Berthhold Reservation v. Wold Eng'ring*, 476 U.S. 877, 890, 892 (1986). For the application of this rule in the employment setting, *see NLRB v. Pueblo of San Juan*, 276 F.3d 1186, 1195 (10th Cir. 2002) (en banc) ("[i]n the absence of clear evidence of congressional intent . . . , federal law will not be read as stripping tribes of their retained sovereign authority to pass right-to-work laws and be governed by them"); *EEOC v. Fond du Lac Heavy Equip. and Constr. Co.*, 986 F.2d 246, 249 (8th Cir. 1993); *EEOC v. Cherokee Nation*, 871 F.2d 937, 939 (10th Cir. 1989); *Penobscot Nation v. Fellencer*, 164 F.3d 706, 709 (1st Cir. 1999).

Supreme Court has recognized a number of such attributes affirming that authority. For example, the Court has held that tribes have the "power to make their own substantive law in internal matters, and to enforce that law in their own forums."[24] Further, the Court has said that tribal courts are "appropriate forums for the exclusive adjudication of [reservation] disputes affecting important personal and property interests of both Indians and non-Indians" within the reservations.[25]

The Court has also recognized that tribes have the "power . . . to raise revenues to pay for the costs of government"[26] — a power directly related to the creation of economic and employment opportunities on their reservations. Finally, the Court has affirmed that tribes have the "power to exclude non-Indians from Indian lands,"[27] which "necessarily includes the lesser power to place conditions on entry, on continued presence, or on reservation conduct."[28]

---

[24] *Santa Clara Pueblo v. Martinez*, 436 U.S. 49, 55-56 (1978).

[25] *Id.* at 65 (footnote and citation omitted). Earlier in the opinion, the Court stated: "[I]n matters involving commercial and domestic relations, subjecting a dispute arising on the reservation to a forum other than the one they have established for themselves may undermine the authority of the tribal court and hence infringe on the right of the Indians to govern themselves." 436 U.S. at 59 (citations, quotations, and footnote omitted).

[26] *See Merrion v. Jicarilla Apache Tribe*, 455 U.S. 130, 144 (1982). In *California v. Cabazon Band of Mission Indians*, the Supreme Court confirmed that this power includes the authority to generate government revenues through reservation gaming operations, free from state regulation, so long as the state where the gaming activity is located does not prohibit all such gaming as a matter of criminal law and public policy. 480 U.S. 202, 211, 216-22 (1986). *See also Indian Country, U.S.A., Inc. v. Oklahoma ex. rel. Oklahoma Tax Comm'n*, 829 F.2d 967, 983 (10th Cir. 1987) (no state jurisdiction over gaming management company operating bingo facility for tribe). Congress reinforced this attribute of tribal sovereignty through its enactment of the comprehensive Indian Gaming Regulatory Act in 1988, 25 U.S.C. §§ 2701-2721 (2018). *See* 25 U.S.C. § 2701(5) (2018) ("Indian tribes have the exclusive right to regulate gaming activity on Indian lands if the gaming activity is not specifically prohibited by Federal law and is conducted within a State which does not, as a matter of criminal law and public policy, prohibit such gaming activity").

[27] *Merrion v. Jicarilla Apache Tribe*, 455 U.S. 130, 141 (1982).

[28] *Id.* at 144. The Navajo Supreme Court, explaining the right to exclude set forth in its 1868 treaty with the United States, has said that "[i]t . . . means that the benefits of

1. Regulatory Authority

It is well-established that tribes have inherent "power to make their own substantive law in internal matters."[29] This includes matters "involving commercial relations" affecting tribal members.[30] But what is the scope of such authority? Any tribe may have, within its reservation or trust lands, tribal and non-tribal members working for the tribe itself, for the tribe's enterprises, for enterprises owned or operated by tribal members, or for enterprises owned or operated by nonmembers. Since tribes have inherent authority to govern relations among and between their members (or citizens) within their territories,[31] it follows

---

the treaty lands, including employment or the fruits of industry, solely belong to the Navajo people" with others admitted to share in those benefits according to the terms of the Navajo Nation. *Arizona Public Service Co. v. Office of Navajo Labor Relations*, No. A-CV-08-87; 17 Indian L. Rptr. 6105, 6106; 6 Nav. R. 246 (Nav. Sup. Ct. 1990) (discussing Margold opinion in delineating inherent powers of Navajo Nation). *See also Cedar Unified School District v. Navajo Nation Labor Comm'n*, No. SC-CV-53-06, slip op., No. SC-CV-54-06, slip op. at ¶¶ 27-28 (Nav. Sup. Ct. 2007) available at www.tribal-institute.org/opinions/2007.NANN.0000018.htm (last visited Jan. 4, 2021) (power of Navajo Nation to exclude nonmembers supports its regulatory authority over employment relations of on-reservation school district owned and operated by the State of Arizona).

[29]The Supreme Court has consistently recognized the "traditional understanding" that each tribe is "a distinct political society, separated from others, capable of managing its own affairs and governing itself."*United States v. Lara*, 541 U.S. 193, 204-05 (2004) (quoting *Cherokee Nation v. Georgia*, 30 U.S. 1, 12-13 (1831)). *See also Santa Clara Pueblo v. Martinez*, 436 U.S. 49, 55-56 (1978) ("[Tribes] have power to make their own substantive law in internal matters, *see Roff v. Burney*, 168 U.S. 218 (1897) (membership); *Jones v. Meehan*, 175 U.S. 1, 29 (1899) (inheritance rules); *United States v. Quiver*, 241 U.S. 602 (1916) (domestic relations), and to enforce that law in their own forums, *see, e.g., Williams v. Lee*, 358 U.S. 217 (1959)"); *Prairie Band Potawatomi Nation v. Wagnon*, 476 F.3d 818 (10th Cir. 2007) (tribal authority to enact motor vehicle registration law for reservation member vehicles is an attribute of sovereignty); *Red Lake Band of Chippewa Indians v. State*, 311 Minn. 241, 243 (1976) (same).

[30]*Santa Clara Pueblo v. Martinez*, 436 U.S. 49, 59-60 (1978) (citing *Williams v. Lee*, 358 U.S. 217, 223 (1959)).

[31]*See generally* REST., LAW OF AMERICAN INDIANS (Tent. Draft No. 2, Mar. 13, 2018) § 20, cmt. c ("tribes retain authority over members or citizens"). This book refers to "tribal members" and "tribal citizens" interchangeably to mean enrolled members of federally recognized Indian tribes.

that they have sovereign authority to regulate labor and employment relations involving their members and the tribe itself or its enterprises within Indian country.[32]

When it comes to tribal authority over nonmembers (or noncitizens), two distinct lines of Supreme Court precedent define the scope of that power. First, an established line of Supreme Court cases confirms the inherent power of tribes to exclude nonmembers from their reservations and the related power to condition their continuing presence when doing business there. These cases include *Worcester v. Georgia*,[33] one of the Court's earliest Indian law decisions, *Williams v.*

---

[32]*See, e.g., EEOC v. Karuk Tribe Hous. Auth.*, 260 F.3d 1071, 1080 (9th Cir. 2001) (tribal member's employment relationship with the tribe's governmental housing authority involved "'purely internal matters' related to the tribe's self-governance"); *Reich v. Great Lakes Indian Fish & Wildlife Comm'n*, 4 F.3d 490, 494-96 (7th Cir. 1993) (employment relations between the commission and game wardens, who were members of tribes that had joined to form a commission to regulate hunting and fishing on tribal lands, involved the sovereign affairs of the tribes); *EEOC v. Fond du Lac Heavy Equip. and Constr. Co., Inc.*, 986 F.2d 246, 249 (8th Cir. 1993) (employment dispute between "an Indian applicant and an Indian tribal employer" engaged in a construction business both on and off the reservation was within the inherent authority of the tribe to resolve); *EEOC v. Cherokee Nation*, 871 F.2d 937, 938-39 (10th Cir. 1989) (employment discrimination dispute involving individual employed in Cherokee Nation's Department of Health and Human Services implicated Cherokee Nation's "treaty-protected right of self-government" and would not be subject to external authority of EEOC; same construction of law would pertain even when "nontreaty matters involving Indians are at issue"); *Donovan v. Navajo Forest Prod. Indus.*, 692 F.2d 709 (10th Cir. 1982) (occupational safety and health matters within tribally-owned lumber mill operating on reservation involved "tribal sovereignty and self-government recognized in the treaty"). *See also Reich v. Mashantucket Sand & Gravel*, 95 F.3d 174, 181 (2d Cir. 1996) (tribe has authority to regulate occupational safety and health matters within tribe-owned sand and gravel company operating on reservation, so long as not inconsistent with federal OSHA law); *Donovan v. Coeur d'Alene Tribal Farm*, 751 F.2d 1113, 1115 (9th Cir. 1985) (tribes have "the inherent sovereign right to regulate the health and safety of workers in tribal enterprises" within the reservation, but on-reservation tribal farm is subject to OSHA requirements); *Arizona Public Service Co. v. Office of Navajo Labor Relations*, 17 Indian L.Rptr. 6105, 6108-10 (Nav. Sup. Ct. 1990) (explaining inherent and treaty-based power of Navajo Nation to regulate employment and civil rights matters within Navajo lands); *Rodriguez v. Wong*, 82 P.3d 263, 266-67 (Wash. Ct. App. 2004) (tribe has inherent authority to regulate employment relationship with non-Indian employee of its Gaming Commission).

[33]31 U.S. 515 (1832).

Lee,[34] and *Merrion v. Jicarilla Apache Tribe*.[35] The common lesson from *Worcester*, *Williams*, and *Merrion* is that, absent a directive from Congress, tribes retain the sovereign authority to exclude nonmembers from the reservation and the "lesser power" to regulate their conduct while they remain.[36]

Nonmembers who enter the reservation to engage in economic activity for personal gain are subject to these attributes of inherent tribal sovereignty.[37] Thus, nonmembers who locate business enterprises within the reservation may be subject to a tribe's labor and employment laws.[38] Likewise, nonmembers who enter the reservation to work for tribal or other reservation enterprises similarly remain subject to the governmental authority of the tribe to exclude such individuals and the "lesser" authority to regulate their employment and labor relations while they remain.[39]

---

[34] 358 U.S. 217 (1959).

[35] 455 U.S. 130 (1982).

[36] *Merrion*, 455 U.S. at 144. For the application of this principle in the employment setting, *see Knighton v. Cedarville Rancheria of Northern Paiute Indians*, 918 F.3d 660, 671-672 (9th Cir. 2019). *See also Water Wheel Camp Recreational Area, Inc. v. LaRance*, 642 F.3d 802, 812-814 (9th Cir. 2011).

[37] *See infra* note 39. *See also White Mountain Apache Tribe v. Smith Plumbing Co.*, 856 F.2d 1301, 1305 (9th Cir. 1988) ("It is well settled that civil jurisdiction over activities of non-Indians concerning transactions taking place on Indian lands 'presumptively lies in the tribal courts unless affirmatively limited by a specific treaty provision or federal statute.'") (quoting *Iowa Mut. Ins. Co. v. LaPlante*, 480 U.S. 9, 18 (1987)) (citations omitted).

[38] *See Plains Commerce Bank v. Long Family & Cattle Co., Inc.*, 128 S. Ct. 2709, 2723 (2008).

[39] *See NLRB v. Pueblo of San Juan*, 276 F.3d 1186, 1192-93 (10th Cir. 2002) (en banc) (describing inherent authority of a tribe to regulate labor relations within nonmember business on reservation); *Arizona Public Service Co.*, 17 Indian L.Rptr. at 6109-10 (discussing inherent authority of Navajo Nation to regulate civil rights and employment relations within non-Indian employer on reservation). As the Ninth Circuit, sitting en banc, and citing *Merrion*, has explained, "[i]f the power to exclude implies the power to regulate those who enter tribal lands, the jurisdiction that results is a consequence of the deliberate actions of those who would enter tribal lands to engage in commerce with the Indians." *Smith v. Salish Kootenai College*, 434 F.3d 1127, 1139

A second line involves more recent cases, stemming from *Montana v. United States*, in which the Court held that a tribe is presumed to not possess regulatory authority over a nonmember on nonmember fee land within the tribe's reservation boundaries, but may (1) "regulate, through taxation, licensing, or other means, the activities of nonmembers who enter consensual relationships with the tribe or its members, through commercial dealing, contracts, leases, or other arrangements" and (2) regulate such noncitizens when their "conduct threatens or has some direct effect on the political integrity, the economic security, or the health or welfare of the tribe."[40] Various justices of the Supreme Court have sent mixed messages about whether these two *Montana* standards now provide the only bases for tribes to regulate the activities of nonmembers, whether on their own fee land or on tribal land.[41] Nevertheless, the Court has not overruled, or even questioned, its historic precedents confirming the inherent authority of tribes to exclude nonmembers and the related authority to condition their economic activity within the reservation.[42]

(9th Cir. 2006) (en banc). *See New Mexico v. Mescalero Apache Tribe*, 462 U.S. 324, 335 (1983) (tribes have authority to regulate "the use of their territory and resources by both members and nonmembers") (citations omitted); *Merrion*, 455 U.S. at 141 ("Nonmembers who lawfully enter tribal lands remain subject to the tribe's power to exclude them. This power necessarily includes the lesser power to place conditions on entry, on continued presence, or on reservation conduct . . ."). *See generally* Kaighn Smith, Jr., *Tribal Self-Determination and Judicial Restraint: The Problem of Labor and Employment Relations Within the Reservation*, 2 MICH. ST. L. REV. 505, 526-30 (2008).

[40]*Montana v. United States*, 450 U.S. 544, 565-66 (1981).

[41]*Compare Nevada v. Hicks*, 533 U.S. 353, 358 n.2 (2001) ("We leave open the question of tribal-court jurisdiction over nonmember defendants in general") and *id*. at 386 (Ginsburg, J., emphasizing the same) *with id*. at 375-86 (Souter, J., with whom Kennedy and Thomas, J.J., concurring) (suggesting that *Montana* standards should apply to determine tribal authority over nonmember activity with land status being one factor in the mix) and *id*. at 387 (O'Connor, J., with whom Stevens and Breyer, J.J., concurring) (asserting that the majority opinion "resolves that *Montana* . . . governs a tribe's civil jurisdiction over nonmembers regardless of land ownership").

[42]Even those justices promoting the view that *Montana*'s standards should provide the sole basis for tribal jurisdiction over nonmembers recognize that tribal power to exclude is "essential to [a] tribe's identity or its self-governing authority." *See Nevada v. Hicks*, 533 U.S. 353, 379 (2001) (Souter, J., joined by Kennedy and Thomas, J.J.,

In sum, to date, the two distinct bases for tribes to regulate nonmember employment relations in Indian country are: (1) inherent authority over nonmember economic activity, implicating the broad power to exclude and the related power to regulate, and (2) inherent authority over nonmember activity on fee lands within the exterior boundaries of Indian reservations, implicating the two *Montana* standards.[43] Given the Supreme Court's mixed messages on the subject, it is prudent to examine any assertion of tribal regulatory authority over nonmembers under the *Montana* standards before concluding, unequivocally, that the exercise of such authority is sound.[44] Indeed, the lower federal courts continue to struggle over the question of whether *Montana*'s consensual relationship and economic security/tribal security/tribal welfare standards displace any general tribal authority over the activities of nonmembers on tribal lands.[45]

---

concurring) (quoting *Oliphant v. Schlie*, 544 F.2d 1007, 1015 (9th Cir. 1976) (Kennedy, J., dissenting)). *See also Duro v. Reina*, 495 U.S. 676, 696 (1990) (the power to exclude non-Indians is a "traditional and undisputed" attribute of tribal self-governance) (citations omitted).

[43] *See Atkinson Trading Co. v. Shirley*, 532 U.S. 645, 651-56 (2001); *Strate v. A-1 Contractors*, 520 U.S. 438, 445-46, 455-56 (1997); *El Paso Natural Gas Co. v. Neztsosie*, 526 U.S. 473, 484-85 n.6-7 (1999).

[44] *See Knighton v. Cedarville Rancheria of Northern Paiute Indians*, 918 F.3d 660, 671-674 (9th Cir. 2019) (employing both (a) the inherent right of tribes to exclude nonmembers from Indian lands, with attendant right to regulate their conduct and (b) the *Montana* tests to confirm tribe's authority to regulate and adjudicate claims against nonmember employee); *Water Wheel Camp*, 642 F.3d at 812-814, 816-819 (same).

[45] *See Window Rock Unified School District v. Reeves*, 861 F.3d 894, 913-914 (9th Cir. 2017) (discussing debates). The Restatement of the American Law Institute concludes that *Montana* has no bearing upon an Indian tribe's inherent authority to govern nonmember conduct on Indian lands and is limited to the factual situation presented by the case: a nonmember's conduct on nonmember fees lands within the exterior boundaries of an Indian reservation. *See* REST., LAW OF AMERICAN INDIANS (Tent. Draft No. 2, Mar. 18, 2018) § 34, cmt. a ("As an attribute of their inherent sovereign authority, Indian tribes retain the power to exclude persons from Indian lands and the concomitant power to regulate conditions on their entry and their right to remain on Indian lands."); *id.* (Tent. Drat No. 4, Apr. 29, 2020) § 52, cmt a ("Indian tribes retain inherent power to govern the economic enterprise of members and nonmembers on Indian lands . . . unless divested of that power by federal law."). More specifically, with respect to tribes' regulatory authority over employment relations, the Restate-

As a general matter, employment relationships fit comfortably within the first *Montana* standard, the consensual relationship basis for tribal authority over nonmembers.[46] Thus, the following employment relations should constitute a "consensual relationship" subject to the labor or employment laws of a tribe under *Montana*:

- Nonmember employers: a nonmember employing tribal members on the nonmember employer's fee land within Indian country or on tribal land leased by the nonmember employer,[47]

- Nonmember employees: a tribe or tribal enterprise employing nonmember employees within Indian country on lands

---

ment provides that unless limited by Congress, "Indian tribes retain inherent sovereign authority to regulate employer-employee relations on Indian lands, including the enactment, implementation, and enforcement of laws governing employment discrimination; wages, hours, and working conditions; and unions and collective bargaining." REST., LAW OF AMERICAN INDIANS (Tent. Draft No. 4, Apr. 29, 2020) § 52, cmt. d.

[46] *See Knighton,* 918 F.3d at 673; *MacArthur v. San Juan County,* 497 F.3d 1057, 1071 (10th Cir. 2007); *Rodriguez v. Wong,* 82 P.3d at 266-267.

[47] *See Plains Com. Bank v. Long Fam. Land & Cattle Co.,* 554 U.S. 316, 335-36 (2008) ("The logic of *Montana* is that . . . a business enterprise employing tribal members . . . may be regulated [by the tribe]"); *Manygoats v. Atkinson Trading Co. Inc.*, No. SC-CV-62-2000, ¶¶ 35-41, at 5 (Nav. Sup. Ct. Aug. 12, 2003) available at http://tribal-institute.org/opinions/2003.NANN.0000016.htm (last visited Jan. 4, 2021) (holding that such an employment relationship falls within *Montana*'s consensual relationship rule); *MacArthur v. San Juan County,* 497 F.3d 1057, 1071-72 (10th Cir. 2007); *FMC v. Shoshone-Bannock Tribes,* 905 F.2d 1311, 1314-15 (9th Cir. 1990). *See also NLRB v. Pueblo of San Juan,* 276 F.3d 1186, 1190-93 (10th Cir. 2002) (en banc) (Pueblo had inherent authority to regulate labor relations at sawmill located within Pueblo lands, employing both tribal members and non-tribal members). If the employer is a state or subdivision of a state, acting in a "governmental capacity," the consensual relationship standard may not operate to establish tribal employment authority over the entity's employment relations. *See MacArthur,* 497 F.3d at 1073-74. However, one court has suggested that a tribe could assert regulatory authority over a state's employment relations on tribal land if the state were engaged in proprietary activities. *Id.* 1074 n.10.

owned by the tribe or its individual members or by the United States in trust for the tribe or its members.[48]

In each of these settings, however, the enacted tribal law must have an obvious nexus to the consensual employment relationship at issue.[49]

Tribal authority over employment relations may also be justified under the second *Montana* standard, recognizing the authority of tribes to regulate nonmembers when their conduct "threatens or has some direct effect on . . . the economic security, or the health or welfare of the tribe."[50] An argument can be made that a nonmember enterprise on tribal lands, employing both members and nonmembers of the tribe, directly affects the economic security and welfare of the tribe, given its impact on the allocation of economic resources within the tribe.[51] The Navajo Supreme Court has had no trouble in reaching such a conclusion.[52]

---

[48]*See Penobscot Nation v. Fellencer*, 164 F.3d 706, 712 (1st Cir. 1999); *Graham v. Applied Geo Technologies*, 593 F. Supp. 2d 915, 919-20 (S.D. Miss. 2008); *Davis v. Mille Lacs Band of Chippewa Indians*, 26 F. Supp. 2d 1175, 1179 (D. Minn. 1998), *aff'd on other grounds*, 193 F.3d 990 (8th Cir. 1999), *cert. denied*, 529 U.S. 1099 (2000).

[49]*See generally* Kaighn Smith, Jr., *Tribal Self-Determination and Judicial Restraint: The Problem of Labor and Employment Relations within the Reservation,* 2 MICH. ST. L. REV. 505, 526-30 (2008).

[50]*Montana*, 450 U.S. at 566 (citations omitted). The U.S. Court of Appeals for the Ninth Circuit invoked this standard to hold that a tribe had authority to regulate (and adjudicate) the conduct of a non-tribal employee of the tribe allegedly engaged in embezzling tribal government funds. *See Knighton v. Cedarville Rancheria of Northern Paiute Indians of the Rancheria,* 918 F.3d 660, 673-674 (9th Cir. 2019). The Washington Court of Appeals has relied upon this standard to confirm a tribe's inherent authority to regulate its commission's employment relations with a non-Indian, exclusive of state authority. *See Rodriquez v. Wong*, 82 P.3d at 267. A number of federal courts recognize the same rule in confirming the inherent authority of tribes to enforce their environmental laws against non-Indian businesses.

[51]*See MacArthur v. San Juan County*, 497 F.3d 1057, 1075 (10th Cir. 2007) (referring to the Navajo Nation's undoubted interest "in regulating employment relationships between its members and non-Indian employers on the reservation"); *NLRB v. Pueblo of San Juan*, 276 F.3d 1186, 1192-93 (10th Cir. 2002) (*en banc*) (recognizing inherent authority of tribe to govern employment relations involving both members and nonmembers within nonmember business on reservation). *See generally* Kaighn Smith,

2. Adjudicatory Authority

The foregoing discussion addresses tribes' authority to regulate labor and employment relations, not the adjudicatory authority of tribal courts or other forums over labor and employment disputes. The Supreme Court has said that a tribe's inherent "adjudicative jurisdiction does not exceed its legislative jurisdiction."[53]

Because Indian tribes have regulatory authority over employment relations between their own tribal citizens and the tribe, its enterprises, or the enterprises owned by other tribal citizens within Indian country, it follows that tribal courts have authority to adjudicate disputes arising out of such employment relations.

The Supreme Court has squarely held that tribal courts have inherent authority to adjudicate claims brought by non-citizens of a tribe against citizens of a tribe arising within Indian country.[54] The Court has not generally addressed tribal court jurisdiction over claims brought by tribes or their citizens against non-citizens arising within Indian country.[55] In one fact-specific case, the Court held that state interests outweighed tribal interests in adjudicating civil rights claims by a tribal citizen against state officers executing a search warrant within an Indian reservation.[56]

The federal circuit courts of appeal have confirmed, however, that absent significant state interests that might thwart the exercise of tribal court jurisdiction, tribal courts have authority to adjudicate claims

---

Jr., *Tribal Self-Determination and Judicial Restraint: The Problem of Labor and Employment Relations within the Reservation*, 2 MICH. ST. L. REV. 505, 526-30 (2008).

[52]*See Manygoats v. Atkinson Trading Co. Inc.*, No. SC-CV-62-2000, ¶¶ 43-44 at 5 (Nav. Sup. Ct. Aug. 12, 2003), available at http://tribal-institute.org/opinions/2003.NANN.0000016.htm (last visited Jan. 4, 2021).

[53]*Strate v. A-1 Contractors*, 520 U.S. 438, 453 (1997).

[54]*Williams v. Lee,* 358 U.S. 217 (1959).

[55]*See Nevada v. Hicks*, 533 U.S. at 358 n.2 ("[W]e have never held that a tribal court had jurisdiction over a nonmember defendant. Typically, our cases have involved claims brought against tribal defendants.").

[56]*See Nevada v. Hicks*, 533 U.S. 353 (2001).

brought by tribes, their wholly-owned enterprises, or by their tribal citizens against non-citizens when the tribe would have regulatory authority over the non-citizen's activity as set out subsection C.1, above.[57]

In the area of labor and employment relations, so long as a tribe is has enacted labor and employment regulations in line with the *Montana* standards, and backed by the principles established by *Worcester*, *Williams*, and *Merrion*, it is likely that tribal courts will have authority to adjudicate employment disputes between members and nonmembers arising under such tribal laws.[58] Case law involving the application of the tribal exhaustion doctrine to employment disputes arising in Indian country, discussed in Chapter 3, provides a good window into the kinds of employment claims that tribal courts likely have jurisdiction to decide.

D. Conclusion

This chapter has focused on the sovereign authority of tribes to govern labor and employment relations within Indian country without considering potential competing federal or state authority over such

---

[57]*See Knighton v. Cedarville Rancheria of Northern Paiute Indians*, 918 F.3d 660 (9th Cir. 2019); *Dolgencorp, Inc. v. Mississippi Band of Choctaw Indians*, 746 F.3d 167 (5 th Cir. 2014); *Water Wheel Camp Recreational Area, Inc. v. LaRance*, 642 F.3d 167 (9th Cir. 2011). *See also Window Rock Unified School District v. Reeves*, 861 F.3d 894 (9th Cir. 2017) (for purposes of applying the tribal exhaustion doctrine, discussed in Chapter 3, it is at least "plausible" that tribal commission would have authority to adjudicate employee claims against school district run by state within Navajo reservation). *See generally* REST., LAW OF AMERICAN INDIANS (Tent. Draft No. 2, Mar. 18, 2018) § 34(c).

[58]*Montana*, 450 U.S. 544; *Worcester*, 31 U.S. 515; *Williams*, 358 U.S. 217; *Merrion*, 455 U.S. 130. *See generally* REST., LAW OF AMERICAN INDIANS (Tent. Draft No. 4, Apr. 29, 2020) § 53(a). In addition to adjudicating violations of tribal civil regulatory laws governing employment relations, tribal courts may have authority to adjust rights and remedies as a matter of common law, such breach of contract or fraud. See *Knighton*, 918 F.3d at 671-676. (fraud and conversion claims). *See generally* REST., LAW OF AMERICAN INDIANS (Tent. Draft No. 4, Apr. 29, 2020) § 53(b). Some courts have held that the application of tribal common law by tribal courts is a form of regulation "by other arrangements" within the *Montana* formulation described in subsection C.1, above. *See, e.g., Smith v. Salish Kootenai College*, 434 F.3d 1127, 1137 (9th Cir. 2006) (en banc) (tort claim for negligent maintenance of vehicle); *Allstate Indemnity Co. v. Stump*, 191 F.3d 1071, 1072 (9th Cir.1999) (bad faith insurance claim).

relations. Given the inherent authority of tribes over their members and over nonmembers under the two distinct lines of Supreme Court authority reviewed in this chapter, there is a solid foundation for tribes to regulate reservation labor and employment relations in general. Whether that regulation is exclusive of state or federal authority is a separate question. Chapter 3 addresses the foundational principles of tribal sovereignty that serve as barriers to the imposition of state and federal authority.

3

DEFENSIVE TRIBAL SOVEREIGNTY: BARRIERS TO STATE AND FEDERAL AUTHORITY OVER LABOR AND EMPLOYMENT RELATIONS IN INDIAN COUNTRY

A. Introduction

Chapter 2 looked at the affirmative power of Indian tribes to regulate labor and employment relations within their territories: the existence and exercise of *affirmative* sovereignty. This chapter shifts gears to examine principles of law that protect tribal authority from being undermined by assertions of state or federal power: the existence and exercise of *defensive* sovereignty. As will be shown, the two concepts (the affirmative and defensive aspects of tribal sovereignty) overlap because the very existence and exercise of tribal sovereignty sets up the basis for its protection from outside forces as a matter of federal law.

One set of legal principles — the infringement and preemption doctrines — establishes potential barriers to state authority over labor and employment relations in Indian country, while another set — the federal infringement standard and the exhaustion doctrine — establishes potential barriers to federal authority over those relations.[1] Although particular treaties or federal statutes may allow state regulatory

---

[1] Inherent tribal sovereignty, like the sovereignty of other governments, includes sovereign immunity from suit. Tribal sovereign immunity from suit is separately discussed in Chapter 4. As explained there, sovereign immunity from suit operates independently as a barrier to lawsuits, whether tribal authority is in competition with external authority or not. *See Miner Elec. Inc. v. Muscogee (Creek) Nation*, 505 F.3d 1007, 1012 (10th Cir. 2007) (distinguishing "two different aspects of an Indian tribe's 'sovereignty': its immunity from suit and the extent of its powers to enact and enforce laws affecting non-Indians"); *In re Greene*, 980 F.2d 590, 595-97 (9th Cir. 1992) (discussing tribal sovereign immunity in relation to other doctrines of tribal sovereignty).

authority over certain tribes, the focus here (as in Chapter 2) is on general principles of federal Indian law.[2]

B. Barriers to State Authority: Infringement and Preemption Doctrines

How does the issue of state authority over labor and employment relations in Indian country arise for decision by a court? Absent an express waiver by a tribe or abrogation by Congress, Indian tribes and their enterprises are immune from suit by state governments.[3] Thus, cases bearing on the issue of whether state laws may govern reservation labor and employment matters involve assertions of state authority over individual tribal members or entities, or nonmember individuals or entities within Indian country.[4]

The original rule, first announced by the Supreme Court in *Worcester v. Georgia*,[5] was that the laws of a state "can have no force" within an Indian tribe's territory absent an express act of Congress or treaty provision.[6] In more recent years, while recognizing that "[t]he policy of leaving Indians free from state jurisdiction and control is

---

[2]Observing that today, "in almost all cases federal treaties and statutes define the boundaries of federal and state jurisdiction,"the Supreme Court relies less upon "platonic notions of Indian sovereignty"and looks more to relevant treaties and statutes in order to discern the limits of state power over Indian affairs. *McClanahan v. State Tax Comm'n. of Arizona*, 411 U.S. 164, 172 & n.8 (1973). Nevertheless, areas of tribal sovereignty that traditionally have remained immune from state control as a matter of federal common law will remain so "except where Congress has expressly provided that State laws shall apply." *Rice v. Rehner*, 463 U.S. 713, 719-20 (1983) (quotations and citation omitted). "Repeal by implication of an established tradition of [tribal] immunity or self-governance is disfavored." *Id.* at 720.

[3]*See generally* Chapter 4, infra.

[4]*See, e.g., White Mountain Apache Tribe v. Bracker*, 448 U.S. 136, 144 (1980). *See also Fisher v. District Court*, 424 U.S. 382 (1976). *But see Rodriguez v. Wong*, 82 P.2d 263 (Wash. Ct. App. 2004) (addressing state authority over employment relations within a tribe without first addressing the issue of sovereign immunity from suit).

[5]31 U.S. 515 (1832).

[6]*Id.* at 520.

deeply rooted in the Nation's history," the Supreme Court has moved away from this absolute rule.[7] Today, in the absence of a clear federal treaty or statute governing the application of state law to a particular matter, the Court recognizes "two independent but related barriers" to the application of state law. "First, the exercise of [state] authority may be preempted by federal law. Second, it may unlawfully infringe on the right of reservation Indians to make their own laws and be ruled by them."[8] These tests, known respectively as "preemption" and "infringement," are unpredictable in their application because they turn on the particular facts presented in each case.

"When on-reservation conduct involving only Indians is at issue, state law is generally inapplicable."[9] Thus, the infringement and preemption standards usually involve state law authority over nonmember reservation activity, sometimes in competition with tribal authority over the same conduct.[10]

1. The Infringement Barrier

The infringement barrier to state authority, grounded in "inherent tribal sovereignty," protects the right of tribes to exercise control

---

[7] *See McClanahan v. Arizona State Tax Comm'n.*, 411 U.S. 164, 168 (1973); *see also Three Affiliated Tribes of the Fort Berthold Reservation v. Wold Eng'g*, 476 U.S. 877, 891 (1986) ("[I]n the absence of federal authorization, . . . all aspects of tribal sovereignty [are] privileged from diminution by the States").

[8] *White Mountain Apache Tribe v. Bracker*, 448 U.S. 136, 142 (1980) (citations omitted).

[9] *Id.* at 144. *See also State ex rel. Peterson v. Dist. Court of Ninth Judicial Dist.*, 617 P.2d 1056, 1069 (Wyo. 1980) (tribal court has exclusive jurisdiction over tort action between tribal members arising on the reservation). *See generally*, American Law Institute, REST., LAW OF AMERICAN INDIANS (Tent. Draft No. 4, 2020) § 37 ("States do not possess civil regulatory authority over tribal members and Indian tribes in Indian country except when: (1) expressly authorized by federal law, or (2) exceptional state interests exist.").

[10] *See generally*, American Law Institute, REST. LAW OF AMERICAN INDIANS (Tent. Draft No. 4, 2020) § 36 ("States have civil regulatory authority over nonmembers in Indian country, except when the state regulation (a) conflicts with an express federal statutory prohibition, (b) is impliedly preempted by federal law, or (c) infringes on tribal self-governance.").

over their reservation affairs free from intrusion by state authority.[11] The rule is stated as follows: "[A]bsent governing Acts of Congress, a State may not act in a manner that infringes on the right of reservation Indians to make their own laws and be ruled by them."[12] Generally, when a matter is subject to governance by a tribe under its inherent sovereign authority (or treaty-protected authority), state law cannot govern the same matter because it would otherwise infringe upon tribal authority.[13]

The Supreme Court articulated the infringement standard in *Williams v. Lee*[14] to bar a state court action brought by a grocery store owner on the Navajo reservation against Navajo tribal members to collect a debt. The Court first made clear that the Navajo Nation had inherent (and treaty-reserved) authority to govern this reservation dispute under its own laws and in its own forum. It then found that the store owner's state court lawsuit would infringe on the Navajo's authority to govern the reservation. The Court said that "to allow the exercise of state jurisdiction here would undermine the authority of the tribal courts over Reservation affairs and hence would infringe on the right of the Indians to govern themselves."[15] The fact that the grocery store owner was not a Navajo citizen was "immaterial"; "[h]e was on the Reservation and the transaction with an Indian took place there."[16] The Court recognized that its decisions "consistently guarded the authority of Indian governments over their reservations."[17] Without the intervention of Congress, the Court would not allow state law to in-

---

[11] *White Mountain Apache Tribe,* 448 U.S. at 142. *See New Mexico v. Mescalero Apache Tribe,* 462 U.S. 324, 334 n.16 (1983).

[12] *See New Mexico v. Mescalero Apache Tribe,* 462 U.S. 324, 332-33 (1983).

[13] *Id.*

[14] 358 U.S. 217 (1959).

[15] *Id.* at 223.

[16] *Id.*

[17] *Id.*

fringe upon the Navajo Nation's right to address the contract dispute under Navajo law within its own judicial forum.[18]

2. The Preemption Barrier

The preemption barrier to the application of state law similarly protects tribal interests in governing particular matters, but focuses more upon interest-balancing in light of congressional policy and law protecting tribal self-governance in particular areas. Importantly, the doctrine of federal preemption of state authority in Indian affairs is substantially different from the application of the preemption doctrine in other contexts, where an express statement by Congress to occupy a field to the exclusion of state law must be found. In Indian affairs, the Supreme Court has "rejected the proposition that in order to find a particular state law to have been preempted by operation of federal law, an express congressional statement to that effect is required."[19]

The Indian law preemption rule is stated as follows: "State jurisdiction is preempted by the operation of federal law if it interferes or is incompatible with federal and tribal interests reflected in federal law, unless the state interests at stake are sufficient to justify the assertion of state authority."[20] This rule, like the infringement standard, does not

---

[18]*Id. See Hatcher v. Harrah's NC Casino Company, LLC*, 610 S.E.2d 210, 214 (N.C. Ct. App. 2005) (casino patron's claim against tribe's reservation gaming facility must be resolved in tribal court; "interests of the Indians outweigh the interests of the state"); *Gallegos v. Pueblo of Tesuque*, 46 P.3d 668, 685-86 (N.M. 2002) (non-Indian claim against tribe for injuries at tribe's gaming facility not subject to state court jurisdiction); *Kizis v. Morse Diesel Int'l, Inc.*, 794 A.2d 498, 505 (Conn. 2002) (same). *See also Iowa Mutual Ins. Co. v. LaPlante*, 480 U.S. 9, 16 (1987) (refusing to construe a statute giving rise to federal court jurisdiction over state law claims, involving parties from different states, in a manner that would allow state law to infringe upon tribal authority unless parties exhaust tribal processes). *See generally* American Law Institute, REST., LAW OF AMERICAN INDIANS, (Tent. Draft No. 4, Apr. 29, 2020) § 39 ("Absent authorization by federal law . . . , states lack civil adjudicatory jurisdiction over causes of action arising on Indian lands . . . against an Indian tribe or its members, [but] States generally have civil adjudicatory authority over causes of action arising in Indian country against nonmembers.").

[19]*White Mountain Apache Tribe*, 448 U.S. at 143-145 (citations omitted).

[20]*Mescalero Apache Tribe*, 462 U.S. at 334.

lend itself to predictable results. Rather, it "call[s] for a particularized inquiry into the nature of the state, federal, and tribal interests at stake, an inquiry designed to determine whether, in the specific context, the exercise of state authority would violate federal law."[21]

In *New Mexico v. Mescalero Apache Tribe*,[22] the Supreme Court applied the preemption doctrine to bar the application of state hunting and fishing laws to nonmember hunting and fishing activities within the reservation of the Mescalero Apache Tribe. Given the Tribe's comprehensive regulation of hunting and fishing, backed by supportive federal programs, the Court held that the tribal interests in retaining exclusive regulatory authority over such activities outweighed the interests of the state in imposing its own laws. The Court held that the Tribe's authority to govern the use of its territory and resources by nonmembers of the Tribe would be undermined by the imposition of New Mexico law.[23] The application of state laws, the Court said, would supplant tribal control by imposing an "inconsistent dual system" of rules.[24]

In *California v. Cabazon Band of Mission Indians*,[25] the Court applied the preemption test to determine whether state gaming regulations could be applied to the gaming operations of an Indian tribe. The case implicated the Cabazon Band's inherent "power ... to raise revenues to pay for the costs of government."[26] Pointing to the strong interest of the Cabazon Band in generating revenue for tribal government and Congressional enactments encouraging such activities, the Court held that the state's asserted interest in regulating the Cabazon Band's bingo games to prevent organized crime was outweighed by

---

[21] *White Mountain Apache Tribe*, 448 U.S. at 145.

[22] 462 U.S. 324 (1983).

[23] *Id.* at 338-41. In addition to regulatory interests, the Court noted the State's interest in generating revenue from licensing fees, which it viewed as the equivalent of a state tax on reservation activities. *See id.* at 343.

[24] *Id.* at 339-40.

[25] 480 U.S. 202 (1986).

[26] *See Merrion v. Jicarilla Apache Tribe*, 455 U.S. 130, 144 (1982).

tribal and federal interests.[27] It struck a balance, and held that the Cabazon Band was free from any state authority over its reservation gaming operations so long as the state did not prohibit all such gaming as a matter of criminal law and public policy.[28] The overlap between the preemption and infringements standards was exhibited by the Court's statement that such state regulation "would impermissibly infringe on tribal government."[29]

3. Application of the Barriers

The interconnected preemption and infringement tests, as barriers to state authority over matters concerning tribes or their reservation affairs, play important roles in the governance of labor and employment relations in Indian country.

A good example is provided by a decision of the Supreme Court of South Dakota in *Sage v. Sicangu Oyate Ho, Inc.*,[30] which involved a state court lawsuit for breach of an employment contract by a teacher who was employed by the St. Francis Indian School on the Rosebud Sioux Indian Reservation. Although the school was operated by a nonprofit corporation, incorporated under the laws of South Dakota, the court viewed it as a tribal entity for the purposes of its jurisdiction analysis.[31] The court held that the state court lacked subject matter jurisdiction over the contract dispute. Echoing the tone of the Supreme Court in *Williams v. Lee*, the court noted that, although the

---

[27] *See Cabazon Band of Mission Indians*, 480 U.S. at 216-22.

[28] *See id.*

[29] *Id.* at 222.

[30] 473 N.W.2d 480, 481 (S.D. 1991).

[31] *Id.* at 483-84 (observing that (1) all of the students at the school were reservation Indians; (2) membership in the corporation was limited to enrolled members of the Rosebud Sioux Tribe who had children in the school and any others they may elect; (3) members of the corporation democratically elected the seven voting members of the school board according to the reservation district they live in, with the exception of one ex officio school board member chosen from the Rosebud Sioux Tribal Education Committee; and (4) current school board members were enrolled members of the tribe).

teacher was not a Rosebud Sioux tribal member, she affirmatively "chose to enter into employment contracts with the school for over a decade" on the reservation.[32] It found state court jurisdiction preempted in light of the inherent authority of the Tribe to govern the dispute and the federal interest in tribal self-government reflected in the funding programs for the school pursuant to the Indian Self-Determination and Education Assistance Act of 1975 (ISDEAA)[33] and the Tribally Controlled Schools Act of 1988.[34]

Another example is the Washington Court of Appeals decision in *Rodriguez v. Wong*.[35] In that case, an employee of the Muckleshoot Indian Tribe's Gaming Commission, a governmental division of the Tribe, sued the director of the Commission in the Washington Superior Court, seeking damages for discrimination under Washington law.[36] Neither the employee nor the director were Muckleshoot tribal members. The court pointed out that the employee had previously asserted claims in accordance with the Commission's personnel manual, which had been approved and adopted by the governing Tribal Council.[37] Under those proceedings, the Commission's Grievance Committee had held a hearing on his complaints and made findings, which, in accordance with the personnel manual, were "final and binding."[38]

---

[32]*Id.* at 482.

[33]25 U.S.C. §§ 5301-5332 (2018).

[34]25 U.S.C. §§ 2501-2511 (2018). The court quoted some of Congress's declarations to promote tribal self-governance pursuant to the ISDEAA. *See Sicangu Oyate Ho Inc.*, 473 N.W.2d at 483. *See also Stathis v. Marty Indian Sch.*, 930 N.W.2d 653 (S.D. 2019) (holding that state court action brought by former principal of tribal school against members of school board for wrongful termination, breach of contract, libel, and other claims preempted by federal law for same reasons).

[35]82 P.3d 263 (Wash. Ct. App. 2004).

[36]*Id.* at 265.

[37]*Id.* at 267.

[38]*Id.* at 265, 267.

The court first held that the Tribe had inherent authority to govern the employment relationship at issue.[39] Next, it addressed whether, considering *Williams v. Lee*, such tribal authority was exclusive of any state jurisdiction, and held that:

> [H]ere the tribe has exercised its jurisdiction to develop its own nondiscrimination and other employment policies, and the State's assertion of jurisdiction would impose state regulations on the tribe whenever nonmembers become employees of the tribe . . . [.] [This] . . . would undermine the right of the tribe to govern reservation affairs.[40]

Few other cases have emerged analyzing the infringement and preemption standards with respect to labor or employment disputes in the tribal setting.[41]

On the separate issue of the application of state regulatory laws to the reservation activities of tribal members in general, the Supreme Court has said that, absent a congressional directive, only "exceptional circumstances" can warrant the assertion of state authority.[42] Thus, where only tribal members and entities are involved in a reservation employment dispute, apart from the obstacles that tribal sovereign

---

[39]*Id.* at 266-67.

[40]*Id.* at 267.

[41]For a general discussion of infringement standards in an employment case, *see South v. Lujan*, 336 P.3d 1000, 1002-1103, 1005-1006 (N.M. 2014) (remanding for factual findings on whether state court jurisdiction over employment discrimination case brought by non-Indian former Sandia Pueblo police officer against chief and captain of police department would infringe upon Pueblo's sovereignty) (discussing cases applying infringement test).

[42]*See California v. Cabazon Band of Mission Indians*, 480 U.S. 202, 214-15 (1987) (quoting *New Mexico v. Mescalero Apache Tribe*, 462 U.S. 324, 331-32 (1983)). *See generally Gobin v. Snohomish County*, 304 F.3d 909, 917 (9th Cir. 2002) (county cannot apply land use regulation to building project of tribal members on their fee land within reservation). *Santa Rosa Band of Indians v. Kings County*, 532 F.2d 655 (9th Cir. 1976) (county land use laws cannot be applied to tribal members on reservation).

immunity may provide, it is likely that state jurisdiction will be found wanting. Where the activities of nonmembers on tribal lands are concerned, important tribal interests may outweigh state interests, especially where congressional policy supports tribal self-government.[43]

Tribes will fare better in maintaining regulatory authority over labor and employment relations within their reservations if they proactively assert their lawmaking authority. Given the fact-driven nature of the infringement and preemption tests, tribes may, in some circumstances, be vulnerable to losing or having to share regulatory authority with states. By having their tribal labor and employment laws in place, tribes will firm up the "tribal interest" side of the balancing equation for the preemption standard and bolster their prospects because they will be exercising the aspect of tribal self-government that would be undermined by the imposition of state authority.

C. Barriers to Federal Authority: Federal Infringement

Federal courts have held that Indian tribes cannot assert sovereign immunity against actions brought against them by the United States or its administrative agencies.[44] Thus, in contrast to lawsuits brought against tribes by individuals or states, tribes are subject to suit by the federal government. The imposition of a particular federal law upon a tribe or activities within its territorial jurisdiction might infringe upon the prerogatives of tribal self-government protected under principles of federal Indian law. Thus, federal courts have developed rules to

---

[43]*See Segundo v. City of Rancho Mirage*, 813 F.2d 1387 (9th Cir. 1987) (declining to apply state rentcontrol laws to nonmember entity operating mobile home park on Indian land held in trust by United States because such laws preempted by federal law, and to do so would undermine tribe's sovereign authority); *Rodriguez v. Wong*, 82 P.3d at 267 ("Were the State to assert jurisdiction over Rodriquez's claims because he is not a member of the tribe, the tribe would be forced either to abandon its own governance and submit to state jurisdiction for all employees, or to apply different sets of employment rules to members and nonmembers"). *See generally Cossey v. Cherokee Nation Enter. LLC*, 212 P.3d 447, 474-78 (Okla. 2009) (Kauger, J., with whom Edmondson, C. J., concurring in part and dissenting in part) (discussing state court cases and other authority bearing on whether tribal court has exclusive jurisdiction over personal injury action against tribe's gaming operation arising on reservation).

[44]*See* Chapter 6.

prevent the infringement in those instances where (a) Congress has failed to indicate its intent to apply a federal statute of general application to tribes or their reservation affairs, and (b) such application has the potential to infringe upon matters of tribal self-government.

This section looks at the emerging rules across the federal circuit courts of appeals with respect to the federal Indian law infringement standard in general. The current state of the law with respect to specific federal labor and employment statutes that are silent with regard to their application to tribes is discussed in detail in Chapters 5 and 6.

1. Supreme Court Decisions Affecting Federal Infringement

While the Supreme Court has not yet directly addressed how to resolve whether a federal law of general application applies to Indian tribes or their reservation affairs, three cases have influenced the lower courts' development of the law in this area.

In *Merrion v. Jicarilla Apache Tribe*, discussed in Chapter 2 in reference to the inherent authority of tribes to exclude nonmembers (and the related authority to regulate their reservation activity), the Court held that an oil and gas company could not prevent the Tribe from imposing its tax law on the company's reservation operations just because the Tribe had not reserved that right in its lease.[45] In addressing the Tribe's inherent authority to tax the company, the Court said, "[b]ecause the Tribe retains all inherent attributes of sovereignty that have not been divested by the Federal Government, the proper inference from silence on this point is that the sovereign power to tax remains intact."[46] While *Merrion* did not involve the issue of whether a federal law of general application would apply to an Indian tribe, the Court's announcement that the recognized attributes of tribal sovereignty cannot be divested by mere silence paved the way for lower courts to pause before allowing federal employment laws that fail to address Indian tribes to infringe upon tribal authority.[47]

---

[45]*Merrion v. Jicarilla Apache Tribe*, 455 U.S. 130, 146 (1982).

[46]*Id.* at 148 n.14.

[47]*See Donovan v. Navajo Forest Products Industries*, 692 F.2d 709, 712 (10th Cir. 1982).

In *Iowa Mutual Insurance Co. v. LaPlante*,[48] the Court considered how to apply the federal statute establishing federal court jurisdiction over cases involving citizens from different states (the "diversity jurisdiction statute") when it could affect an attribute of tribal sovereignty: the authority of tribal courts to resolve on-reservation disputes similar to those at issue in *Williams v. Lee*, discussed above. The Court noted that Congress had not considered the application of the diversity jurisdiction statute to reservation affairs involving Indians.[49] Pointing out that "[t]ribal authority over the activities of non-Indians on reservation lands is an important part of tribal sovereignty," the Court said, citing *Merrion*, that "the proper inference from silence" on Congress's part was that the diversity jurisdiction statute would not apply to infringe the authority of a tribe to adjudicate matters within its jurisdiction in the first instance.[50]

The Court's messages in *Merrion* and *Iowa Mutual* — that congressional silence cannot signal an undermining of established tribal authority — might appear in conflict with language the Court used in an earlier decision, *Federal Power Commission. v. Tuscarora Indian Nation*.[51] In *Tuscarora*, the Court stated that it was "well settled by many decisions of this Court that a general statute in terms applying to all persons includes Indians and their property interests."[52] Notably, that case did not involve the activities of a tribe within Indian country. At issue was whether land owned by the Tuscarora Nation in fee could be condemned (and subsequently flooded) to make way for a dam pursu-

---

[48] 480 U.S. 9 (1987).

[49] *Id.* at 18.

[50] *Id.* Accord *Michigan v. Bay Mills Indian Community*, 572 U.S. 782, 790 (2014) (stating that it is an "enduring principle of Indian law" that "courts will not lightly assume that Congress . . . intends to undermine Indian self-government").

[51] 362 U.S. 99 (1960). This conflict is flagged by the Tenth Circuit in one of the first decisions to address the application of a federal employment law of general application to an Indian tribe. *See Donovan v. Navajo Forest Prods. Inds.*, 692 F.2d 709, 713 (10th Cir. 1982) ("*Merrion,* in our view, limits or, by implication, overrules *Tuscarora*").

[52] *Tuscarora Indian Nation*, 362 U. S. at 116.

ant to the Federal Power Act. The Court held that Federal Power Act restrictions applicable to "reservations," defined as lands in which the United States holds a proprietary interest, did not apply to the Tuscarora Nation's fee lands.[53] The Nation could not assert governmental authority over the land; in that sense, it was not acting as a sovereign, but as an ordinary landowner.[54] The Court's statement that "a general statute in terms applying to all persons includes Indians and their property interests" thus does not apply in the context of a tribe's own sovereign activities within its established territorial jurisdiction. In any event, the *Tuscarora* Court's statement certainly was not material to its decision.[55] Thus, it may be considered "dictum" (not a legal holding).[56]

The lower federal courts have taken differing approaches to applying the *Tuscarora* Court's dictum to the issue of whether federal labor or employment laws of general application apply to Indian tribes or their enterprises. None have presumed that it operates on its own accord to impose silent federal laws upon the employment relations of an Indian tribe or its enterprises within Indian country.

---

[53] *See id.* at 105-06, 115.

[54] *See generally*, Wenona Singel, *Labor Relations and Tribal Self-Governance*, 80 N.D.L. REV. 691, 703 (2004).

[55] For a discussion of the precise issue in *Tuscaora* and the manner it was addressed, rendering it immaterial to the activities of an Indian tribe acting as a sovereign, *see* Kaighn Smith Jr., *When Congress Forgets: Breaking Through Congress's Failure to Mention Indian Tribes in Federal Employment Laws*, FED. LAW., March/April 2021, at 8, 9–10.

[56] Courts question the extent to which this dictum should be accepted as authoritative. *See San Manuel Indian Bingo & Casino v. N.L.R.B.*, 475 F.3d 1306, 1311 (D.C. Cir. 2007) ("Tuscarora's statement is of uncertain significance, and possibly dictum, given the particulars of that case."); *EEOC v. Cherokee Nation*, 871 F.2d 937, 938 n.2 (10th Cir. 1989) (questioning "the continuing vitality of the *Tuscarora* dictum" in light of subsequent Supreme Court decisions); *United States v. Winnebago Tribe of Nebraska*, 542 F.2d 1002 (8th Cir. 1976) (same). *See generally Multimedia Games, Inc. v. WLGC Acquisition Corp.*, 214 F.Supp.2d 1131, 1136 (N.D.Okla. 2001) (discussing the Tenth Circuit's treatment of the *Tuscarora* dictum).

2. Varying Approaches to the Application of General Federal Labor and Employment Laws to Tribes and Tribal Enterprises

If the Supreme Court's broad dictum in *Tuscarora* — that federal laws of general application presumptively apply "to Indians" — is taken as a statement of law, then it is hard to reconcile it with the Court's subsequent pronouncement in *Merrion* and *Iowa Mutual* that congressional silence should not be construed to allow the undermining of attributes of tribal sovereignty.[57] The challenge of such reconciliation has played out in the context of the application of federal labor and employment laws to Indian tribes and their enterprises within Indian country. The resulting contradictory approaches of the federal circuit courts of appeals are described below.[58]

a. Ninth, Second, and Sixth Circuits: Federal Law Applies Absent Interference with Treaty or "Purely Intramural Matter"

In *Donovan v. Coeur d'Alene Tribal Farm*,[59] the Ninth Circuit addressed whether the Occupational Safety and Health Act of 1970 (OSHA)[60] — a federal law of general application, which is silent with respect to its application to tribes — may be applied to a reservation

---

[57] *Merrion*, 455 U.S. at 148-49; *Iowa Mut. Ins. Co.*, 480 U.S. at 18. *See also Bay Mills Indian Community*, 572 U.S. at 789-90 ("courts will not lightly assume that Congress in fact intends to undermine Indian self-government") (citing *Santa Clara Pueblo v. Martinez*, 436 U.S. 49, 58-60 (1978); *Iowa Mut. Ins. Co. v. LaPlante*, 480 U.S. at 18; *United States v. Dion*, 476 U.S. 734, 738–739 (1986)).

[58] *See* Chapter 6 for a discussion of how the different approaches have worked in reference to specific federal laws. For a general overview see Alex T. Skibine, *Practical Reasoning and the Application of General Federal Regulatory Laws to Indian Nations*, 22 WASH. & LEE J. CIVIL RTS. & SOC. JUST. 123, 124–25 (2016).

[59] 751 F.2d 1113 (9th Cir. 1985).

[60] 29 U.S.C. §§ 651-678 (2018).

farm owned and operated by the Coeur d'Alene Tribe.[61] The Ninth Circuit's starting point was the Supreme Court's dictum in *Tuscarora*.[62] Even though, as noted above, *Tuscarora* involved lands held in fee, the Ninth Circuit relied on the case to presume that OSHA would apply to the Tribe's on-reservation farm unless the Tribe could satisfy one of three exceptions. The Court said:

> A federal statute of general applicability that is silent on the issue of applicability to Indian tribes will not apply to them if: (1) the law touches "exclusive rights of self governance in purely intramural matters"; (2) the application of the law to the tribe would "abrogate rights guaranteed by Indian treaties"; or (3) there is proof "by legislative history or some other means that Congress intended the law not to apply to Indians on their reservations. . . ." In any of these three situations, Congress must *expressly* apply a statute to Indians before we will hold that it reaches them.[63]

The Ninth Circuit then said the first exception did not apply "[b]ecause the Farm employs non-Indians as well as Indians, and because it is in virtually every respect a normal commercial farming enterprise."[64] The Court's emphasis on the farm's employment of "non-Indians" ignores the critical importance of tribal authority over nonmembers within Indian country to protect the integrity of tribal communities.[65] In addition, its emphasis on the "commercial-looking" na-

---

[61] OSHA applies to an "organized group of persons . . . engaged in a business affecting commerce who has employees . . . ," but expressly excludes "the United States or any State or political subdivision of a State." 29 U.S.C. § 652.

[62] *Coeur d'Alene Tribal Farm*, 751 F.2d at 1115-16.

[63] *Id.* at 1116 (quoting *United States v. Farris*, 624 F.2d 890, 893-94 (9th Cir. 1980)).

[64] *Id.*

[65] As discussed in Chapter 2, Indian tribes have inherent sovereign authority to exclude nonmembers from their territories and to govern their activities while they re-

ture of the farm ignores the critical importance of enterprises owned and controlled by Indian tribes for generating tribal government revenues due to their lack of a tax base.[66] Because the Tribe had no treaty to protect itself from the operation of OSHA, the court held that the Tribe was subject to the law.[67]

The identified "exceptions" applied by the court in *Coeur d'Alene Farm* originated in an earlier Ninth Circuit case, *United States v. Farris*, involving the application of federal criminal laws to activities of individual tribal citizens within the reservation.[68] In that case, the court relied on *Tuscarora* to conclude that the individuals were subject to federal criminal prosecution unless one of these exceptions could be identified.[69] Commentators have criticized the Ninth Circuit for extending the *Farris* rule in this manner because it ignores a critical distinction: Indian tribes are not individuals; they are sovereign governments.[70]

---

main. *Merrion v. Jicarilla Apache Tribe*, 455 U.S. 130, 144–45 (1982). The leading treatise in the field of federal Indian laws describes this inherent sovereignty as "intimately tied to a tribe's ability to protect the integrity and order of its territory and the welfare of its members, it *is an internal matter* over which the tribes retain sovereignty." COHEN'S HANDBOOK OF FEDERAL INDIAN LAW § 4.01[2][e] at 221 (Nell Jessup Newton et al. eds., 2012) (emphasis added).

[66]*See Michigan v. Bay Mills Indian Cmty.*, 572 U.S. 782, 810 (2014) (Sotomayer, J., concurring) ("[T]ribal business operations are critical to the goals of tribal self-sufficiency because such enterprises in some cases may be the only means by which a tribe can raise revenues.").

[67]*Id.* at 1116-17.

[68]*United States v. Farris*, 624 F.2d 890 (9th Cir. 1980).

[69]*Id.* at 893.

[70]*See generally* Vicki J. Limas, *Application of Federal Labor and Employment Statutes to Native American Tribes: Respecting Sovereignty and Achieving Consistency*, 26 ARIZ. ST. L.J. 681, 745-746 (1994) (criticizing subsequent opinions following *Farris* rationale); Kaighn Smith Jr., *When Congress Forgets: Breaking Through Congress's Failure to Mention Indian Tribes in Federal Employment Laws,* FED. LAW., March/April 2021, at 9-10 (describing lack of foundation for Coeur d'Alene Farm formulation and racial distinctions it has engendered); Kaighn Smith Jr., *Tribal Self-Determination and Judicial Restraint: The Problem of Labor and Employment Relations Within the Reservation*, 2 MICH. ST. L. REV. 505, 538-39 (2008) (criticizing opinions following *Farris* rationale).

Nevertheless, the unexamined extrapolation of the *Farris* formulation beyond individual tribal citizens to Indian tribes has found traction beyond the Ninth Circuit. The United States Court of Appeals for the Second Circuit followed the *Farris/Coeur d'Alene Farm* approach in concluding that the Department of Labor could impose OSHA upon the on-reservation activities of a sand and gravel company owned and operated by the Mashantucket Pequot Tribal Nation that employed nonmembers of the Nation.[71] The United States Court of Appeals for the Sixth Circuit likewise followed this approach in allowing the National Labor Relations Board to invoke the National Labor Relations Act of 1935 (NLRA) — a law that generally applies to all employers, but excludes states[72] — to strike down the operational labor laws of the Little River Band of Ottawa Indians as an "unfair labor practice" because the Band's laws varied from the NLRA.[73]

---

[71] *Reich v. Mashantucket Sand & Gravel*, 95 F.3d 174 (2d Cir. 1996). Citing *Montana*, the Second Circuit said "limitations on tribal authority are particularly acute where non-Indians are concerned." *Id.* at 180. In so doing, the court overlooked the fact that *Montana* addressed only the Crow Nation's authority over the activities of nonmembers on their own fee lands, *see supra* at 32. It also failed to appreciate the clear import of a tribe's inherent sovereign authority to regulate nonmembers within reservation and trust lands set out by the Supreme Court in *Merrion*, *see supra* at 31. Further, even if *Montana*'s "general proposition" governed tribal authority over nonmembers within a tribe's reservation and trust lands, *Montana* confirmed that (even on non-member fee lands) Indian tribes have inherent sovereign authority to regulate contractual relationships between the tribe or its enterprises and nonmembers, *see supra* at 32 and an employment relationship is just that, *see Knighton v. Cedarville Rancheria of Northern Paiute Indians*, 918 F.3d 660, 673 (9th Cir. 2019).

[72] *See* 29 U.S.C. § 152.

[73] *NLRB v. Little River Band of Ottawa Indians Tribal Government* 788 F.3d 537 (6th Cir. 2015) (discussed in more detail in Chapter 7). Failing to appreciate the Supreme Court's clear recognition, in *Merrion,* that Indian tribes retain inherent sovereign authority to govern the right of non-tribal citizens to enter their reservations and trust lands (and to regulate their conduct while they remain), *see supra* note 65, the Sixth Circuit rested its decision on the view that the Band's sovereign interests were not significant because "[t]he Supreme Court has long been suspicious of tribal authority to regulate the activity of non-members and is apt to view such power as implicitly divested . . . . " *Id.* at 544. *See also id.* at 546 (tribal power of nonmembers is at the "periphery" of "inherent tribal sovereignty").

b. Tenth and Eighth Circuits: If the Application of Federal Law Will Undermine Tribal Sovereignty, The Law Will Not Apply Absent a Clear Congressional Directive

The Tenth Circuit has rejected the *Tuscarora* dictum as a starting point for determining when a federal law of general application may be applied to tribal activities within reservations. In *Donovan v. Navajo Forest Products Industries*,[74] a case with facts very similar to *Coeur D'Alene Farm*, the Tenth Circuit held that OSHA could not be applied to a forest products enterprise owned and operated by the Navajo Nation on its reservation because to do so would undermine the Navajo Nation's sovereign authority to exclude nonmembers from tribal lands.

Consistent with the Ninth Circuit's second exception in *Coeur d'Alene Farm*, the Tenth Circuit first refused to apply the *Tuscarora* presumption if the application of OSHA, which says nothing about its application to Indian tribes or their wholly-owned enterprises, would impair an express treaty provision.[75] Going further, the Tenth Circuit said that, in light of *Merrion*, the *Tuscarora* presumption should have no force when the application of such a general federal law could "dilute" the inherent authority of tribes to exclude nonmembers or to condition their presence within the reservation.[76] Given the Supreme Court's recognition, in *Merrion*, that "an Indian tribe's power to exclude non-Indians from tribal lands is an inherent attribute of tribal sovereignty, essential to a tribe's exercise of self-government and territorial management," the Tenth Circuit refused to allow OSHA to undermine that aspect of the Navajo Nation's sovereignty without a clear directive from Congress.[77] The court explained:

---

[74]*Donovan v. Navajo Forest Prods. Inds.*, 692 F.2d 709, 712 (10th Cir. 1982).

[75]*Id.* at 711.

[76]*Id.* at 712.

[77]*Id.* at 712 (citing *Merrion v. Jicarilla Apache Tribe*, 455 U.S. 130, 141 (1982) (emphasis omitted). In *Coeur d'Alene Farm*, the NinthCircuit said that it disagreed with the Tenth Circuit's decision in *Navajo Forest Products Industr* to the extent that the Tenth

> The United States retains legislative plenary power to divest Indian tribes of any attributes of sovereignty.... Absent some expression of such legislative intent, however, we shall not permit divestiture of the tribal power to manage reservation lands so as to exclude non-Indians from entering thereon merely on the predicate that federal statutes of general application apply to Indians just as they do to all other persons ... unless Indians are expressly excepted therefrom. We believe that *Merrion* ... settled that issue in favor of the tribes."[78]

The Tenth Circuit later made clear, in *NLRB v. Pueblo of San Juan*,[79] that the *Tuscarora* dictum cannot be used to displace a tribe's exercise of inherent regulatory authority — in that case, the regulation of reservation labor organizations.[80] Noting "the absence of clear evidence of congressional intent," the court refused to uphold a challenge to the Pueblo's exercise of such authority;[81] congressional silence, the court said, will "not work a divestiture of [that] tribal power."[82]

Circuit's decision was "not tied to the existence of an express treaty right." *Coeur d'Alene Farm,* 751 F.2d at 1117 n.3.

[78]*Donovan,* 692 F.2d at 714. *See also EEOC v. Cherokee Nation,* 871 F.2d 937, 939 (10th Cir. 1989) (when there is no clear indication of congressional intent to abrogate tribal sovereignty, the court will protect it from infringement by federal authority exercised under the Age Discrimination in Employment Act, which fails to address tribes).

[79]276 F.3d 1186 (10th Cir. 2002) (en banc) (discussed in more detail in Chapter 7).

[80]*Id at* 1199.

[81]*Id.* at 1195. The Pueblo passed a so-called right-to-work-ordinance, prohibiting agreements between management and labor organizations that would require union membership or the payment of union dues, and enforced that law against an on-reservation lumber mill employing Pueblo citizens and non-citizens. *See id.* The Pueblo's law is similar to state right-to-work laws, and the NLRA expressly allows states to enact such laws. *Id.* at 1190 n.3.

[82]*Id.* at 1196. The Tenth Circuit later explained, "[i]n this circuit, respect for Indian sovereignty means that federal regulatory schemes do not apply to tribal governments

In *E.E.O.C. v. Fond du Lac Heavy Equipment and Construction Co.*, the Eighth Circuit followed the general approach of the Tenth Circuit.[83] That case presented the question of whether another federal law, the Age Discrimination in Employment Act of 1967 (ADEA),[84] should be applied to an Indian tribe's on-reservation enterprise.[85] The ADEA, like OSHA, is silent about its application to tribes.[86] The Eighth Circuit held that if application of the ADEA would undermine the exercise of tribal self-government, Congress's silence must be viewed as rendering the ADEA ambiguous, and the court must thus refrain from reading into it any intent to undermine tribal sovereignty absent a clear indication from Congress.[87] Decades later, the Eighth Circuit also followed this approach in an OSHA case involving a fishing enterprise owned by the Red Lake Band of Chippewa Indians operating within the Band's reservation and employing only citizens of the Band.[88]

Thus, the Tenth and Eighth Circuits, in contrast to the Ninth, Second, and Sixth Circuits consider, in the first instance, whether the imposition of a federal labor or employment law of general application would interfere with tribal sovereignty, established by treaty or by common law. If it would, these circuits view Congress's silence as ambiguous, and hold the law inapplicable, absent some other clear directive from Congress. By adopting the *Tuscarora* dictum with the

---

exercising their sovereign authority absent express congressional authorization." *Dobbs v. Anthem Blue Cross & Blue Shield*, 600 F.3d 1275, 1283 (10th Cir. 2010).

[83]*E.E.O.C. v. Fond du Lac Heavy Equip. & Constr. Co.*, 986 F.2d 246 (8th Cir. 1993) (discussed in more detail in Chapter 6).

[84]29 U.S.C. §§ 621-634 (2018).

[85]*See Fond du Lac Heavy Equip. & Constr. Co.*, 986 F.2d 246 (8th Cir. 1993).

[86]Like OSHA and the NLRA, the ADEA applies generally to "employers," but excludes the United States, states, and political subdivisions of states. *See* 29 U.S.C. § 630(b).

[87]*Id.* at 249.

[88]*Scalia v. Red Lake Nation Fisheries, Inc.*, No. 19-3373, 2020 WL 7083327 (8th Cir. Dec. 4, 2020).

qualifications developed in *Farris*, the Ninth, Second, and Sixth Circuits presume that such laws apply to tribes, unless a tribe establishes one of the three *Farris* exceptions.

c. Seventh Circuit: Uncertainty

In *Reich v. Great Lakes Indian Fish and Wildlife Commission*,[89] the U.S. Court of Appeals for the Seventh Circuit addressed whether the United States Department of Labor could impose the Fair Labor Standards Act of 1938 (FLSA)[90] (addressing overtime pay and minimum wages) upon a consortium of Indian tribes that employed a number of game wardens to oversee the Tribes' fish and wildlife resources. The court concluded that the Tribes' authority over the wages and hours of the game wardens reflected the "sovereign functions of tribal government."[91] Tracking the Tenth Circuit and Eighth Circuit approaches, it went on to hold that, absent a clear expression of congressional intent, federal courts must presume that Congress would not undermine such an exercise of sovereignty.[92] Because the Department of Labor could not show such intent on the part of Congress, the court refused to impose the FLSA upon the tribes.[93]

Several years later, in *Menominee Tribal Enterprises v. Solis*,[94] however, the Seventh Circuit retreated, somewhat, from the favorable stance it took for tribal authority in *Reich*. In *Menominee*, Seventh Circuit upheld the application of OSHA to a sawmill owned and controlled by the Menominee Tribe within the Tribe's reservation and employing only tribal citizens.[95] In a short decision, the court started

---

[89] *Reich v. Great Lakes Indian Fish & Wildlife Comm'n*, 4 F.3d 490 (7th Cir. 1993).

[90] 29 U.S.C. §§ 201-219 (2018).

[91] *Id.* 494-95.

[92] *Id.* (following *EEOC v. Cherokee Nation*, 871 F.2d 937 (10th Cir. 1989)).

[93] *Id.*

[94] 601 F.3d 669, 670 (7th Cir. 2010) (discussed in more detail in Chapter 6).

[95] *Id.*

its opinion with a formulation based on the *Farris/Coeur d'Alene Farm* approach:

> Statutes of general applicability that do not mention Indians are nevertheless usually held to apply to them. . . . But there are exceptions; a statute of general applicability will be held inapplicable to Indians if it would interfere with tribal governance . . . . Or if it would clash with rights granted Indians by other statutes or by treaties with Indian tribes (which are the legal equivalent of federal statutes . . . . Or if there is persuasive evidence that Congress did not intend by its silence that the statute would apply to Indians.[96]

The court found no treaty right protecting the Tribe's sawmill from OSHA, nor any indication that Congress did not intend the law to apply to tribes.[97] In considering whether any interference with tribal government was at stake, the court simply said, "[t]he Menominees' sawmill is just a sawmill, a commercial enterprise."[98]

Notably, the *Menominee Tribal Enterprises* court referred to "interfere[nce] with tribal governance" as an "exception" to the "general applicability" rule without narrowing it to "purely intramural matters" under the *Farris/Coeur d'Alene Farm* formulation.[99] Thus, the Seventh

---

[96]*Id.* at 670-71 (citations omitted).

[97]*Id.* at 671-72. The Seventh Circuit observed that *Mashantucket* involved the employment of "non-Indians," and then stated "[s]ince non-Indians are not subject to tribal jurisdiciton, the [Mashantucket] enterprise could not be thought part of the tribe's governmental structure." *Id.* at 673. As noted above, *supra* note 71, given the Supreme Court's standing decision in *Merrion* and the "first exception" set forth in its decision in *Montana*, "non-Indians" clearly are subject to tribal jurisdiction under certain circumstances.

[98]*Id.* at 671. This statement overlooks the importance of reservation tribal enterprises for the generation of tribal governmental revenues. *See supra* note 66.

[99]*Menominee Tribal Enterprises*, 601 F.3d at 671. *See also Smart v. State Farm Ins. Co.*, 868 F.2d 929, 932-34 (7th Cir. 1989) (applying *Farris/Coeur d'Alene Farm* approach to application of ERISA to health clinic). *But see Great Lakes Indian Fish & Wildlife*

Circuit still appears open to protecting tribal authority from federal agency interference in settings where tribes exercise their inherent regulatory authority in accord with the Supreme Court decisions described in Chapter 2.[100]

d. D.C. Circuit: Degree of Infringement Affects Outcome

The D.C. Circuit has taken a third approach. In *San Manuel Indian Bingo and Casino v. NLRB*,[101] it held that the NLRA[102] could be applied to a tribe's on-reservation gaming operation. While conceding that such gaming is "governmental" because its purpose is to generate revenue to support tribal government services, the court nevertheless characterized it as principally "commercial" in nature and therefore not sufficiently at the core of tribal sovereignty to warrant protection from the imposition of the NLRA.[103] Unlike the Ninth, Second, and Sixth Circuits, the D.C. Circuit did not accept the *Tuscarora* dictum as a useful starting point because (a) it had no real bearing on the Supreme Court's conclusion in that case, and (b) it appeared in conflict with subsequent Supreme Court decisions recognizing that, in the absence of a "clear expression of Congressional intent," courts must re-

---

Comm'n, 4 F.3d at 495 (criticizing *Smart*, 868 F.2d at 936, for failing to recognize that "Indian tribes, like states, are quasi-sovereigns entitled to comity," and holding that a court must not apply a federal employment statute in a manner that would "intrude on the sovereign functions of tribal government" without a strong indication from Congress).

[100]*See Great Lakes Indian Fish & Wildlife Comm'n*, 4 F.3d at 494-95 (the "'inherent sovereignty' of Indian tribes . . . extends to the kind of regulatory functions exercised by the Commission with respect to both Indians and non-Indians"; court will not construe FLSA to "invade the central regulatory functions of a sovereign entity").

[101]475 F.3d 1306 (D.C. Cir. 2007).

[102]29 U.S.C. §§ 151-169 (2018).

[103]*San Manuel*, 475 F.3d at 1312-13.

frain from imposing a federal statute upon a tribe if it will impair tribal sovereignty.[104]

But neither did the D.C. Circuit proceed, like the Tenth and Eighth Circuits, to first consider whether an established attribute of tribal sovereignty (like the power to regulate reservation economic activity) would be placed in jeopardy by the application of federal law. Rather, it suggested that tribal sovereignty can be evaluated concentrically, with "traditional customs and practices" within the reservation at the core, and "commercial activities that tend to blur any distinction between tribal government and a private corporation" at the periphery.[105] Those at the core could warrant protection, but those at the periphery, depending on the facts presented, might not.[106] In *Michigan v. Bay Mills Indian Community*,[107] Justice Sotomayor explained the importance of tribal governmental enterprises for the generation of governmental revenues, a view that contradicts the D.C. Circuit's notion that tribal gaming should be characterized as a "commercial" in nature.[108]

---

[104] *See San Manuel*, 475 F.3d at 1311 (citing *Santa Clara Pueblo v. Martinez*, 436 U.S. 49, 59-60 (1978)); 1317 (referencing "presumption" against undermining tribal sovereignty).

[105] *See id*. at 1312-14.

[106] *See id*. at 1314-15 (noting that no clear infringement of tribal sovereignty at issue; and if any, it was "modest").

[107] 572 U.S. 782 (2014).

[108] Justice Sotomayor wrote:
> [T]ribal gaming operations cannot be understood as mere profit-making ventures that are wholly separate from the Tribes' core governmental functions. A key goal of the Federal Government is to render Tribes more self-sufficient, and better positioned to fund their own sovereign functions, rather than relying on federal funding .... And tribal business operations are critical to the goals of tribal self-sufficiency because such enterprises in some cases may be the only means by which a tribe can raise revenues.

Id. at 810 (Sotomayor, J., concurring) (quotations and citations omitted). The Restatement of the Law of American Indians similarly provides:
> [A]n Indian tribe's operation of a casino pursuant to its inherent authority codified by Congress in the Indian Gaming Regulatory Act, 25 U.S.C. § 2710 et seq.

* * *

It remains to be seen which, if any, of the various approaches of the federal circuit courts will be adopted by the Supreme Court as the rule of decision when a federal labor or employment law, otherwise silent with regard to its application to Indian tribes, will apply to tribes or their enterprises. Most commentators endorse the approach of the Tenth and Eighth Circuits.[109]

("IGRA"), is a governmental undertaking for a governmental purpose: to generate revenues to support governmental services.
American Law Institute, REST., LAW OF AMERICAN INDIANS (Tent. Draft No. 4, Apr. 29, 2020) § 52, cmt. (c).

[109] *See, e.g.*, William Buffalo & Kevin J. Wadzinski, *Application of Federal and State Labor and Employment Laws to Indian Tribal Employers*, 25 U. MEM. L. REV. 1365 (1995); Kristen E. Burge, Comment, *ERISA and Indian Tribes: Alternative Approaches for Respecting Tribal Sovereignty*, 2000 WIS. L. REV. 1291 (2000); Vicki J. Limas, *Application of Federal Labor and Employment Statutes to Native American Tribes: Respecting Sovereignty and Achieving Consistency*, 26 ARIZ. ST. L.J. 681 (1994); Brian P. McClatchey, *Why Tribally-Owned Businesses Are Not "Employers": Economic Effects, Tribal Sovereignty, and NLRB v. San Manuel Band of Mission Indians*, 43 IDAHO L. REV. 127 (2006); Ann Richard, Note, *Application of the National Labor Relations Act and the Fair Labor Standards Act to Indian Tribes: Thwarting the Economic Self-Determination of Tribes*, 30 AM. INDIAN L. REV. 203 (2005-2006); Wenona T. Singel, *Labor Relations and Tribal Self-Governance*, 80 N.D. L. REV. 691 (2004); Alex Tallchief Skibine, *Applicability of Federal Laws of General Application to Indian Tribes and Reservation Indians*, 25 U.C. DAVIS L. REV. 85 (1991); Kaighn Smith Jr., *When Congress Forgets: Breaking Through Congress's Failure to Mention Indian Tribes in Federal Employment Laws*, FED. LAW., March/April 2021; Bryan H. Wildenthal, *Federal Labor Law, Indian Sovereignty, and the Canons of Construction*, 86 OR. L. REV. 413 (2007); Symposium, *Labor and Employment Laws in Indian Country*, 2 MICH. ST. L. REV. 435 (2008).

Language in recent Supreme Court decisions supports this view. *See McGirt v. Oklahoma*, 140 S. Ct. 2452, 2477 (2020) (statating that the Court "has long required a clear expression of the intention of Congress before" the federal government may undermine tribal sovereignty); *id.* at 2477 (citing *Ex parte Crow Dog*, 109 U.S. 556, 572 (1883)) (quotations omitted); *Michigan v. Bay Mills Indian Cmty*, 572 U.S. 782, 790 (2014) (stating that a congressional decision to undermine tribal sovereignty "must be clear," and this "rule of construction reflects an enduring principle of Indian law: [that] courts will not lightly assume that Congress in fact intends to undermine Indian self-government") (citing *Iowa Mut. Ins. Co. v. LaPlante*, 480 U.S. 9, 18 (1987)).

D. Deference to Tribal Court Authority: The Exhaustion Doctrine

The tribal court exhaustion doctrine operates as a separate barrier to state or federal court proceedings involving tribal employment relations. The doctrine is grounded in the federal policy of protecting and supporting tribal self-government and the authority of tribal courts over reservation affairs. It fits within the general category of defensive sovereignty with respect to reservation labor and employment relations because it may prevent a federal or state court from entertaining a case otherwise within its jurisdiction until legal remedies in a tribal judicial forum have been exhausted.

1. The Roots and Elements of the Tribal Court Exhaustion Doctrine

The Supreme Court established the exhaustion doctrine in *National Farmers Union Insurance Companies v. Crow Tribe of Indians*.[110] The case involved a claim by an insurance company that the tribal court of the Crow Tribe lacked jurisdiction over a case involving a nonmember defendant on the Crow reservation.[111] The Court held that the federal court had authority to decide the issue because the case raised a question of federal Indian law: the scope of the tribal court's authority over a nonmember (federal question jurisdiction).[112] How-

---

[110] 471 U.S. 845 (1985).

[111] Leroy Sage, a Crow Indian minor, was struck by a motorcycle in the parking lot of his elementary school while returning from a school activity. The school was operated by the Lodge Grass School District No. 27, a political subdivision of the State of Montana. *Nat'l. Farmers Union Ins. Co. v. Crow Tribe of Indians*, 471 U.S. 845, 847 (1985). It was located on land owned by the State of Montana, but within the exterior boundaries of the Crow Indian Reservation. *Id.* Sage, through his guardian, a Crow tribal member, sued the school district in the Crow Tribal Court. He won a default judgment against it and proceeded to execute the judgment against school property. *Id.* At that point, the school and its insurance company, National Farmers Union, brought an action in the federal court against the tribal court plaintiff, the tribal court judges, and the members of the Crow Tribal Council, claiming that, as a matter of federal Indian law, the tribal court had no authority to adjudicate the case. *Id.* at 848.

[112] *Id.* at 852-53.

ever, it held that the tribal court should have the first opportunity to decide the scope of its jurisdiction. The Supreme Court explained:

> We believe that examination should be conducted in the first instance in the Tribal Court itself. Our cases have often recognized that Congress is committed to a policy of supporting tribal self-government and self-determination. That policy favors a rule that will provide the forum whose jurisdiction is being challenged the first opportunity to evaluate the factual and legal bases for the challenge . . . . Exhaustion of tribal court remedies, moreover, will encourage tribal courts to explain to the parties the precise basis for accepting jurisdiction, and will also provide other courts with the benefit of their expertise in such matters in the event of further judicial review.[113]

On the other hand, the Court said that its announced exhaustion requirement would not be required where (a) the assertion of tribal jurisdiction is motivated by bad faith or a desire to harass, (b) the action is "patently violative of express jurisdictional prohibitions," or (c) exhaustion would be futile because of the lack of an adequate opportunity to challenge the court's jurisdiction.[114] Absent one of those exceptions, the federal court must stay the federal case or dismiss without prejudice to await the exhaustion of tribal court proceedings.[115]

In *Iowa Mutual Insurance Co. v. LaPlante*, the Supreme Court extended the doctrine to federal court actions invoking federal court jurisdiction when a controversy involves citizens of different states, known as diversity jurisdiction.[116] That case involved a claim by an insurance company asserting that it had no duty to defend a claim in-

---

[113]*Id.* at 856-57.

[114]*Id.* at 857 n.21.

[115]*Id.* at 857.

[116]480 U.S. 9 (1987).

volving an accident arising on the Blackfeet reservation between a tribal member plaintiff (LaPlante) and a ranch that operated as a Montana corporation.[117] The Supreme Court said that civil jurisdiction over the activities of nonmembers within Indian reservations "presumptively lies in the tribal courts unless affirmatively limited by a specific treaty provision or federal statute," and that the proper inference from Congress's silence on the subject was that this jurisdiction remained intact.[118] Extending the principles of *National Farmers Union* to the case before it, the Court held that the federal district court was required to stay Iowa Mutual's federal case or dismiss it without prejudice to allow the exhaustion of tribal court remedies.[119] The Court rejected Iowa Mutual's arguments that such exhaustion should not be required in order to protect it "against local bias and incompetence" within the tribal court, stating that such assertions were "not among the exceptions to the exhaustion requirement established in *National Farmers Union*" and "would be contrary to the congressional policy promoting the development of tribal courts."[120] It also pointed out that the Indian Civil Rights Act of 1968 (ICRA)[121] "provides non-Indians

---

[117] In that case, Edward LaPlante, a member of the Blackfeet Indian Tribe, was employed by a ranch located on the Blackfeet Indian Reservation and owned by members of the Tribe. He was injured when the cattle truck he drove as part of his work for the ranch "jackknifed." The accident occurred on the reservation. Iowa Mutual Insurance Company (an Iowa company) insured the ranch and attempted, unsuccessfully, to settle the claim. Thereafter, LaPlante and his wife brought a lawsuit in the Blackfeet Tribal Court against the ranch (a Montana corporation) and its tribal member owners for personal injury. They also asserted a claim against Iowa Mutual for compensatory and punitive damages for badfaith refusal to settle. *Iowa Mut. Ins. Co. v. LaPlante*, 480 U.S. at 9, 11-12. After the tribal court denied Iowa Mutual's motion to dismiss for lack of subject matter jurisdiction, Iowa Mutual sued the LaPlantes, the ranch, and the ranch owners in federal court, asking for a declaratory judgment that it had no duty to defend or indemnify the ranch or its owners because the injuries sustained by the LaPlantes fell outside the coverage of the applicable insurance policies. *Id*. at 13.

[118] *Id*. at 18.

[119] *Id*. at 18-19.

[120] *Id*.

[121] 25 U.S.C. §§ 1301-02 (2018).

with various protections against unfair treatment in the tribal courts."[122]

Since *Iowa Mutual* and *National Farmers Union*, the Supreme Court has clarified that exhaustion is not a jurisdictional prerequisite to a federal court proceeding to decide a case over which federal question or federal diversity jurisdiction exists. In *Strate v. A-1 Contractors*,[123] the Court explained that the exhaustion doctrine applied as a matter of comity out of respect for tribal self-government.[124] In addition to the three exceptions stated in *National Farmers*, the Court added a fourth exception to the exhaustion rule: exhaustion of tribal court remedies is not required when it is plain that federal law provides no basis for tribal governance over a nonmember's conduct.[125]

The lower federal courts have filled out the contours of the exhaustion doctrine.[126] They have held that it should be expansively ap-

---

[122]*Iowa Mut. Ins. Co.*, 480 U.S. at 19.

[123]520 U.S. 438 (1997).

[124]*Id.* at 451.

[125]*Id.* at 459 n.14. *See also Nevada v. Hicks*, 533 U.S. 353, 369 (2001) (exhaustion not required when it is clear that tribal court lacks jurisdiction so that exhaustion "would serve no purpose other than delay").

[126]In the Ninth Circuit, absent one of the four exceptions, exhaustion of tribal court remedies is required unless it is "plain that the tribal courts lack jurisdiction over the dispute."*Boozer v. Wilder*, 381 F.3d 931, 936 (9th Cir. 2004); *e.g., Ford Motor Co. v. Todecheene*, 488 F.3d 1215, 1216 (9th Cir. 2007). In the Tenth Circuit, when the activity at issue arises on the reservation or involves a "reservation affair," comity concerns "almost always dictate that the parties exhaust their tribal remedies before resorting to the federal forum." *E.g., Kerr-McGee Corp. v. Farley*, 115 F.3d 1498, 1507 (10th Cir. 1997); *Texaco v. Zah*, 5 F.3d 1374, 1377-78 (10th Cir. 1993); *Burlington N. R.R. Co. v. Crow Tribal Council*, 940 F.2d 1239 (9th Cir. 1991). Whether a particular case presents a "reservation affair" may turn on whether the claims at issue implicate the interests of tribal members. *See Kerr-McGee*, 115 F.3d at 1508 (considering the interest of the tribe in protecting and vindicating the rights of its residents when evaluating whether the case presented a reservation affair); whether a case implicates tribal law or policy, *see Navajo Nation v. Intermountain Steel Bldgs.*, 42 F. Supp.2d 1222, 1229 (D. N.M. 1999) (considering whether tribal law is at issue in determining whether the case presents a reservation affair); whether a tribal court proceeding involving the same parties is pending, *see Hartman v. Kickapoo Tribe Gaming Comm'n.*, 176 F.Supp.2d 1168, 1181 n. 6 (D.Kan. 2001), *aff'd*, 319 F.3d 1230 (10th Cir. 2003); or

plied to require the exhaustion of tribal court remedies for any given dispute, not just issues of jurisdiction.[127] And, as a general rule, after exhaustion of tribal adjudicatory processes, a reviewing federal court will not disturb the tribal court's judgment unless, as a matter of federal law, the tribal court lacked subject matter jurisdiction or there is a "valid reason" not to give deference to the tribal court's decision.[128]

Several state courts, like federal courts, apply the tribal exhaustion doctrine.[129] Thus, when a state court has jurisdiction over a claim arising in Indian country over which a tribal forum has colorable jurisdiction and none of the exceptions apply, the state court should stay or dismiss the case without prejudice to allow the exhaustion of tribal remedies.[130]

---

whether resolution of the dispute involves interpretations of tribal law, *see generally Johnson v. Harrah's Kansas Casino Corp.*, No. 04-4142-JAR, 2006 WL 463138, *10 (D.Kan. Feb. 23, 2006). The doctrine may operate, however, whether a pending tribal court action exists or not. *See, e.g., Garcia v. Akwesasne Hous. Auth.*, 268 F.3d 76, 81-82 (2d Cir. 2001); *Ninigret Dev. Corp. v. Narragansett Indian Wetuomuck Hous. Auth.*, 207 F.3d 21, 31 (1st Cir. 2000); *United States v. Tsosie*, 92 F.3d 1037, 1041 (10th Cir. 1996); *Crawford v. Genuine Parts Co.*, 947 F.2d 1405, 1407 (9th Cir. 1991). It also operates to require the exhaustion of available tribal administrative proceedings, not just tribal court proceedings. *See generally Burlington N. R.R. Co. v. Crow Tribal Council*, 940 F.2d 1239, 1246-47 (9th Cir. 1991); *Janis v. Wilson*, 521 F.2d 724, 726-27 (8th Cir. 1975); *Middlemist v. Sec'y. of Interior*, 824 F. Supp. 940, 945 (D. Mont. 1993); *Takes Gun v. Crow Tribe of Indians*, 448 F. Supp. 1222, 1226-27 (D. Mont. 1978).

[127]*See, e.g., Brown v. Washoe Hous. Auth.*, 835 F.2d 1327, 1328 (10th Cir. 1988); *United States ex rel. Kishell v. Turtle Mountain Hous. Auth.*, 816 F.2d 1273, 1276-77 (8th Cir. 1987); *Wellman v. Chevron U.S.A.*, 815 F.2d 577, 578-79 (9th Cir. 1987).

[128]*Attorney's Process & Investigation Serv. Inc. v. Sac & Fox Tribe of Mississippi in Iowa*, 609 F.3d 927, 942 (8th Cir. 2010). *See Burrell v. Armijo*, 456 F.3d 1159, 1173 (10th Cir. 2006) (rejecting on due process grounds the tribal court's sovereign immunity decision in subsequent federal court action, in which plaintiff asserted same federal civil rights claims against tribal officials that had been asserted and exhausted in tribal court).

[129]*See, e.g., Harvey v. Ute Indian Tribe of Uintah & Ouray Reservation*, 416 P.3d 401, 417–21; *Klammer v. Lower Sioux Convenience Store*, 535 N.W.2d 379 (Minn. 1995). *See generally* Pete Heidepriem, *Tribal Remedies, Exhaustion, and State Courts*, 44 AM. INDIAN L. REV. 241, 256-271 (2020).

[130]*See Harvey*, 416 P.3d at 417-21.

2. The Exhaustion Doctrine and Labor and Employment Disputes in Indian Country

When a federal or state court holds that tribal exhaustion is required before a reservation labor or employment dispute may proceed before it, there is, at the very least, a colorable argument that tribal jurisdiction may be asserted over the dispute at issue in accord with the legal principles discussed in Chapter 2.[131] As such, cases applying the doctrine to reservation labor and employment disputes present a measure of the scope of tribal sovereign authority over labor and employment relations in Indian country.

Federal courts have stayed or dismissed cases involving employment-relations disputes within reservations under the tribal exhaustion doctrine in the following settings:

- *Window Rock Unified Sch. Dist. v. Reeves*:[132] Navajo citizen and non-Navajo citizen employees of school districts that are operated by the State of Arizona on leased lands within the Navajo Reservation brought employment-related claims against the districts before the Navajo Nation's Labor Counsel. The school districts sued the officers of the Counsel in federal court, claiming that the Navajo Nation did not have jurisdiction to adjudicate the employees' claims. The Ninth Circuit, resting on the Navajo Nation's inherent right to exclude non-tribal citizens from the Navajo Reservation and to regulate their conduct while they remain, held that the Counsel had "colorable or plausible" jurisdiction over the claims and that state interests were not significantly implicated so as to thwart Navajo jurisdiction.[133]

---

[131]*See Graham v. Applied Geo Technologies Inc.*, 593 F. Supp.2d 915, 920 (S.D. Miss. 2008) (applying *Montana* factors discussed in Chapter 2 to decide if there was a colorable argument for tribal jurisdiction warranting exhaustion).

[132]861 F.3d 894 (9th Cir. 2017), as amended (Aug. 3, 2017).

[133]*Id.* at 898-904.

- *Duncan Energy Co. v. Three Affiliated Tribes of Ft. Berthold Reservation:*[134] A non-Indian energy company's challenge to tribal law requiring it to give employment preferences to tribal members and imposing production tax was held subject to tribal court exhaustion. The company operated oil and gas wells within a quadrant of the Fort Berthold Reservation under leases from non-Indian landowners. The Ninth Circuit held "this dispute over tribal taxation and employment rights to be a dispute arising on the Reservation that raises questions of tribal law and jurisdiction that should first be presented to the tribal court."[135]

- *Hartman v. Kickapoo Tribe Gaming Commission:*[136] A non-member employed at the Tribe's casino sued the Tribe, its gaming commission, state gaming regulators, and federal gaming regulators, claiming that their suspension of her gaming license violated her due process rights under the federal Constitution and violated the Indian Gaming Regulatory Act of 1988 (IGRA).[137] Before proceeding in federal court, she sued tribal defendants in tribal court, alleging due process violations. The court held that the exhaustion doctrine required dismissal of claims against tribal defendants. Since the dispute arose on the reservation and was a "reservation affair," the court had "no discretion not to defer" to the tribal court.[138]

- *Sharber v. Spirit Mountain Gaming Inc.:*[139] Employee of tribal gaming facility brought action against the casino in

---

[134] 27 F.3d 1294 (8th Cir. 1994).

[135] *Id.* at 1300 (citations omitted).

[136] 176 F. Supp.2d 1168 (D.Kan. 2001), *aff'd* 319 F.3d 1230 (10th Cir. 2003).

[137] 25 U.S.C. §§ 2701-21 (2018).

[138] *Hartman*, 176 F. Supp.2d at 1181 (citations omitted).

[139] 343 F.3d 974, 975 (9th Cir. 2003).

federal court, claiming violations of the Family and Medical Leave Act of 1993 (FMLA).[140] The district court decided that the tribal court should first address its jurisdiction over the FMLA claim and whether the casino had sovereign immunity, and dismissed the case for lack of subject matter jurisdiction. The Ninth Circuit affirmed the district court's decision to apply the exhaustion doctrine, but reversed that part of the decision holding that dismissal was for lack of subject matter jurisdiction because the exhaustion doctrine does not affect a federal court's subject matter jurisdiction.[141]

- *Rassi v. Fed. Program Integrators, LLC*:[142] Nonmember of Penobscot Nation employed within the Penobscot Indian Reservation by subsidiary of the Nation's corporation, formed under section 17 of Indian Reorganization Act, brought civil rights and other claims against corporation.[143] The federal district court dismissed the case under the exhaustion doctrine.[144]

- *Abdo v. Fort Randall Casino*:[145] A former manager of an on-reservation casino operated by the Yankton Sioux Tribe brought action against the casino and the Tribe for breach of employment contract and wrongful termination. The parties disputed whether the contract was a casino management agreement subject to IGRA or a garden-variety employment contract. The federal district court held that, under the circumstances, it would abstain to allow exhaus-

---

[140] 29 U.S.C. §§ 2601, 2611-19, 2631-36 (2018).

[141] *Sharber*, 343 F.3d at 976.

[142] 69 F. Supp. 3d 288 (D. Me. 2014).

[143] *See id.* at 290.

[144] *See id.* at 293-294.

[145] 957 F. Supp. 1111 (D.S.D. 1997).

tion of tribal remedies. "[T]he instant case involves the Yankton Sioux Tribe and the tribally owned and operated Fort Randall Casino, and the dispute arises from Tribal government activity involving a project located within the borders of the reservation."[146] Thus, the court stayed further proceedings to allow "determination by the Tribal Court of the Court's jurisdiction and the legal validity of the management contract under applicable tribal law."[147]

- *Graham v. Applied Geo Technologies, Inc.*:[148] A non-Indian employee of a tribally-owned business operating on reservation claimed race discrimination. The court held that dismissal of the claim was warranted under the exhaustion doctrine and required the employee to exhaust tribal court remedies before bringing discrimination claims under Title VII and § 1981.[149] Referencing *Montana* standards, the court held that there is a "colorable claim of tribal court jurisdiction so that the requirement of exhaustion applies."[150]

- *Prescott v. Little Six, Inc.*:[151] Little Six, Inc. (LSI), a corporation organized under the laws of the Shakopee Mdewakanton Sioux (Dakota) Community, operated a casino on the Tribe's reservation and administered employee benefit plans for casino employees. The Tribe was the sole shareholder of LSI. Former executive employees of LSI at the casino brought a federal court action against LSI, claiming violations of the federal Employee Retirement In-

---

[146]*Id.* at 1113.

[147]*Id.* at 1114.

[148]593 F. Supp.2d 915 (S.D. Miss. 2008).

[149]*Id.* at 919-22.

[150]*Id.* at 920.

[151]897 F. Supp. 1217 (D. Minn. 1995).

come Security Act of 1974 (ERISA).[152] There were a number of actions related to the claims pending in the tribal court. The federal court observed that while federal courts have exclusive jurisdiction to award equitable relief for ERISA violations, they did not have exclusive jurisdiction "to determine whether an ERISA plan exists or whether benefits were wrongfully denied."[153] The tribal court was free to determine that issue, and, indeed, the defendants claimed that ERISA would not apply to the benefit plans in question because they did not comply with tribal law.[154] With tribal law implicated, and a proceeding pending in the tribal court, the federal court held that the case should be dismissed to allow the exhaustion of tribal remedies.[155]

- *Geroux v. Assurant, Inc.*:[156] A tribal member, employed on the reservation of the Keweenau Bay Indian Community by the Tribe, brought a tribal court action seeking unpaid disability benefits. The federal court held that the action could not be removed to federal court under a theory of ERISA preemption and that the exhaustion of tribal court remedies was required to allow the tribal court to assess its own jurisdiction, including the issue of ERISA preemption.[157]

---

[152] Pub. L. No. 93-406, 88 Stat. 829.

[153] *Prescott,* 897 F. Supp. at 1222.

[154] *Id.* at 1223.

[155] *Id.* at 1222-24.

[156] No. 2:08-cv-00184, 2009 WL 4068700 (W.D. Mich. Nov. 23, 2009).

[157] *Id.* at *3-5.

Federal courts have refused to apply the exhaustion doctrine to disputes involving employment relations affecting tribes in the following cases:

- *State of Montana Department of Transportation v. King:*[158] The State of Montana sued tribal officials to enjoin them from enforcing tribal employment preference law on a state highway construction project crossing the reservation. The federal court held that tribal exhaustion was not necessary because the tribe lacked "regulatory authority over nonmembers for activities on reservation land owned by non-Indians."[159]

- *Garcia v. Akwesasne Housing Authority:*[160] A nonmember executive director of Akwesasne Tribal Housing Authority sued the Housing Authority and its chairman in federal court, claiming age discrimination, violation of due process rights under both the federal Constitution and the Indian Civil Rights Act, breach of contract, and tort. The district court dismissed the complaint under the tribal exhaustion doctrine and sovereign immunity. The Second Circuit held that the exhaustion doctrine did not bar the suit because (a) the case involved a non-tribal plaintiff; (b) there was no pending tribal proceeding addressing the controversy; and (c) the federal action did not implicate tribal law.[161] The court found that the plaintiff's claims against the Housing Authority were barred by sovereign immunity but that her claims against the individual defendant could proceed.[162]

---

[158] 191 F.3d 1108 (9th Cir. 1999).

[159] *Id.* at 1113 (citing *Montana v. United States*, 450 U.S. 544, 563-65 (1981)).

[160] 268 F.3d 76 (2d Cir. 2001).

[161] *Id.* at 82-84.

[162] *Id.*

- *Tidwell v. Harrah's Kansas Casino Corp.*:[163] A nonmember brought an action against her employer, Harrah's Kansas Casino Corporation, a non-Indian corporation, claiming discrimination in violation of state and federal law. Harrah's operated a casino for the Prairie Band Potawatomi Nation on its reservation. The federal district court held that the exhaustion doctrine did not apply because (a) the dispute was between two non-Indians; (b) it involved federal law without implicating tribal law or policy; and (c) there was no pending action in the tribal court involving the same controversy.[164]

- *Johnson v. Harrah's Kansas Casino Corp.*:[165] For "substantially the same reasons discussed in *Tidwell*, the Court declined to dismiss this suit based on considerations of comity."[166] A nonmember was employed by Harrah's Kansas Casino Corporation (a Nevada corporation), which operated a casino on the reservation of the Prairie Band Potawatomi Nation under a management agreement with the Tribe. She brought federal and state law discrimination claims against Harrah's in federal court. The court held that the case did not present a "reservation affair" warranting application of the exhaustion doctrine. According to the court, the case did not implicate tribal law or policy, there was no pending action in the tribal court, and the case did not implicate the interests of tribal members.[167]

---

[163] 322 F. Supp.2d 1200 (D. Kan. 2004).

[164] *Id.* at 1204-05. While it may not have affected the outcome, the court erroneously stated that Harrah's "owned" the casino, which would violate IGRA if true. *See id.* at 1205 *and compare* 25 U.S.C. § 2710(b)(2)(A). It also failed to recognize that the casino was located on reservation or trust land, as required by IGRA. *See id.* at 1205 *and compare* 25 U.S.C. §§ 2703(4); 2710(b)(1); 2710(d)(1).

[165] No. 04-4142-JAR, 2006 WL 463138, *10 (D.Kan. Feb. 23, 2006).

[166] *Id.* at *10.

[167] *Id.*

- *Hines v. Grand Casinos of Louisiana LLC - Tunica-Biloxi:*[168] Grand Casinos of Louisiana LLC entered into a Management and Construction Agreement with the Tunica-Biloxi Indian Tribe for the operation of the Tribe's casino on the reservation pursuant to IGRA. Under the terms of the agreement, Grand Casinos had "exclusive responsibility" to select, control, and discharge employees at the casino. A nonmember brought an action in the federal court against Grand Casinos, claiming she suffered sexual harassment by a supervisor in violation of federal law.[169] She also commenced an action for employment discrimination in the tribal court against Grand Casinos and the Tribe. Grand Casinos filed a motion to dismiss the federal court case, claiming (a) that the Tribe was her employer under the terms of the management agreement and (b) that the exhaustion doctrine applied. The Fifth Circuit held that the Tribe's interests were not implicated in the federal court case. First, although the Tribe paid the employee's salary, withheld her taxes, and paid for her benefits, under the common-law "control test," Grand Casinos was her employer as a matter of law. Second, the court said that the "exhaustion doctrine is inapposite" in this setting.[170]

- *Krempel v. Prairie Island Indian Community:*[171] Krempel, a resident of Wisconsin, brought an action in Minnesota state court against the Prairie Island Indian Community, his former employer, and Anne Burr, his former supervisor, a Minnesota resident. He alleged sexual harassment, gender and sexual orientation discrimination, defamation, and promissory estoppel, all under Minnesota law, arising out of his employment at the Tribe's Treasure Island Casino,

---

[168] No. 01-30692, 2002 WL 180364 (5th Cir. Jan. 4, 2002).

[169] *Id.* at *1-2.

[170] *Id.* at *2-3.

[171] 125 F.3d 621 (8th Cir. 1997).

located on the reservation.[172] The defendants removed the case to federal court on the basis of diversity jurisdiction. The Tribe did not assert sovereign immunity from suit.[173] Although the Tribe had begun the process of developing a judicial system, it was not fully operational at the time of removal. The federal district court dismissed the case without prejudice under the exhaustion doctrine. It said, "This case involves claims of wrongful conduct by a Casino employee on tribal property. Because the conduct of tribal employees and the operation of the Casino are issues which clearly implicate tribal law, the tribal court is the proper forum for plaintiff to first raise his claims."[174] The Eighth Circuit reversed. It held that the exhaustion doctrine was inapplicable under the Supreme Court's futility exception because there was no tribal court system in place.[175]

- *Vance v. Boyd Mississippi Inc.*:[176] A nonmember employee of Silver Star Casino, owned by the Mississippi Band of Choctaw Indians and located on the Choctaw Tribal Reservation, brought an action for pregnancy discrimination (under federal law) against Boyd Mississippi, Inc., which operated the casino under a management agreement with the Tribe. Boyd moved to dismiss pursuant to the exhaustion doctrine. The court held that the exhaustion of tribal remedies was not required. There was no pending tribal court action, and the case did not implicate tribal law or policy. Rather, it was "between two non-Indians, concerning only

---

[172]*Krempel v. Prairie Island Indian Cmty.*, 888 F. Supp. 106, 107 (D.Minn. 1995).

[173]*Id.*

[174]*Id.* at 109.

[175]*Krempel v. Prairie Island Indian Cmty.*, 125 F.3d 621, 624 (8th Cir. 1997) ("we hold as a matter of law that Krempel, who had filed a timely claim in an existing forum, was not required to exhaust tribal remedies at a later time when the tribal court came into existence").

[176]923 F. Supp. 905 (S.D. Miss. 1996).

issues of federal law, which happened to arise on the Reservation in a business owned by the Tribe but which is managed by a non-Indian corporation."[177]

- *Myrick v. Devils Lake Sioux Manufacturing Corp.*:[178] A tribal member and resident of the Devils Lake Sioux Indian Reservation brought an action in the federal court against Devils Lake Sioux Manufacturing Corporation, a North Dakota corporation, presumably operating on the reservation. The Devils Lake Sioux Tribe owned 51 percent of the corporation, and Brunswick Corporation, a Delaware corporation, owned the other 49 percent. The plaintiff claimed age and race discrimination under federal law, violations of the Fair Labor Standards Act,[179] and breach of contract. The federal district court denied the defendants' motion to dismiss the action under the exhaustion doctrine on the grounds that there was "no attack or challenge to the jurisdiction of the tribal court," neither the tribe nor an arm of the tribe was a party, and the case predominately presented issues of federal law.[180]

E. Conclusion

This chapter has outlined the law establishing barriers to state and federal authority over labor and employment relations within Indian country. The established infringement and preemption barriers to state law authority are more stable than the barriers to federal authority; the federal courts are fractured with respect to the rule that governs the latter. When the barriers break down, concurrent authority— between a state and a tribe, or between a federal agency and a tribe— may exist over a given on-reservation labor or employment matter.

---

[177]*Id.* at 911.

[178]718 F. Supp. 753 (D.N.D. 1989).

[179]29 U.S.C. §§ 201-19 (2018).

[180]*Myrick*, 718 F. Supp. at 755.

And when concurrent jurisdiction exists, courts may invoke the exhaustion doctrine to allow tribal remedies to run their course.

The existence of governing tribal law over reservation labor and employment matters will likely become a critical factor in applying infringement and preemption barriers to state authority and the federal infringement standard. Such law may enhance balancing tests in favor of tribal self-government. Further, the existence of an enforceable remedy under tribal law in a tribal forum may cause federal and state courts to pause before adjudicating an on-reservation employment dispute under the exhaustion doctrine.

Chapter 2 examined the legal underpinnings of affirmative tribal sovereignty for tribes to govern reservation labor and employment relations. This chapter has examined defensive aspects of tribal sovereignty: legal standards that prevent state or federal authorities from intruding upon tribal self-government. Chapter 4 turns to the operation of tribal sovereign immunity from suit as a distinct, defensive barrier to the authority of federal, state, and tribal courts.

4

DEFENSIVE TRIBAL SOVEREIGNTY: SOVEREIGN IMMUNITY AND TRIBAL EMPLOYMENT DISPUTES

A. Introduction

In addition to the barriers to state and federal regulatory authority over on-reservation labor and employment relations discussed in Chapter 3, sovereign immunity stands as a separate barrier to the authority of courts over disputes involving such relations. Unless unambiguously waived by a tribe or by Congress, sovereign immunity bars suits by individuals and state agencies in any court (federal, state, or tribal) against an Indian tribe.[1] Federal courts have held, however, that sovereign immunity does not prevent the United States or its agencies from bringing lawsuits against tribes.[2]

This chapter sets forth the basic law of tribal sovereign immunity and its application to reservation labor and employment matters. A recurring question that arises in this setting is whether sovereign immunity applies to bar lawsuits against tribal officials or tribal enterprises. The answer affects the ability of employees to bring legal claims to obtain relief for alleged workplace wrongs, such as discrimination or breach of contract. This chapter initially describes the basic principles of tribal sovereign immunity. It then examines when sovereign immunity applies to bar suits against tribal officials, individuals, and enterprises. Lastly, it considers waivers of sovereign immunity

---

[1]*Michigan v. Bay Mills Indian Cmty.*, 572 U.S. 782 (2014); *C & L Enterprises, Inc. v. Citizen Band Potawatomi Indian Tribe of Oklahoma*, 532 U.S. 411 (2001); *Kiowa Tribe of Okla. v. Mfg. Tech's., Inc.*, 523 U.S. 751 (1998).

[2]For further discussion of federal agency lawsuits against tribes and tribal enterprises, *see* Chapter 6.

and the related problem of forum selection for the resolution of disputes.

B. Sovereign Immunity: Basic Principles

Indian tribes possess the common law immunity from suit traditionally enjoyed by sovereign powers.[3] This stems from tribes' status as independent sovereign nations pre-dating the formation of the United States.[4] Sovereign immunity bars any lawsuit, other than one brought by the federal government, against Indian tribes and their governmental units, absent an unequivocal waiver of the immunity either by the tribe itself or by Congress.[5] A tribe's sovereign immunity from suit bars actions by individuals or state agencies against tribes for any type of activity, whether deemed "commercial" or "governmental,"[6] and whether such activity occurs within or outside of Indian country.[7]

Tribal sovereign immunity is generally viewed as a jurisdictional barrier to the authority of courts and other tribunals exercising adjudi-

---

[3]*See Bay Mills Indian Cmty.,* 572 U.S. at 788-789; *Okla. Tax Comm'n v. Citizen Band Potawatomi Indian Tribe of Okla.*, 498 U.S. 505, 510 (1991); *Santa Clara Pueblo v. Martinez*, 436 U.S. 49, 58-59 (1978).

[4]*Santa Clara Pueblo v. Martinez*, 436 U.S. 49, 58 (1978).

[5]*Okla. Tax Comm'n v. Citizen Band Potawatomi Indian Tribe of Okla.*, 498 U.S. 505, 510 (1991).

[6]*Id.*; *Native American Distributing v. Seneca-Cayuga Tobacco Co.*, 546 F.3d 1288, 1292-93 (10th Cir. 2008).

[7]*Bay Mills Indian Cmty.,* 572 U.S. at 790; *Kiowa Tribe of Okla.*, 523 U.S. at 755. The Supreme Court has long held that Congress, not the Court, should be the branch of government to make the policy judgments about any retrenchment from the established contours of tribal sovereign immunity. *See id.* at 758 ("we defer to the role Congress may wish to exercise in this important judgment"). Indeed, given Congress's commitment to enhancing the sovereignty of Indian tribes through its numerous enactments in the "modern era" of federal Indian policy discussed in Chapter 1, the Court has said "we are not disposed to modify the long-established principle of tribal sovereign immunity." *Oklahoma Tax Com'n v. Citizen Band Potawatomi Indian Tribe of Oklahoma*, 498 U.S. 505, 510 (1991).

catory functions.[8] It applies to any claim for relief against Indian tribes and their governing bodies.[9] That is, unless it is waived, courts and tribunals have no *power* to proceed against a tribe.[10] Simply stated, with the exception of lawsuits brought by the United States or its agencies, courts have no authority to entertain an action against Indian

---

[8]*See Puyallup Tribe, Inc. v. Dep't of Game of State of Wash.*, 433 U.S. 165, 172 (1977) ("Absent an effective waiver or consent, it is settled that a state court may not exercise jurisdiction over a recognized Indian tribe"); *Miner Elec., Inc., v. Muscogee (Creek) Nation*, 505 F.3d. 1007, 1009-11 (10th Cir. 2007); *Lewis v. Norton*, 424 F.3d 959, 961 (9th Cir. 2005); *Garcia v. Akwesasne Hous. Auth.*, 268 F.3d 76, 84 (2d Cir. 2001); *Black Hills Inst. of Geological Research v. U.S. Dept. of Justice*, 967 F.2d 1237, 1240 n.5 (8th Cir. 1992). *But see Meyers v. Oneida Tribe of Indians of Wis.*, 836 F.3d 818 (7th Cir. 2016) (sovereign immunity does not implicate subject matter jurisdiction because it can be waived).

[9]*See Citizen Band Potawatomi Indian Tribe of Okla. v. Okla. Tax Comm'n*, 969 F.2d 943, 948 n.5 (10th Cir. 1992); *Black Hills Inst. of Geological Research v. U.S. Dept. of Justice*, 967 F.2d 1237, 1240 n.5 (8th Cir. 1992); *Maynard v. Narragansett Indian Tribe*, 798 F. Supp. 94, 96 n.1 (D.R.I. 1992).

[10]In fact, in cases where the tribe is clearly the named defendant, courts may presume there is a jurisdictional obstacle unless the plaintiff affirmatively pleads some grounds for finding a waiver. *See Wichita & Affiliated Tribe of Okla. v. Hodel*, 788 F.2d 765, 773 (D.C. Cir. 1986); *Seneca-Cayuga Tribe of Okla. v. State ex rel. Thompson*, 874 F.2d 709, 715-16 (10th Cir. 1989). Further, courts will not imply a waiver of immunity based on "policy concerns, perceived inequities arising from the assertion of immunity, or the unique context of the case." *Multimedia Games, Inc., v. WLGC Acquisition Corp.*, 214 F. Supp.2d 1131, 1139 (N.D. Okla. 2001) (*quoting Ute Distrib. Corp. v. Ute Indian Tribe*, 149 F.3d 1260, 1267 (10th Cir. 1998)). Where sovereign immunity (and therefore lack of subject matter jurisdiction) is present, parties may be left without remedies or forums to enforce their rights. *See, e.g., Kiowa Tribe of Okla. v. Mfg. Tech's., Inc.*, 523 U.S. 751, 755 (1998); *Okla. Tax Comm'n v. Potawatomi Indian Tribe*, 498 U.S. 505, 514 (1991); *U.S. v. U.S. Fid. & Guar. Co.*, 309 U.S. 506, 513 (1940); *Ute Distrib. Corp. v. Ute Indian Tribe*, 149 F.3d 1260, 1266 n.8 (10th Cir. 1998) ("The proposition that tribal immunity is waived if a party is otherwise left without a judicial remedy is inconsistent with [Supreme Court precedent]"); *Fluent v. Salamanca Indian Lease Auth.*, 928 F.2d 542, 547 (2d Cir. 1991) ("Sovereign immunity may leave a party with no forum for that party's claims.") (quotations omitted); *Makah Indian Tribe v. Verity*, 910 F.2d 555, 560 (9th Cir. 1990) (same); *E.F.W. v. St. Stephen's Mission Indian High School*, 51 F.Supp.2d 1217, 1228 (D. Wyo. 1999).

tribes unless the tribe or Congress has expressly abrogated the tribe's immunity.[11]

Importantly, sovereign immunity only arises if there is an action in a court or "quasi-judicial" tribunal. In other words, it operates solely as a constraint upon judicial authority. Whether a particular law may *apply* to a tribe is therefore a separate question from whether such a law may be enforced against a tribe *in court*.[12] It is only in the latter context that sovereign immunity comes into play. While seemingly incongruous, courts have said that just because Congress imposes the requirements of a particular law upon Indian tribes, that does not mean that Congress also abrogates tribal sovereign immunity with respect to lawsuits brought by individuals under that law.[13]

As discussed below, unless expressly waived by Congress or by a tribe, the doctrine of tribal sovereign immunity generally bars suits against Indian tribes, tribal enterprises, tribal officials, and tribal employees. However, there are important limitations to the doctrine of tribal sovereign immunity. It does not bar suits against tribal officials or employees in their individual capacities when the tribe is not the "real party in interest."[14] Nor does it bar a suit for prospective injunctive relief to prevent tribal officials from violating applicable federal

---

[11] *See Seneca-Cayuga Tribe of Okla. v. State ex rel. Thompson*, 874 F.2d 709, 715 n.7 (10th Cir. 1989); *Meier v. Sac & Fox Indian Tribe of Miss. in Iowa*, 476 N.W.2d 61, 64 (Iowa 1991).

[12] "There is a difference between the right to demand compliance with state laws and the means available to enforce them." *Kiowa Tribe of Okla. v. Mfg. Tech's., Inc.*, 523 U.S. 751, 755 (1998) (citing *Okla. Tax Comm'n v. Citizen Band Potawatomi Indian Tribe of Okla.*, 498 U.S. 505, 514 (1991)).

[13] *Garcia v. Akwesasne Hous. Auth.*, 268 F.3d 76, 86 n.5 (2d Cir. 2001) ("the fact that a statute applies to Indian tribes does not mean that Congress abrogated tribal immunity in adopting it") (quoting *Bassettt v. Mashantucket Pequot Tribe*, 204 F.3d 343, 357 (2d Cir. 2000)); *Fla. Paraplegic Ass'n, Inc., v. Miccosukee Tribe of Indians of Fla.*, 166 F.3d 1126, 1130 (11th Cir. 1999) ("whether an Indian tribe is *subject* to a statute and whether the tribe may be *sued* for violating the statute are two entirely different questions"). *But see Narragansett Indian Tribe v. Rhode Island*, 449 F.3d 16, 24 (1st Cir. 2006) (en banc) (rejecting distinction with respect to application of state law and sovereign immunity from judicial enforcement of state law).

[14] *Lewis v. Clarke*, 137 S. Ct. 1285, 1291 (2017).

law. Further, it may not apply to bar suits against entities that are not considered "arms of the tribe." These limitations warrant close examination given their effect upon employment-related controversies.

C. Sovereign Immunity: Individual Capacity and *Ex Parte Young* Lawsuits

With two notable exceptions discussed below, tribal government officials are generally entitled to immunity from suit when they act in their official capacity and within the scope of their authority.[15] Courts have applied tribal sovereign immunity to protect not only high-ranking tribal government officials, but also lower-level employees working for tribes.[16] They have also held that tribal attorneys, when acting as representatives of tribes and within the scope of their authority, enjoy the tribe's sovereign immunity from suit.[17] Such immunity also protects tribal government officials and representatives from being

---

[15]*See, e.g., Native American Distrib. v. Seneca-Cayuga Tobacco Co.*, 546 F.3d 1288, 1296-97 (10th Cir. 2008); *Chayoon v. Chao*, 355 F.3d 141, 143 (2d Cir. 2004), *cert. denied*, 543 U.S. 966 (2004); *Hardin v. White Mountain Apache Tribe*, 779 F.2d 476, 478 (9th Cir. 1985); *Romanella v. Hayward*, 933 F.Supp. 163, 167 (D.Conn. 1996), *aff'd*, 114 F.3d 15 (2d Cir. 1997).

[16]*Bassett v. Mashantucket Pequot Museum & Research Ctr., Inc.*, 221 F. Supp.2d 271, 277-78 (D. Conn. 2002); *Filer v. Tohono O'Odham Nation Gaming Enter.*, 129 P.3d 78, 85-86 (Ariz. Ct. App. 2006). *Compare Baugus v. Brunson*, 890 F.Supp. 908, 911 (E.D. Cal. 1995) (suggesting that tribal immunity extends only to high-level government officials) *and Turner v. Martire*, 97 Cal. Rptr. 2d 863, 869 (Cal. Ct. App. 2000) (disagreeing with *Baugus* and applying functional test).

[17]*See Catskill Dev. LLC v. Park Place Entm't. Corp.*, 206 F.R.D. 78, 90-91 (S.D.N.Y. 2002) (citations omitted). *See also Gaming Corp. of America v. Dorsey & Whitney*, 88 F.3d 536, 550 (8th Cir. 1996) ("Tribes need to be able to hire agents, including counsel, to assist in the process of regulating gaming. As any government with aspects of sovereignty, a tribe must be able to expect loyalty and candor from its agents. If the tribe's relationship with its attorney, or attorney advice to it, could be explored in litigation in an unrestricted fashion, its ability to receive candid advice essential to [developing gaming] would be compromised"); *Baugus v. Brunson*, 890 F.Supp. 908, 911 (E.D. Cal. 1995) (tribal representative need not be a tribal member to enjoy tribe's sovereign immunity).

compelled by subpoenas to give testimony in civil cases as nonparty witnesses.[18]

1. Individual Capacity Lawsuits

Individuals who have no relationship to tribal government do not enjoy the sovereign immunity belonging to the tribe and its officials.[19] Thus, if tribal officials or employee takes action *as an individual* — not as a tribal official or employee — they may be subject to suit in their individual (or "personal") capacity, even for damages.[20] Whether sovereign immunity blocks lawsuits for money damages against tribal officials or employees turns on whether the tribe is the "real party in interest."[21] If the relief sought by the lawsuit would have a direct effect on the tribe's property or fiscal resources, the tribe is the real party in interest and the suit is barred by sovereign immunity.[22] Sovereign immunity in these cases does not turn on whether the alleged wrongdo-

---

[18] *See Alltel Commc'ns, LLC v. DeJordy,* 675 F.3d 1100, 1106 (8th Cir. 2012); *Catskill Dev. LLC v. Park Place Entm't. Corp.,* 206 F.R.D. 78, 86-88 (S.D.N.Y. 2002); *but see Bonnet v. Harvest,* 741 F.3d 1155, 1162 (10th Cir. 2014) (holding tribe's agency immune from subpoena, but suggesting, without deciding, that tribal officials may not have such immunity); *Great W. Casinos, Inc., v. Morongo Band of Mission Indians,* 88 Cal. Rptr. 2d 828, 840 (Cal. Ct. App. 1999), *cert. denied,* 531 U.S. 812 (2000).

[19] *Puyallup Tribe, Inc., v. Dept. of Game of Wash.,* 433 U.S. 165, 173 (1977) ("[T]he [tribe's] successful assertion of tribal sovereign immunity in this case does not impair the authority of the state court to adjudicate the rights of the individual defendants over whom it properly obtained personal jurisdiction"); *United States v. James,* 980 F.2d 1314, 1319 (9th Cir.1992) ("Tribal immunity does not extend to the individual members of the tribe").

[20] *Lewis v. Clarke,* 137 S. Ct. 1285, 1291 (2017); *see also Native American Distrib. v. Seneca-Cayuga Tobacco Co.,* 546 F.3d 1288, 1297 (10th Cir. 2008); *Burrell v. Armijo,* 456 F.3d 1159, 1174 (10th Cir. 2006), *cert. denied,* 549 U.S. 1167 (2007); *Garcia v. Akwesasne Hous. Auth.,* 268 F.3d 76, 88 (2d Cir. 2001) (allowing suit to proceed against tribal officer in personal capacity).

[21] *Lewis v. Clarke,* 137 S. Ct. at 1290-1291; *Pistor v. Garcia,* 791 F.3d 1104, 1112 (9th Cir. 2015).

[22] *See Maxwell v. Cty. of San Diego,* 708 F.3d 1075, 1088 (9th Cir. 2013).

ing of the official or employee occurred within the scope of their duties, but whether the remedy sought is against the tribe.[23]

In *Larimer v. Konocti Vista Casino Resort, Marina & RV Park*,[24] a former employee of a tribal casino resort sued the resort and its chief executive officer for breach of contract and failure to pay overtime wages in violation of the Fair Labor Standards Act. The court found that the resort was an arm of the tribe and, therefore, had sovereign immunity from suit.[25] It separately found that the plaintiff's claims were "indistinguishable from his claims against the Tribe" and, therefore, payment was "in effect sought from the Tribe's treasury."[26] Thus, because the Tribe was the real party in interest, the claims against the chief executive officer were barred by sovereign immunity.[27]

---

[23]*Lewis v. Clarke*, 137 S. Ct. at 1290. As the Ninth Circuit has explained:
> By its essential nature, an individual or personal capacity suit against an officer seeks to hold the officer personally liable for the wrongful conduct taken *in the course of her official duties*. As the officer *personally* is the target of the litigation, she may not claim sovereign immunity – and that is so regardless of whether she was acting under color of tribal or state law at the time of the wrongful conduct in question.

Pistor v. Garcia, 791 F.3d 1104, 1114 (9th Cir. 2015) (emphasis in original); *see also Native Am. Distrib. v. Seneca-Cayuga Tobacco Co.*, 546 F.3d 1288, 1296 (10th Cir. 2008) ("The general bar against official-capacity claims . . . does not mean that tribal officials are immunized from individual-capacity suits arising out of actions they took in their official capacities."); *but see Cosentino v. Fuller*, 189 Cal. Rptr. 3d 15, 24 (Ct. App. 2015), as modified on denial of reh'g (June 22, 2015), as modified (June 25, 2015) ("When tribal officials act in their official capacity and within their scope of authority they are protected by sovereign immunity."); *Turner v. Martire*, 82 Cal. App. 4th 1042, 1054, 99 Cal. Rptr. 2d 587, 595 (2000), as modified on denial of reh'g (Aug. 14, 2000) (same).

[24]814 F. Supp. 2d 952 (N.D. Cal. 2011).

[25]*Id.* at 955.

[26]*Id.* at 957.

[27]*Id.*

2. The *Ex Parte Young* Doctrine

The *Ex Parte Young* doctrine establishes an exception to the general rule of immunity for tribal officials. This doctrine, grounded in federal constitutional law, allows suits to proceed against state officials who have violated, or threaten to violate, federal law.[28] It operates on a "fiction" that state officers who would violate federal law cannot be considered to act as *bona fide* state officials because they would be acting in an unlawful, illegitimate manner.[29] This fiction has the practical effect of allowing federal courts to enforce federal law against errant state officials notwithstanding the barrier to suits against states provided by the Eleventh Amendment, but it allows only for prospective injunctive relief to prevent the officer from acting in violation of federal law; immunity from monetary damages remains intact.[30]

In *Santa Clara Pueblo v. Martinez*, the Supreme Court stated, without explanation, that the *Ex Parte Young* doctrine may be applied to tribal officials to allow federal court suits against them if a plaintiff seeks declaratory or injunctive relief to prevent an alleged violation of federal law.[31] Thus, the federal courts now consistently hold that tribal sovereign immunity does not bar suits against tribal officials when a plaintiff seeks only injunctive relief and alleges that a tribal official is acting in violation of federal law.[32] (Non-tribal employers have in-

---

[28]*Ex Parte Young*, 209 U.S. 123 (1908) (suit may proceed in federal court against a state official to prevent official from violating federal law, notwithstanding the Eleventh Amendment, which forbids individuals to sue states in federal court).

[29]*See Agua Caliente Band of Cahuilla Indians v. Hardin*, 223 F.3d 1041, 1045 (9th Cir. 2000).

[30]*See Verizon Maryland, Inc., v. Pub. Serv. Comm'n of Maryland*, 535 U.S. 635, 645 (2002).

[31]*Santa Clara Pueblo v. Martinez*, 436 U.S. 49, 59 (1978).

[32]*See Santa Clara Pueblo*, 436 U.S. at 59; *Dawavendewa v. Salt River Project Agric. Improvement & Power Dist.*, 276 F.3d 1150, 1160 (9th Cir. 2002); *Garcia v. Akwesasne Hous. Auth.*, 268 F.3d 76, 88 (2d Cir. 2001); *Tamiami Partners Ltd. v. Miccosukee Tribe of Indians of Florida*, 177 F.3d 1212, 1225 (11th Cir. 1999); *N. States Power Co. v. Prairie Island Mdewakanton Sioux Indian Cmty.*, 991 F.2d 458, 460 (8th Cir.1993). Courts have also said that the doctrine allows suits for injunctive relief to proceed against tribal

voked the doctrine to challenge assertions of tribal authority over their reservation employment relations.[33]) While application of the *Ex Parte Young* doctrine in these cases means that sovereign immunity does not bar such claims, the plaintiff must still establish that the federal law alleged to have been violated applies to the tribal setting, an issue implicating the principles discussed in Chapter 3.[34]

There is an important qualification to the application of the *Ex Parte Young* exception to the sovereign immunity of tribal officials: if the relief requested in a lawsuit against a tribal official will require affirmative actions by a tribal government or affect the disposition of tribal government property, the lawsuit will still be barred by sovereign immunity.[35]

Garcia v. Akwesasne Housing Authority[36] is a good example of a tribal employment case involving both official and individual capacity claims.[37] In *Garcia*, a former executive director of the Akwesasne Tribal Housing Authority sued the Housing Authority and its chairman in federal court, claiming (among other things) age discrimina-

---

officials if they seek to enforce a tribal law they have no authority to enact. *See Baker Elec. Co-op, Inc., v. Chaske*, 28 F.3d 1466, 1471-72 (8th Cir. 1994).

[33]*See Salt River Project Agr. Imp. & Power Dist. v. Lee,* 672 F.3d 1176, 1180 (9th Cir. 2012).

[34]*See Garcia v. Akwesasne Hous. Auth.*, 268 F.3d 76, 87-88 (2d Cir. 2001) (pointing out that a case may proceed against an official, but the federal law must be shown to apply and there must be a cause of action). Part II of this book addresses whether specific federal labor and employment laws may be applied to tribes or their enterprises.

[35]*Dawavendewa v. Salt River Project Agric. Improvement & Power Dist.*, 276 F.3d 1150, 1160 (9th Cir. 2002) ("a suit may be barred, even if the officer being sued has acted unconstitutionally or beyond his statutory powers, when the requested relief will require affirmative actions by the sovereign or disposition of unquestionably sovereign property"); *Tamiami Partners Ltd. v. Miccosukee Tribe of Indians of Florida*, 177 F.3d 1212, 1225-26 (11th Cir. 1999); *Taylor v. Ala. Intertribal Council Title IV*, 261 F.3d 1032, 1036 (11th Cir. 2001) (per curiam).

[36]268 F.3d 76 (2d Cir. 2001).

[37]*See also Morrison v. Viejas Enterprises,* No. 11CV97 WQH BGS, 2011 WL 3203107, at *4 (S.D. Cal. July 26, 2011) (suggesting that tribal officials could be subject to suit for declaratory or injunctive relief under Family Medical Leave Act).

tion, civil rights violations, and breach of contract. The court held that Congress did not waive the Housing Authority's sovereign immunity pursuant to the Native American Housing Assistance and Self-Determination Act of 1996 (NAHASDA).[38] However, under the *Ex Parte Young* doctrine, sovereign immunity did not bar the plaintiff's claims for injunctive relief against the chairman in his official capacity.[39] While sovereign immunity from suit could be avoided for those claims, the plaintiff still was required to show that the federal law underlying his claims against the chairman applied in the tribal setting.[40] Finally, the court held that sovereign immunity did not prevent the plaintiff from proceeding with his claims for money damages against the chairman in his individual capacity.[41]

D. Sovereign Immunity: Tribal Enterprises

The existence of sovereign immunity operates as a kind of proxy for whether any given employer has a sovereign status, either as the tribe itself, or as an arm of the tribe. That status has significance for a wide range of issues. For instance, if an employing entity has the sovereign status belonging to a tribe, the *Montana* test[42] for the assertion of tribal regulatory authority over nonmembers (discussed in Chapter 2) may be more readily satisfied because there will be a direct consensual relationship between nonmember employees and the tribe (or a sovereign arm of the tribe).[43] Further, if a particular employing entity has the sovereign status of a tribe, then a tribe enacting laws to afford employees enforceable workplace rights and remedies may need to waive

---

[38] 25 U.S.C. §§ 4101-4243 (2018).

[39] *Garcia*, 268 F.3d at 87-88.

[40] *See id.* at 87-88.

[41] *Id.*

[42] *Montana v. United States*, 450 U.S. 544, 565-66 (1981).

[43] *See Knighton v. Cedarville Rancheria of Northern Paiute Indians*, 918 F.3d 660, 673 (9th Cir. 2019); *Graham v. Applied Geo Technologies, Inc.*, 593 F. Supp.2d 915, 919-20 (S.D. Miss. 2008).

the entity's sovereign immunity from suit to render the laws effective, unless the tribe decides to leave tribal officials subject only to injunctive relief under principles discussed above.[44]

The precise standards governing when tribal enterprises have sovereign immunity from suit are not crystal clear. When tribes directly engage in economic activities, absent an unequivocal waiver, they enjoy sovereign immunity from suit.[45] However, tribes may choose to act through wholly-owned tribal corporations, through corporations chartered under tribal law,[46] through corporations organized under the Indian Reorganization Act of 1934 (IRA),[47] or through corporations or-

---

[44]*See* Chapter 8 for further examination.

[45]*See Kiowa Tribe of Okla. v. Mfg. Tech's., Inc.*, 523 U.S. 751 (1998); *Native American Distrib. v. Seneca-Cayuga Tobacco Co.*, 546 F.3d 1288, 1293-96 (10th Cir. 2008). *See also Chance v. Coquille Indian Tribe*, 963 P.2d 638, 639 (Or. 1998) ("tribal immunity extends to agencies, entities, and enterprises that a tribe creates pursuant to the tribe's powers of self-government").

[46]*See generally,* REST., LAW OF AMERICAN INDIANS (Tent. Draft No. 4, Apr. 29, 2020) §§ 50-54 (discussing variety of tribal enterprises and whether they have sovereign immunity). There is a general consensus across the federal and state courts that a corporation organized under tribal law, controlled by the tribe, and operated for the tribe's governmental purpose will be deemed to enjoy the sovereign immunity of the tribe. *See Wright v. Colville Tribal Enter. Corp.*, 147 P.3d 1275, 1280 (Wash. 2006) (tribal sovereign immunity protects tribal governmental corporations owned and controlled by a tribe and created under its own tribal laws; tribal corporation must explicitly hold itself out as a separate and distinct entity in order to waive immunity); *Altheimer & Gray v. Sioux Mfg. Corp.*, 983 F.2d 803, 809-10 (7th Cir. 1993), *cert. denied*, 510 U.S. 1019 (1993); *Multimedia Games, Inc., v. WLGC Acquisition Corp.*, 214 F.Supp.2d 1131, 1135 (N.D. Okla. 2001) (Miami Tribe of Oklahoma Business Development Authority, a corporation formed under tribal law for economic development, has sovereign immunity from suit under copyright and other commercial claims because it is "a subordinate economic enterprise and political subdivision of the Miami Tribe"); *Hagen v. Sisseton-Wahpeton Cmty. College*, 205 F.3d 1040 (8th Cir. 2000) (community college chartered as nonprofit corporation under tribal law has sovereign immunity of tribe); *Elliott v. Capital Int'l Bank & Trust*, 870 F.Supp. 733, 733-35 (E.D. Tex. 1994); *Duluth Lumber & Plywood Co. v. Delta Dev., Inc.*, 281 N.W.2d 377, 378, 383-84 (Minn. 1979).

[47]Many tribes adopted corporate charters to pursue economic development under Section 17 of the Indian Reorganization Act of 1934, 25 U.S.C. §§ 5123, 5124 (2018). Oklahoma tribes may charter corporations under 25 U.S.C. § 5203 (2018), a provision of the Oklahoma Indian Welfare Act, and such corporations have the same status as

ganized under state law.⁴⁸ Whether a particular tribal entity enjoys sovereign immunity may turn on whether the entity at issue can be considered the tribe itself or a separate entity, whether the tribe owns and controls the entity, and whether the net revenues of the entity fund the tribe's governmental operations.⁴⁹

IRA Section 17 corporations. Absent a clear waiver in the corporate charter, by contract, or by tribal law, Indian tribes' IRA Section 17 corporations enjoy sovereign immunity from suit. *See Amerind Risk Mgmt. Corp. v. Malaterre*, 633 F.3d 680, 685 (8th Cir. 2011); *Memphis Biofuels, LLC v. Chickasaw Nation Indus., Inc.*, 585 F.3d 917, 920-921 (6th Cir. 2009); *Bales v. Chickasaw Nation Indus.*, 606 F. Supp. 2d 1299, 1304 (D.N.M. 2009). *See also Rassi v. Fed. Program Integrators, LLC*, 69 F. Supp. 3d 288, 291–92 (D. Me. 2014) (absent a clear waiver, state limited liability corporation —wholly owned by Indian tribe's IRA Section 17 corporation and controlled by latter's board, and formed to generate governmental revenues and tribal employment — has sovereign immunity from employee claims). *But see GNS, Inc. v. Winnebago Tribe of Nebraska*, 866 F. Supp. 1185, 1188-1189 (N.D. Iowa 1994) (finding that incorporation under IRA Section 17 waives sovereign immunity).

⁴⁸A number of courts have held that nonprofit corporations organized by tribes under state law to promote tribal interests have sovereign immunity from suit. *See, e.g., Manzano v. S. Indian Health Council, Inc.*, 2021 WL 2826072, at *6 (S.D. Cal. July 7, 2021) (holding that state non-profit corporation formed and controlled by consortium of tribes to provide health care services to tribal citizens has sovereign immunity from suit and that incorporation under state law does not constitute a waiver of sovereign immunity); *Matyascik v. Arctic Slope Native Ass'n, Ltd.*, 2019 WL 3554687, at *2–3 (D. Alaska Aug. 5, 2019) (same; discussed in the text below). *Ransom v. St. Regis Mohawk Educ. & Cmty. Fund, Inc.*, 658 N.E.2d 989, 993 (N.Y. 1995) (holding that nonprofit corporation organized by tribe under state law to promote governmental interests possesses sovereign immunity). *See also Pink v. Modoc Indian Health Project, Inc.*, 157 F.3d 1185 (9th Cir. 1998) (holding that off-reservation nonprofit corporation formed and controlled by two Indian tribes to provide health services is "tribe" for purposes of immunity from employment discrimination claim); *Giedosh v. Little Wound School Board, Inc.*, 995 F. Supp. 1052 (D.S.D. 1997) (holding that nonprofit corporation organized under state law is considered a "tribe" for purposes of immunity from employment discrimination claim). *See generally*, REST., LAW OF AMERICAN INDIANS (Tent. Draft No. 4, Apr. 29, 2020) § 54 (discussing sovereign immunity of corporations and other business association formed by tribes under state law).

⁴⁹*See, e.g., Hagen v. Sisseton-Wahpeton Cmty. Coll.*, 205 F.3d 1040 (8th Cir. 2000); *Trudgeon v. Fantasy Springs Casino*, 84 Cal. Rptr.2d 65 (Cal. Ct. App. 1999); *Gavle v. Little Six, Inc.*, 555 N.W.2d 284 (Minn. 1996); *Ransom v. St. Regis Mohawk Educ. and Cmty. Fund*, 658 N.E.2d 989 (N.Y. 1995). Alaska Native Corporations (ANCs) under the Alaska Native Claims Settlement Act of 1971, 43 U.S.C. §§ 1610-1629h (2018) are

1. **Sovereign Immunity and "Arms of Tribes"**

Courts have developed a variety of tests to decide whether a particular entity, operating to serve a tribe's economic interests, enjoys sovereign immunity as an "arm" of the tribe.[50] The United States Supreme Court has yet to address this issue.

In *Wright v. Colville Tribal Enterprise Corp.*,[51] a race discrimination case brought by a former employee of a tribal corporation, the Washington Supreme Court held that the corporation enjoyed the sovereign immunity of the Tribe because it was owned and controlled by the Tribe and established under tribal law.[52] It rejected the multifactor considerations of other courts in favor of this "bright-line rule."[53] Because, as a matter of tribal law, the tribal government of the Confederated Tribes of the Colville Reservation created, owned, and controlled the corporation, the court held that the corporation enjoyed the protection of the Tribe's sovereign immunity from suit.[54]

In *Matyascik v. Arctic Slope Native Ass'n, Ltd.*,[55] a medical doctor formerly employed by a regional health organization established by a consortium of federally recognized Indian tribes, sued the organization for breach of contract, conversion, and other causes of action under state and federal law. The defendant was a nonprofit corporation

---

private corporations and do not have sovereign immunity. *See Aleman v. Chugach Support Servs., Inc.*, 485 F.3d 206, 213 (4th Cir. 2007).

[50] *See, e.g., Wright v. Colville Tribal Enter. Corp.*, 147 P.3d 1275 (Wash. 2006); *Runyon v. Ass'n of Village Council Presidents*, 84 P.3d 437 (Alaska 2004); *Trudgeon v. Fantasy Springs Casino*, 84 Cal. Rptr.2d 65, 69 (Cal. Ct. App. 1999); *Galve v. Little Six, Inc.*, 555 N.W.2d 284, 294 (Minn. 1996); *Ransom v. St. Regis Mohawk Educ. & Cmty. Fund, Inc.*, 658 N.E.2d 989, 992-93 (N.Y. 1995); *Dixon v. Picopa Constr. Co.*, 772 P.2d 1104, 1109 (Ariz. 1989).

[51] 147 P.3d 1275 (Wash. 2006).

[52] *Id.* at 1279.

[53] *Id.* at 1279 n.3.

[54] *Id.* at 1279.

[55] No. 2:19-CV-0002-HRH, 2019 WL 3554687, at *1 (D. Alaska Aug. 5, 2019).

formed under state law by eight tribes, the member tribes' governing bodies authorized the corporation to receive certain federal funds to provide health services to their tribal members, and the corporation was controlled by a Board of Directors, consisting of elected or appointed members from each of the eight consortium tribes."[56]

The court applied a multifactor test used by a number of federal circuit courts of appeals to determine whether entities are "arms of the tribes" entitled to sovereign immunity:

> (1) the method of creation of the economic entities; (2) their purpose; (3) their structure, ownership, and management, including the amount of control the tribe has over the entities; (4) the tribe's intent with respect to the sharing of its sovereign immunity; and (5) the financial relationship between the tribe and the entities.[57]

---

[56] *Matyascik v. Arctic Slope Native Ass'n, Ltd.,* 2019 WL 3554687, at *2–3 (D. Alaska Aug. 5, 2019). *See Manzano v. S. Indian Health Council, Inc.,* 2021 WL 2826072, at *6 (S.D. Cal. July 7, 2021) (holding that incorporation under state law does not constitute a waiver of sovereign immunity).

[57] *Id.,* 2019 WL 3554687, at *2 (quoting *White v. Univ. of Calif.,* 765 F.3d 1010, 1025 (9th Cir. 2014). In *Breakthrough Mgmt. Grp., Inc. v. Chukchansi Gold Casino and Resort,* 629 F.3d 1173, 1187 (10th Cir. 2010), the Tenth Circuit employed the same five factors and a sixth factor: whether granting immunity would be consistent with the federal policies surrounding tribal sovereign immunity. In *People v. Miami Nation Enterprises* 386 P.3d 357 (Cal. 2016), the California Supreme Court adopted essentially the same five factors. In *Williams v. Big Picture Loans, LLC,* 929 F.3d 170, 177 (4th Cir. 2019), the Fourth Circuit adopted "the first five *Breakthrough* factors to analyze arm-of-the-tribe sovereign immunity" and said that the "sixth *Breakthrough* factor, whether the purposes underlying tribal sovereign immunity would be served by granting an entity immunity, overlaps significantly with the first five *Breakthrough* factors [and] inform[s] the entire analysis." In *Hwal'Bay Ba: J Enterprises, Inc. v. Jantzen in & for Cty. of Mohave,* 458 P.3d 102 (Ariz. 2020), the Supreme Court of Arizona applied the *Breakthrough* factors to decide whether a tribal corporation operating a white water rafting company and sued by a guest for injuries had proved the requisite "arm of the tribe" elements for sovereign immunity. Because the coporation had not submitted evidence to show whether the corporation's revenues funded tribal government, the Court held that case could proceed against the corporation without the constraints of sovereign immunity, at least until such evidence was presented.

The plaintiff conceded that the first four factors tipped in favor of the defendant corporation having sovereign immunity, but argued that the corporate form protected the tribes from financial liability and, therefore, warranted a determination that the corporation was not an "arm" of the tribes.[58] The federal court disagreed, relying upon testimony of the corporation's chief executive officer that the corporation's budget depended on "federal funds provided to benefit its member tribes and their tribal members" and that a damages award against the corporation would harm funding for the tribes.[59] Thus, the court dismissed the case, finding that the corporation enjoyed sovereign immunity and had not waived it.[60]

The Restatement of the Law of American Indians distills the test for determining whether a tribal entity is an "arm of the tribe" and therefore entitled to sovereign immunity as follows:

> In cases where the close connection between an Indian tribe and its unincorporated subdivision, agency, or instrumentality is not plain, the subdivision, agency, or instrumentality in question will be deemed to be an "arm of the tribe" and, therefore, imbued with the tribe's sovereign immunity if (1) the entity is controlled by the governing body of the tribe, (2) the tribe owns the entity, and (3) a substantial portion of the net revenues earned by the entity inure to the tribe.[61]

---

[58] *Id.* at *4.

[59] *Id.* at *3 (citing *Barron v. Alaska Native Tribal Health Consortium*, 373 F. Supp. 3d 1232, 1240 (D. Alaska 2019)) (observing that this factor weighs in favor or sovereign immunity).

[60] *Id.* at *4.

[61] REST., LAW OF AMERICAN INDIANS (Tent. Draft No. 4, Apr. 29, 2020) § 56, cmt. (d).

2. Tribal Gaming Enterprises and Sovereign Immunity

Courts consistently hold that sovereign immunity applies to economic enterprises created by tribes to own and operate gaming facilities pursuant to IGRA.[62]

Allen v. Gold Country Casino[63] is a good example of a tribal employment case raising this issue. In *Allen*, a former security guard sued a tribal casino owned and operated by the Tyme Maidu Tribe of the Berry Creek Rancheria for workplace discrimination and other claims. While he conceded that the Tribe itself had sovereign immunity, he sought to distinguish the Tribe's casino. The Ninth Circuit explained that

> when the tribe establishes an entity to conduct certain activities, the entity is immune if it functions as an arm of the tribe. . . . The question is not whether the activity may be characterized as a business . . . but whether the entity acts as an arm of the tribe so that its activities are properly deemed to be those of the tribe.[64]

The court went on to announce that the Tribe's operation of a gaming facility under the terms of the IGRA clearly qualified as an activity that was part of the tribal government:

> [T]he Casino is not a mere revenue-producing tribal business (although it is certainly that). The IGRA provides for the creation and operation of Indian casinos to promote "tribal economic development, self-sufficiency, and strong tribal governments." One of the principal purposes of the IGRA is "to

---

[62]*See, e.g., Breakthrough Mgmt. Grp., Inc. v. Chukchansi Gold Casino & Resort*, 629 F.3d 1173, 1192-1193 (10th Cir. 2010); *Allen v. Gold Country Casino,* 464 F.3d 1044, 1046-47 (9th Cir. 2006).

[63]464 F.3d 1044, 1046-47 (9th Cir. 2006).

[64]*Id.* at 1046 (citations omitted).

insure that the Indian tribe is the primary beneficiary of the gaming operation...."

With the Tribe owning and operating the Casino, there is no question that these economic and other advantages inure to the benefit of the Tribe. Immunity of the Casino directly protects the sovereign Tribe's treasury, which is one of the historic purposes of sovereign immunity in general....[65]

The lessons from *Allen* do not extend to non-Indian management companies that operate tribal gaming facilities under IGRA. Such companies are unlikely to enjoy the sovereign immunity of tribes.[66] Indeed, pursuant to IGRA, they are prohibited from having any "proprietary interest" in tribal gaming operations,[67] and this eliminates a critical element of the "arm of the tribe" analysis: ownership by a federally recognized Indian tribe.

E. Waivers of Sovereign Immunity

A waiver of sovereign immunity cannot be implied; "it must be unequivocally expressed"[68] or "clear"[69] and properly authorized.[70] Any

---

[65] *Id.* at 1047 (citations omitted).

[66] *See Johnson v. Harrah's Kansas Casino Corp.*, No. 04-4142-JAR, 2006 WL 463138, at *8 (D. Kan. Feb. 23, 2006).

[67] 25 U.S.C. § 2710(b)(2)(A).

[68] *Santa Clara Pueblo v. Martinez*, 436 U.S. 49, 58-59 (1978).

[69] *C & L Enter., Inc., v. Citizen Band Potawatomi Indian Tribe of Okla.*, 532 U.S. 411, 418 (2001).

[70] *See, e.g., Memphis Biofuels, LLC v. Chickasaw Nation Industries, Inc.*, 585 F.3d 917, 922 (6th Cir. 2009) (citing cases); *Native American Distrib. v. Seneca-Cayuga Tobacco Co.*, 546 F.3d 1288, 1295 (10th Cir. 2008); *Sanderlin v. Seminole Tribe of Fla.*, 243 F.3d 1282, 1287-88 (10th Cir. 2001) (tribal government official's execution of federal funding agreement providing for application of certain federal laws to tribe could not constitute waiver of tribe's sovereign immunity with respect to suits under those laws). A

ambiguities with respect to a waiver will be resolved in favor of preserving the immunity,[71] and the party seeking to establish the waiver bears the burden of proving it.[72] Moreover, unlike states and state entities imbued with sovereign immunity, Indian tribes and tribal entities that enjoy sovereign immunity do not waive their immunity by removing a case from state court to federal court.[73]

Valid waivers may be set out in the corporate charters of tribal corporations,[74] in contracts properly entered into by a tribe or an arm of a tribe authorized to waive sovereign immunity,[75] or by a tribal reso-

---

"sue and be sued" provision that authorizes a tribal entity to consent to suit does not constitute a waiver of immunity absent evidence that a tribal official has invoked that power. *Ransom v. St. Regis Mohawk Educ. & Cmty. Fund, Inc.*, 658 N.E.2d 989, 995 (N.Y. 1995). *See also Hagen v. Sisseton-Wahpeton Cmty. Coll.*, 205 F.3d 1040, 1044 (8th Cir. 2000) (authorization in tribal college's charter to "waive any immunity from suit" did not itself effect a waiver); *Chance v. Coquille Indian Tribe*, 963 P.2d 638, 640-42 (Or. 1998) (authorization in tribal ordinance for tribal officials to consent to suit is not itself a waiver of immunity).

[71]*Ramey Constr. Co. v. Apache Tribe of the Mescalero Reservation*, 673 F.2d 315, 320 (10th Cir. 1982); *Maryland Cas. Co. v. Citizens Nat'l. Bank of W. Hollywood*, 361 F.2d 517, 521 (5th Cir. 1966) *cert. denied*, 385 U.S. 918 (1966); *accord S. Unique, Ltd., v. Gila River Pima-Maricopa Indian Cmty.*, 674 P.2d 1376, 1381 (Ariz. Ct. App. 1983); *Long v. Chemehuevi Indian Reservation*, 171 Cal. Rptr. 733, 735 (Cal. Ct. App. 1981).

[72]*Montoya v. Chao*, 296 F.3d 952, 955 (10th Cir. 2002). The defense of sovereign immunity typically is raised in a motion to dismiss. If there are factual disputes about a sovereign immunity waiver or other issues bearing on the issue of sovereign immunity, the court has wide discretion to allow affidavits or take evidence to decide the issue. *See, e.g., Veeder v. Omaha Tribe of Nebraska*, 864 F. Supp. 889, 894 (N.D. Iowa 1994); *Wright v. Colville Tribal Enter. Corp.*, 147 P.3d 1275, 1281-82 (Wash. 2006) (Madsen, J., concurring); *Smith v. Hopland Band of Pomo Indians*, 115 Cal. Rptr.2d 455, 460 (Cal. Ct. App. 2002).

[73]*Contour Spa at the Hard Rock, Inc. v. Seminole Tribe of Fla.*, 692 F.3d 1200, 1208 (11th Cir. 2012).

[74]*See Native Am. Distrib. v. Seneca-Cayuga Tobacco Co.*, 546 F.3d 1288, 1293 (10th Cir. 2008).

[75]*See C & L Enterprises, Inc. v. Citizen Band Potawatomi Indians*, 532 U.S. 411 (2001).

lution or law.[76] On the other hand, a promise to follow federal employment discrimination laws in an employee handbook or in a federal funding contract will not suffice to waive sovereign immunity.[77]

1. The Effect of "Sue and Be Sued" Clauses

Although some courts have held that the "sue and be sued" clause of model charters establishing Section 17 IRA corporations waives any sovereign immunity such entities possess,[78] a majority of courts have held that such clauses, authorizing the corporation "to sue and be sued in courts of competent jurisdiction within the United States" only authorize the corporation to waive sovereign immunity.[79] Similar clauses

---

[76]*Stifel, Nicolaus & Co. v. Lac du Flambeau Band of Lake Superior Chippewa Indians,* 807 F.3d 184, 202 (7th Cir. 2015), as amended (Dec. 14, 2015); *Madewell v. Harrah's Cherokee Smokey Mountains Casino,* No. 2:10CV8, 2010 WL 2574079, at *3 (W.D.N.C. May 3, 2010), report and recommendation adopted, 730 F. Supp. 2d 485 (W.D.N.C. 2010).

[77]*Nanomantube v. Kickapoo Tribe in Kansas,* 631 F.3d 1150, 1152 (10th Cir. 2011) (holding that employee handbook provision stating that tribe's gaming enterprise "will comply with the provisions of Title VII of the Civil Rights Act of 1964 and 1991" does not waive sovereign immunity); *Gilbertson v. Quinault Indian Nation,* 495 F. App'x 779, 779–80 (9th Cir. 2012) ("language of the employee handbook stating that employees are 'protected' by Title VII" was not "sufficiently clear" to waive sovereign immunity); *Allen v. Gold Country Casino,* 464 F.3d 1044, 1047 (9th Cir. 2006) (holding that neither statement in form employment application that employee could be terminated "for any reason consistent with applicable state or federal law," nor Employee Orientation Booklet, stating that tribal employer would "practice equal opportunity employment and promotion regardless of race, religion, color, creed, national origin ... and other categories protected by applicable federal laws" sufficiently clear to waive immunity); *Sanderlin v. Seminole Tribe of Fla.,* 243 F.3d 1282, 1287-88 (10th Cir. 2001) (holding that federal funding agreement providing for application of certain federal laws not a waiver of the tribe's sovereign immunity with respect to suits under those laws); *Dillon v. Yankton Sioux Tribe Housing Authority,* 144 F.3d 581, 583 (8th Cir.1998) (same).

[78]*See, e.g., Parker Drilling Co. v. Metlakatla Indian Cmty.,* 451 F. Supp. 1127, 1131-35 (D. Alaska 1978); *S. Unique, Ltd. v. Gila River Pima-Maricopa Indian Cmty.,* 674 P.2d 1376, 1383-84 (Ariz. Ct. App. 1983).

[79]*See Bruguier v. Lac du Flambeau Band of Lake Superior Chippewa Indians,* 237 F. Supp. 3d 867, 872-73 & n.2 (W.D. Wis. 2017). *See generally Validity and Construction of Indian Reorganization Act,* 28 A.L.R. Fed. 563, § 27 (2008) (citing cases holding that

in model ordinances for tribal housing authorities that Indian tribes have established, and receive federal funding for, have led to mixed decisions. Many tribal housing authorities were formed at a time when the United States Department of Housing and Urban Development (HUD) required tribes to enact a model ordinance as a precondition for the receipt of federal funds.[80] These model ordinances provided that a subject tribe's governing body

> hereby gives its irrevocable consent allowing [the tribal housing authority] to sue or be sued in its corporate name, upon any contract, claim or obligation arising out of its activities under the ordinance and hereby authorizes [the tribal housing authority] to agree by contract to waive any immunity from suit which it might otherwise have . . . ; but the Tribe shall not be liable for the debts or obligations of [the tribal housing authority].[81]

Some courts have held that this provision waives the sovereign immunity of a tribal housing authority for lawsuits arising out of any of its activities.[82] Others have held that it is insufficient to waive such immunity, but merely authorizes a housing authority to waive its im-

---

broad "sue and be sued" clauses waive sovereign immunity). *Id.* at § 28 (citing cases holding that such clauses do not waive sovereign immunity). *See generally* F. COHEN, HANDBOOK OF FEDERAL INDIAN LAW § 7.05(1)(c) (2012) ("The weight of authority is to find that the charters do not themselves waive immunity, but rather authorize the housing authority to waive immunity by contract.")

[80] *See* 42 C.F.R. § 950 (1995) (superceded).

[81] *See, e.g., Garcia v. Akwesasne Hous. Auth.*, 268 F.3d 76, 86-87 (2d Cir. 2001); *Ninigret Dev. Corp. v. Narragansett Indian Wetuomuck Hous. Auth.*, 207 F.3d 21, 30 n.6 (1st Cir. 2000); *Dillon v. Yankton Sioux Tribe Hous. Auth.*, 144 F.3d 581, 582-83 (8th Cir. 1998) (same); *Snowbird Constr. Co., Inc., v. United States,* 666 F. Supp. 1437, 1441 (D. Idaho 1987) (same).

[82] *See Snowbird Constr. Co., Inc., v. United States,* 666 F. Supp. 1437, 1441 (D. Idaho 1987).

munity by contract.[83] One court has said that this provision merely authorizes a waiver by contract and, unless the contract provides otherwise, only for suits in a tribal forum.[84]

In the context of an employment dispute, the Eighth Circuit Court of Appeals addressed this issue in *Dillon v. Yankton Sioux Tribe Housing Authority*.[85] In *Dillon*, a former employee claimed employment discrimination against the Housing Authority in federal court. He asserted that the "sue and be sued" clause in the Tribe's ordinance, modeled on HUD's language, constituted a waiver of sovereign immunity. The Eighth Circuit held that the Housing Authority retained sovereign immunity unless it entered into a contract with the employee providing for an express waiver. The Second Circuit reached the same conclusion in *Garcia v. Akwesasne Housing Authority*,[86] discussed above.

In *Rassi v. Fed. Program Integrators, LLC*,[87] the U.S. District Court for the District of Maine held that a "sue and be sued" clause in a tribal corporation's articles of incorporation designating United States federal courts to be among the courts of competent jurisdiction for *all matters* relating to [the Small Business Administration's] programs, including, but not limited to, [section] 8(a)," was a waiver of sovereign immunity for claims under the False Claims Act brought by a former employee against the corporation.[88] The court said that the phrase "all matters relating to ... program participation" was sufficiently clear and broad to encompass the claims.[89]

---

[83]*See Garcia*, 268 F.3d at 87; *Ninigret Dev. Corp. v. Narragansett Indian Wetuomuck Hous. Auth.*, 207 F.3d 21, 30 (1st Cir. 2000); *Dillon v. Yankton Sioux Tribe Hous. Auth.*, 144 F.3d 581, 583-84 (8th Cir. 1998).

[84]*Garcia*, 268 F.3d at 87. *See also Robles v. Shoshone-Bannock Tribes*, 876 P.2d 134, 136 (Idaho 1994) ("sue and be sued" clause does not mean suit against tribal corporation may proceed in state rather than tribal court).

[85]144 F.3d 581, 584 (8th Cir. 1998).

[86]268 F.3d 76, 87 (2d Cir. 2001).

[87]69 F. Supp. 3d 288 (D. Me. 2014).

[88]*Id.* at 292 (emphasis added).

[89]*Id.*

2. Arbitration Clauses and Contractual Waivers

In *C & L Enterprises, Inc., v. Citizen Band Potawatomi Indian Tribe of Oklahoma*,[90] the Supreme Court addressed a tribe's contractual waiver of tribal sovereign immunity. The Tribe entered a contract with the plaintiff, C & L Enterprises, Inc. (C & L), for the construction of a roof on a bank owned by the Tribe in Oklahoma. The contract was a standard form agreement of the American Institute of Architects, and provided that (a) "all claims arising out of the contract shall be decided by arbitration in accordance with the Construction Industry Arbitration Rules of the American Arbitration Association," (b) any "award entered by the arbitrator shall be final and judgment may be entered upon it . . . in any court having jurisdiction thereof," and (c) the "contract shall be governed by the law of the place where the Project is located."[91] After signing the contract, the Tribe decided it preferred a different roofing material, solicited new bids, and retained another contractor.[92] When C & L invoked the arbitration clause, the Tribe refused to arbitrate, and the arbitrator proceeded to award C & L damages for breach of contract and attorney fees.[93] C & L then filed suit against the Tribe in Oklahoma state court to enforce the award, and the Tribe responded that it had not waived sovereign immunity in any court under the terms of the contract; it had only agreed to arbitrate.[94]

A unanimous Supreme Court held that the Tribe's contract with C & L constituted a "clear" waiver of sovereign immunity from suit in Oklahoma state court.[95] It pointed out that (a) the Tribe proposed the contract, which included the clause stating that it was "governed by the law of the place where the Project is located," and (b) Oklahoma law clearly provided that "the making of an agreement . . . providing for

---

[90] 532 U.S. 411 (2001).

[91] *Id.* at 415-16.

[92] *Id.* at 416.

[93] *Id.*

[94] *Id.* at 421-22.

[95] *Id.* at 423.

arbitration in this state confers jurisdiction on the court to enforce the agreement . . . and to enter judgment on an award thereunder."[96] The Court said it had "no occasion to decide" whether an Indian tribe's generalized consent to suit, without specification of forum, would limit a waiver of sovereign immunity only to suit in tribal court, but in the case before it, the Court said, the Tribe "plainly consented to suit in Oklahoma state court."[97]

The Ninth Circuit's decision in *Allen v. Gold Country Casino*,[98] discussed above,[99] illustrates the law governing waivers of sovereign immunity in the employment setting. The plaintiff claimed that, even if the casino had the sovereign immunity of the Tribe (as the court concluded it did), a waiver could be found in a provision of his employment application stating that he could be fired "for any reason consistent with applicable state or federal law," or from language in an Employee Orientation Booklet stating that the Tribe would "practice equal opportunity employment . . . protected by applicable federal laws."[100] The Ninth Circuit held that these statements were insufficiently "clear" to establish a waiver of immunity.[101] While they "might imply a willingness to submit to federal lawsuits," the court pointed out, "waivers of tribal sovereign immunity may not be implied."[102] The court distinguished *C & L Enterprises* because, unlike the contract at issue in that case, the employment documents at issue in *Allen* contained no "phrase clearly contemplating suits against the Casino."[103]

---

[96] *Id.* and *see id.* at 415 for quoted text.

[97] *Id.* at 421 n.4.

[98] 464 F.3d 1044 (9th Cir. 2006).

[99] *See supra* Section D.

[100] *Id.* at 1047.

[101] *Id.* (citing and quoting *C & L Enter., Inc., v. Citizen Band Potawatomi Indian Tribe of Okla.*, 532 U.S. 411, 418 (2001)).

[102] *Id.* (citing *Santa Clara Pueblo v. Martinez*, 436 U.S. 49, 58 (1978)).

[103] *Id.*

3. Forum Selection Clauses

When a tribal entity enjoys sovereign immunity from suit, two separate issues of jurisdiction arise: not only will *any* court lack jurisdiction to entertain a lawsuit against the entity in the absence of an unequivocal waiver by the tribe (or abrogated by Congress), but a state court may also lack jurisdiction if there is no forumselection clause to confer authority upon the court by agreement of the tribe.[104] Stated another way, even if the entity waived sovereign immunity, under the infringement doctrine discussed in Chapter 3, absent consent by the tribe, a state court could lack jurisdiction over the claim.[105] In *C & L Enterprises*, the Supreme Court held that the tribe's contract not only clearly waived its immunity from suit, but it also provided that Oklahoma state courts would have authority to enforce an arbitration award.[106] Because the asserted breach of contract at issue arose outside of Indian country, the Court had no occasion to address whether a tribal forum would have competing jurisdiction over the claim.[107]

A tribe's clear contractual consent to resolve a dispute through arbitration may waive its immunity with respect to an arbitration award, but a contractual provisionstating that judgment on the award "may be entered in accordance with the applicable law in any court having jurisdiction thereof" may not necessarily confer jurisdiction upon a state

---

[104]*See Garcia v. Akwesasne Hous. Auth.*, 268 F.3d 76, 86 (2d Cir. 2001) (inquiry into a purported waiver "encompasses not merely whether [a tribe] may be sued, but where it may be sued").

[105]Indian tribes may consent to state court jurisdiction over claims arising within Indian country over which they would ordinarily exercise exclusive jurisdiction. *See, e.g., Ute Indian Tribe of Uintah v. Lawrence*, 312 F. Supp. 3d 1219, 1224, 1259-1270 (D. Utah 2018); *Outsource Servs. Mgmt., LLC v. Nooksack Bus. Corp.*, 333 P.3d 380, 381-384 (Wash. 2014) (en banc).

[106]*C & L Enter., Inc.*, 532 U.S. at 423.

[107]As discussed in Chapter 3, absent agreement by an Indian tribe to allow a state court to adjudicate a claim brought by a nonmember agaisnt a tribal citizen arising within the tribe's reservation, state court jurisdiction is barred for it would infringe upon the inherent authority of the tribe to adjudicate the dispute.

court in the absence of an express waiver of tribal court jurisdiction.[108] Conversely, a contractual designation of a forum for dispute resolution in a form contract may not, alone, be effective to waive sovereign immunity if there is no clear manifestation of intent by a tribe to agree to such a waiver.[109] Since the designation of a forum for resolving a dispute typically is set forth in a contract, the issues surrounding such designations usually emerge out of contract disputes, including employment contracts.[110]

F. Conclusion

The doctrine of tribal sovereign immunity, viewed in the overall context of reservation labor and employment relations, falls within the general category of "defensive tribal sovereignty," for it stands as a barrier to judicial authority (*i.e.,* the authority of the federal, state, and tribal courts) over any employer that is imbued with such immunity. Because it can prevent state and federal courts from taking jurisdiction over reservation employment disputes, it stands as an additional barrier to "external" authority over such disputes—in addition to the infringement, preemption, and exhaustion doctrines explored in Chapter 3.

---

[108]*See Oglala Sioux Tribe v. C & W Enter., Inc.*, 516 F. Supp.2d 1044, 1051 (D.S.D. 2007).

[109]*See Breakthrough Mgmt. Group, Inc., v. Chukchansi Gold Casino & Resort*, No. CIV.A. 06-cv-01596-MSK-KLM, 2007 WL 2701995, at *5 (D.Colo. Sept. 12, 2007) (form contract providing "the sole and exclusive venue for any and all disputes involving . . . this Agreement shall be the state and federal courts located within the state of Colorado" insufficient to waive sovereign immunity). *Compare ValU-Constr. Co. v. Rosebud Sioux Tribe*, 146 F.3d 573, 576-78 (8th Cir. 1998) (waiver found where tribe agreed to arbitration clause) *with Pan American Co. v. Sycuan Band of Mission Indians*, 884 F.2d 416, 418-20 (9th Cir. 1989) (finding no waiver from similar arbitration clause). *See also Ninigret Dev. Corp. v. Narraganset Indian Wetuomuck Hous. Auth.*, 207 F.3d 21, 30-31 (1st Cir. 2000) (finding waiver from arbitration clause and comparing cases); *Am. Indian Agric. Credit Consortium, Inc., v. Standing Rock Sioux Tribe*, 780 F.2d 1374 (8th Cir. 1985) (promissory note, providing that, in the event of a collection action, the law of the District of Columbia would apply, insufficient to waive sovereign immunity).

[110]*See, e.g., Calvello v. Yankton Sioux Tribe*, 899 F. Supp. 431, 434 (D.S.D. 1995).

Principles of "affirmative tribal sovereignty," discussed in Chapter 2, provide the grounds for tribes to regulate and adjudicate labor and employment relations under tribal law and in tribal forums.[111] In exercising this affirmative sovereignty, Indian tribes face important policy considerations in deciding whether to waive sovereign immunity when the employment relationship they regulate involves the tribe itself or a tribal entity imbued with sovereign immunity. Failure to waive that immunity, of course, likely leaves employees without a judicial remedy. But if tribes do not provide employees with rights and remedies for workplace harms, federal agencies may seek to fill the gap by imposing federal law upon reservation employment relations.

With no tribal law in place, the federal courts considering the propriety of such an imposition may see no "infringement" of tribal self-government at stake and thereby allow federal authority to proceed. Thus, when it comes to determining jurisdiction over labor and employment relations in Indian country, the exercise of "affirmative tribal sovereignty" may directly affect the workings of the principles of "defensive tribal sovereignty" explored in Chapter 3. Finally, waivers of sovereign immunity may be needed to ensure that workplace rights and remedies are fairly enforceable in tribal forums under tribal law.

Appendix A, "Variables Affecting the Governance of Labor and Employment Relations in Indian Country," maps out the legal standards affecting tribal, federal, and state authority over various employment relations in Indian country. It provides a convenient summary of many of the concepts covered in Part I.

---

[111]Part II of this book explores what tribes are doing to regulate labor and employment relations in Indian country through the exercise of such affirmative sovereignty.

PART II

FEDERAL AUTHORITY AND LABOR AND EMPLOYMENT RELATIONS IN INDIAN COUNTRY

Federal laws affecting labor and employment relations in Indian country can be broken down into three categories: (1) *civil rights*, which encompass all forms of employment discrimination that Congress has chosen to address through a variety of laws; (2) *labor and employment laws*, which generally address the terms and conditions of employment, such as workplace safety, hours and minimum wages, and family medical leave; and (3) *labor unions and collective bargaining*, an area governed by one federal law: the National Labor Relations Act.

Each of these areas presents specific opportunities and challenges for tribes in exercising affirmative sovereignty. As set forth in Chapter 2, tribal nations have inherent sovereign authority to enact laws governing these matters within Indian country. At the same time, federal agencies are not shy about seeking to impose the federal laws they administer against tribes or their enterprises. Tribes cannot defend against federal agency enforcement actions with sovereign immunity. Whether these agencies succeed or not in any given case can have significant implications for tribal self-government.

Importantly, the law determining the outcome of many such cases is in a state of flux. In some of its enactments, Congress has expressly excluded tribes. In others, however, it has failed to consider tribal nations at all, while clearly intending to exclude other sovereign governments. Federal courts have struggled to set coherent standards for applying certain federal labor and employment laws to Indian tribes and their enterprises when Congress has failed to signal its intent. The question may well be resolved by the Supreme Court, unless Congress amends its laws to indicate its intent. In the meantime, if tribal nations fail to exercise affirmative sovereignty to govern labor and employment relations matters in Indian country, the courts may perceive that there is a "gap" for federal agencies to fill.

The following three chapters address the application of federal laws to tribal employment relations in the three categories noted above: civil rights, federal labor and employment laws addressing the terms and conditions of employment, and unions and collective bargaining. In each area, there is room for the exercise of affirmative tribal sovereignty under the principles discussed in Chapter 2. In each area, there are also potentially competing federal authorities. The law will be shaped as the resulting tensions play out. Thus, Part II shows that there are abounding challenges to tribal sovereignty ahead. Part III will turn to the developing tribal law governing labor and employment relations in Indian country. The very development of such tribal laws could "fill the gap" and therefore deter courts from allowing federal agencies to infringe on the exercise of tribal sovereignty in these areas.

5

CIVIL RIGHTS AND TRIBAL EMPLOYMENT

A. Introduction

When we think of "civil rights," we typically think of protections afforded to individuals by the United States Constitution that check abuses of power by governmental authorities: for example, due process of law, freedom of speech, and equal protection of the laws. These protections are found in the Bill of Rights and the Fourteenth Amendment. Pursuant to federal constitutional law, these rights constrain governmental employers in their relations with employees in the public sector. Thus, governmental employers must provide public employees with "due process" if they have a property interest in their employment. Pursuant to the First Amendment, they cannot discipline employees for exercising their rights of free speech.Under the Equal Protection Clause, they cannot discriminate against employees on the basis of such things as race, sex, or national origin. Apart from the United States Constitution, certain federal statutes, most prominently Title VII of the Civil Rights Act of 1964,[1] provide additional protections against employment discrimination in both the public and private sectors.

The Bill of Rights and the Fourteenth Amendment do not apply to Indian tribes, nor does Title VII. As "separate sovereigns predating the Constitution," Indian tribes are not constrained by the constitutional provisions "framed specifically as limitations on federal or state authority,"[2] and Congress expressly excluded tribes from the provisions of Title VII.[3]

---

[1] 42 U.S.C. §§ 2000e–2000e-17 (2018).

[2] *Santa Clara Pueblo v. Martinez*, 436 U.S. 49, 55-56 (1978).

[3] 42 U.S.C. § 2000e(b) (2018).

In 1968, however, Congress enacted the Indian Civil Rights Act of 1968 (ICRA)[4] to impose constraints upon tribal governments tracking the Bill of Rights and the Fourteenth Amendment.[5] ICRA has significant implications for the rights of employees of tribal governments. Further, in contrast to Title VII, a number of federal "civil rights" statutes protect against employment discrimination without mentioning tribes. Courts have grappled with whether such statutes may govern the tribal employment setting.

This chapter first examines the operation of ICRA, and then looks at other federal statutes protecting civil rights in the employment setting and their application to Indian tribes and their enterprises.

B. The Indian Civil Rights Act of 1968

The Indian Civil Rights Act protects the civil rights of employees within the governmental operations of tribes in a number of categories similar to those provided to state or federal employees under the United States Constitution.

ICRA provides, in pertinent part, that:

> [n]o Indian tribe in exercising powers of self-government shall —
> (1) make or enforce any law prohibiting the free exercise of religion, or abridging the freedom of speech, or of the press, or the right of the people peaceably to assemble and to petition for a redress of grievances;
> (2) violate the right of the people to be secure in their persons, houses, papers, and effects against unreasonable search and seizures, nor issue warrants, but upon probable cause, supported by oath or affirmation, and particularly describing the place to be searched and the person or thing to be seized;

---

[4] 25 U.S.C. §§ 1301-03 (2018).

[5] *See Martinez*, 436 U.S. at 66-69 (discussing legislative history).

. . .

> (8) deny to any person within its jurisdiction the equal protection of its laws or deprive any person of liberty or property without due process of law. . . .[6]

Subsection 1 tracks the First Amendment. Under the First Amendment, government employees have brought suit against their employers for adverse employment decisions based upon an unlawful violation of their freedom of speech.[7] Subsection 2 tracks the Fourth Amendment. Under that provision, government employers are constrained in their ability to search or interfere with the reasonably expected privacy rights of their employees, including in the administration of drug tests.[8] Subsection 8 tracks the due process and equal protection provisions of the Fourteenth Amendment, which has given rise to lawsuits by public employees when they have suffered adverse employment action without due process (*i.e.*, the deprivation of a "property right" in employment)[9] or in violation of equal protection (*i.e.*, discriminatory treatment on the basis of sex, race, religion, or national origin).[10]

1. Non-Enforcement of ICRA in Federal Court

In the first ten years after Congress's enactment of ICRA, the federal courts enforced it against Indian tribes and tribal officials, albeit

---

[6]25 U.S.C. § 1302 (2018).

[7]*See, e.g., Ceballos v. Garcetti*, 361 F.3d 1168 (9th Cir. 2004); *Roldan-Plumey v. Cerezo-Suarez*, 115 F.3d 58, 61-62 (1st Cir. 1997). *See generally* William A. Herbert, *The First Amendment and Public Sector Labor Relations*, 19 LAB. LAW. 325, 325-51 (2004).

[8]*See, e.g., Knox County Educ. Ass'n. v. Knox County Bd. of Educ.*, 158 F.3d 361 (6th Cir. 1998); *Am. Fed. of Gov't Employees Local 1533 v. Cheney*, 754 F. Supp. 1409, 1426-27 (N.D. Cal. 1990).

[9]*See, e.g., Cleveland Bd. of Educ. v. Loudermill*, 470 U.S. 532, 542 (1985) (public employee's "property interest" in job gives employee right to due process from governmental employer).

[10]*See Notari v. Denver Water Dep't*, 971 F.2d 585, 587 (10th Cir. 1992) (race and sex discrimination claims by public employees grounded in Equal Protection Clause).

with a self-conscious recognition that American constitutional concepts could not be grafted onto ICRA and applied within culturally distinct tribal communities.[11] In 1978, the Supreme Court held in *Santa Clara Pueblo v. Martinez* that, with the exception of petitions for release by persons held by tribes against their will (known as *habeas corpus*), ICRA could be enforced only within tribal forums.[12] *Santa Clara Pueblo* was a landmark decision, for it recognized that the process of defining the contours of individual rights against tribal government authority implicated important issues of tribal sovereignty.[13] The Court held that "tribal forums are available to vindicate rights created by the ICRA" for Indians and non-Indians alike.[14] Thus, absent the extraordinary circumstance of a persons being physically held against their will, affirmative claims under ICRA must be resolved within tribal communities themselves, without external interference.[15] One federal court has held, however, that ICRA can be raised as a defense to a federal court action brought by an Indian tribe to enforce tribal law.[16]

---

[11] *See, e.g., Janis v. Wilson*, 385 F. Supp. 1143 (D.S.D. 1974); *McCurdy v. Steele*, 353 F. Supp. 629 (D. Utah 1973).

[12] 436 U.S. 49 (1978).

[13] *See Santa Clara Pueblo*, 436 U.S. at 65-66. The Court ruled that Martinez's claims (that the Pueblo's membership law, giving more favorable treatment to Pueblo men who married outside the Pueblo than women who did the same) could proceed against the Pueblo's governor under the *Ex Parte Young* doctrine examined in Chapter 4. The Court was persuaded, however, that if such claims proceeded in a non-tribal forum, essential attributes of tribal sovereignty would suffer unintended harm. "Even in matters involving commercial and domestic relations," the Court wrote, "we have recognized that subjecting a dispute arising on the reservation among reservation Indians to a forum other than the one they have established for themselves may undermine the authority of the tribal court and hence infringe on the right of the Indians to govern themselves." *Santa Clara Pueblo*, 436 U.S. at 59 (citations and quotations omitted).

[14] *Id.* at 65, 69.

[15] *Id.* at 71-72. Chapter 8 explores a variety of Indian tribal laws protecting civil rights in the employment setting.

[16] *See Santa Ynez Band of Mission Indians v. Torres*, 262 F. Supp. 2d 1038, 1044 (C.D. Cal. 2002).

a. *Dry Creek* Exception

The Tenth Circuit recognized a limited exception to the holding of *Santa Clara Pueblo* precluding ICRA enforcement in federal court in *Dry Creek Lodge, Inc. v. Arapahoe and Shoshone Tribes*.[17] Under the extraordinary facts presented, the court held that non-Indians' ICRA claims could go forward in the federal court even though there was no petition for *habeas corpus*. In *Dry Creek*, non-Indians built a small commercial camping lodge on fee land they owned within the boundaries of the Wind River Reservation of the Shoshone and Arapahoe Indian Tribes.[18] A dirt road linked the lodge to the nearest highway and traversed the property of a family of tribal members.[19] On the day the lodge formally opened, the Tribes, at the request of the family, blocked the access road. The Dry Creek Lodge brought an action in tribal court to open the access road.[20] The tribal court, however, held that it lacked jurisdiction to entertain the lawsuit without the consent of the tribal council.[21] The tribal council refused to grant its consent and directed the parties to attempt to resolve their differences on their own.[22] Unable to resolve the dispute and frustrated, the Dry Creek Lodge owners proceeded to file suit in federal court.[23] The Tenth Circuit held that the extraordinary facts presented, showing that the Dry Creek Lodge owners were being forcibly deprived of their personal

---

[17] 623 F.2d 682 (10th Cir. 1980) ("*Dry Creek Lodge II*"), *cert. denied*, 449 U.S. 1118 (1981).

[18] *Id.* at 683-84. *See also Dry Creek Lodge, Inc. v. U.S.*, 515 F.2d 926, 931 (10 th Cir. 1975) ("*Dry Creek Lodge I*") (earlier decision describing facts of the case).

[19] *Dry Creek Lodge I*, 515 F.2d at 931; *Dry Creek Lodge II*, 623 F.2d at 683-84.

[20] *See Dry Creek Lodge I*, 515 F.2d at 931; *Dry Creek Lodge II*, 623 F.2d at 683-84.

[21] *See id.*

[22] *See id.*

[23] *See id.*

and property rights without any available tribal remedy, warranted the court allowing their federal action to proceed under ICRA.[24]

No federal court decision since *Dry Creek* has held that an ICRA claim, other than a petition for *habeas corpus* relief, may proceed in federal court. Other federal courts have suggested that the *Dry Creek* decision was wrongly decided.[25] The Tenth Circuit itself has emphasized "the minimal precedential value of *Dry Creek*,"[26] and noted that "[w]ith the exception of *Dry Creek* itself, we have *never* found federal jurisdiction based on the *Dry Creek* exception."[27]

2. Tribal Court Enforcement of ICRA

Indian tribes have not been consistent in their views about whether ICRA had "the substantial and intended effect of changing the law which [tribal] forums are obliged to apply," as the Supreme Court stated in *Santa Clara Pueblo*.[28] Some tribal courts have refused to enforce ICRA without a clear waiver of sovereign immunity by the tribal government.[29] Other tribal courts have had no trouble finding that ICRA

---

[24]*Dry Creek Lodge II*, 623 F.2d at 685. Judge Holloway dissented, arguing that *Santa Clara Pueblo* left no room for the exception carved out by the majority's decision. *Id.* at 685-86 (Holloway, J., dissenting).

[25]*See R.J. Williams Co. v. Fort Belknap Hous. Auth.*, 719 F.2d 979, 981 (9th Cir. 1983), cert. denied, 472 US 1016 (1985) (*Santa Clara Pueblo* forecloses any federal court action under ICRA other than *habeas corpus* petitions).

[26]*Ordinance 59 Ass'n v. U.S. Dep't. of the Interior Secretary*, 163 F.3d 1150, 1158-59 (10th Cir. 1998). *See also Walton v. Tesuque Pueblo*, 443 F.3d 1274, 1278 (10th Cir. 2006) ("in the twenty-six years since *Dry Creek*, . . . we have never found the rule to apply.")

[27]*Id.* at 1159.

[28]*Santa Clara Pueblo*, 436 U.S. at 65.

[29]*See, e.g., Kotch v. Absentee Shawnee Tribe*, 3 Okla. Trib. 184, 195 (Absentee Shawnee Tribe Sup. Ct. 1993); *Pawnee Tribe v. Franseen*, 19 Indian L. Rptr 6006, 6008 (Ct. Indian App.-Pawnee 1991); *Bd. of Trustees of Sisseton-Wahpeton Cmty Coll. v. Wynde*, 18 Indian L. Rptr. 6033, 6035 (Northern Plains Intertribal Ct. App. 1990); *Johnson v. Navajo Nation*, No. A-CV-16-85; 14 Indian L. Rptr. 6037; 5 Nav. R. 192 (Navajo Sup. Ct. 1987) available at http://www.tribalinstitute.org/opinions/1987.NANN.0000011.htm; *McCormick v. Election Comm.*, 1 Okla. Trib. 8, 19 (Ct. Indian Offens-

waives tribal sovereign immunity for enforcement in tribal court.[30] It can be argued that, if tribes fail to provide a clear avenue for resolution of civil rights claims (under ICRA or tribal laws) or assert barriers such as sovereign immunity, they may be perceived as lacking in fair procedures and respect for basic civil rights, and thereby face attempts by disgruntled individuals to obtain a federal court remedy.[31] Chapter 8 explores what a number of tribes have done to clarify the enforcement of ICRA or to provide workplace rights and remedies for employees claiming discrimination or other "civil rights" violations.

---

es—Sac. & Fox 1980). *See also Long v. Mohegan Tribal Gaming Auth.*, 25 Indian L. Rptr. 6111 (Mohegan Gaming Disputes Trial Ct. 1997) (noting Tribe's adoption of ICRA remedies under constitution, but reserving judgment on whether Tribe waived sovereign immunity for ICRA claims). *But see* REST., LAW OF AMERICAN INDIANS § 23, cmt a (Tent. Draft No. 2, March 13, 2018) ("In accordance with congressional plenary power to regulate tribal sovereignty . . . tribal courts apply and interpret ICRA.").

[30]*See, e.g., Johnson v. Mashantucket Pequot Gaming Enter.*, No. MPCA-96-1008; 1 Mashantucket Rptr 15; 25 Indian L. Rptr. 6011 (Mashantucket Pequot Tribal Ct., June 11, 1996) available at http://www.tribal-institute.org/opinions/1996.NAMP.0000002.htm; *Oglala Sioux Tribal Personnel Bd. v. Red Shirt*, 16 Indian L. Rptr. 6052, 6053 (Oglala Sioux Ct. App. 1983); *Works v. Fallon Paiute-Shoshone Tribe*, 24 Indian L. Rptr. 6033, 6033 (Inter-tribal Ct. App. Nev. 1997); *Dupree v. Cheyenne River Hous. Auth.*, 16 Indian L. Rptr. 6106, 6108-09 (Cheyenne River Sioux Ct. App. 1988); and Colville Tribal Civil Rights Act (1988), available at http://www.narf.org/nill/Codes/colvillecode/title_1_5.pdf (Confederated Tribes of the Colville Reservation adopting ICRA language and waiving sovereign immunity from claims for declaratory and/or injunctive relief). *See generally* Frank Pommersheim, *Tribal Court Jurisprudence: A Snapshot from the Field*, 21 VT. L. REV. 7, 22-23 & n.44 (1997) (collecting cases).

[31]*See generally* Kaighn Smith, Jr., *Ethical "Obligations" and Affirmative Tribal Sovereignty: Some Considerations for Tribal Attorneys,* Conference Paper, Federal Bar Association, 31st Annual Indian Law Conference, Albuquerque, NM, April 7, 2006, *reprinted in* Matthew L. M. Fletcher, American Indian Tribal Law, 217 (2011); Vicki J. Limas, *Employment Suits Against Indian Tribes: Balancing Sovereign Rights and Civil Rights,* 70 Denv. U. L. Rev. 359, 359-92 (1993).

C. Federal Civil Rights Laws and Tribal Employment

1. Federal Civil Rights Acts

In the absence of tribal law, employees may seek to invoke federal statutes that protect civil rights in the workplace. While Congress expressly excluded Indian tribes from Title VII and the employment discrimination provisions of the Americans with Disabilities Act (ADA),[32] it failed to account for tribes or their enterprises in numerous other civil rights statutes that apply across American workplaces. Federal courts have had to struggle with the scope of the "Indian tribe" exemptions under Title VII and the ADA. Thus, the law is still very much a work in progress with respect to the application of federal employment laws protective of civil rights to Indian tribes and their reservation enterprises.

During the Civil War era, Congress enacted several laws protecting newly freed slaves from discriminatory treatment. These laws include 42 U.S.C. § 1983 (Section 1983), prohibiting state officials and municipalities from violating federal constitutional protections;[33] 42 U.S.C. § 1981 (Section 1981), prohibiting race discrimination in contracts;[34] and 42 U.S.C. § 1985 (Section 1985), prohibiting conspiracies to

---

[32] 42 U.S.C. §§ 12101–213 (2018). The ADA's exclusion of tribes appears at 42 U.S.C. § 12111(5)(B)(i).

[33] 42 U.S.C. § 1983 (2018). Section 1983 provides, in pertinent part, as follows:
> Every person who, under color of any . . . [state law] subjects, or causes to be subjected, any citizen of the United States or other person within the jurisdiction thereof to the deprivation of any rights, privileges, or immunities secured by the Constitution and laws, shall be liable to the party injured in an action at law. . . .

Id.

[34] 42 U.S.C. § 1981 (2018). Section 1981 provides, in pertinent part, as follows:
> (a) Statement of equal rights
> All persons within the jurisdiction of the United States shall have the same right in every State and Territory to make and enforce contracts, to sue, be parties, give evidence, and to the full and equal benefit of all laws and proceedings for the security of persons and property as is enjoyed by white citizens, and shall be subject to like punishment, pains, penalties, taxes, licenses, and exactions of every kind, and to no other.
> (b) "Make and enforce contracts" defined

deprive individuals of equal protection under the law.³⁵ To date, the federal courts have refused to enforce these laws against Indian tribes, tribal officials, and subdivisions of tribal governments, including Indian housing authorities.³⁶

The logic of these decisions is noteworthy. To assert a claim under either Section 1983 or Section 1985, a plaintiff must allege a violation of a federal constitutional right.³⁷ As the Supreme Court said in

> For purposes of this section, the term "make and enforce contracts" includes the making, performance, modification, and termination of contracts, and the enjoyment of all benefits, privileges, terms, and conditions of the contractual relationship.
> (c) Protection against impairment
> The rights protected by this section are protected against impairment by nongovernmental discrimination and impairment under color of State law.
> *Id.*

³⁵42 U.S.C. § 1985 (2018). Section 1985(3) provides, in pertinent part, as follows:
> If two or more persons in any State or Territory conspire ... for the purpose of depriving, either directly or indirectly, any person or class of persons of the equal protection of the laws, or of equal privileges and immunities under the laws ... , whereby another is injured in his person or property, or deprived of having and exercising any right or privilege of a citizen of the United States, the party so injured or deprived may have an action for the recovery of damages occasioned by such injury or deprivation, against any one or more of the conspirators.

Id.

³⁶*See Nero v. Cherokee Nation of Okla.*, 892 F.2d 1457 (10th Cir. 1989) (Tribe not subject to race discrimination claims under Sections 1981, 1983, and 1985 for denying membership to descendants of former slaves owned by tribe); *Wheeler v. Swimmer*, 835 F.2d 259, 262 (10th Cir. 1987) (Tribe not subject to claims under Section 1985 for alleged wrongful conduct of tribal election); *R.J. Williams Co. v. Fort Belknap Hous. Auth.*, 719 F.2d 979 (9th Cir. 1983), *cert. denied*, 472 U.S. 1016 (1985); *Wardle v. Ute Indian Tribe*, 623 F.2d 670 (10th Cir. 1980) (Tribe not subject to Section 1981 race discrimination claim for terminating white police officer); *Montgomery v. Flandreau Santee Sioux Tribe*, 905 F. Supp. 740, 745 (D.S.D. 1995) (Tribe not subject to Section 1985 claim for alleged favoritism in distribution of casino profits). *But see Aleman v. Chugach Support Serv., Inc.*, 485 F.3d 206, 210-11 (4th Cir. 2007) (wholly owned subsidiary of Alaska Native Corporation operating for-profit construction business in Maryland subject to race discrimination suit under Section 1981 even though exempt from suit under Title VII).

³⁷*Wheeler v. Swimmer*, 835 F.2d 259, 262 (10th Cir. 1987).

Santa Clara Pueblo, however, Indian tribes and tribal officials acting under color of tribal authority are not subject to the constitutional provisions that constrain the power of states.[38] When asserted against tribal authority, these protections are available to individual Indians and non-Indians "only to the extent incorporated in ICRA."[39] Since *Santa Clara Pueblo* holds that ICRA provisions, other than *habeas corpus* petitions, are enforceable only within tribal forums, federal courts will not allow what cannot occur under ICRA to occur under Section 1983 or Section 1985. In short, there is no federal constitutional basis to allow suits to proceed against tribal authorities under Sections 1983 and 1985.[40] In addition, Section 1983 requires that any alleged violation of federal law be under "color of state law." Unless acting in concert with state officials, tribal authorities cannot be said to act "under color of state law" because tribes are not states.[41]

Section 1981, on its face, does not have the same constraints (*i.e.*, state action and violation of a federal constitutional provision) as actions under Sections 1983 and 1985. However, it has been held not to apply to tribal employment. The issue was addressed for the first time by the Tenth Circuit in *Wardle v. Ute Indian Tribe*.[42] In *Wardle*, the tribe terminated the plaintiff, a non-Indian police officer, and gave his job to a tribal member. The plaintiff sued the tribe for race discrimination under Section 1981 and other statutory and constitutional provisions. The Tenth Circuit rejected his claim, holding that he had no federal cause of action under Section 1981.[43] The court explained:

---

[38]*Santa Clara Pueblo*, 436 U.S. at 71-72.

[39]*Nero v. Cherokee Nation of Okla.*, 892 F.2d 1457, 1462 (10th Cir. 1989).

[40]*See Delorge v. Mashantucket Pequot Gaming Enter.*, No. MPTC-CV-97-114, ¶¶ 50-63, 3 Mashantucket Rptr. 1 (Mashantucket Pequot Tribal Ct. July 23, 1997) available at http://www.tribal-institute.org/opinions/1997.NAMP.0000038.htm.

[41]*See Burrell v. Armijo*, 456 F.3d 1159, 1174 (10th Cir. 2006); *R.J. Williams Co. v. Fort Belknap Hous. Auth.*, 719 F.2d 979, 982 (9th Cir. 1983).

[42]623 F.2d 670 (10th Cir. 1980).

[43]The district court had dismissed the case on several grounds: lack of a federally protected right, sovereign immunity, and failure to exhaust tribal remedies. The

The statutory provisions upon which plaintiff relies do not provide him a cause of action, even assuming that these provisions would otherwise apply to Indian tribes and that the discharge in this case was racially discriminatory . . . . Each of the statutes invoked by plaintiff is a broad, general provision guaranteeing equal rights and equal protection or prohibiting racial discrimination. These broad civil rights provisions do not specifically prohibit preferential employment of tribal members by Indian tribes. On the other hand, 42 U.S.C. § 2000e specifically exempts Indian tribes from compliance with the prohibition against discriminatory discharge from employment. Under such circumstances, the specific provisions control over the more general ones.[44]

In *Stroud v. Seminole Tribe of Florida*,[45] the federal district court likewise rejected a race discrimination claim under Section 1981 and other federal civil rights provisions brought by the Tribe's former education director, who asserted she was fired because she was white. The court held that Congress had not "expressly or impliedly extended Section 1981 to the employment practices of the Indian tribes."[46]

Tenth Circuit agreed with the district court's first ground, the absence of any federal cause of action, and saw no need to decide the other issues. *Wardle*, 623 F.2d at 672.

[44] *Id.* at 673 (citing *Morton v. Mancari*, 417 U.S. 535, 550-51 (1974)).

[45] 606 F. Supp. 678 (S.D. Fla. 1985).

[46] *Id.* at 679-80 (citing *Wardle*, 623 F.2d at 673). *See Taylor v. Alabama Intertribal Council Title IV JTPA*, 261 F.3d 1032, 1035-36 (11th Cir. 2001) ("it would be wholly illogical to allow plaintiffs to circumvent the Title VII bar against race discrimination claims based on a tribe's Indian employment preference programs simply by allowing a plaintiff to style his claim as § 1981 suit"; intertribal consortium, organized to promote tribes' business opportunities were "entitled to the same protections as a tribe itself"). *See Delorge v. Mashantucket Pequot Gaming Enter.*, No. MPTC-CV-97-114, ¶¶ 78-86 (Mashantucket Pequot Tribal Ct. July 23, 1997) (rejecting application of Section 1981 to tribal gaming commission).

In *Yashenko v. Harrah's NC Casino Co. LLC*,[47] the U.S. Court of Appeals for the Fourth Circuit explored the application of Section 1981 to a tribal employment setting in some detail. Yashenko was the Manager of Employee Relations at the Eastern Band of Cherokee Indians' gaming facility, which was overseen by Harrah's under a management agreement with the Band. Harrah's implemented the Band's employment preference laws at the casino. After he was discharged from employment, Yashenko sued Harrah's under Section 1981, claiming that he was discriminated against on the basis of race because his employment contract was subject to tribal employment preferences. The federal district court held that Yashenko could not proceed under Section 1981 because Congress had expressed its intent, through Title VII, that tribes enjoy exemptions from such suits.[48] On appeal, the Fourth Circuit did not reach the issue. Instead, it held, along lines similar to a Ninth Circuit decision, *Dawavendewa v. Salt River Project Agric. Improvement & Power Dist.*,[49] discussed in Chapter 10, that the Band was an indispensable party that could not be joined because of its sovereign immunity. The court said the Band was "indispensable" because, among other things, an adverse Section 1981 judgment would "prejudice the Tribe's economic interests in the Management Agreement with Harrah's and its interests as a sovereign in negotiating contracts and governing its reservation."[50]

The lessons of *Morton v. Mancari*,[51] a Supreme Court case also discussed in Chapter 10, are reflected in these decisions: the application of Section 1981 to tribal employment decisions would fly in the face of specific Congressional enactments protecting the employment deci-

---

[47] 446 F.3d 541 (4th Cir. 2006).

[48] *Id.* at 552 n.2 (citing *Yashenko v. Harrah's NC Casino Co., LLC*, 352 F. Supp. 2d 653, 663 (W.D.N.C. 2005)).

[49] 154 F.3d 1117 (9th Cir. 1998), *cert. denied*, 528 U.S. 1098 (2000).

[50] *Id.* at 553.

[51] 417 U.S. 535 (1974).

sions of tribal government from external scrutiny under constitutional or civil rights standards.[52]

2. Federal Employment Discrimination Laws

The most well-known federal employment discrimination law is Title VII of the Civil Rights Act of 1964, which prohibits adverse employment actions against employees on the basis of race, color, sex (including pregnancy), religion, national origin, and ancestry.[53] Sexual harassment falls under the category of sex discrimination. The ADA prohibits employment discrimination on the basis of disability and requires employers to provide reasonable accommodations for employees with disabilities.[54] Remedies for violations of Title VII or the ADA may include reinstatement and back pay or "front pay," if reinstatement is not feasible, emotional distress, punitive damages, and attorney fees.[55] Lawsuits may be brought against employers by individual employees or by the Equal Employment Opportunity Commission (EEOC) on their behalf.

A third federal statute, the Age Discrimination in Employment Act of 1967 (ADEA),[56] prohibits employment discrimination on the basis of age. The ADEA, like Title VII and the ADA, may be enforced by individuals claiming to have suffered age discrimination, or by the EEOC on their behalf. Remedies available for violations of the ADEA are similar to those for violations of Title VII and the ADA. Finally, a number of federal statutes prohibit employment discrimina-

---

[52]*See Wardle*, 623 F.2d at 673 (citing *Mancari,* 417 U.S. at 547-48). *See also Graham v. Applied Geo Tech. Inc.*, 593 F. Supp.2d 915, 921 (S.D. Miss. 2008) (non-Indian in reservation-based consensual employment relationship with "a tribal entity that may fairly be treated for tribal jurisdiction purposes as the Tribe" must exhaust tribal remedies for alleged race discrimination, including claim under Section 1981).

[53]42 U.S.C. §§ 2000e–2000e-17 (2018).

[54]*See* 42 U.S.C. §§ 12101–12213 (2018).

[55]In 1991, Congress qualified the liability standards for the recovery of certain remedies under Title VII and the ADA. *See* 42 U.S.C. § 1981a (2018).

[56]29 U.S.C. §§ 621-34 (2018).

tion for recipients of federal funds. This section addresses legal issues for the tribal employment setting under each of these categories of federal employment discrimination law.

3. Exemptions of "Indian Tribes" Under Title VII and the ADA

The most often-invoked federal employment discrimination law, Title VII, excludes "Indian tribes" from its provisions.[57] Senator Mundt of South Dakota, who introduced this exemption, stated that it was to protect "the welfare of our oldest and most distressed American minority, the American Indians," and to allow them to "conduct their own affairs" without facing the liabilities imposed under the Act.[58] Title VII additionally exempts any employer "on or near" an Indian reservation from any liability under that statute for treating non-Indians differently than Indians if such treatment is pursuant to "any publicly announced employment practice of such business or enterprise under which a preferential treatment is given to any individual because he is an Indian living on or near a reservation."[59] (The operation of this latter exemption is discussed in Chapter 10.) The ADA, which prohibits employment discrimination on the basis of disability and requires employers to provide reasonable accommodations for employees

---

[57] The exemption appears in the definition of "employer":
 For the purposes of this subchapter—
 (b) The term "employer" means a person engaged in an industry affecting commerce who has fifteen or more employees for each working day in each of twenty or more calendar weeks in the current or preceding calendar year, and any agent of such a person, *but such term does not include . . . an Indian tribe.*
42 U.S.C. § 2000e(b)(1) (2018) (emphasis added). Congress specifically addressed the application of this exemption for Alaska Native Corporations (ANCs) in the Alaska Native Claims Settlement Act by providing that if an ANC owns at least 25 percent of the employer, the exemption applies. 43 U.S.C. § 1626(g) (2018).

[58] 110 Cong. Rec. 13702 (1964).

[59] 42 U.S.C. § 2000e-2(i) (2018). *See Little v. Devils Lake-Sioux Mfg. Corp.*, 607 F. Supp. 700 (D.N.D. 1985) (on-reservation manufacturing company, owned 51 percent by tribe and 49 percent by non-Indian corporation, and subject to Indian employment preference laws, not subject to race discrimination claim for denying grievance to former white employee).

with disabilities, likewise expressly excludes Indian tribes from its provisions.[60]

Congress's express exclusion of "Indian tribes" from the definition of employers covered by Title VII and the ADA leaves open the question of what entities may be considered "Indian tribes" for the purpose of that exclusion. Thus far, the courts have read these exemptions liberally and generally applied them to businesses that are significantly controlled by tribes or that function to enhance tribal government interests.[61]

A sampling of the cases follows:

- *Dille v. Council of Energy Resource Tribes*:[62] Council of Energy Resource Tribes, a consortium of 39 tribes under the control of the member tribes, exempt as "Indian tribe" under Title VII.

- *Duke v. Absentee Shawnee Tribe of Oklahoma Housing Authority*:[63] Absentee Shawnee Housing Authority, created pursuant to Oklahoma law as a state agency to provide lowincome housing to tribal members, exempt as Indian tribe under Title VII. The "mere organization of such an entity under state law does not preclude its characterization as a tribal organization"; as "an enterprise designed to further the economic interests of the Absentee Shawnee tribe" and subject to its "exclusive control," the Housing Authori-

---

[60] *See* 42 U.S.C. § 12111(5)(B)(i) (2018) (term "employer" does not include an Indian tribe). Congress has not exempted Alaska Native Corporations from the employment discrimination provisions of the ADA. *See Pearson v. Chugach Gov't Servs. Inc.*, 669 F. Supp. 2d 467, 475–76 (D. Del. 2009) (rejecting extension of ANC exclusion from Title VII to employment discrimination under ADA).

[61] *But see Portico Reality Services Office Fox v. Portico Reality Servs. Off.*, 739 F. Supp. 2d 912, 914 (E.D. Va. 2010) (narrowly construing limited exclusion of Alaska Native Corporations (ANCs) from Title VII; holding that Alaska limited liability company indirectly owned by ANC not within that exclusion).

[62] 801 F.2d 373 (10th Cir. 1986).

[63] 199 F.3d 1123 (10th Cir. 1999).

ty would be exempt from Title VII claims under the "Indian tribe" exemption.[64]

- *EEOC v. Navajo Health Foundation-Sage Memorial Hospital Inc.*:[65] Nonprofit corporation incorporated under state law, but wholly owned and controlled by Navajo Nation to provide health services to tribal members, is an "Indian tribe" under Title VII.

- *Hagen v. Sisseton-Wahpeton Community College*:[66] College chartered by tribe as a nonprofit corporation to provide post-secondary education to tribal members on the Lake Traverse Reservation has sovereign immunity from race discrimination suits brought pursuant to state and federal law. (College's board of trustees consisted of one enrolled member from each of the Tribe's seven districts.)

- *Pink v. Modoc Indian Health Project Inc.*:[67] Off-reservation nonprofit corporation, formed and controlled by two Indian tribes to provide health services, exempt as "Indian tribe" under Title VII.

- *Curtis v. Sandia Casino*:[68] Casino owned and operated by the Pueblo of Sandia exempt under Title VII and ADA.

- *Giedosh v. Little Wound School Board*:[69] On-reservation school board, a nonprofit corporation, incorporated under the laws of South Dakota, was exempt as an "Indian tribe" under Title VII. Important factors for the decision: (a) the

---

[64]*Id.* at 1125.

[65]No. CV-06-2125-PCT-DGC, 2007 WL 2683825 (D. Ariz. Sept. 7, 2007).

[66]205 F.3d 1040 (8th Cir. 2000).

[67]157 F.3d 1185 (9th Cir. 1998).

[68]No. 02-2274, 2003, WL 21386332 (10th Cir. June 17, 2003) (unpublished).

[69]995 F. Supp. 1052 (D.S.D. 1997).

board was made up of members of the tribe; (b) it furthered important tribal interests, i.e., the educational development of the children living in Indian country; (c) it contracted with the Bureau of Indian Affairs under the Indian Self-Determination and Education Assistance Act; (d) the school that the board administered was chartered by the tribe; and (e) the school was required to comply with tribal ordinances and regulations.[70]

- *Barker v. Menominee Nation Casino:*[71] Menominee Nation Casino and Menominee Tribal Gaming Commission, organized as subordinate economic enterprises of the Menominee Indian Tribe, exempt as "Indian tribe" under Title VII.

- *Myrick v. Devils Lake Sioux Manufacturing Corp.:*[72] North Dakota corporation, owned 51 percent by Devils Lake Sioux Tribe and 49 percent by a Delaware corporation and engaged in manufacturing on reservation, not exempt as "Indian tribe" under Title VII.[73]

---

[70]*Id.* at 1057-59. The U.S. District Court for the District of New Mexico followed the reasoning of *Giedosh* in holding that an on-reservation school district organized as a nonprofit corporation under state law and controlled by Navajo tribal members elected in accordance with Navajo law was an "Indian tribe," excluded from Title VII. See *Jim v. Shiprock Associated Sch., Inc.*, 2019 WL 2285918, at *5 (D.N.M. May 29, 2019), *aff'd,* 833 F. App'x 749 (10th Cir. 2020).

[71]897 F. Supp. 389 (E.D. Wis. 1995).

[72]718 F. Supp. 753 (D.N.D. 1989).

[73]*Compare Little v. Devils Lake-Sioux Manufacturing Corp.*, 607 F. Supp. 700 (D.N.D. 1985) (same company exempt from discrimination when following Indian employment preference policy) and *Devils Lake Sioux Manufacturing Corp.*, 243 NLRB 29 (1979) (same company subject to National Labor Relations Act).

- *Setchell v. Little Six, Inc.*:[74] Little Six, Inc., d/b/a Mystic Lake Casino, a corporation wholly owned by the Mdewakanton Sioux Community and incorporated under tribal law, but holding a Minnesota license to do business in Minnesota as a "foreign corporation," falls within "Indian tribe" exemption of ADA.

As a general rule, these cases show that in discerning whether a particular employer qualifies as an "Indian tribe" for the exemptions under the ADA and Title VII, courts consider the same factors that determine whether a particular entity is an "arm of the tribe" for the purposes of sovereign immunity from suit. Thus, there is an overlap between the standards used to determine whether a particular entity falls within the "Indian tribe" exemption from liability under Title VII and the ADA and whether such an entity qualifies as an "arm of the tribe" with sovereign immunity from suit, which is addressed in Chapter 4.[75]

4. The Age Discrimination in Employment Act of 1967

The Age Discrimination in Employment Act of 1967 (ADEA)[76] does not, by its terms, exclude Indian tribes. It is administered by the EEOC separately from Title VII. The EEOC has sought to impose the ADEA upon tribes or tribal enterprises on three occasions in three separate U.S. Courts of Appeals, thus far without success.[77] But the

---

[74] No. C4-95-2208, 1996 WL 162560 (Minn. Ct. App. Apr. 9, 1996).

[75] *See McCoy v. Salish Kootenai Coll., Inc.*, 334 F. Supp. 3d 1116, 1121 (D. Mont. 2018), *aff'd*, 785 F. App'x 414 (9th Cir. 2019) (applying "arm of the tribe" standards to decide whether tribal college incorporated under tribal and state law is an "Indian tribe" excluded from liability under Title VII.)

[76] 29 U.S.C. §§ 621-634 (2018).

[77] *See EEOC v. Karuk Tribe Hous. Auth.*, 260 F.3d 1071 (9th Cir. 2001); *EEOC v. Fond du Lac Heavy Equip. & Constr. Co.*, 986 F.2d 246 (8th Cir. 1993), *EEOC v. Cherokee Nation*, 871 F.2d 937 (10th Cir. 1989). *See also Cano v. Cocopah Casino*, No. CV-06-2120-PHX-JAT, 2007 WL 2164555 (D. Ariz. July 25, 2007) (refusing to dismiss application of ADEA to tribe-owned and operated casino).

courts were divided in two of these cases, and each case turned largely on the particular facts presented.

The cases are briefly summarized here:

- *EEOC v. Karuk Tribe Housing Authority:*[78] This case involved a claim of age discrimination by a member of the Karuk Tribe against the Tribe's housing authority. The Ninth Circuit applied its *Coeur d'Alene Tribal Farm*[79] framework, discussed in Chapter 3, for determining whether a federal law of general application could apply to an Indian tribe. (It considered the tribal housing authority to be a branch of the Tribe.) Under the circumstances of the case — an intra-tribal dispute, a housing authority involved in governmental (as opposed to commercial) activities, and the availability of a tribal process to resolve the dispute — the court held that the ADEA did not apply. The court concluded that the case involved "purely intramural matters" touching on the Tribe's "exclusive rights of self-governance."[80]

- *EEOC v. Fond du Lac Heavy Equipment and Construction Co.:*[81] The EEOC brought suit against a tribally-owned construction company and the tribe on behalf of a tribal member who claimed he was denied employment on the basis of his age. Tracking the Tenth Circuit standard, the Eighth Circuit held that if the ADEA were applied to the Tribe and its business, it would interfere with the "inherent" right of the Tribe to resolve "an intramural matter that has traditionally been left to the tribe's self-government."[82] One judge dissented, arguing that Con-

---

[78] 260 F.3d 1071 (9th Cir. 2001).

[79] *Donovan v. Coeur d'Alene Tribal Farm*, 751 F.2d 1113 (9th Cir. 1985).

[80] *Karuk Tribe Hous. Auth.*, 260 F.3d at 1082.

[81] 986 F.2d 246 (8th Cir. 1993).

[82] *Id.* at 248-49.

gress's failure to exempt tribes from the ADEA, while clearly doing so with respect to Title VII, showed that it intended to apply the ADEA to tribes.[83]

- *EEOC v. Cherokee Nation*:[84] This was the first case to address the application of the ADEA to tribes. The Tenth Circuit found that applying the ADEA to the Cherokee Nation would interfere with the treaty right of the Tribe "to make and carry into effect all such laws as they may deem necessary for the government and protection of the persons and property within their own country."[85] Employing the rule that any ambiguities must be resolved to preserve "traditional notions of sovereignty and with the federal policy of encouraging tribal independence," the court concluded that Congress's silence about the application of the ADEA to Indian tribes rendered its intent ambiguous.[86] The court resolved the ambiguity in favor of the Tribe, and held that the ADEA did not apply. As in the *Fond du Lac Heavy Equipment* case, one judge dissented, arguing that Congress's failure to exclude tribes from the ADEA as it had done under Title VII showed its intent to apply the ADEA to tribes.[87]

These cases reflect the operation of the federal infringement standards discussed in Chapter 3. The dissents in *Cherokee Nation*[88] and *Fond du Lac Heavy Equipment*,[89] and the fact-specific nature of

---

[83] *Id.* at 251 (Wollman, J., dissenting).

[84] 871 F.2d 937 (10th Cir. 1989).

[85] *Id.* at 938 n.2.

[86] *Id.* at 939.

[87] *Id.* at 939-42 (Tacha, J., dissenting).

[88] *Id.*

[89] 986 F.2d at 251 (Wollman, J., dissenting).

their resolution, leave in limbo the law concerning the application of the ADEA to tribes and tribal enterprises.[90]

5. Federal Employment Discrimination Laws Tied to Federal Funding

Section 504 of the Rehabilitation Act of 1973[91] prohibits recipients of federal funds from discriminating against employees on the basis of disability.[92] The Age Discrimination Act of 1975 (not to be confused with the ADEA) prohibits age discrimination by such recipients.[93] Employees have attempted to invoke these provisions against tribes that receive federal funds. Thus far, the courts have held that these laws do not waive tribal sovereign immunity.[94] Indeed, by their terms,

---

[90]*Compare E.E.O.C. v. Forest Cty. Potawatomi Cmty.*, 2014 WL 1795137, at *3 (E.D. Wis. May 6, 2014) (holding that Indian tribe is a "person" for the purpose of the definition of an "employer" under the ADEA; applying *Coeur d'Alene Tribal Farm* standards discussed in Chapter 3) *with Delorge v. Mashantucket Pequot Gaming Enter.*, No. MPTC-CV-97-114, ¶¶ 96-102 (Mashantucket Pequot Tribal Ct. July 23, 1997) (ADEA cannot be applied to tribal gaming commission).

[91]*Pub.* L. No. 93-112, § 504, 87 Stat. 394, 394 (1973).

[92]As the Supreme Court has summarized:
> Section 504 ... provides, *inter alia*, that no "otherwise qualified handicapped individual," as defined in 29 U.S.C. § 706(7), shall, solely by reason of his handicap, be excluded from participation in any program receiving federal financial assistance. Section 706(7)(B) defines "handicapped individual" to mean any person who "(i) has a physical ... impairment which substantially limits one or more of [his] major life activities, (ii) has a record of such an impairment, or (iii) is regarded as having such an impairment."

School Bd. of Nassau County, Fla. v. Arline, 480 U.S. 273, 273 (1987).

[93]*See* 42 U.S.C. §§ 6101-6107 (2018).

[94]*See Garcia v. Akwesasne Hous. Auth.*, 268 F.3d 76, 85-86 (2d Cir. 2001) (Native American Housing Assistance and Self-Determination Act of 1996, and implementing regulation, requiring compliance with Age Discrimination Act of 1975, did not waive sovereign immunity); *Sanderlin v. Seminole Tribe of Fla.*, 243 F.3d 1282 (11th Cir. 2001) (federal funding contract for tribal police department requiring compliance with Section 504 of the Rehabilitation Act did not constitute waiver of tribal sovereign immunity). *See also Nanomantube v. Kickapoo Tribe in Kansas*, 631 F.3d 1150, 1153 (10th Cir. 2011) (Tribe's agreement in employee handbook "to comply with the provi-

these statutes apply only to state or local government recipients of federal funding.[95] Indian tribes are neither.[96]

Certain other federal laws may, from time to time, be incorporated by reference into federal funding contracts involving Indian tribes. So-called Public Law 638 contracts, entered into pursuant to the Indian Self-Determination and Education Assistance Act,[97] under which tribes receive federal funding for governmental services, may contain "boilerplate" antidiscrimination provisions generally applicable to recipients of federal funds, such as Executive Order 11246 (prohibiting employment discrimination by federal procurement contractors) or Section 504 of the Rehabilitation Act (prohibiting disability discrimination).[98] It would be inconsistent with Congress's express goals of protecting tribes from employment discrimination lawsuits to impose these laws upon tribes as a result of such boilerplate language. No cases have been found in which these laws have been enforced against tribes or tribal agencies by virtue of their reference in government funding contracts.

Regulations promulgated under the Native American Housing Assistance and Self-Determination Act (NAHASDA)[99] by the U.S. Department of Housing and Urban Development (HUD) provide, in question/answer format, as follows:

---

sions of Title VII of the Civil Rights Act of 1964 and 1991" is not a waiver of sovereign immunity).

[95] Rehabilitation Act of 1973, 29 U.S.C. § 794(b) (2018); Age Discrimination Act of 1975, 42 U.S.C. § 6107(4) (2018).

[96] *See White Mountain Apache Tribe v. Bracker*, 448 U.S. 136, 143 (1980) (tribes are not states); *Wheeler v. U.S.*, 435 U.S. 313 (1978) (tribes are not local governments).

[97] 25 U.S.C. §§ 5301-5351 (2018).

[98] *See generally* Vicki Limas, *Sovereignty as a Bar to Enforcement of Executive Order 11246 in Federal Contracts with Native American Tribes*, 26 N.M. L. Rev. 257, 279-92 (1996).

[99] 25 U.S.C. §§ 4101-4243 (2018).

Sec. 1000.12. What nondiscrimination requirements are applicable?

(a) The requirements of the Age Discrimination Act of 1975 (42 U.S.C. 6101-07) and HUD's implementing regulations in 24 CFR part 146.

(b) Section 504 of the Rehabilitation Act of 1975 (29 U.S.C. 794) and HUD's regulations at 24 CFR part 8 apply.

(c) The Indian Civil Rights Act (Title II of the Civil Rights Act of 1968; 25 U.S.C. 1301-03), applies to federally recognized Indian tribes that exercise powers of self-government.

(d) Title VI of the Civil Rights Act of 1964 (42 U.S.C. 2000d) and Title VIII of the Civil Rights Act of 1968 (42 U.S.C. 3601 et seq.) apply to Indian tribes that are not covered by the Indian Civil Rights Act. However, the Title VI and Title VIII requirements do not apply to actions by Indian tribes under Section 201(b) of NAHASDA.[100]

Whether, and how, these regulations would be enforced against a tribe or its "tribally designated housing entity" is open to question. Subsection (d) appears out of place because the Indian Civil Rights Act, by its terms, applies to all tribal governments.[101] And it is doubtful that Title VI would apply to federally recognized Indian tribes or their des-

---

[100] 24 C.F.R. § 1000.12 (2010). *See also* 25 U.S.C. § 4114(b) (2018) (labor standards for recipients); 24 C.F.R. § 1000.16 (2010) ("What labor standards are applicable?").

[101] *See* 25 U.S.C. § 1302 (2018). Further, the NAHASDA statute itself requires tribally designated housing authorities to certify compliance with ICRA "to the extent that such title is applicable." 25 U.S.C. § 4112(c)(5)(A) (2018).

ignated housing authorities.[102] While noncompliance with these laws might place agency funding at risk,[103] it is unlikely that these provisions create a private right of action or a waiver of sovereign immunity for individuals to sue tribal housing entities or officials.[104]

D. Conclusion

For many, the concept of "civil rights" in the United States is fundamental to what it means to be American. The fact that Indian tribes are governments predating the formation of the United States and therefore not constrained by the constitutional provisions that constrain the states and the federal government is fundamental to the nature of Indian tribal sovereignty. But there is a tension between these two realities in the workplaces of Indian tribes. The economic power that tribes have realized in the "modern era" of Indian self-determination, particularly from the enactment of IGRA,[105] has placed them under scrutiny with respect to their employment relations with non-Indians. Thus, tribes are challenged to answer the question of what rights and remedies they provide to protect civil rights in the workplace if they face no constraints under the United State Constitution, if they are excluded from arguably the most important civil rights

---

[102] 42 U.S.C. § 2000d (2018) prohibits "race, color, or national origin" discrimination by any "program or activity receiving Federal financial assistance." Like the Age Discrimination Act of 1975, 42 U.S.C. §§ 6101-6107 (2018), and Section 504 of the Rehabilitation Act, *Pub.* L. No. 93-112, § 504, 87 Stat. 394, 394 (1973), the term "program or activity" in Title VII is defined as those of instrumentalities or agencies of state or local governments. 42 U.S.C. § 2000d-4a (2018). Indian tribes are neither.

[103] *See* Native American Housing Assistance and Self-Determination Act, 25 U.S.C. § 4161 (2018) (remedies for noncompliance).

[104] *See Santa Clara Pueblo v. Martinez*, 436 U.S. 49, 60-72 (1978) (setting out requirement for Congress to establish an enforceable private right of action and holding that the Indian Civil Rights Act does not create such right of action against tribal officials other than for *habeas corpus* relief); *Garcia v. Akwesasne Hous. Auth.*, 268 F.3d 76, 86 (2d Cir. 2001) (the NAHASDA regulations quoted in the text do not constitute a waiver of sovereign immunity).

[105] *See* Chapter 1, Section D for a discussion of the "modern era" of federal Indian policy.

laws governing the employment setting (Title VII and the ADA), and if the ICRA protections cannot be enforced in the federal courts. Tribes are beginning to answer that question by enacting a variety of laws to protect the civil rights of employees in Indian country.[106]

---

[106] *See* Chapter 8.

6

FEDERAL LAWS GOVERNING EMPLOYMENT TERMS AND CONDITIONS AND TRIBAL EMPLOYMENT

A. Introduction

Chapter 3 described legal barriers to federal authority over the labor and employment relations of Indian tribes when Congress fails to explicitly address tribes within legislation. It further outlined the differing approaches of the federal courts of appeals in addressing those barriers. Chapter 5 discussed federal laws designed to protect civil rights (*e.g.*, workplace sex, race, and disability discrimination). This chapter looks at federal laws that regulate employment terms and conditions (*e.g.*, safety and health; wages and hours). Chapter 7 will consider the federal law regulating unions and collective bargaining: the National Labor Relations Act.

As discussed in Chapter 4, it is clear that none of these federal laws—insofar as they provide for private lawsuits—can be enforced against an Indian tribe by individuals because Congress did not expressly waive the sovereign immunity of tribes under these laws. Congress's 2006 amendment to the Employee Retirement Income Security Act of 1974 (ERISA),[1] discussed below, however, is one exception.

Notwithstanding their immunity from suits by individuals, tribes may face actions by the federal agencies administering labor and employment laws because tribes do not have sovereign immunity from lawsuits brought by the United States and its agencies.[2] It is in this set-

---

[1] 29 U.S.C. §§ 1001-1461 (2018).

[2] *See EEOC v. Karuk Tribe Hous. Auth.*, 260 F.3d 1071, 1075 (9th Cir. 2001). *Compare Larimer v. Konocti Vista Casino Resort, Marina & RV Park*, 814 F. Supp. 2d 952 (N.D. Cal. 2011) (tribe's sovereign immunity from suit bars individual's lawsuit against tribe under Fair Labor Standards Act).

ting that courts have decided the issue of whether federal laws that generally govern hours, wages, and working conditions, without mentioning Indian tribes, nevertheless apply to tribes. These federal labor and employment laws are often referred to as laws "of general application."[3] Appendix B provides a chart of most of these laws as well as Title VII to show the issues they address, the federal agencies administering the laws, how each law is enforced, and the remedies that each law provides.

B. Occupational Safety and Health Act

Congress enacted the Occupational Safety and Health Act of 1970 (OSHA)[4] to ensure safe and healthful working conditions for employees.[5] The Occupational Safety and Health Administration oversees enforcement and administration of OSHA in states that do not have their own qualifying programs.[6] Congress expressly excluded the federal government as well as state and local governments from the requirements of OSHA, but it failed to address whether OSHA applies to Indian tribes or their enterprises.[7]

---

[3] *See Donovan v. Navajo Forest Prod. Indus.*, 692 F.2d 709, 711 (10th Cir. 1982). Federal labor and employment laws that exclude state and local governments, or the federal government, cannot accurately be characterized as federal laws of "general application" for the very reason that they exclude governmental employers. *See N.L.R.B. v. Pueblo of San Juan*, 280 F.3d 1278, 1283 (10th Cir. 2000), *on reh'g en banc*, 276 F.3d 1186 (10th Cir. 2002). Thus, commentators criticize courts that automatically invoke the *Coeur d'Alene Tribal Farm* formulation for deciding cases about the application of labor and employment statutes to Indian tribes and their economic enterprises when the law would not apply to similarly situated states or state enterprises. *See* Alex T. Skibine, *Practical Reasoning and the Application of General Federal Regulatory Laws to Indian Nations*, 22 WASH. & LEE J. CIVIL RTS. & SOC. JUST. 123, 174–75 (2016); Kaighn Smith Jr., *When Congress Forgets: Breaking Through Congress's Failure to Mention Indian Tribes in Federal Employment Laws*, FED. LAW., March/April 2021, at 8, 8–9.

[4] 29 U.S.C. §§ 651-678 (2018).

[5] *Id.* § 651(b).

[6] *See id.* §§ 659, 667(b).

[7] *Id.* § 652(5).

Five federal circuit courts of appeals have addressed the application of OSHA to tribal enterprises with differing results. The Ninth Circuit's decision in *Coeur d'Alene Tribal Farm*[8] and the Tenth Circuit's decision in *Navajo Forest Products Industries*[9] are discussed in Chapter 3. These cases involved very similar facts — an on-reservation, tribally owned business that employed both Indians and non-Indians and engaged in interstate commerce — but came to opposite conclusions because of the different legal standards applied.

The Ninth Circuit presumed OSHA applied to the Coeur d'Alene Tribal Farm and left the farm with the burden of showing one of three exceptions: (1) that application of OSHA to the farm would intrude upon an exclusive right of self-governance in a "purely intramural matter," (2) that application of OSHA to the farm would thwart a treaty right, or (3) that Congress did not intend the law to apply to Indians on their reservations.[10] The farm sought to establish the first exception, but was unable to do so.[11] The court found that the farm's commercial purpose and its employment of "non-Indians" undermined its ability to show that its activities were "intramural" or related to self-government.[12]

---

[8]*Donovan v. Coeur d'Alene Tribal Farm*, 751 F.2d 1113 (9th Cir. 1985).

[9]*Donovan v. Navajo Forest Prods. Indus.*, 692 F.2d 709, 712 (10th Cir. 1982).

[10]*Coeur d'Alene Tribal Farm*, 751 F.2d at 1116.

[11]*Id.* at 1116-17.

[12]*Id.* Courts' use of the term "non-Indians" has been flagged as a race-based distinction of dubious relevance to the legal issue presented in these cases. *See* Kaighn Smith Jr., *When Congress Forgets: Breaking Through Congress's Failure to Mention Indian Tribes in Federal Employment Laws,* Fed. Law., March/April 2021, at 8, 10 (discussing the problem of injecting the racial distinction of "non-Indians" into the legal formulation for deciding whether federal laws that are silent about their application to Indian tribes apply to tribes). The cases under review contemplate the scope of a federally recognized Indian tribe's authority over employment relations within its sovereign territory. As set forth in Chapter 2, the scope of that authority may turn on whether the entity or individual at issue is considered a member (or citizen) of the tribe asserting authority, but the racial classification of "Indian" or "non-Indian" has no bearing on the question.

The Tenth Circuit, however, reached the opposite conclusion with respect to Navajo Forest Products Industries because it found, in the first instance, that the Navajo Nation had retained its sovereign right to prevent outsiders from interfering with reservation affairs.[13] The Tenth Circuit rejected the Ninth Circuit's presumption, grounded in dictum from the Supreme Court's opinion in *Tuscarora Indian Nation*,[14] that a federal law of general application applies to Indian tribes and their reservation businesses.[15]

The Second Circuit has sided with the Ninth Circuit. In *Reich v. Mashantucket Sand & Gravel*,[16] the Second Circuit concluded that a tribally owned construction company, operating on the Mashantucket Pequot Tribal Nation's reservation and employing "non-Indians," was subject to OSHA under the Ninth Circuit standard.[17] Contrary to the Supreme Court's decisions in *Merrion v. Jicarrilla Apache Tribe*[18] and *Montana v. United States*,[19] discussed in Chapter 2, the court said that "limitations on tribal authority are particularly acute where non-Indians are concerned."[20]

---

[13]*Navajo Forest Prods. Indus.*, 692 F.2d at 712.

[14]*Fed. Power Comm'n v. Tuscarora Indian Nation*, 362 U.S. 99 (1960).

[15]*Navajo Forest Prods. Indus.*, 692 F.2d at 711. *See also U.S. Dept. of Labor v. Occupational Safety & Health Rev. Comm'n*, 935 F.2d 182 (9th Cir. 1991) (OSHA applies to tribal lumber mill operating on reservation, notwithstanding treaty right to exclude non-Indians from reservation). For a further discussion of *Tuscarora Indian Nation* see Chapter 3, Section C.

[16]95 F.3d 174, 176 (2d Cir. 1996).

[17]*Id.* at 181 ("the nature of MSG's work, its employment of non-Indians, and the construction work on a hotel and casino that operates in interstate commerce—when viewed as a whole, result in a mosaic that is distinctly inconsistent with the portrait of an Indian tribe exercising exclusive rights of self-governance in purely intramural matters").

[18]455 U.S. 130, 144 (1982).

[19]450 U.S. 544, 564-65 (1981).

[20]*Id.* at 180.

In *Menominee Tribal Enterprises v. Solis*,[21] the Seventh Circuit addressed whether OSHA applied to a sawmill owned and operated by the Menominee Indian Tribe on its reservation, employing only tribal members. The court largely tracked the *Coeur d'Alene Tribal Farm* formulation. The fact that the Tribe employed only its own citizens made no difference to the court; it held that because the sawmill was "commercial," it could not fit within the self-governance exception for presumed applicability under that formulation.[22] Finding no interference with tribal self-government or rights guaranteed to the Tribe by treaty or statute, the court held that the sawmill was subject to OSHA.[23]

In 2020, the U.S. Court of Appeals for the Eighth Circuit addressed whether a fishing enterprise owned by the Red Lake Band of Chippewa Indians operating within the Band's reservation and employing only tribal members was subject to OSHA.[24] Two tribal members drowned while fishing for the enterprise, and the Labor Department sought to fine the enterprise for failing to provide the workers with appropriate personal flotation devices.[25] The Eighth Circuit held that Congress's silence about OSHA's application to Indian tribes and their enterprises could not be construed to impose the require-

---

[21] 601 F.3d 669 (7th Cir. 2010) (Posner, J.).

[22] *See id.* at 674.

[23] *Id.* at 673. The court pointed out that the lawyer for the Tribe said that the sawmill "makes every effort to comply with OSHA," that it "seeks the advice of the Occupational Safety and Health Administration," and that "its objection is merely to having to pay fines if it fails to comply." *Id.* at 673. The court then observed:
> The sawmill's output (some $20 million worth in 2005, the latest date for which the record contains such data) is sold in interstate commerce, in competition with sawmills owned by non-Indian enterprises. Exempting a sawmill owned by an Indian tribe from the obligations that OSHA imposes on its competitors seems hardly necessary to implement the Restoration Act or the Management Plan, let alone the 1856 treaty or any earlier treaty.

Id. For an additional discussion of the *Menominee Tribal Enterprises* decision see Chapter 3, Section C(2)(c).

[24] *Scalia v. Red Lake Nation Fisheries, Inc.*, 982 F.3d 533, 535–36 (8th Cir. 2020).

[25] *See id.*

ments of OSHA upon the Band's fishing enterprise.[26] The court reasoned that the employment relations at issue were internal matters implicating core matters of tribal sovereignty and application of OSHA would infringe on that sovereignty; Congress's silence would not suffice to allow that infringement.[27] It further found that the Band's treaty right to fish bolstered the view that the enterprise should be free from OSHA.[28] This decision appears at odds with the Seventh Circuit's decision *Menominee Tribal Enterprises*: both involved on-reservation tribal enterprises employing only tribal members and came to opposite conclusions.

C. Fair Labor Standards Act

Pursuant to the Fair Labor Standards Act of 1938 (FLSA),[29] Congress established minimum nationwide standards for wages and overtime pay, and administrative procedures through which workers may seek compensation for qualifying work time.[30] The FLSA's provisions also deal with child labor, equal pay, and other compensation issues.[31]

---

[26] *See id.*

[27] *Id.* The Eighth Circuit followed its earlier precedent, *EEOC v. Fond du Lac Heavy Equip. & Constr. Co.,* 986 F.2d 246 (8th Cir. 1993), addressing whether application of the Age Discrimination in Employment Act (ADEA) applied to an enterprise of the Fond du Lac Band of Lake Superior Chippewa Indians. (The ADEA, like OSHA, fails to mention Indian tribes, but exempts states and the United States. *See* 29 U.S.C. § 152.) *Fond du Lac* involved an ADEA claim brought against the enterprise by the EEOC on behalf of Band citizen. The Eighth Circuit refused to apply the ADEA, stating that "[s]ubjecting such an employment relationship ... to federal control and supervision dilutes the sovereignty of the tribe." *Fond du Lac Heavy Equip,* 986 F.2d at 249. *Red Lake Nation Fisheries* further solidifies the Eighth Circuit's stance that "[f]or a statute of general applicability to apply to Indian self-government," the court will look for either an "explicit statement of Congress" or "evidence of congressional intent to abrogate." *Red Lake Nation Fisheries, Inc.,* 982 F.3d at 535 (quoting and citing *United States v. Dion,* 476 U.S. 734, 739-40 (1986)).

[28] *See id.*

[29] 29 U.S.C. §§ 201-19 (2018).

[30] *Id.* §§ 206, 207, 216(c).

[31] *Id.* §§ 206(d)(1), 212, 216(d).

Congress exempted certain classes of employees (*e.g.*, salaried professionals) from some of the FLSA's provisions.[32] It did not expressly address the application of the FLSA to Indian tribes. Thus far, only the Seventh Circuit and the Ninth Circuit have addressed the applicability of the FLSA to tribes.

The Seventh Circuit first addressed the issue in *Reich v. Great Lakes Indian Fish & Wildlife Commission*,[33] which involved game wardens employed by the Great Lakes Indian Fish & Wildlife Commission, a consortium of thirteen tribes that was organized to oversee tribal hunting and fishing rights in the Great Lakes region.[34] In concluding that the FLSA would not apply to these employees, the Seventh Circuit emphasized two things: first, the activity at issue involved the tribes' sovereign right to regulate their property interests, and second, the FLSA would not apply to similarly situated employees of state governments.[35] The majority opinion, written by Judge William Posner, showed signs of agreement with the Tenth and Eighth Circuits' approaches in a setting where a federal law of general application — like the FLSA — would affect the "inherent authority" of the tribes.[36]

The decision was not unanimous. A dissenting judge would have reached a different result under the Ninth Circuit's *Coeur d'Alene Tribal Farm* standard.[37] In apparent response to that dissent, the majority qualified its decision by distinguishing the cases relied upon by

---

[32]*Id.* §§ 203(e)(3)-(5), 213.

[33]4 F.3d 490 (7th Cir. 1993).

[34]*Id.* at 492.

[35]*See id.* at 494-95.

[36]*See id.* at 494 (regulatory function within the "inherent authority" of tribes cannot be impaired by application of FLSA in the absence of an express directive by Congress even in the absence of a specific treaty right); *id.* at 496 (agreeing with Tenth Circuit's approach in *EEOC v. Cherokee Nation*, 871 F.2d 937 (10th Cir. 1989)). *But see Menominee Tribal Enterprises v. Solis*, 601 F.3d 669 (7th Cir. 2010) (discussed above in reference to OSHA). For an additional discussion of *Reich, see* Chapter 3, Section C(2)(c).

[37]*Reich v. Great Lakes Indian Fish & Wildlife Comm'n*, 4 F.3d at 496-504 (Coffey, J., dissenting).

the dissent on the ground that "the employees in those cases were engaged in routine activities of a commercial or service character, namely lumbering and health care, rather than of a governmental character."[38]

Ten years later, in *Snyder v. Navajo Nation*,[39] the Ninth Circuit addressed the application of the FLSA to law enforcement officers employed by the Navajo Nation. The court affirmed the district court's holding that the FLSA did not apply to the plaintiffs because "law enforcement [is] an intramural matter" under the *Coeur d'Alene Tribal Farm* case.[40] Although tribal law enforcement officers traveled off the reservation to assist in the investigation of crimes affecting the reservation and Navajo citizens, the court held that their activities constituted a "traditional government function" that must be exempt from federal laws of general application in order to protect tribes' "exclusive rights of self-governance in purely intramural matters."[41]

In its 2009 decision in *Solis v. Matheson*,[42] the Ninth Circuit considered the application of the FLSA to a smoke shop owned and operated by an enrolled member of the Puyallup Tribe on the Puyallup Reservation. The court again applied the *Coeur d'Alene Tribal Farm* standards.[43] This time, however, in addressing the "[s]elf-government and [i]ntramural [a]ffairs [e]xception" to its presumption of applicabil-

---

[38]*Id.* at 495 (distinguishing *Smart v. State Farm Ins. Co.*, 868 F.2d 929 (7th Cir. 1989); *Donovan v. Coeur d'Alene Tribal Farm*, 751 F.2d 1113 (9th Cir. 1985); *U.S. Dept. of Labor v. OSHRC*, 935 F.2d 182 (9th Cir. 1991); *Lumber Indus. Pension Fund v. Warm Springs Forest Prods. Indus.*, 939 F.2d 683 (9th Cir. 1991)). *See also Menominee Tribal Enterprises v. Solis*, 601 F.3d 669, 673-74 (7th Cir. 2010) (sawmill owned and operated by tribe on reservation subject to OSHA) (discussed above in reference to OSHA).

[39]382 F.3d 892, 894 (9th Cir. 2004).

[40]*Id.* (citing *Donovan v. Coeur d'Alene Tribal Farm*, 751 F.2d 1113 (9th Cir. 1985)).

[41]*Id.* at 895-96 (quoting *Coeur d'Alene Tribal Farm*, 751 F.2d at 1116).

[42]563 F.3d 425 (9th Cir. 2009).

[43]*Id.* at 430. *See also Chao v. Matheson*, No. C06-5361RBL, 2007 WL 1830738, at *1, *4 (W.D. Wash. June 25, 2007) (holding tribal member business subject to FLSA).

ity,⁴⁴ the court considered whether application of the FLSA would clash with the regulatory authority of the Tribe. The court said:

> [A]lthough the Supreme Court has found that Indian tribes have a strong interest as a sovereign in regulating economic activity involving its own members within its own territory and . . . may enact laws governing such activity, the Mathesons do not argue that the Puyallup Tribe enacted a different wage and hour law that applied in place of the FLSA, nor do they assert that the FLSA does not preempt any such law. Thus, there is no evidence in the record that the Puyallup Tribe has acted on its right of self-governance in the field of wage and hours laws and specifically with respect to overtime.
>
> Because the Puyallup Tribe has not enacted wage and hour laws, the holdings of the cases discussed above lead this court to conclude that the overtime provisions of the FLSA apply to the Mathesons and the intramural affairs exception does not.⁴⁵

The court also considered whether, under the principles of *Montana v. United States*,⁴⁶ discussed in Chapter 2, the Tribe exercised governmental authority that could be thwarted by the application of the FLSA to the tribal member's reservation business. But there was "no evidence that the Puyallup Tribe asserted regulatory authority over employment and wages for non-Indians,"⁴⁷ and, the court observed, "*Montana* only applies insofar as the tribe in question is seeking to as-

---

⁴⁴*Matheson*, 563 F.3d at 430.

⁴⁵*Id.* at 433-34 (citations and quotations omitted).

⁴⁶450 U.S. 544, 565-66 (1981).

⁴⁷*Matheson*, 563 F.3d at 436.

sert regulatory authority over the activities of a nonmember."[48] These observations might suggest that the Ninth Circuit would have been open to reaching a different result if the Puyallup Tribe had regulated the minimum wages and overtime pay for employees at the smoke shop in accordance with its own laws.

D. Family Medical Leave Act

Congress passed the Family Medical Leave Act of 1993 (FMLA)[49] to ensure that specified employees would not lose their job security if they needed a reasonable amount of time off to deal with personal or family medical problems.[50] The Act makes it unlawful for "any employer to interfere with, restrain, or deny the exercise of or the attempt to exercise, any right provided under [the FMLA]."[51] The FMLA provides covered employees with up to twelve workweeks of unpaid, job-protected leave per year and requires employers to maintain group health benefits during the required leave.[52] Congress included certain federal employers as well as state and local governments within the definition of employers subject to the Act.[53] The Department of Labor enforces the FMLA and has promulgated regulations interpreting its provisions.[54]

No court has yet addressed the applicability of the FMLA to tribes or their enterprises when an action under the FMLA is commenced by a federal agency. Two cases have held, however, that lawsuits brought under the FMLA by individuals against tribes or their enterprises are

---

[48]*Id.* (citation and quotation omitted) (citing and quoting *MacArthur v. San Juan County*, 497 F.3d 1057, 1067, 1069 (10th Cir. 2007), *cert. denied*, 552 U.S. 1181 (2008)).

[49]29 U.S.C. §§ 2601-2654 (2018).

[50]*Id.* § 2601(b).

[51]*Id.* § 2615 (a)(1).

[52]*Id.* §§ 2612, 2614.

[53]29 U.S.C. § 2611 (4)(A)(iii).

[54]*See id.* §§ 2617(b), 2654.

barred by the doctrine of tribal sovereign immunity.⁵⁵ In a third case, the FMLA was applied to a management company in charge of a tribe's gaming operations (including employee relations), but the issue of whether, as a matter of law, the FMLA should apply in that setting was not raised.⁵⁶ A federal district court held that an Alaska Native Corporation, operating a Delaware-based military subcontracting business, was subject to suit by a nonmember employee under the FMLA.⁵⁷

E. Employee Retirement Income Security Act

Congress enacted the Employee Retirement Income Security Act of 1974 (ERISA)⁵⁸ to regulate private sector pensions and other benefits.⁵⁹ This includes requiring specific disclosure about the details and

---

⁵⁵In *Chayoon v. Chao*, 355 F.3d 141 (2d Cir. 2004), the Second Circuit affirmed the dismissal of an FMLA action brought by an employee of the Mashantucket Pequot Tribal Nation's Foxwoods Casino Resort and the Tribal Council. The court held that sovereign immunity barred Chayoon's action because Congress did not unequivocally waive tribal sovereign immunity pursuant to the FMLA. *Id*. at 143. It further said, "Chayoon cannot circumvent tribal immunity by merely naming officers or employees of the Tribe when the complaint concerns actions taken in defendants' official or representative capacities and the complaint does not allege they acted outside of the scope of their authority." *Id*. (The sovereign immunity of tribal officials is discussed in more detail in Chapter 4.) In *Myers v. Seneca Niagara Casino*, 488 F. Supp. 2d 166 (N.D.N.Y. 2006), the federal district court likewise dismissed an FMLA claim brought against a tribal gaming facility on the ground of sovereign immunity. In *Sharber v. Spirit Mountain Gaming, Inc.*, 343 F.3d 974 (9th Cir. 2003) (per curiam), the Ninth Circuit applied the exhaustion doctrine (discussed in Chapter 3) to stay a similar FMLA case brought against a tribal gaming facility. Rather than rule on the issue of sovereign immunity or consider whether the FMLA applied to the casino, the court held that the case should be stayed to give the tribal court the first opportunity to decide whether to address the controversy. *Id*. at 975-76.

⁵⁶*See Yashenko v. Harrah's NC Casino Co., LLC*, 446 F.3d 541, 543-45 (4th Cir. 2006).

⁵⁷*Pearson v. Chugach Gov't Servs. Inc.*, 669 F. Supp. 2d 467, 476-77 (D. Del. 2009).

⁵⁸29 U.S.C. §§ 1001-1461 (2018).

⁵⁹*Id*. §§ 1001-1001b.

finances of benefit plans for employees and their beneficiaries.[60] Congress also established standards to prevent and remedy the misuse of plan assets.[61] ERISA gives plan participants the right to sue employers or other entities involved in managing benefit plans for wrongfully withheld benefits or for breaches of fiduciary duty.[62] Congress allocated responsibilities for enforcing and interpreting various aspects of ERISA to the Treasury Department, the Department of Labor, and the Pension Benefit Guaranty Corporation.[63]

In 2006, Congress amended the definition of "governmental plans," which are exempt from ERISA, to include certain plans of Indian tribes.[64] It exempted any:

> plan which is established and maintained by an Indian tribal government . . . , a subdivision of an Indian tribal government . . . , or an agency or instrumentality of either, and all of the participants of which are employees of such entity substantially all of whose services as such an employee are in the performance of essential governmental functions but not in the performance of commercial activities (whether or not an essential government function).[65]

Prior to this amendment, Congress had given no indication of whether ERISA applied to Indian tribes or their enterprises. The cases decided before the 2006 amendment on the question of ERISA applicability to tribes or their enterprises are instructive, for they add to the general body of federal court cases grappling with whether federal

---

[60] *Id.* § 1021.

[61] *Id.* §§ 1109, 1132.

[62] *Id.* § 1132.

[63] *See, e.g., id.* §§ 1201, 1204.

[64] Pub. L. No. 109-280, § 906(a)(2)(A), 120 Stat. 780 (codified as amended at 29 U.S.C. § 1002(32) (2018)).

[65] 29 U.S.C. § 1002(32).

employment laws that fail to address Indian tribes and tribal entities nevertheless apply to them.

1. Application to Tribal Enterprises Before 2006 Amendment

In two of the four cases that arose prior to the amendment, courts held that ERISA applied to tribal employers on Indian reservations.[66] First, in *Smart v. State Farm Insurance Co.*,[67] the Seventh Circuit considered whether ERISA applied to a benefit plan for an employee of a reservation-based health center owned and operated by the Lac du Flambeau Band of Lake Superior Chippewa Tribe.[68] The employee had a dispute with the non-Indian health insurance carrier for the center, not with the center itself.[69] The court concluded that application of ERISA to the plan, under the circumstances presented, would not interfere with the Tribe's right of self-governance.[70] The court continued, "ERISA does not broadly and completely define the employment relationship"; it "merely requires reporting and accounting standards for the protection of the employees."[71] It also pointed out that the dispute was "not between the Chippewa Health Center and Smart."[72]

---

[66]*See Lumber Indus. Pension Fund v. Warm Springs Forest Prods. Indus.*, 939 F.2d 683 (9th Cir. 1991) (applying ERISA to tribally owned lumber mill); *Smart v. State Farm Ins. Co.*, 868 F.2d 929 (7th Cir. 1989) (applying ERISA to tribal health center); *Prescott v. Little Six Inc.*, 387 F.3d 753 (8th Cir. 2004) (declining to apply ERISA to tribal casino); *Colville Confederated Tribes v. Somday*, 96 F. Supp. 2d 1120 (E.D. Wash. 2000) (declining to apply ERISA to tribal government employees).

[67]868 F.2d 929 (7th Cir. 1989).

[68]*Id.* at 930.

[69]*Id.* at 930-31.

[70]*Id.* at 935-36.

[71]*Id.*

[72]*Id.* at 936. In *Reich v. Great Lakes Indian Fish & Wildlife Comm'n*, 4 F.3d 490 (7th Cir. 1993), discussed above in reference to the FLSA, the Seventh Circuit limited language from its opinion in *Smart*, stating that the assertion in *Smart* that "'federalism

Second, in *Lumber Industry Pension Fund v. Warm Springs Forest Products Industries*,[73] the Ninth Circuit considered whether ERISA applied to a pension fund for employees of Warm Springs Forest Products Industries, a tribally owned and operated sawmill located on the Warm Springs Indian Reservation.[74] Pursuant to a tribal ordinance, the mill shifted fund payments for tribal member employees to a tribal pension plan.[75] The fund sued under ERISA to get the contributions back.[76] The Ninth Circuit applied its *Coeur d'Alene Tribal Farm* standards to hold, with little analysis, that ERISA applied to the mill.[77] The court said the mill was "not protected from such [ERISA] liability under the self-government exception [to the general application of federal laws to tribes]."[78]

A district court within the Ninth Circuit has taken a different approach. In *Colville Confederated Tribes v. Somday*,[79] the Colville Confederated Tribes sued their former executive director in federal court for a declaratory judgment that its retirement plan was not subject to ERISA and won. Rather than apply the Ninth Circuit's *Coeur d'Alene Tribal Farm* test for determining whether a federal law of general application applies to tribal employers, the court simply concluded that

---

uniquely concerns States; there simply is no Tribe counterpart,' *goes too far*." 4 F.3d at 495 (emphasis added; citation to *Smart* omitted). The court continued:
> Indian tribes, like states, are quasi-sovereigns entitled to comity[, and] [c]omity argues for allowing the Indians to manage their own police as they like . . . until and unless Congress gives a stronger indication than it has here that it wants to intrude on the sovereign functions of tribal government.

Id.

[73] 939 F.2d 683 (9th Cir. 1991).

[74] *Id.* at 684.

[75] *Id.* at 684-85.

[76] *Id.* at 684.

[77] *Id.* at 685-86.

[78] *Id.* at 685.

[79] 96 F. Supp. 2d 1120 (E.D. Wash. 2000).

the plan fell within ERISA's exemption for "governmental plans" at that time.[80]

Finally, in *Prescott v. Little Six, Inc.*,[81] the Eighth Circuit held that, because the Shakopee Mdewakanton Court of Appeals had found that the retirement plans at issue — affecting executive-level employees at Little Six, Inc., the gaming facility of the Shakopee Mdewakanton Sioux (Dakota) Community — were not authorized under tribal law, there was no benefit plan on which to rest an ERISA action.[82] "Because as a matter of tribal law no benefit plan exists," the court held, "there is nothing here to which ERISA could apply."[83] In an earlier decision in the same case, the federal district court refused to entertain the ERISA case in federal court until the plaintiffs exhausted tribal court remedies even though the initial question of whether an ERISA plan existed presented a question of federal law.[84]

2. Application to Tribal Enterprises After 2006 Amendment

As noted above, the 2006 amendment to the "governmental plan" exception exempts from ERISA coverage employee benefit plans administered by Indian tribal governments or their subdivisions, agencies, or instrumentalities, but only if the services of the affected employees are "in the performance of essential governmental functions

---

[80]*Id.* at 1131. ERISA, at the time, defined an exempt "governmental plan" as "a plan established or maintained for its employees by the Government of the United States, by the government of any State or political subdivision thereof, or by any agency or instrumentality of any of the foregoing." 29 U.S.C. § 1002(32). The Pension Benefit Guaranty Corporation, the federal agency charged with administering ERISA, concluded that the Tribes' plan fell within that definition, and the federal district court agreed. *See Colville Confederated Tribes v. Somday*, 96 F. Supp. 2d at 1130.

[81]387 F.3d 753 (8th Cir. 2004).

[82]*Id.* at 758.

[83]*Id.*

[84]*See Prescott v. Little Six Inc.*, 897 F. Supp. 1217 (D. Minn. 1995).

but not in the performance of commercial activities (whether or not an essential government function)."[85]

To date, only the Tenth Circuit has dealt with the operation of this amendment. In *Dobbs v. Anthem Blue Cross & Blue Shield*,[86] the court addressed whether the amendment would apply retroactively to claims brought by an employee of the Southern Ute Indian Tribe concerning his loss of health insurance. The amendment was not enacted until after Dobbs filed his claims, but the court concluded that the 2006 amendment applied to Dobbs's claims.[87] While that conclusion, by itself, is not of particular importance, the court's reasoning is significant because it reconfirms the Tenth Circuit's approach to the application of general federal labor or employment laws to tribes and their enterprises, previously discussed in Chapter 3. This reasoning stands in distinct contrast to the Ninth Circuit's approach under *Coeur d'Alene Tribal Farm*. Thus, it warrants attention.

Whether or not the 2006 amendment applied retroactively to Dobbs's claims turned on whether the amendment simply clarified the existing law or represented a substantive change in the law.[88] Before the 2006 amendment, ERISA was silent with regard to its application to Indian tribes. The pre-amendment language excluded only the employee benefit plans of the "Government of the United States , . . . the government of any State or political subdivision thereof, or . . . [an] agency or instrumentality of any of the foregoing."[89] Thus, the issue presented for the Tenth Circuit in deciding whether the 2006 amendment would apply retroactively was whether, notwithstanding congressional silence on the issue, the employee benefit plans of tribal governments were exempt from ERISA before the amendments.[90] If they were, the 2006 amendment simply clarified the law and, by not creat-

---

[85] 29 U.S.C. § 1002(32) (2018) (emphasis added).

[86] 600 F.3d 1275 (10th Cir. 2010).

[87] *Id*. 1296-97.

[88] *Id*. at 1281-84.

[89] 29 U.S.C. § 1002(32) (2018).

[90] *See Dobbs*, 600 F.3d 1281-84.

ing or eliminating substantive rights, could be applied retroactively to Dobbs's claims.[91]

The Tenth Circuit restated its approach to deciding when federal laws of general application may be applied to Indian tribes:

> In this circuit, respect for Indian sovereignty means that federal regulatory schemes do not apply to tribal governments exercising their sovereign authority absent express congressional authorization. Although our early cases relied in part on treaties that expressly protected Indian tribes' sovereignty, we later recognized that a treaty was not a necessary prerequisite to exemption . . . .
>
> Applying certain federal regulatory schemes to Indian tribes would impinge upon their sovereignty by preventing tribal governments from freely exercising their powers, including the "sovereign authority to regulate economic activity within their own territory." For this reason, ERISA would not apply to insurance plans purchased by tribes for employees primarily engaged in governmental functions unless Congress expressly or necessarily preempted Indian tribal sovereignty. Applying ERISA to such plans would prevent tribal governments from purchasing insurance plans for governmental employees in the same manner as other government entities, thus treating tribal governments as a kind of inferior sovereign. We do not assume Congress intended to infringe on Indian tribal sovereignty in this manner absent an express statement or strong evidence of congressional intent.[92]

---

[91] *See id.*

[92] *Id.* at 1283-84 (citations and footnotes omitted).

The court, therefore, reconfirmed what it had implicitly decided when the case was previously before it: that the 2006 amendment to ERISA applied retroactively because it merely clarified the established law (in the Tenth Circuit) that, given Congress's silence on the subject, ERISA could not be applied to the employee benefit plans of Indian tribal governments.[93]

Beyond this, the Tenth Circuit clarified the substance of the 2006 amendment. The federal district court had concluded that the plan at issue for Dobbs fell within the exemption for tribal governmental plans because Dobbs's job involved assisting in the management of the Tribe's treasury, which would be considered an "essential government function," and not a "commercial" activity.[94] The Tenth Circuit pointed out, however, that the district court had misunderstood the test for ascertaining the ERISA exemption pursuant to the amendment:

> As amended, § 1002(32) defines "governmental plan" to include "a plan which is established and maintained by an Indian tribal government," but only when "all of the participants" in the plan are employees "substantially all of whose services as such an employee are in the performance of essential governmental functions but not in the performance of commercial activities (whether or not an essential government function)." Thus a plan qualifies as a governmental plan only if it is established and maintained by an Indian tribal government and all of the participants are employees primarily engaged in essential governmental functions rather than commercial activities.[95]

This would require the district court, on remand from the Tenth Circuit, to undertake a fact-specific inquiry regarding the job duties of

---

[93]*Id.* at 1283-85.

[94]*Id.* at 1286.

[95]*Id.* at 1285.

all the employees covered by the same plan as Dobbs.[96] Only in this way can a decision be reached on "whether all plan participants are employees 'substantially all of whose services . . . are in the performance of essential governmental functions but not in the performance of commercial activities (whether or not an essential government function)."'[97]

Other federal courts have begun to address the operation of the 2006 amendment. The following are examples:

- *Bolssen v. Unum Life Insurance Co. of America:*[98] Disability plan covering plaintiff, employed as custodian of Oneida Tribe's casino and other casino employees, was not exempt from ERISA as a governmental plan under the amendment.

- *Stopp v. Mutual of Omaha Life Insurance Co.:*[99] Plaintiff served as administrative assistant to the Tribal Council of the Agua Caliente Band of Cahuilla Indians, working on governmental affairs. He participated in a benefits plan covering the Tribe's casino employees. Out of the 1,998 employees covered by the plan, 1,900 were employed in the casino facility. The federal district court held that ERISA covered the plan under the 2006 amendment, and even if the amendment did not apply retroactively to cover the plan, it would still be subject to ERISA under the pre-amendment law.[100]

---

[96]*Id.* at 1285-86.

[97]*Id.* (quoting 29 U.S.C. § 1002(32)) (emphasis omitted).

[98]629 F.Supp.2d 878, 881-83 (E.D. Wis. 2009).

[99]No. CIV-09-221-FHS, 2010 WL 1994899 (E.D. Okla. May 18, 2010).

[100]*Id.* at *2-3.

- *Coppe v. Sac & Fox Casino Healthcare Plan*:[101] The court held that a nonmember employee of a tribal health consortium, who was covered by a benefits plan that is not excluded from ERISA as a "governmental plan," need not exhaust tribal remedies in tribal court before commencing an ERISA action in federal court. The court said that "Congress has preempted the tribe's adjudicatory authority over ERISA claims and, therefore, exhaustion of tribal remedies is not required."[102]

F. Other Laws

There is limited case law on the application of other federal employment laws addressing employment terms and conditions that fail to mention Indian tribes.

The federal district court for the district of Wyoming addressed application of the 2010 Affordable Care Act (ACA), requiring certain employers to provide health insurance coverage to their employees or pay a fine,[103] in the 2015 case of *N. Arapaho Tribe v. Burwell*,[104] The court held that the Northern Arapaho Tribe was subject to the requirements of the ACA even though the Act fails to include tribes. The court applied the *Coeur d'Alene Tribal Farm* framework and rejected the Tribe's argument that under Tenth Circuit precedent it should be free from the ACA requirements because their imposition would infringe upon the Tribe's inherent sovereignty.[105]

---

[101] 2015 WL 1137733 (D. Kan. Mar. 13, 2015).

[102] *Id.* at *1, *4-*5.

[103] *See* 42 U.S.C. § 18081(f)(2)(A) (2018).

[104] 118 F. Supp. 3d 1264 (D. Wyo. 2015).

[105] *See id.* at 1285-86 (D. Wyo. 2015). For a general discussion of the ACA's application to tribal employers *see* Rachel Sibila, *"Play or Pay": Interpreting the Employer Mandate of the Patient Protection and Affordable Care Act As It Relates to Tribal Employers,* 39 Am. Indian L. Rev. 235 (2015) (concluding that Congress's failure to expressly include Indian tribes should render them free from the ACA's employer mandates).

The federal district court for the southern district of California addressed the Uniformed Services Employment and Reemployment Rights Act (USERRA), prohibiting discrimination against past and current members (and applicants) of the uniformed services,[106] in the 2021 case of *Manzano v. S. Indian Health Council, Inc.*[107] The court held that USERRA's broad definition of "employer," which includes states and the federal government,[108] did not abrogate tribal sovereign immunity.[109]

G. Conclusion

Congress failed to address Indian tribes and their enterprises in a host of federal laws addressing the terms and conditions of employment. This leaves it up to the courts to determine whether, in the face of such Congressional oversight, a given law should apply to tribes or their enterprises. The law surrounding this problem is complex, inconsistent across the federal courts, and unpredictable. Outcomes may differ, depending upon which circuit court of appeals will ultimately rule on the issue. Indeed, a case arising in New Mexico or Oklahoma, which would be governed by the law of the Tenth Circuit, could turn out differently than a case arising in the Ninth Circuit.

A consistent emerging consideration for all courts, however, is whether the imposition of the federal law in question may infringe upon the exercise of tribal sovereignty. If the imposition of federal law

---

[106] *See* 38 U.S.C.A. § 4303(4)(A) (2018).

[107] 2021 WL 2826072 (S.D. Cal. July 7, 2021).

[108] USERRA defines "employer," in relevant part, as:
> any person, institution, organization, or other entity that pays salary or wages for work performed or that has control over employment opportunities, including-
> (i) a person, institution, organization, or other entity to whom the employer has delegated the performance of employment-related responsibilities;
> (ii) the Federal Government;
> (iii) a State;

38 U.S.C.A. § 4303.

[109] *Manzano*, 2021 WL 2826072, at *11.

upon a reservation employment relationship would undermine tribal regulatory authority exercised in accordance with established principles of tribal sovereignty as expressed in a tribal employment law, courts may be more hesitant to allow the federal law to apply.

7

THE NATIONAL LABOR RELATIONS ACT AND TRIBAL EMPLOYMENT

A. Introduction

Congress enacted the National Labor Relations Act (NLRA)[1] in 1935 to quell industrial strife and improve relations between private sector workers and their employers through collective bargaining.[2] The NLRA establishes the right of private sector employees to organize and join unions, and to engage in collective bargaining with employers. Congress empowered the National Labor Relations Board (NLRB) to administer and enforce the NLRA.[3] The NLRB oversees elections establishing unions.[4] It also adjudicates claims of "unfair labor practices," which may be brought by unions or employers for alleged violations of the duties under the NLRA.[5] Once a union is elected to represent a bargaining unit within an employer, the NLRA requires employers and unions to "bargain in good faith" in order to enter into a collective bargaining agreement.[6] Failure to bargain in good

---

[1] 29 U.S.C. §§ 151-169 (2018). Congress enacted the Labor Management Relations Act of 1947, 29 U.S.C. §§ 141-197(2018), to amend the NLRA and to provide supplemental remedies and procedures to further the purposes of the NLRA.

[2] *See* 29 U.S.C. § 151.

[3] *Id.* § 153.

[4] *Id.* § 159.

[5] *Id.* § 160.

[6] *Id.* § 158(a)(5).

faith, and other unfair labor practices, can trigger sanctions and enforcement orders issued by the NLRB.[7]

Congress expressly excluded federal government agencies, federal government corporations, states, and political subdivisions of states from the NLRA by excluding them from the definition of "employer."[8] But it failed to mention Indian tribes or their enterprises. Labor organizing within governmental employers (the public sector) is not addressed in the NLRA. It has been addressed by some states, however, in ways that differ substantially from the NLRA. For example, contrary to the NLRA,[9] which guarantees the right of private sector employees to strike, some states prohibit strikes against state government operations.[10] It is a federal crime for employees to strike against the federal government.[11]

For seventy-two years after the enactment of the NLRA, the NLRB did not view Indian tribes or their on-reservation enterprises as subject to the Act; tribes are governments, and the NLRA is a private sector law. Things changed, however, in 2007 with the D.C. Circuit's decision in *San Manuel Indian Bingo & Casino v. NLRB*.[12] That decision upheld the NLRB's assertion of jurisdiction over union organizing activity at the gaming operations of the San Manuel Band of Mission Indians. It arose out of an appeal by the Band of the NLRB's deci-

---

[7]*Id.* § 160.

[8]The NLRA defines "employer," in pertinent part, as follows:
    (1) The term "person" includes one or more individuals, labor organizations, partnerships, associations, corporations, legal representatives, trustees, trustees in cases under Title 11, or receivers.
    (2) The term "employer" includes any person acting as an agent of an employer, directly or indirectly, but shall not include the United States or any wholly owned Government corporation, or any Federal Reserve Bank, or any State or political subdivision thereof, . . .
Id. § 152(2).

[9]*See* 29 U.S.C. § 163 (2018).

[10]*See, e.g.,* IOWA CODE ANN. § 20.12 (2017).

[11]*See* 5 U.S.C. § 7311(3) (2018).

[12]475 F.3d 1306 (D.C. Cir. 2007).

sion to reverse its decades-old view that Congress did not intend the NLRA to apply to Indian tribes within their reservations. In so doing, the NLRB joined the Department of Labor and the Equal Employment Opportunity Commission (EEOC) in seeking to impose the laws it administers upon Indian tribes and their enterprises within Indian country, without any express guidance by Congress.

Notwithstanding Congress's exclusion of state and federal governments from the NLRA,[13] the D.C. Circuit allowed the NLRB to impose its authority upon the operations of a tribal government, at least when they involve the generation of government revenues pursuant to the Indian Gaming Regulatory Act (IGRA).[14] For advocates of tribal self-determination, the *Coeur d'Alene Tribal Farm*[15] and *Mashantucket Sand & Gravel*[16] decisions, discussed in Chapters 3 and 6, had signaled a potential threatening trend, but the *San Manuel* decision opened the door to far more serious intrusions into tribal sovereignty. It empowered non-Indian enterprises — labor unions — to operate within the jurisdictions of Indian tribes under the protection of a federal agency, the NLRB, in ways that impact the distribution of governmental resources generated by tribes.

The *San Manuel* decision and others in its wake present significant challenges to tribes in deciding how to address labor relations and collective bargaining within their jurisdictions. But, as in the case of the unsettled law surrounding the application of other federal employment laws that fail to address Indian tribes, there are significant counter precedents. Thus, the Supreme Court is likely to have the final word.[17] Two other federal circuit courts of appeals, the Sixth and the Ninth Circuits, have allowed the application of the NLRA to tribal

---

[13] 29 U.S.C. § 152(2) (2018).

[14] *San Manuel Indian Bingo & Casino*, 475 F.3d at 1311-16.

[15] *Donovan v. Coeur d'Alene Tribal Farm*, 751 F.2d 1113 (9th Cir. 1985).

[16] *Reich v. Mashantucket Sand & Gravel*, 95 F.3d 174, 176 (2d Cir. 1996).

[17] *See generally, Tribal Power, Worker Power: Organizing Unions in the Context of Native Sovereignty*, 134 HARV. L. REV. 1162, 1168 (2021) (describing the "fractured circuit split").

gaming facilities.[18] The Sixth Circuit was splintered.[19] The NLRB separately declined to apply the NLRA to the gaming operations of the Chickasaw Nation, invoking the "treaty-rights exception" to the presumption that "silent" federal laws apply to Indian tribes under the *Coeur d'Alene Tribal Farm* formulation discussed in Chapter 3.[20]

A 2002 decision of the Tenth Circuit in *NLRB v. Pueblo of San Juan*,[21] paved another approach that is contrary to the decisions of the D.C., Sixth, and Ninth Circuits. That decision suggests that if application of the NLRA would intrude upon the sovereign prerogatives of an Indian tribe, a clear directive from Congress must be found before a federal agency can apply the law and abrogate those prerogatives.[22] In

---

[18] *See Pauma v. Nat'l Lab. Rels. Bd.*, 888 F.3d 1066 (9th Cir. 2018); *Nat'l Lab. Rels. Bd. v. Little River Band of Ottawa Indians Tribal Gov't*, 788 F.3d 537 (6th Cir. 2015); *Soaring Eagle Casino & Resort v. N.L.R.B.*, 791 F.3d 648 (6th Cir. 2015).

[19] *Nat'l Lab. Rels. Bd. v. Little River Band of Ottawa Indians Tribal Gov't*, 788 F.3d 537, 556-65 (6th Cir. 2015) (McKeague, J., dissenting "[b]ecause the majority's decision impinges on tribal sovereignty, encroaches on Congress's plenary and exclusive authority over Indian affairs, conflicts with Supreme Court precedent, and unwisely creates a circuit split"); *Soaring Eagle Casino & Resort v. N.L.R.B.*, 791 F.3d 648 (6th Cir. 2015) (disagreeing with the reasoning of *Little River Band* majority decision, but following it as precedent).

[20] *WinStar World Casino*, 362 N.L.R.B. No. 109, 2014-2015 NLRB Dec. ¶ 15,968 (June 4, 2015).

[21] 276 F.3d 1186 (10th Cir. 2002) (en banc).

[22] One commentator aptly describes the tension between the *San Manuel* and *San Juan* decisions as follows:
> If Indian nations are covered by the NLRA, as *San Manuel* holds, they cannot at the same time be exempt from it, as *San Juan* implies.... If Indian nations are analogous to governmental entities ... that possess power to regulate private-sector labor-management relations through right-to-work laws, as *San Juan* holds, it follows that they would be analogous to governmental entities excluded from coverage of the NLRA ..., which possess power to regulate fully their own labor relations. But if Indian nations are "employers" subject to the NLRA ..., as *San Manuel* holds, they cannot at the same time enact right-to-work laws regulating labor relations.

Vicki J. Limas, *The* Tuscar*organization of the Tribal Workforce*, 2008 MICH. ST. L. REV. 467, 481 (2008). The inherent sovereign authority of Indian tribes to enact laws governing reservation labor and employment is addressed in Chapter 2.

that case, the Tenth Circuit upheld a law enacted by the Pueblo that guaranteed the right of employees within its territorial jurisdiction to work for an employer without having to join a union. The Pueblo's so-called right-to-work ordinance was similar to laws enacted in many states across the nation to prohibit private sector employers and unions from entering into agreements that require employees to join unions. While such a tribal law is not expressly allowed under the terms of the NLRA, the Tenth Circuit held that it was enacted pursuant to the Pueblo's inherent authority to govern economic relationships within its jurisdiction.[23] The court then rejected the NLRB's arguments that such tribal authority was preempted by the NLRA.[24]

This chapter first sets forth the history of the NLRB's approach to the application of the NLRA to Indian tribes or their enterprises, both within reservations and off-reservation, an important backdrop to the present setting. It then turns to a more detailed account of the application of the NLRA within Indian country.[25]

B. Early NLRB Concerns

When the NLRB first considered the issue in 1976, the Board concluded that tribal governmental entities operating within Indian reservations should be treated the same as states or federal entities and therefore excluded in the same manner from the NLRA.[26] Tribal governments, in the view of the Board, were exempt from the NLRA to the same extent as "any state or political subdivision thereof."[27]

Thus, in the early cases, when faced with the application of the NLRA to on-reservation enterprises associated with tribal governments, the issue of concern to the NLRB was whether the employing entity could be considered the tribal government or should be treated

---

[23]*Id.* at 1190-93.

[24]*Id.* at 1194-200.

[25]Chapter 9 surveys tribal lawmaking in the area of on-reservation labor relations.

[26]*Fort Apache Timber Co.*, 226 NLRB 503 (1976).

[27]*Id.* at 506 n.5.

as a separate entity. A separate concern was how to treat the off-reservation operations of tribal governments.

1. Determining Whether a Tribal Enterprise is Part of Government

The NLRB first addressed this issue in 1976 in *Fort Apache Timber Co.*,[28] a case involving a logging operation of the White Mountain Apache Tribe. Applying the standard developed by the Supreme Court in *NLRB v. Natural Gas Utility District*[29] governing the economic activities of state governments, the Board held that the timber company would be considered an exempt governmental employer if it was (1) created directly by the Tribe, so as to constitute a department or administrative arm of the government, or (2) "administered by individuals who are responsible to public officials or to the general electorate."[30]

The Fort Apache Timber Company was an on-reservation enterprise of the White Mountain Apache Tribe and wholly owned by the Tribe.[31] Its employees were on the payroll of tribal government, and the tribal council set the wages and conditions of employment. The Board explained that, because "the Fort Apache Timber Company is an entity administered by individuals directly responsible to the Tribal Council . . . [it is] exempt as a governmental entity recognized by the United States, to whose employees the NLRA was never intended to apply."[32]

---

[28]*Fort Apache Timber Co.*, 226 NLRB 503 (1976).

[29]402 U.S. 600 (1971).

[30]*Fort Apache Timber Co.*, 226 NLRB 503, 504 n.5, 506 n.22 (1976).

[31]*Id.* at 503.

[32]*Fort Apache Timber Co.*, 226 NLRB 503, 506 n.22 (1976). In *Roberson v. Confederated Tribes of the Warm Springs Reservation of Oregon*, 103 L.R.R.M. (BNA) 2749; No. 79-546, 1980 U.S. Dist. LEXIS 9991(D. Ore. Feb. 4, 1980), a federal district court followed the Board's reasoning in *Fort Apache Timber Co.* in a case involving the application of the NLRA to Warm Springs Forest Products Industries (WSFPI). It held that, if the Tribe operated WSFPI pursuant to its corporate charter under Section 17 of the Indian Reorganization Act of 1934 (IRA), 25 U.S.C. § 477, it would be treated as a private sector "employer" under the NLRA, but if WSFPI were an arm of the

The NLRB reached a different result in 1979 in *Devils Lake Sioux Manufacturing Corp.*[33] The employer in that case was a North Dakota corporation formed by the Sioux Indian Tribal Council and Brunswick Corporation, a private business corporation.[34] The Tribe owned 51 percent of the stock in the company, and the Brunswick Corporation owned 49 percent of the stock.[35] The nine-member board of directors consisted of four representatives of the tribal council and five Brunswick officials.[36] Brunswick managed the company under a management contract according to policies set by the board of directors.[37] The company leased land on the reservation, where it manufactured camouflage material.[38]

The Tribe and Brunswick argued that the case was controlled by *Fort Apache Timber Co.*, asserting that Devils Lake Sioux Manufacturing, like Fort Apache Timber Company, was an on-reservation tribal enterprise, operating under the direction and control of the tribal council.[39] The NLRB disagreed and found that Devils Lake Sioux Manufacturing Corporation, unlike Fort Apache Timber Company, was "completely managed and operated by the Brunswick Corpora-

---

Tribe, it would not. *Id*. The *Roberson* case is further discussed in Chapter 7, Section G. Chapter 3 discusses IRA Section 17 corporations in the context of sovereign immunity.

[33] 243 NLRB 163 (1979).

[34] *Id*. at 163.

[35] *Id*.

[36] *Id*.

[37] *Id*.

[38] *Id*.

[39] *Id*.

tion."[40] Thus, it held that the corporation was an "employer" subject to the NLRA.[41]

A third case, *Southern Indian Health Council*,[42] involved a nonprofit, on-reservation health clinic operated by a consortium of seven tribes. A board of directors, made up of appointees from the member tribes, controlled the clinic and its personnel matters.[43] The NLRB held that the case was controlled by *Fort Apache Timber Co.,* not *Devils Lake Sioux Manufacturing*.[44] It concluded that the clinic was, in effect, controlled by the seven member tribes through their appointments to the board.[45] Since it was, therefore, controlled by the tribal governments, it was not an "employer" under the Act.[46]

In sum, the NLRB's first approach to applying the NLRA to the on-reservation activities of Indian tribes tracked its approach to the activities of state governments. So long as the employing entity could be considered an arm of the tribal government under the *Natural Gas Utility* factors, the NLRA's exemption for states and the federal government would apply equally to tribes.

---

[40] *Id.*

[41] *Id.* at 163-64. *See also Roberson v. Confederated Tribes of the Warm Springs Reservation of Oregon*, 103 L.R.R.M. (BNA) 2749 (D.Ore. 1980), (IRA Section 17 corporation subject to suit as "employer" for breach of collective bargaining agreement under Section 301 of the Labor Management Relations Act, 29 U.S.C. § 185(a) (2006)). *Cf. Myrick v. Devils Lake Sioux Mfg. Corp.*, 718 F. Supp. 753 (D.N.D. 1989) (allowing claims to go forward against the same corporation as that in *Devils Lake Sioux Manufacturing Corp.*, 243 NLRB 163 (1979), under Title VII and the ADEA).

[42] 290 NLRB 436 (1988).

[43] *Id.* at 436.

[44] *Id.* at 437.

[45] *Id.*

[46] *Id.* The NLRB said that the Act's exemption for state and political subdivisions applied because "the directors of the Employer are directly appointed by, and subject to removal by, the governing bodies of the member tribes." *Id. Cf. Dille v. Council of Energy Res. Tribes*, 801 F.2d 373 (10th Cir. 1986) (council of thirty-nine tribes is "tribe" exempt from definition of employer under Title VII).

2. Determining Whether the Government Exemption Extends to Tribal Entities Off-Reservation

Under the NLRB's decision in *Fort Apache Timber Co.*, it would logically follow that the NLRA's government exemption should apply to Indian tribes wherever they operate; indeed, a state's extraterritorial activities would not affect its exemption from the NLRA.[47] This territorial issue arose in *Sac & Fox Industries Ltd.*,[48] a case involving the off-reservation manufacturing operations of a nonprofit tribal corporation that was wholly owned by the Sac and Fox Indian Tribe of Oklahoma. While the day-to-day operations of the corporation were managed by a non-tribal member, the corporation's labor policies were set by the Tribe.[49] Thus, the organizational structure of the entity was very similar to the health clinic in *Southern Indian Health Council*.[50] The NLRB's regional director held that the corporation was an exempt governmental entity under the Act, but the NLRB, upon review, reversed.[51]

The NLRB distinguished *Fort Apache* and *Southern Indian Health* on the ground that those cases involved the on-reservation activities of tribal governments.[52] It analyzed the case under the Ninth Circuit's *Coeur d'Alene Tribal Farm* standards, qualifying the *Tuscarora* dictum, as previously described in Chapters 3 and 6.[53] Applying those factors, the Board found that: (1) application of the NLRA to the Tribe's off-reservation enterprise would not touch matters of tribal self-

---

[47] *See San Manuel Indian Bingo & Casino v. NLRB*, 475 F.3d 1306, 1309 (D.C. Cir. 2007) (pointing out that logic of *Fort Apache Timber* not limited to on-reservation tribal government enterprises).

[48] 307 NLRB 241 (1992).

[49] *Id.* at 242.

[50] 290 NLRB 436 (1988).

[51] *Id.* at 243-44.

[52] *Id.* at 242-44.

[53] *Id.* at 243-44.

government because the enterprise was involved in "a normal manufacturing operation," a majority of its employees were non-tribal members, and the NLRA would not completely define relations between the employees and the tribe; (2) the NLRA's effects would not extend to "purely intramural matters," such as tribal membership, inheritance, or domestic relations;[54] (3) application of the Act to the enterprise would not interfere with a treaty right of the Tribe; and (4) there was no indication of congressional intent not to apply the NLRA to tribes' off-reservation activities.[55]

A dissenting Board member argued that the majority's decision was inconsistent with *Fort Apache Timber Co.*[56] Certainly, the Board's adoption of the *Coeur d'Alene Tribal Farm* approach, leaving the Tribe with the burden of establishing one of three factors to escape NLRB jurisdiction, showed that the Board was prepared to depart from the more straightforward *Natural Gas Utility* test applied in *Fort Apache Timber Co.*[57]

The NLRB's retreat from the *Fort Apache Timber* approach was further confirmed in *Yukon Kuskokwim Health Corp.*,[58] where it held that an off-reservation health clinic, formed and controlled by a group of Alaska Native tribes to provide health services to tribal members, was subject to the NLRA. The Board refused to entertain an argument that because the clinic provided a governmental service — the provision of health care services to tribal members under a federal government contract — it should be treated differently than *Sac & Fox Industries Ltd.*[59] The NLRB held that it would not extend the NLRA's government exemption to Indian tribes when the employment activity

---

[54] *Id.* at 244.

[55] *Id.* at 244-45.

[56] *Id.* at 245-47.

[57] 226 NLRB 503, 504 n.5, 506 n.22 (1976).

[58] 328 NLRB 761 (1999).

[59] *Id.* at 763-64.

is off-reservation.⁶⁰ This decision was affirmed by the D.C. Circuit.⁶¹ In 2003, the Ninth Circuit held that under the *Coeur d'Alene Tribal Farm* standards, the NLRB did not plainly lack jurisdiction over a similar off-reservation tribal health care facility operated by a nonprofit corporation.⁶²

In sum, by the time the *San Manuel* case came before the Board, the model adopted by the NLRB (and affirmed by the federal circuit courts of appeals) for determining whether the NLRA applied to the labor relations of employing tribal entities turned, in the first instance, on whether the employment activity was on- or off-reservation. The NLRA would apply to any off-reservation activity, regardless of the nature of the employing entity. Whether the NLRA would apply to labor relations within an on-reservation tribal entity, on the other hand, would turn on whether the employer would be considered the tribal government under the *Natural Gas Utility* factors.⁶³

C. The NLRB's Change of Course: Indian Gaming

In its 2004 decision in *San Manuel Bingo & Casino*,⁶⁴ the NLRB abandoned its earlier precedents and held that Indian tribes are gener-

---

⁶⁰*Id.* at 764.

⁶¹*See Yukon-Kuskokwim Health Corp. v. NLRB*, 234 F.3d 714 (D.C. Cir. 2000). The D.C. Circuit remanded the case to the Board to address the clinic's argument that it should benefit from the NLRA's exemption for the federal government because it took over the federal government's operation of the health care services at issue, pursuant to a contract under the Indian Self-Determination Act. *See id.* at 718.

⁶²*NLRB v. Chapa De Indian Health Program, Inc.*, 316 F.3d 995 (9th Cir. 2003).

⁶³The view that an Indian tribe loses its sovereign character (thereby triggering NLRA application) by operating outside of its own jurisdiction is arguably at odds with two Supreme Court decisions discussed in Chapter 2, *Michigan v. Bay Mills Indian Cmty.*, 572 U.S. 782 (2014) and *Kiowa Tribe of Okla. v. Mfg. Tech's., Inc.*, 523 U.S. 751 (1998), both holding that tribal sovereign immunity is intact whether a tribe or its instrumentality operates on or off-reservation. Further, the NLRA's exclusion of states cannot turn on where a given state (or state instrumentality) has employees; if the logic for exempting tribes from the NLRA is that they are governments, it should make no difference where they are located.

⁶⁴341 NLRB 1055 (2004).

ally subject to the NLRA. The case involved an unfair labor practice charge brought by the Hotel Employees & Restaurant Employees International Union (HERE) against the on-reservation gaming operations of the San Manuel Band of Serrano Mission Indians.[65] Under the Band's compact with the State of California, entered into pursuant to IGRA, the Band agreed to allow union organizing at its gaming facility.[66] HERE claimed that the Band gave preferential treatment to the Communications Workers of America in its organizational efforts and thereby violated the NLRA.[67] The Band responded that its operation of on-reservation gaming for the congressionally mandated purpose of generating revenue for the tribal government was exempt from the NLRA under the rationale of *Fort Apache Timber Co.* and *Southern Indian Health Council*.[68]

The NLRB reviewed its prior decisions and found the reasoning of its precedents erroneous.[69] It reversed its view that Indian tribes were implicitly included in the NLRA exemption for governments.[70] Resorting to a "plain language" interpretation of that exemption, the Board said that its scope was limited to "the United States or any wholly owned Government corporation . . . or any State or political subdivision thereof," and that Indian tribes do not fit those descriptions.[71] It added that the fact that a tribe engages in an employment activity within the reservation makes no difference:

> In *Fort Apache*, the Board provided no authority for the proposition it ultimately adopted—that the text

---

[65] *Id.*

[66] Chapter 9 describes the model ordinance that the San Manuel Band and other tribes agreed to enact under the California gaming compacts.

[67] *San Manuel Indian Bingo & Casino*, 341 NLRB 1055, 1055 (2004).

[68] *See id.*

[69] *Id.* at 1056-59.

[70] *Id.*

[71] *Id.* at 1058 (quoting 29 U.S.C. § 152(2)).

of Section 2(2) [29 U.S.C. § 152(2)], and the Board's interpretation of that text, can support an exemption based on the location of the employer at issue. . . . [T]he Act does not explicitly exempt Indian tribes—wherever they operate. Nor does the precedent support the finding of implicit exemptions or exemptions by analogy based on an employer's location, or any other factor. Accordingly, we overrule prior precedent to the extent it holds otherwise.[72]

Next, the Board rejected its earlier view, expressed in *Fort Apache Timber Co.*, that tribal government operations within Indian reservations are generally free from federal authority in the absence of a specific congressional enactment.[73] Instead, the Board decided that it should follow language from the Supreme Court's decision in *Tuscarora* suggesting that "a general statute in terms applying to all persons includes Indians and their property interests."[74]

It limited that formulation, however, by adopting the *Coeur d'Alene Tribal Farm* qualifications as it had done in *Sac & Fox Industries Ltd*.[75] Resting principally on the Ninth Circuit and Second Circuit precedents that applied the *Coeur d'Alene Tribal Farm* analysis, the Board claimed there was "broad consensus" across the courts of appeals with respect to its approach.[76] Having adopted the *Coeur d'Alene Trib-*

---

[72] *Id.* at 1059.

[73] *Id.*

[74] *Id.* (quoting *Federal Power Comm'n v. Tuscarora Indian Nation*, 362 U.S. 99, 116 (1960)).

[75] *Id.* at 1059-60.

[76] *Id.* at 1060. Such a claim is incorrect. As the D.C. Circuit stated in its review of the NLRB's decision, "out-of-circuit precedent is inconsistent as to the application of general federal laws to Indian tribes." *San Manuel Indian Bingo & Casino v. NLRB*, 475 F.3d 1306, 1311 (D.C. Cir. 2007). The disparate approaches across the circuits are set out in Chapter 3. *See generally, Tribal Power, Worker Power: Organizing Unions in the Context of Native Sovereignty,* 134 HARV. L. REV. 1162, 1168 (2021) (describing the "fractured circuit split").

al Farm standard, the NLRB easily concluded that the Band's gaming facility would not escape NLRB jurisdiction.[77]

D. The D.C. Circuit's Decision in *San Manuel*

The San Manuel Band appealed the NLRB's decision to the D.C. Circuit, which affirmed the Board's jurisdiction, but under a slightly different approach than *Coeur d'Alene Tribal Farm*.[78] The court's first concern was to determine whether the application of the NLRA to the Band's gaming facility would interfere with tribal self-government. The court conceded that the Band's gaming was "governmental" because its purpose was to generate revenue to support tribal government services. But it held to the view that such gaming was nevertheless "commercial" in nature and therefore not sufficiently at the core of tribal sovereignty to warrant protection from its abrogation caused by the application of the NLRA.[79]

The D.C. Circuit said:

> [T]he NLRA does not impinge on the Tribe's sovereignty *enough* to indicate a need to construe the statute narrowly against the application to employment at the Casino. First, operation of a casino is not a traditional attribute of self-government. Rather, the casino at issue here is virtually identical to scores of purely commercial casinos across the country. Second, the vast majority of the Casino's employees and customers are not

---

[77]*San Manuel Indian Bingo & Casino*, 341 NLRB 1055, 1062 (2004) ("application of the *Tuscarora-Coeur d'Alene* standard poses no impediment to the assertion of the Board's jurisdiction"). The NLRB's decision in *San Manuel* has been criticized by commentators. *See generally*, Wenona T. Singel, *Labor Relations and Tribal Self-Governance*, 80 N.D. L. REV. 691 (2004); Anna Wermuth, *Union's Gamble Pays Off: In San Manuel Indian Bingo & Casino, the NLRB Breaks the Nation's Promise and Reverses Decades-Old Precedent to Assert Jurisdiction Over Tribal Enterprises on Indian Reservations*, 21 LAB. LAW. 81 (2005).

[78]475 F.3d 1306 (D.C. Cir. 2007).

[79]*Id*. at 1314-15.

members of the Tribe, and they live off the reservation. For these reasons, the Tribe is not simply engaged in internal governance of its territory and members, and its sovereignty over such matters is not called into question. Because applying the NLRA to San Manuel's Casino would not impair tribal sovereignty, federal Indian law does not prevent the Board from exercising jurisdiction.[80]

To arrive at this conclusion, the court construed the Supreme Court's precedents on tribal sovereignty as establishing a continuum, with "traditional customs and practices" within the reservation community at the core, and off-reservation or "commercial activities that tend to blur any distinction between tribal government and a private corporation" at the periphery.[81] The court suggested that "traditional customs and practices" were deserving of most protection, but that if a tribe operated in a "commercial capacity," tribal sovereign concerns were at their weakest. [82] In this way — by minimizing the impact of imposing the NLRA upon the Band's attributes of sovereignty — the court reasoned that it was not necessary to invoke a presumption that Congress's silence about the application of the NLRA to tribes constituted an ambiguity.[83] By reasoning that there was no material intrusion upon tribal self-government, the court found no reason to look for

---

[80]*Id.* at 1315 (emphasis added).

[81]*See id.* at 1314.

[82]*See id.* at 1312-13. The D.C. Circuit's characterization of Indian gaming under the Indian Gaming Regulatory Act (IGRA) as "commercial," not "governmental," is at odds with the pronounced purpose of, and requirements of, that statute, *see* 25 U.S.C. § 2702(1) (stating purpose to promote "strong tribal governments"); § 2710(b)(2)(B) (net revenues from gaming must support tribal government). *See also Michigan v. Bay Mills Indian Cmty.,* 572 U.S. 782, 807-10 (2014) (Sotomayor, J., concurring) (Tribes engage in enterprises because they are often the only means for generating governmental revenue).

[83]*Id.* at 1311-15.

an unambiguous pronouncement by Congress to apply the NLRA to tribes.[84]

The court did make note of the fact that, pursuant to its IGRA compact with California, the Band enacted its own labor ordinance to govern labor relations. However, the court held that any conflict between the NLRA rules and the Band's ordinance was "probably modest" and "secondary to a commercial undertaking."[85] Thus, the court had no occasion to address what the outcome would be if a particular tribal law governing on-reservation labor or employment relations conflicted with the application of the NLRA in a more than "modest" manner.[86]

E. Tribal Authority Over On-Reservation Labor Relations: The Tenth Circuit's Decision in *Pueblo of San Juan* and the Sixth Circuit's Decision in *Little River Band of Ottawa Indians*

If, in accordance with the D.C. Circuit's *San Manuel* decision, the requirement of a clear statement by Congress operates only when application of the NLRA intrudes "enough" upon the prerogatives of a tribal government, that standard might well be met if such an application would thwart a tribe's labor law enacted pursuant to its inherent

---

[84]*Id.* at 1317. Like the NLRB's decision in *San Manuel*, the D.C. Circuit's decision has been criticized by scholars of Indian law. *See, e.g.*, Bryan H. Wildenthal, *Federal Labor Law, Indian Sovereignty, and the Canons of Construction*, 86 OR. L. REV. 413 (2007).

[85]*San Manuel Indian Bingo & Casino v. NLRB*, 474 F.3d at 1315.

[86]In *NLRB v. Fortune Bay Resort Casino*, 688 F. Supp.2d 858 (D. Minn. 2010), the District of Minnesota enforced a subpoena issued by the NLRB against the Fortune Bay Resort Casino, the IGRA gaming facility of the Bois Forte Band of Chippewa Indians. The district court held that the NLRB had lawful authority to issue the subpoena to explore its jurisdiction to proceed with an unfair labor practice charge brought by a tribal member against the casino. *Id.* at 979-82. As in *San Manuel Indian Bingo & Casino v. NLRB*, there was no significant clash between a tribal law governing labor relations and the application of the NLRA in that case.

sovereign authority.[87] As discussed at the outset of this chapter, in contrast to the D.C. Circuit's decision in *San Manuel*, the Tenth Circuit's decision in *NLRB v. Pueblo of San Juan*[88] established that the NLRA cannot preempt a tribal law enacted pursuant to inherent tribal sovereignty, in that case, the Pueblo's right-to-work law. The case warrants a full description.

In 1996, Ohkay Owingeh, then referred to as "Pueblo of San Juan," enacted a "right-to-work" law that prohibited so-called union security agreements for any employees, tribal or non-tribal, employed in businesses on tribal lands.[89] The Tribe leased land to a lumber company, and the lease prohibited the company from entering "into any contract or other arrangement which would require a tribal member to be a member of a union."[90] The NLRB sued the Tribe in federal court to enjoin enforcement of the ordinance and lease provisions, claiming that they were preempted by the NLRA.[91]

The Tenth Circuit, sitting en banc, ruled in favor of Ohkay Owingeh, holding that "it retains the sovereign power to enact its right-to-work ordinance, and to enter into the lease agreement with

---

[87] Of course, such a "sliding scale" approach is at odds with the NLRB's *Fort Apache Timber* decision, which held that Indian tribes should simply be treated as exempt governments, just like states and their political subdivision, and instruments of the federal government.

[88] 276 F.3d 1186 (10th Cir. 2002) (en banc).

[89] *Id.* at 1189. Under the NLRA, an employer and a union may agree, as part of a collective bargaining agreement, to require employees, as a condition of their continued employment, to become members of the union that represents them. *See* 29 U.S.C. § 158(a)(3). These are known as "union security agreements." The NLRA allows states and territories to enact laws that prohibit such agreements, 29 U.S.C. § 164(b), and such laws are generally referred to as "right-to-work" laws because they ensure that the right to work is not affected by union membership. Some of the policy debates surrounding the enactment of right-to-work laws are explored in Chapter 9.

[90] *Pueblo of San Juan*, 276 F.3d at 1189.

[91] *Id.* at 1187.

right-to-work provisions, because Congress has not made a clear retrenchment of such tribal power."[92]

The court's analysis proceeded in three parts. First, it held that the Tribe had inherent authority to regulate labor relations (for both tribal members and non-tribal members) within a business operating on tribal lands within the reservation.[93] Second, applying longstanding canons of construction protecting tribal self-government, the court held that "[i]n the absence of clear evidence of congressional intent . . . , federal law will not be read as stripping tribes of their retained sovereign authority to pass right-to-work laws and be governed by them."[94] Third, the court said that the proper inference to draw from Congress's silence about whether the NLRA could preempt the Tribe's right-to-work law was that it could "not work a divestiture of [that] tribal power."[95]

The court then went on to reject the NLRB's argument that the Tribe's law should be deemed preempted pursuant to the language in *Tuscarora*: "that a general statute in terms applying to all persons includes Indians and their property interests."[96] The Tenth Circuit distinguished *Tuscarora* on the ground that it dealt solely with a tribe's claim to property, not with a tribe's sovereign authority to govern.[97] "We are convinced [that the *Tuscarora* language] does not apply," the court said, "where an Indian tribe has exercised its authority as a sovereign—here, by enacting a labor regulation."[98]

Rather than leave the Tribe with the burden of showing an exception to the *Tuscarora* presumption of federal law applicability under

---

[92]*Id.* at 1191.

[93]*Id.* at 1193.

[94]*Id.* at 1195.

[95]*Id.* at 1196.

[96]*Id.* at 1198 (quoting *Fed. Power Comm'n. v. Tuscarora Indian Nation*, 362 U.S. 99, 116 (1960)).

[97]*Id.* at 1199.

[98]*Id.*

the *Coeur d'Alene Tribal Farm* approach, the Tenth Circuit imposed the burden on the NLRB to show that Congress intended to preempt the Tribe's sovereign authority to enact its right-to-work law.[99] It held that Ohkay Owingeh had a "strong interest as a sovereign in regulating economic activity" and that the NLRB failed to carry its burden of showing that Congress intended to preempt the Tribe's law.[100]

Pueblo of San Juan did not involve the actual application of the NLRA to an Indian tribe; rather, it presented the question of whether the NLRA preempted a tribal labor law enacted pursuant to a tribe's inherent sovereign authority. But the issues can become intertwined, and that was the case in *N.L.R.B. v. Little River Band of Ottawa Indians Tribal Government*.[101] The Band enacted a Fair Employment Practices Code (FEPC) to govern labor and employment relations within its public sector, including within its IGRA gaming operation, the Little River Casino Resort.[102] The FEPC includes laws governing labor organizing and collective bargaining similar to those of states that allow labor organizing. Like other public sector labor laws, the Little River Band's labor law varies from the NLRA. For example, it prohibits strikes.[103] Referring to unique concerns about substance use within the tribal community, the Band's law also prohibits collective bargaining over drug testing standards in a manner that would conflict with the policies of the Band.[104]

In 2013, the NLRB issued an unfair labor practice decision against the Band's government, holding that the tribal government violated the NLRA by applying its own labor law to its on-reservation IGRA

---

[99]*Id.* at 1190-92, 1196-97.

[100]*Id.* at 1200.

[101]788 F.3d 537 (6th 2015).

[102]*See* Little River Band of Ottawa Indians, Fair Employment Practices Code, available at https://lrboi-nsn.gov/government/tribal-code/ (last visited Oct. 18, 2021).

[103]*See id.* § 16.06(c).

[104]See id. § 16.19.

gaming operation, the Little River Casino Resort, in a manner that varied from the NLRA.

On appeal to the Sixth Circuit, the Band relied heavily upon *Pueblo of San Juan*, pointing out that the FEPC exemplified the exercise of the Band's inherent sovereign authority, and under the Tenth Circuit's standard, that authority could not be preempted by the NLRA absent a clear expression of intent by Congress, an intent found nowhere in the NLRA. "It is hard to imagine a greater affront a sovereign's authority (and its dignity)," the Band argued in its brief, "than to topple its own, carefully thought-out policy judgments in these areas and to substitute those of another power."[105]

The Sixth Circuit's three-judge panel ruled 2-1 against the Band. The majority found that the Band's sovereign interests were not significant because its laws applied to non-members. The majority wrote, "[t]he Supreme Court has long been suspicious of tribal authority to regulate the activity of non-members and is apt to view such power as implicitly divested . . . ."[106] With that premise in hand, it applied the *Coeur d'Alene Tribal Farm* framework and held that the NLRB could properly strike down the Band's laws that vary from the NLRA as unfair labor practices.[107] In a strongly worded dissent, Judge David McKeague pointed to the Supreme Court's decision in *Merrion,* discussed in Chapter 3, where the Court held that Indian tribes retain inherent sovereign authority to govern the right of non-tribal citizens to enter their reservations and trust lands and to regulate their conduct while they remain.[108] Following the Tenth Circuit's approach in *Pueblo of San Juan,* he wrote that absent a clear expression of intent by Congress, the NLRB could not thwart the Band's exercise of its inherent authority to enact and enforce its FEPC, and Congress provided no

---

[105] Brief of Petitioner/Cross-Respondent Little River Band of Ottawa Indians Tribal Government, Docket No. 13-1464 at PageID# 49, accessible at https://ecf.ca6.uscourts.gov/n/beam/servlet/TransportRoom (last visited Oct. 18, 2021).

[106] *Little River Band of Ottawa Indians Tribal Government,* 788 F.3d at 544. *See also id.* at 546 (tribal power of non-members is at the "periphery" of "inherent tribal sovereignty").

[107] *Id.* at 551-552.

[108] *Merrion v. Jicarilla Apache Tribe,* 455 U.S. 130, 144 (1982).

such clear expression of intent in the NLRA.[109] The Band petitioned the Supreme Court for review, but the Court declined.[110]

F. Other Cases

1. *Soaring Eagle Casino v. NLRB*[111] and the Sixth Circuit Split

Less than a month after the panel issued its decision in *Little River Band,* a separate three-judge panel of the Sixth Circuit decided *Soaring Eagle Casino v. NLRB.*[112] That case involved a garden-variety NLRB unfair labor practice against the IGRA gaming facility of the Saginaw Chippewa Tribe of Michigan. Unlike *Little River Band,* there was no competing tribal law at issue; the NLRB simply sought to stop the casino from prohibiting union solicitation in violation of the NLRA.[113] The three-judge panel examined the law and voiced the view that the majority decision that had just issued in *Little River Band* was wrongly decided.[114] It concluded that "the approach . . . most consistent with Supreme Court precedent and Congress's supervisory role over the scope of Indian sovereignty" required the conclusion that (a) the Tribe exercised inherent sovereign authority of the employment relations at the casino and (b) absent a clear expression of intent by Congress, the NLRA could not be imposed upon the Tribe to displace that sovereign authority. In this light, the *Soaring Eagle Casino* panel aligned itself with Judge McKeague's dissent in *Little River Band* and with the

---

[109] *Little River Band of Ottawa Indians Tribal Government,* 788 F.3d at 561-62.

[110] *See Little River Band of Ottawa Indians Tribal Gov't v. N.L.R.B.,* 136 S. Ct. 2508 (2016).

[111] 791 F.3d 648 (2015).

[112] 791 F.3d 648 (2015).

[113] *See id.* at 654-55.

[114] *See id.* at 662-75.

Tenth Circuit's approach in *Pueblo of San Juan*.[115] The panel said it was powerless to follow its reasoning, however, because it was constrained, by circuit precedent, to follow the panel majority's decision in *Little River Band*.[116] Like the Little River Band, the Soaring Eagle Casino sought review by the Supreme Court, but the Court declined.[117]

2. The Ninth Circuit's Doubling Down on the *Coeur d'Alene Tribal Farm* Framework

The Ninth Circuit has, so far, had the last word on the subject. In 2018, it decided *Pauma v. National Labor Relations Board*,[118] involving an asserted unfair labor practice by Casino Pauma, the IGRA gaming operation of the Pauma Band of Luiseno Mission Indians. The NLRB found that the casino (or "the Band") violated the NLRA by improperly restricting union solicitation, and the Band appealed to the Ninth Circuit.[119] The Ninth Circuit applied its *Coeur d'Alene Tribal Farm* framework. Observing that "the Casino employs 462 employees, five of whom are members of the Pauma Band" and that "the vast majority of employees and managers are not members of any Native American Tribe," the court easily concluded that the casino's labor relations did not involve "exclusive rights of self-governance in purely intramural matters" under that framework.[120] The Band could not point to a treaty right that would be abrogated by application of the NLRA to its casino.[121] Thus, it could not invoke either of the two principal exceptions

---

[115] For a commentary on *Soaring Eagle Casino* and the conflicting approaches of other circuits, *see generally* Alex T. Skibine, *Practical Reasoning and the Application of General Federal Regulatory Laws to Indian Nations*, 22 WASH. & LEE J. CIVIL RTS. & SOC. JUST. 123 (2016).

[116] *Soaring Eagle Casino*, 791 F.3d at 675.

[117] *Soaring Eagle Casino & Resort v. N.L.R.B.*, 136 S. Ct. 2509 (2016).

[118] 888 F.3d 1066 (9th Cir. 2018).

[119] *Id.* at 1071.

[120] *Id.* at 1077.

[121] *Id.*

to the presumed application of a general federal labor law to an Indian tribe or its enterprise under the Ninth Circuit's *Coeur d'Alene Tribal Farm* framework.[122] The Band petitioned the Supreme Court for review, but the Court, once again, declined.[123]

3. *Chickasaw Nation d/b/a Winstar World Casino:* The "Treaty Rights Exception"[124]

The first (and so far only) case in which an Indian tribe has prevailed under the treaty rights exception within the *Coeur d'Alene Farm* framework – that federal statutes of "general applicability" apply to Indian tribes unless the application would thwart a treaty right or interfere with "exclusive rights of self-governance in purely intramural matters"[125] – issued in 2015. This was the same year as the *Little River Band* and *Soaring Eagle Casino* cases.[126] Like *Soaring Eagle Casino*, *Pauma*, and *San Manuel Band*, the case involved a garden-variety unfair labor practice charge against a tribe's IGRA gaming facility, the Winstar World Casino of the Chickasaw Nation.[127] The Nation invoked the provisions of its 1830 treaty with the United States through which it relinquished its lands in Mississippi. That treaty provided, in pertinent part, that

> no Territory or State shall ever have a right to pass laws for the government of the [Nation]; . . . the U.S.

---

[122]*Id.*

[123]*Casino Pauma v. N.L.R.B.*, 139 S. Ct. 2614 (2019).

[124]*Chickasaw Nation d/b/a Winstar World Casino and International Brotherhood of Teamsters Local 886,* 362 NLRB 942 (2015).

[125]*See supra* 52-55, discussing the *Coeur d'Alene Tribal Farm* framework.

[126]*Chickasaw Nation d/b/a Winstar World Casino and International Brotherhood of Teamsters Local 886,* 362 NLRB 942 (2015) ("*Chickasaw Nation*").

[127]On the stipulated record before the NLRB, the charge was described as being based on management's "informing casino employees that because of the Nation's tribal sovereignty, they did not have the protection of the Act." *Id.*

shall forever secure said [Nation] from, and against, all laws except such as from time to time may be enacted in their own National Councils, not inconsistent with the Constitution, Treaties, and Laws of the United States; and except such as may, and which have been enacted by Congress, to the extent that Congress under the Constitution are required to exercise a legislation over Indian Affairs.[128]

The treaty further provided that "wherever well founded doubt shall arise" concerning the construction of the treaty, "it shall be construed most favorably towards" the Nation.[129] Because the NLRA is not a law enacted by Congress in its exercise of legislative authority over Indian affairs, the NLRB held that this specific treaty provision guaranteed the right of the Chickasaw Nation to operate the casino on its lands free from the application of the NLRA.[130] In light of this decision, it is likely that a handful of other tribes with similar treaty provisions can argue that they are not subject to the NLRA.[131]

G. Conclusion

As pointed out in Chapter 1, federal Indian law reflects history. The history of the NLRB's application of the NLRA to Indian tribes shows a relatively recent about-face on the issue of whether the NLRA applies to Indian tribal governments. Clearly, the advent and success of Indian gaming has caused the NLRB to rethink its views on tribal

---

[128]*Id.* at 942 (quoting 1830 Treaty of Dancing Rabbit Creek).

[129]*Id.* (quoting same).

[130]*Id.* at 945.

[131]*See* Briana Green, San Manuel's *Second Exception: Identifying Treaty Provisions That Support Tribal Labor Sovereignty,* 6 MICH. J. ENVTL. & ADMIN. L. 463 (2017). Treaty arguments were also made by the Saginaw Chippewa Tribe in *Soaring Eagle Casino,* but were (over one dissenting judge) unsuccessful. *See Soaring Eagle Casino,* 791 F.3d at 656-61 (majority's rejection of treaty argument) *and id.* at 675-77 (White, J., dissenting, accepting treaty argument).

sovereignty and the scope of its jurisdiction over the labor relations of Indian tribes.[132] There are good reasons to think it is wrong to do so. IGRA gaming reflects the exercise of inherent tribal sovereignty: the generation of revenues to support governmental services by Indian tribes, many of whom have no appreciable tax base or other ways to raise such revenues.[133]

In 2018, notwithstanding hard-fought efforts, Congress failed to enact the Tribal Labor Sovereignty Act[134] to amend the NLRA to clarify that Indian tribes, as sovereign governments, should be treated in the same manner as states and the federal government: excluded from the definition of "employer" under the NLRA.[135]

A comparison of the Tenth Circuit's decision in *Pueblo San Juan* with the District of Columbia Circuit's decision in *San Manuel,* and the deep split within the Sixth Circuit between the *Little River Band* and *Soaring Eagle Casino* panels, shows that the law remains in a state of

---

[132] In its *San Manuel* decision, the NLRB said: "As tribal businesses have grown and prospered, they have become significant employers of non-Indians and serious competitors with non-Indian owned businesses." *San Manuel Indian Bingo & Casino,* 341 NLRB 1055, 1056 (2004).

[133] RESTATEMENT OF THE LAW OF AMERICAN INDIANS (Tent. Draft No. 4, April 29, 2020) § 46, cmt. c ("[A]n Indian tribe's operation of a casino pursuant to its inherent authority codified by Congress in . . . [IGRA] . . . is a governmental undertaking for a governmental purpose: to generate revenues to support governmental services.") *See California v. Cabazon Band of Mission Indians,* 480 U.S. 202, 222 (1987) (state regulation of reservation gaming by tribe to generate governmental revenues would "impermissibly infringe upon tribal government"); *New Mexico v. Mescalero Apache Tribe,* 462 U.S. 324, 335 (1983) (tribes have inherent authority to "regulate economic activity within the reservation" and to raise revenues to support tribal government). *See also Michigan v. Bay Mills Indian Cmty.,* 572 U.S. 782, 810 (2014) ("tribal business operations are critical to the goals of tribal self-sufficiency because such enterprises in some cases may be the only means by which a tribe can raise revenues") (citations and quotations omitted).

[134] H.R. 511, 114th Cong. § 2 (2015); S. 248, 114th Cong. § 2 (2015); H.R. 986, 115th Cong. § 2 (2017); S. 63, 115th Cong. § 2 (2017).

[135] *See* Noam Scheiber, *Senate Bill to Curtail Labor Rights on Tribal Land Falls Short,* N.Y. Times, April 16, 2018.

flux.[136] As discussed in Chapter 2, the precedents of the Supreme Court support the view that Indian tribes exercise of regulatory authority over reservation labor and employment relations pursuant to their inherent sovereign authority, which remains intact absent express abrogation by Congress. Whether tribes will ultimately be free to govern labor relations and collective bargaining involving their employees without the imposition of the NLRA, or whether the NLRA will always trump that exercise of inherent tribal sovereignty, remains an unanswered question – one that, absent clarification by Congress, may still reach the Supreme Court.

---

[136]*See generally* Limas, *supra* note 21 at 481.

PART III

TOWARD TRIBAL LABOR AND EMPLOYMENT LAW

Aside from the law of domestic relations, there may be no more important area of law affecting a person's identity and economic security than the law of labor and employment relations. As discussed in Chapter 2, Indian tribes may engage in substantial lawmaking in this area pursuant to their inherent sovereignty. There is no reason why they should not do so, especially when they may otherwise face the assertion of regulatory authority by outside federal agencies. By enacting laws to protect employees' rights, tribes can also foster healthy and productive workplaces.[1] The areas in which such laws may be enacted can be broken down into three discrete categories.

1. *Civil Rights and Employment Discrimination.* This category includes laws prohibiting workplace discrimination on the basis of sex, age, disability, race, color, religion, national origin, sexual orientation, or other classifications, and/or protecting employee rights of privacy, speech, or due process. Such laws may include the provision of tribal court remedies for employees who suffer discrimination on these bases. A prominent example is sex discrimination, including harassment by co-workers or supervisors. As discussed in Chapter 5, federal laws protecting against such workplace sex discrimination, as well as dis-

---

[1] *See generally* Wenona T. Singel, *Indian Tribes and Human Rights Accountability*, 49 SAN DIEGO L. REV. 567, 584-585 (2012) (describing explosion of tribal employment and need for tribal government accountability).

crimination on the basis of race, color, religion, ancestry, national origin, and disability do not apply to tribes or entities that they own and control. As also discussed in Chapter 5, Congress failed to address tribes in federal age discrimination laws; so the applicability of those laws to tribes and their instrumentalities is uncertain. There is no impediment to tribal lawmaking in these areas, and Indian tribes' civil rights codes or constitutional provisions may already provide certain rights to tribal government employees who suffer from these forms of discrimination. Chapter 8 looks at the laws of a number of tribes in this area, as well as selected substantive issues that arise in employment discrimination disputes.

2. *Labor Unions and Collective Bargaining.* With the success of tribal economic development (particularly Indian gaming), union activity in Indian country has increased. In response, tribes have begun to enact their own laws to govern labor relations and collective bargaining, in much the same way that the federal government and states regulate these matters in their public sectors.

As discussed in Chapter 7, the decision of the United States Court of Appeals for the Tenth Circuit in *National Labor Relations Board v. Pueblo of San Juan*,[2] supports the view that, pursuant to their inherent sovereignty, tribes retain the power to govern labor relations within their reservation enterprises.[3] In much the same way that states govern labor relations and collective bargaining within their revenue-generating ventures,[4] tribes possess the sovereign authority to do the same within theirs, including within gaming facilities operating pursuant to the Indian Gaming Regulatory Act of 1988 (IGRA).[5] The question then arises whether the National Labor Relations Act (NLRA) preempts such tribal laws, even though the Act fails to mention Indian tribes while excluding the two other sovereign govern-

---

[2] 276 F.3d 1186 (10th Cir. 2002) (en banc).

[3] *See id.* at 1192-93.

[4] *See New York City Off-Track Betting Corp. v. Loc. 2021 of Dist. Council 37, Am. Fed'n of State, Cty. & Mun. Emp. (AFSCME), AFL-CIO*, 416 N.Y.S.2d 974 (Sup. Ct. 1979).

[5] 25 U.S.C. §§ 2701-21 (2018).

ments in this country – states and the federal government – from its coverage.[6]

The Tenth Circuit requires a clear expression of intent by Congress for such preemption. Statutory silence, exemplified by Congress's failure to mention Indian tribes in statutes such as the Occupational Safety and Health Act (OSHA) and the NLRA that otherwise exclude states and the federal government, will not do.[7] As discussed in Chapter 7, the Sixth Circuit's decision in *National Labor Relations Bd. v. Little River Band of Ottawa Indians Tribal Government*,[8] upholding a National Labor Relations Board decision to strike down the Band's labor laws as applied to its IGRA gaming operations to the extent that those tribal laws vary from the NLRA, is in tension with the Tenth Circuit's clear statement rule. Thus, the law is in a state of flux.

But just because the law is in flux does not mean that Indian tribes cannot not exercise their inherent sovereign authority over labor relations. Indeed, in light of the Tenth Circuit's decision in *Pueblo of San Juan*, tribes within the Tenth Circuit may have an open road to govern reservation labor relations within their reservation enterprises. Tribes in other federal circuit courts of appeals that have yet to rule need not hesitate just because of legal uncertainty. On the contrary, it makes sense for tribes to enact and implement their own labor laws and assert their authority to do so rather than remain docile.[9] Chapter 9 looks at

---

[6] Tribes can be described as the "third sovereign" in this country, alongside states and the federal government. *See* Justice Sandra Day O'Connor, *Lessons from the Third Sovereign: Indian Tribal Courts*, 33 TULSA L.J. 1 (1997). The Tenth Circuit observes that Indian tribes "have a status higher than that of states. They are subordinate and dependent nations possessed of all powers as such only to the extent that they have expressly been required to surrender them by the superior sovereign, the United States." *N.L.R.B. v. Pueblo of San Juan*, 276 F.3d 1186, 1192 n.6 (10th Cir. 2002) (quoting *Native Am. Church of N. Am. v. Navajo Tribal Council*, 272 F.2d 131, 134 (10th Cir. 1959)).

[7] *See N.L.R.B. v. Pueblo of San Juan*, 276 F.3d at 1195; *Donovan v. Navajo Forest Prod. Indus.*, 692 F.2d 709, 714 (10th Cir. 1982) (rejecting application of OSHA to tribal instrumentality absent clear expression of intent by Congress; silence will not suffice).

[8] 788 F.3d 537 (6th Cir. 2015).

[9] *See* Introduction to Chapter 8.

what tribes have done in this field and explores some of the substantive issues surrounding tribes' regulation of unions and collective bargaining.

3. *Wages, Hours, and Working Conditions.* This category includes OSHA;, addressing workplace safety matters; the Fair Labor Standards Act, addressing minimum wages and overtime; and the federal Family Medical Leave Act, addressing medical leave for employee. Like the NLRA, these federal laws fail to mention Indian tribes. This category will not be separately treated; for the same principles that govern the sovereign authority of Indian tribes to enact and implement public sector labor laws akin to the NLRA also govern the ability of Indian tribes to enact and implement laws in these areas. The preemption question has yet to emerge in these areas as it has in the context of tribal laws governing unions and collective bargaining. But the same split across the federal circuit courts of appeals described above, with the *Little River Band of Ottawa Indians Tribal Government* decision pitted against *Pueblo of San Juan,* would likely play out were a federal agency to challenge tribal laws governing wages, hours, and working conditions on the ground that they vary from federal laws governing the same areas, albeit without mentioning Indian tribes. Thus, tribes within the jurisdictions of the Tenth Circuit and federal circuit courts of appeals that have yet to address whether Congress must clearly express an intent to preempt tribal laws should have no hesitation enacting laws to govern wages, hours, and working conditions.[10]

---

[10]The Klamath Tribes, the Suquamish Tribe, the Squaxin Island Tribe, and the Jamestown S'Klallam Tribe are examples of tribes that have enacted enforceable laws governing minimum wages, overtime, and family medical leave. Sometimes these laws incorporate federal law by reference, but provide remedies tailored to their communities. *See* Klamath Tribal Code, Title 6, §§ 41.10-41.19, 41.20-41.30 (available at https://klamathtribalcourts.com/tribal-laws/) (last visited Nov. 20, 2021); Suquamish Tribal Code, Chapters 18.2-18.4 (available at https://suquamish.nsn.us/home/government/suquamish-tribal-code/) (last visited Nov. 20, 2021); Squaxin Island Tribe Labor and Employment Code, Chapters 12.03-12.07 (available at https://library.municode.com/tribes_and_tribal_nations/squaxin_island_tribe/codes/code_of_ordinances (last visited Nov. 20, 2021); Jamestown S'Klallam Tribe, Tribal Code, Title 3 – Labor Code, available at https://jamestowntribe.org/wp-content/uploads/2018/05/Title_03_Labor_Code_9_12_14.pdf (last visited Nov. 20, 2021). Appendix C also provides numerous examples of tribal laws, including those addressing wages, hours, and working conditions.

8

DEVELOPING TRIBAL LAW: CIVIL RIGHTS AND EMPLOYMENT DISCRIMINATION

A. Introduction

As discussed in Chapter 2, tribes have the power to govern reservation labor and employment relations. Case law discussed in Chapter 3 further suggests that the more tribes govern these relations, the better situated they will be to resist attempts by federal agencies to impose laws from the outside.[1] By adopting such laws, tribes can ensure that their workplaces are fair and thereby maintain a more productive and high-quality workforce while furthering tribal values of respect and care for others.[2] Finally, if a tribe has enacted its own law governing

---

[1] *See Solis v. Matheson*, 563 F.3d 425, 430-34 (9th Cir. 2009) (holding that FLSA applies to Indian employer on reservation, but pointing out that the outcome could be different if a tribe had its own law governing wages and hours); *see also NLRB v. Pueblo of San Juan*, 276 F.3d 1186, 1199 (10th Cir. 2002) (stating that the Supreme Court's dictum in *Fed. Power Comm'n v. Tuscarora Indian Nation*, 362 U.S. 99, 116 (1960) on the general application of federal laws to Indians "does not apply where an Indian tribe has exercised its authority as a sovereign—here, by enacting a labor regulation—rather than in a proprietary capacity such as that of employer or landowner."); *EEOC v. Karuk Tribe Hous. Auth.*, 260 F.3d 1071, 1081 (9th Cir. 2001) ("The intramural nature of the dispute here is underscored by the fact that the Tribe has an established internal process for adjudicating such matters"). *See generally* Ezekiel J. N. Fletcher, *De Facto Judicial Preemption of Tribal Labor and Employment Law*, 2008 MICH. ST. L. REV. 435, 440 (2008) (recommending enactment of tribal employment law to prevent federal intrusion into tribal sovereignty). *But see Nat'l Lab. Rels. Bd. v. Little River Band of Ottawa Indians Tribal Gov't*, 788 F.3d 537, 554 (6th Cir. 2015) (allowing NLRB to strike down tribal laws that vary from the NLRA notwithstanding Congress's failure to address Indian tribes in the NLRA).

[2] *See* Kaighn Smith, Jr., *Ethical "Obligations" and Affirmative Tribal Sovereignty: Some Considerations for Tribal Attorneys*, Federal Bar Association, 2006 Annual Indian Law

the issues, it may argue in the face of claims brought by a federal agency (like the EEOC) that the agency proceedings must be stayed or dismissed pending the employee's exhaustion of tribal remedies, a procedural barrier to federal authority discussed in Chapter 3.[3]

Chapter 5 looked at the issue of civil rights in tribal employment by examining sources of federal law protecting the civil rights of employees from adverse governmental action, protections initially grounded in the Bill of Rights and the Fourteenth Amendment to the United States Constitution, and reflected in the Indian Civil Rights Act of 1968 (ICRA).[4] These protections include due process of law (where "property interests" in employment are at stake), equal protection (i.e., protection against discrimination on the basis of race, sex, religion, or national origin), freedom of speech, and freedom from unreasonable searches and seizures.[5] As discussed in Chapter 5, violations

---

Conference, Conference Materials at 532-43 (Albuquerque, N.M. 2006) *reprinted in* Matthew L. M. Fletcher, AMERICAN INDIAN TRIBAL LAW, 217 (2011) (discussing ethical considerations of tribal attorneys to advocate for fair employment practices laws). *See generally* Mark D. Rosen, *Multiple Authoritative Interpreters of Quasi-Constitutional Federal Law: Tribal Courts & the Indian Civil Rights Act,* 69 FORDHAM L. REV. 479, 487 (2000) (discussing how tribal court interpretations of Indian Civil Rights Act provisions reflect the unique values of individual tribes and do not necessarily reflect protections afforded by similar provisions of the federal constitution); Scott D. Danahy, *License to Discriminate: The Application of Sovereign Immunity to Employment Discrimination Claims Brought by Non-Native American Employees of Tribally Owned Businesses,* 25 FLA. ST. U.L. REV. 679 (1998) (exploring the clash between tribal sovereign immunity and non-Indian employees' discrimination suits against tribal government employers).

[3]*See, e.g., Graham v. Applied Geo Tech. Inc.*, 593 F. Supp.2d 915 (S.D. Miss. 2008); *Garcia v. Akwesasne Hous. Auth.*, 268 F.3d 76, 89-90 (2d Cir. 2001) (Katzmann, J., concurring); *Davis v. Mille Lacs Band of Chippewa Indians*, 26 F. Supp. 2d 1175 (D. Minn. 1998), *aff'd.*, 193 F.3d 990 (8th Cir. 1999).

[4]25 U.S.C. §§ 1301-1303 (2018).

[5]Section 1302 of ICRA provides, in pertinent part:
No Indian tribe in exercising powers of self-government shall—
(1) make or enforce any law prohibiting the free exercise of religion, or abridging the freedom of speech . . .;
(2) violate the right of the people to be secure in their persons, houses, papers, and effects against unreasonable search and seizures . . .;
. . .

of these constitutional rights by non-Indian governmental bodies or officials may be actionable pursuant to 42 U.S.C. § 1983, and, with respect to race discrimination, pursuant to 42 U.S.C. § 1981.[6] In the wake of the Supreme Court's landmark decision in *Santa Clara Pueblo v. Martinez*[7] — reconfirming that tribes are not subject to the constitutional provisions that constrain the authority of the states or the federal government — federal courts have refused to impose these laws upon the operations of tribal governments.[8] With the sole exception of petitions for *habeas corpus* relief, tribes retain exclusive governmental authority to decide how to enforce the provisions of ICRA within their territories.

The concept of "civil rights" in the employment setting may encompass not only protections against the types of discrimination most often associated with the Equal Protection Clause (sex, race, color, religion, or national origin),[9] but also protections against discrimination on

---

(8) deny to any person within its jurisdiction the equal protection of its laws or deprive any person of liberty or property without due process of law....
Id. § 1302. Subsection (1), of course, tracks the First Amendment of the U.S. Constitution. Similarly, subsection (2) tracks the Fourth Amendment, and subsection (8) tracks the Equal Protection and Due Process clauses of the Fourteenth Amendment.

[6]The protections against sex, race, color, national origin, and religious discrimination by state government employers guaranteed by the Equal Protection Clause of the United States Constitution run parallel to similar protections under Title VII of the Civil Rights Act of 1964, 42 U.S.C. §§ 2000e-2000e-17 (2018), and may be separately enforced against state actors pursuant to 42 U.S.C. § 1983. *See Notari v. Denver Water Dep't*, 971 F.2d 585, 587 (10th Cir. 1992).

[7]436 U.S. 49 (1978).

[8]*See, e.g., Nero v. Cherokee Nation of Okla.*, 892 F.2d 1457 (10th Cir. 1989); *R.J. Williams Co. v. Fort Belknap Hous. Auth.*, 719 F.2d 979 (9th Cir. 1983); *Wardle v. Ute Indian Tribe*, 623 F.2d 670 (10th Cir. 1980); *Stroud v. Seminole Tribe of Florida*, 606 F. Supp. 678, 679-80 (S.D. Fla. 1985).

[9]*See* U.S. Const. amend. XIV, § 1. These categories of discrimination are known as "suspect classifications" under federal constitutional law. They are reviewed by courts under a "strict scrutiny" standard, and may give rise to remedies if a government employer takes an adverse employment action on the basis of any such classification. Adverse employment actions may include such things as failing to hire, promote, or train an employee; discharging or laying off an employee; declining seniority or benefits to an employee; or leaving an employee subject to harassment or a hostile

the basis of age, disability, or other classifications.[10] Apart from the restraint upon governments found in the Equal Protection Clause of the United States Constitution, federal law separately protects against discrimination on the basis of sex, race, color, religion, and national origin, in both the public and private sectors pursuant to Title VII of the Civil Rights Act of 1964.[11] It likewise protects against disability discrimination in both public and private employment settings pursuant to the Americans with Disabilities Act of 1990 (ADA),[12] and against age discrimination in those sectors pursuant to the Age Discrimination in Employment Act of 1976 (ADEA).[13] Congress excluded Indian tribes from claims of sex, race, color, national origin, and religious discrimination under Title VII, and from disability discrimination claims under the ADA. Congress failed, however, to address the application of the ADEA to Indian tribes.

---

work environment. *See* BARBARA LINDEMANN & PAUL GROSSMAN, EMPLOYMENT DISCRIMINATION LAW 1075-468 (4th ed. 2007). Tribes may or may not classify various kinds of discrimination in ways similar to federal law. *See* Ann E. Tweedy, *Sex Discrimination Under Tribal Law*, 36 WM. MITCHELL L. REV. 392, 407-08 (2010).

[10]Under the Equal Protection Clause, government discrimination on the basis of disability, age, or sexual orientation does not give rise to "strict scrutiny" review by the courts, but must still be justified by having some rational relationship to a legitimate governmental purpose. *See* Tweedy, *supra* note 19 at 584-86, 621, 815-16.

[11]42 U.S.C. §§ 2000e-2000e-17 (2018). The same standards that govern the operation of the Equal Protection Clause of the Fourteenth Amendment with regard to state government actors, also apply to the operation of the Fifth Amendment's equal protection provision with regard to federal government actors. *See Adarand Constructors, Inc. v. Pena*, 515 U.S. 200, 201 (1995).

[12]42 U.S.C. §§ 12101-12113 (2018).

[13]29 U.S.C. §§ 621-634 (2018). While the Eleventh Amendment presents impediments to direct actions brought by individuals against states under the ADA and the ADEA in federal court, the EEOC, as an agency of the United States, may bring actions against state and local governments under these laws. Public employees can bring actions against state officials under the *Ex Parte Young* doctrine, discussed in Chapter 4, to seek prospective relief for constitutional violations, and they can seek damages for such violations against persons acting under color of state law pursuant to 42 U.S.C. § 1983, discussed in Chapter 5.

By expressly excluding tribes from the most central federal employment discrimination laws, Title VII and the ADA, Congress respected the authority of tribes to decide, under their own community norms and policy judgments, whether and how to remedy tribal workplace discrimination on the basis of sex, race, national origin, color, religion, and disability.[14] Congress's failure to address the application of the ADEA to Indian tribes leaves uncertainty about the application of this law to tribes and their enterprises, at least when the Equal Employment Opportunity Commission (EEOC) brings the action, because, as discussed in Chapter 6, in that setting, tribes cannot claim sovereign immunity from suit. Tribes can, however, enact their own laws governing age discrimination, and if they do, courts may be less ready to impose the ADEA upon tribes' reservation enterprises at the behest of the EEOC.[15]

In short, there are internal and external imperatives, grounded in fundamental principles of tribal sovereignty, for Indian tribes to enact their own laws protecting against employment discrimination. First, the enactment of such laws can foster workplace harmony and security for employees in accordance with tribal values.[16] Second, the enact-

---

[14]*See* 42 U.S.C. § 2000e(b) (excluding Indian tribes from definition of "employer" under Title VII); 42 U.S.C. § 12111(5)(B)(i) (excluding Indian tribes from the definition of "employer" under ADA). The scope of Congress's exclusion of "Indian tribes" from the ADA and Title VII is discussed in Chapter 5. Courts have liberally construed that exclusion to include tribal corporations and other entities that further the interest of tribal governments. Thus, opportunities for tribes to enact laws without confronting an assertion of concurrent federal law authority are wide open for these employing entities. This may include tribes' IGRA gaming enterprises. *See Barker v. Menominee Nation Casino*, 897 F. Supp. 389 (E.D. Wis. 1995). *But see Tidwell v. Harrah's Kansas Casino Corp.*, 322 F. Supp.2d 1200 (D. Kan. 2004) (casino management company subject to Title VII claim, given its control over employment decisions at tribe's IGRA gaming facility).

[15]*See, e.g., EEOC v. Karuk Tribe Hous. Auth.*, 260 F.3d 1071, 1081-82 (9th Cir. 2001); *EEOC v. Fond du Lac Heavy Equip. & Constr. Co. Inc.*, 986 F.2d 246, 249-50 (8th Cir. 1993).

[16]*See generally* Matthew L.M. Fletcher, *Tribal Employment Separation: Tribal Law Enigma, Tribal Governance Paradox, and Tribal Court Conundrum*, 38 MICH. J. L. REFORM 273, 273-74 (2005) (external rules may destroy cultural norms and tribal communities).

ment of such laws may fill a void and stem pressures from the outside to impose federal laws on tribes. The enactment of such laws (depending on their design) could generate new avenues for litigation and accompanying costs. But to the extent that such laws promote the values of the tribal nation enacting them and add to the protection of tribal sovereignty, those costs may well be acceptable.

* * *

Section B of this chapter looks at how a variety of tribes have addressed the issue of employment discrimination, whether through the provision of remedies under tribal constitutional provisions or ICRA, both of which constrain the actions of tribal government, or through the enactment of specific tribal laws similar to Title VII, the ADA, or the ADEA. What is clear from this survey is that there is no set model or path for any given tribe. This is not a field in which "one size fits all"; every tribe is unique and will design its laws to reflect its own priorities and values.[17]

Section C selects key issues that arise in the provision of remedies for employment discrimination that any tribe (or its courts) is likely to grapple with as the law develops. The substantive issues chosen for discussion are: (a) how principles of sovereign immunity may or may not apply in relation to the relief a tribal forum may award for civil rights violations; (b) the protection of due process rights of tribal employees; (c) the protection of free speech rights for tribal employees; and (d) the allocation of the burden of proof in employment discrimination cases.

B. Civil Rights Protections for Employees Under Tribal Law

Tribes generally provide two basic paths to remedy employment discrimination or civil rights violations. First, some tribes provide tribal court jurisdiction to enforce an equal protection clause under a tribal constitution or ICRA. Such a provision may be interpreted by the tribal court to prohibit discrimination against governmental employees on the basis of race, sex, religion, color, or national origin. Separate provi-

---

[17] *See generally* Ann E. Tweedy, *Sex Discrimination Under Tribal Law*, 36 WM. MITCHELL L. REV. 392, 416 (2010) (noting that tribes "take diverse approaches to the issue of sex discrimination").

sions of a tribal constitution may likewise afford employees rights of due process, free speech, and freedom from unreasonable searches and seizures, as ICRA does in constraining tribal government action.[18]

Second, some tribes have legislative enactments that expressly provide remedies for the same forms of discrimination covered by a tribal constitution or ICRA, and additionally provide remedies for other forms of discrimination not typically covered by constitutional provisions, such as age, disability, sexual orientation, or other classifications. Such protections may be extended to cover private sector employers within the jurisdiction of the tribe, not just governmental employees covered by ICRA or constitutional provisions.

As described below, tribal law regimes reflect a mixture of these two paths, with significant variations in the degree of detail and scope of application.[19]

---

[18]This chapter touches upon all of these civil rights in the tribal employment setting, with the exception of the protection against unreasonable searches and seizures, which is typically found alongside due process and equal protection clauses in the civil rights codes and constitutions of tribes. While there is little case law on the subject to date, such a provision likely restricts tribal government employers in such things as searching computers of employees or mandating drug tests. *See Osfield v. Mashantucket Pequot Gaming Enterprise,* 6 Mash. App. 1 (Mash. Pequot Ct. App. 2013); *Palencia v. Pojoaque Gaming Inc.,* 28 Indian L. Rptr. 6149 (Pueblo of Pojoaque Tribal Ct. 2001).

[19]For relatively recent tribal laws protecting employees from employment discrimination in streamlined codes, *see* Klamath Tribal Code, Title 6, §§ 41.01-41.09 (available at https://klamathtribalcourts.com/tribal-laws/) (last visited Nov. 20, 2021); Suquamish Tribal Code, Chapters 18.1 and 18.4 (available at https://suquamish.nsn.us/home/government/suquamish-tribal-code/) (last visited Nov. 20, 2021); Squaxin Island Tribe Labor and Employment Code, Chapters 12.02 and 12.07 (available at https://library.municode.com/tribes_and_tribal_nations/squaxin_island_tribe/codes/code_of_ordinances (last visited Nov. 20, 2021).

1. Navajo Nation

   a. The Navajo Bill of Rights: Protections for Government Employees

In 1967, prior to the enactment of ICRA, the Navajo Nation Tribal Council adopted the Navajo Nation Bill of Rights, which is likely the most longstanding codified law governing civil rights protections for all persons (including employees) within an Indian nation.[20] The Navajo Bill of Rights contains substantially the same rights as those found in ICRA, and the Navajo Supreme Court has declared that the "Navajo courts have always been available for the enforcement of civil rights created by the ICRA and the Navajo Bill of Rights."[21]

---

[20] *See* 1 N.N.C. §§ 1-9 (1967).

[21] *Johnson v. Navajo Nation*, No. A-CV-16-85, ¶ 48; 5 Nav. R. 192, 200; 14 Indian L. Rptr. 6037 (Nav. Sup. Ct. 1987) available at www.tribal-institute.org/opinions/1987.NANN.0000011.htm (last visited Nov. 25, 2021). The Navajo Nation Bill of Rights provides in part:
   § 3. Denial or abridgment of rights on basis of sex; equal protection and due process of Navajo Nation law:
   Life, liberty, and the pursuit of happiness are recognized as fundamental individual rights of all human beings. Equality of rights under the law shall not be denied or abridged by the Navajo Nation on account of sex nor shall any person within its jurisdiction be denied equal protection in accordance with the laws of the Navajo Nation, nor be deprived of life, liberty or property, without due process of law. Nor shall such rights be deprived by any bill of attainder or ex post facto law.
   § 4. Freedom of religion, speech, press, and the right of assembly and petition:
   The Navajo Nation Council shall make no law respecting an establishment of religion, or prohibiting the free exercise thereof; or abridging the freedom of speech, or of the press; or the right of people peaceably to assemble, and to petition the Navajo Nation government for a redress of grievances.
1 N.N.C. §§ 3-4.

i. The Navajo Sovereign Immunity Act: Waiver of Immunity for Money Damages

In 1986, the Navajo Nation Tribal Council amended the Navajo Sovereign Immunity Act to allow certain suits against the Navajo Nation and its enterprises for damages for civil rights violations to the extent of insurance coverage, and the law mandates such coverage.[22] The act provides, in pertinent part:

> Subject to all other provisions of this Act, the express coverage of any commercial liability policy insuring the Navajo Nation or of any self-insurance program established by the Navajo Nation, for sum which the Navajo Nation as insured shall become legally obligated to pay as damages ... *shall include liability for such actual monetary loss and damage which is established by clear and convincing evidence, to be the direct and proximate result of the wrongful deprivation or impairment of civil rights as set forth in Chapter 1 of Title 1 of the Navajo Tribal Code, the Bill of Rights of the Navajo Nation.* In the sound exercise of judicial discretion, the Courts of the Navajo Nation may, to the extent deemed proper and appropriate in any action for damages for wrongful deprivation or impairment of civil rights as provided herein, award necessary costs of suit and/or reasonable fees, based upon time and value, incurred for legal representation; or require each or any party thereto, to bear their own respective costs and/or legal fees incurred therein.[23]

---

[22] *See Johnson*, No. A-CV-16-85 at ¶ 53; 5 Nav. R. at 194 (citing Navajo Tribal Council Resolution, CD-60-86, December 11, 1986).

[23] 1 N.N.C. §554(F)(5) (emphasis added).

The Navajo Supreme Court has held that under this section, plaintiffs who suffer civil rights violations may recover for "pain and suffering" and "emotional distress" if proven by clear and convincing evidence.[24] The Navajo Supreme Court has also said that the protections provided by "ICRA and the Navajo Bill of Rights may . . . be enforced against Navajo Nation officials under the Navajo Sovereign Immunity Act."[25]

In any action brought in the Navajo Nation courts by an employee against the Navajo Nation or one of its commissions, agencies, or subordinate economic organizations in which a violation of civil rights is at issue, the court first determines the scope of insurance coverage in relation to the asserted claims.[26] In light of the above-quoted provision of the Navajo Sovereign Immunity Act, "insurance policy provisions effectively become part and parcel of the waiver of sovereign immunity."[27]

---

[24]*Navajo Nation v. Crockett*, No. SC-CV-14-94, ¶¶ 68-70; 7 Nav. R. 237, 245; 24 Indian L. Rptr. 6027 (Nav. Sup. Ct. 1996) http://tribal-institute.org/opinions/1996.NANN.0000006.htm (last visited Nov. 25, 2021) *See also Manuelito v. Kellogg*, No. WR-CV-217-87 ¶¶ 41, 43-44; 6 Nav. R. 508, 511 (Window Rock Navajo Dist. Ct. 1989), available at http://tribal-institute.org/opinions/1989.NANN.0000024.htm (last visited Nov. 25, 2021) (former public safety officials of the Navajo Nation may proceed with claims that their terminations violated due process and equal protection when insurance policy at issue covered personal injury, and "personal injury" was defined to include "[m]ental [i]njury" and "[m]ental [a]nguish").

[25]*See Johnson*, No. A-CV-16-85 at ¶ 55; 5 Nav. R. at 200 n.6.

[26]*See Kellogg*, No. WR-CV-217-87 at ¶¶ 35-45; 6 Nav. R. at 510-511.

[27]*Kellogg*, No. WR-CV-217-87 at ¶ 39; 6 Nav. R. at 510. In *Kellogg*, the court also held that the suit could proceed against the officers responsible for implementing the terminations, in their official capacities, without the constraint of sovereign immunity that they would otherwise enjoy. *Id.* at ¶ 59; 6 Nav. R. at 513. The Nation could be named as a codefendant, given its ultimate responsibility for the claims, but it was not an indispensable party. *Id.* at ¶¶ 58-62; 6 Nav. R. at 513-14.

ii. Sovereign Immunity: Civil Rights Claims Versus Employment Claims

In *Raymond v. Navajo Agricultural Products Industry*,[28] the Navajo Supreme Court did not view sexual harassment as a civil rights claim grounded in a violation of equal protection (gender discrimination). In that case, a female employee claimed that she suffered from an illegal termination, involving sexual harassment, at the Navajo Agricultural Products Industry (NAPI), an enterprise of the Navajo Nation. NAPI's insurance policy excluded liability for

> employment-related or personnel practices, policies, acts, errors or omissions including but not limited to . . . termination of employment . . . [and] coercion, criticism, demotion, promotion, evaluation, reassignment, discipline, defamation, harassment, humiliation, discrimination, . . . or consequential injury as a result of [the] above.[29]

The court held that Raymond's claims, including the claim for sexual harassment, "are either expressly excluded or not included in the policy's coverage."[30] Thus, it effectively construed her sexual harassment claim as an excluded "employment-related" claim. The court pointed out, however, that "[u]nder section 354(f)(5) of the [Navajo Sovereign Immunity] Act, the Nation's commercial liability policies must contain a provision covering damages resulting from 'wrongful deprivation of civil rights,'"[31] and that the policy in question contained such a provision as follows:

---

[28]No. SC-CV-26-94; 7 Nav. R. 142 (Nav. Sup. Ct. 1995) available at www.tribal-institute.org/opinions/1995.NANN.0000013.htm (last visited Nov. 24, 2021).

[29]*Raymond*, No. SC-CV-26-94 at ¶ 26; 7 Nav. R. at 143-44.

[30]*Raymond*, No. SC-CV-26-94 at ¶ 27; 7 Nav. R. at 144.

[31]*Raymond*, No. SC-CV-26-94 at ¶¶ 29-30; 7 Nav. R. at 144-45.

> Public Officials' Errors and Omissions means any and all Wrongful Acts by an Insured in the discharge of duties for the Named Insured . . . Wrongful Act includes actual or alleged violations of . . . civil rights . . . .[32]

The court also said that actions for injunctive and other equitable relief may be brought against Navajo officials to prevent civil rights violations pursuant to 1 N.N.C. § 354(g)(1). Nevertheless, the court construed all of Raymond's claims as employment claims, not as civil rights claims, and held that sovereign immunity barred her suit.[33]

In *Navajo Nation v. Crockett*,[34] the Navajo Supreme Court held that employees' claims that they were terminated in violation of their due process and free speech rights under the Navajo Bill of Rights were not excluded (as in *Raymond*) from NAPI's insurance coverage as employment-related claims. Instead, the court found that they were in the nature of civil rights claims falling within the above-quoted language for policy coverage.

In *Crockett*, employees prevailed in a jury trial against NAPI on claims that they were fired for speaking out at a Navajo Nation Council meeting about alleged mismanagement (environmental and safety issues) at NAPI.[35] NAPI appealed, claiming sovereign immunity under the theory that, as in *Raymond*, the plaintiffs' claims were not civil rights claims, but employment claims, expressly excluded by the policy.

---

[32]*Id.*

[33]The court said that Raymond's sole remedy was to seek review of her termination under the Navajo Preference in Employment Act (NPEA), which provides, in pertinent part, that "[A]ll employers shall not penalize, discipline, discharge, nor take any adverse action against any Navajo employee without just cause."15 N.N.C. § 608(B)(4). Claimants may file a charge with the Office of Navajo Labor Relations, the agency responsible for the monitoring and enforcement of the NPEA. *See* 15 N.N.C. § 610 (A)-(B). Raymond, however, failed to meet the filing deadline for such a charge.

[34]SC-CV-14-94, ¶¶ 38-54; 7 Nav. R. 237; 24 Indian L. Rptr. 6027 (Nav. Sup. Ct. 1996) available at www.tribal-institute.org/opinions/1996.NANN.0000006.htm (last visited Nov. 25, 2021).

[35]*See id.* No. SC-CV-14-94 at ¶¶ 11, 38-54, 72; 7 Nav. R. at 238.

The Navajo Supreme Court disagreed:

> [S]ubsection 354(f)(5) requires the Nation to carry liability insurance to cover civil rights claims and any damages arising therefrom.... It also modifies and limits the requirement in section 354(f) that the Nation may only be sued for claims expressly covered by its policy.
>
> The employees' claims are framed as civil rights claims, notably for violations of *freedom of speech* and *due process of law*. NAPI admits that its insurance covers civil rights claims, but argues that the employees' claims arise from employment termination and not civil rights, and therefore are expressly excluded under its policy. NAPI's policy does exclude "any liability arising out of any . . . employment related or personnel practices, policies, acts, errors or omissions including termination of employment . . . [and] compensation."
>
> . . . In *Raymond*, we agreed with the district court that the plaintiff's claims were "employment related", and not civil rights claims. . . . In contrast, the employees in this case properly raised civil rights claims in their complaint and the district court decided they were civil rights claims.
>
> The district court has the duty to make that determination . . . . Accordingly, this case is a civil rights case, and not an employment case . . . .[36]

---

[36]*Id*. No. SC-CV-14-94 at ¶¶ 27-30; 7 Nav. R. at 237-39 (emphasis added). The court noted that NAPI's insurance policy provides coverage for federal or state civil rights violations. They held that this was just boilerplate language and interpreted it to include violations of Navajo Nation law. "Thus," the court said, "the Nation's immunity from suit [was] waived under the Act's insurance exception." *Id*. No. SC-CV-14-94 at ¶ 33; 7 Nav. R. at 239.

b. Navajo Nation Preference in Employment Act: "Just Cause" and Other Protections for Public and Private Sector Employees

Beyond the provision of judicial remedies for civil rights violations involving employees of the Navajo Nation or its commissions, agencies, and enterprises, Navajo law protects employees within the Navajo reservation from "prejudice, intimidation, and [] sexual harassment" pursuant to the Navajo Preference in Employment Act (NPEA).[37] NEPA also provides that, with the exception of certain Navajo Nation government employees, all employees within the Navajo Reservation may not be terminated without "just cause."[38]

The NPEA established the Office of Navajo Labor Relations (ONLR) to enforce these laws.[39] For non-Navajo Nation government employees, the ONLR may act upon the complaint of an individual or take action upon its own initiative.[40] NPEA also established the Navajo Nation Labor Commission (NNLC) as the adjudicatory body to hear complaints brought by the ONLR or individual non-Navajo Nation government employees.[41] The NNLC has authority to issue determinations and enforcement orders for violations of the Navajo Na-

---

[37] 15 N.N.C. §§ 604(B)(8-9), as amended by Navajo Nation Council Resolution CMA-13-16 (March 23, 2016). In addition to requiring Navajo hiring preferences for all employers, the NPEA provides, in pertinent part, that:
> All employers shall use non-discriminatory job qualifications and selection criteria in employment [and] ...
> [a]ll employers shall maintain a safe and clean working environment and provide employment conditions [that] are free of prejudice, intimidation, and including sexual harassment.

Id. §§ 604(B)(7), (9), as amended by Navajo Nation Council Resolution No. CMA-13-16 (March 23, 2016). *See generally* Paul Spruhan, *Tribal Labor and Employment Law: The Navajo Preference in Employment Act*, ARIZONA ATTORNEY, Vol. 58, No. 11, July-August 2022, at 44 (explaining operation of NPEA).

[38] 15 N.N.C. §§ 604(B)(4).

[39] *Id.* § 201.

[40] *Id.* § 610(B)(1).

[41] *Id.* § 301.

tion's employment laws.[42] Its decisions are subject to judicial review before the Navajo Nation Supreme Court.[43] Navajo Nation government employees follow the grievance process set out in the applicable personnel policies manual.[44] For executive and legislative employees, the Office of Hearings and Appeals (OHA), an administrative tribunal set up under the Office of the President and Vice-President, hears such grievances.[45] Similarly, OHA's decisions can be appealed to the Navajo Supreme Court.[46]

The NPEA prohibits any waiver of its requirements or protections by contract.[47] Any contract provision that is inconsistent or conflicts with the requirements of NPEA "shall be legally invalid and unenforceable and the Act shall prevail and govern the subject of the inconsistency or conflict."[48] Further, the Navajo Supreme Court has held that NPEA's "just cause" provision applies to all employees within the Nation, though the NPEA exempts certain Navajo Nation government employees from this requirement by classifying them as "at-will."[49] When an employee claims that an employer has failed to provide just cause for termination or other disciplinary action, has not provided a workplace free from harassment, or otherwise has violated

---

[42] *Id.* § 612.

[43] *See id.* § 613(A).

[44] 15 N.N.C. § 614, as amended by Navajo Nation Council Resolution No. CO-48-14 (October 23, 2014).

[45] Navajo Nation Personnel Policies Manual, § XIV(I).

[46] 15 N.N.C. § 614(C).

[47] *Id.* § 609.

[48] *Id.* § 609(A); *see generally Cedar Unified Sch. Dist. v. Navajo Nation Labor Comm'n*, No. SC-CV-53-06, slip op., No. SC-CV-54-06, slip op. at ¶¶ 27-28 (Nav. Sup. Ct. 2007) available at www.tribal-institute.org/opinions/2007.NANN.0000018.htm (last visited Nov. 25, 2021).

[49] *Cedar Unified Sch. Dist.*, No. SC-CV-53-06; No. SC-CV-54-06, at ¶ 31; 15 N.N.C. § 604(B)(8) (as amended by Navajo Nation Council Resolution No. CO-60-17 (October 17, 2017).

the Act, the burden of proof rests with the employee.[50] Although the law originally required clear and convincing evidence, employees now need only prove their claim by a preponderance of the evidence.[51]

2. Mashantucket Pequot Tribal Nation

a. Mashantucket Pequot Civil Rights Code: Protections for Government Employees

In 2000, the Mashantucket Pequot Tribal Nation enacted its Civil Rights Code to provide judicial remedies for violations by the Nation of individuals' rights of free speech, due process, equal protection, and other rights similar to those guaranteed by the Bill of Rights of the U.S. Constitution and the ICRA.[52] Since such civil rights check the power of governments, it makes sense that any action brought under the Mashantucket Pequot Civil Rights Code must be brought against the Nation itself.[53]

The statute of limitations for claims under the Mashantucket Pequot Civil Rights Code is one year. No claim can be brought unless a plaintiff first files a Notice of Claim within 180 days after the claim

---

[50] 15 N.N.C. §611(B), as amended by Navajo Nation Council Resolution No. CMA-13-16 (March 23, 2016).

[51] *Id.*

[52] 20 M.P.T.L., ch.1 §§ 1-6, available at http://www.mptnlaw.com/TribalLaws.htm (last visited Nov. 25, 2021).

[53] The provisions of the Mashantucket Pequot Civil Rights Code track those of the ICRA and the Bill of Rights, providing, in pertinent part, as follows:
    1. Civil Rights
    a. The Tribe shall not:
(1) make or enforce any law prohibiting the free exercise of religion or abridging the freedom of speech, or of the press, or the right of the people to peaceably assemble and to petition for a redress of grievances;
(2) violate the right of the people to be secure in their persons, houses, papers, and effects against unreasonable search and seizures . . . . ;
(8) deny to any person within its jurisdiction the equal protection of its laws or deprive any person of liberty or property without due process of law.
Id. 20 M.P.T.L. § 1.

accrues, setting forth the details of the claim, including the "name of any officer, agent, servant, employee or the division, agency, committee, office, entity or instrumentality of the Tribe involved, if known."[54]

Unlike the Navajo Nation's law, actions brought under the Mashantucket Pequot Civil Rights Code are subject to a bench trial and may not be tried to a jury.[55] The law allows plaintiffs to recover "for actual damages resulting from a violation of the [civil] rights," as well as for "pain and suffering or mental anguish provided that, in no event shall the total award of actual damages plus pain and suffering for injuries arising from the set of facts and circumstances alleged in the complaint exceed the amount of $250,000."[56] Finally, the act allows the recovery of attorney fees against the Tribe at the discretion of the court but only "when the court determines that the action(s) of the Tribe were wholly unreasonable and particularly egregious."[57] If the Tribe prevails, attorney's fees may be awarded to the Tribe "only upon a finding that the plaintiff's claim is frivolous, unreasonable or without foundation in the law or fact."[58] Punitive damages may not be recovered.[59]

In *Barnes v. Mashantucket Pequot Tribal Nation*,[60] the Mashantucket Pequot Tribal Court addressed a discrimination claim brought by an African American, invoking the equal protection provision of the Tribe's Civil Rights Code. Citing to a decision of the Hopi Appeals Court, the court recognized the claim, consistent with federal courts' construction of the parallel language of the Equal Protection Clause of the United States Constitution, stating:

---

[54]*Id.* § 3(d), (f).

[55]*Id.* § 4(a).

[56]*Id.* § 3(e)(2).

[57]*Id.* § 3(e)(3).

[58]*Id.*

[59]*Id.* § 3(e)(5)(ii).

[60]No. CV-GC-2006-153; 34 Indian L. Rptr. 6072 (Mashantucket Pequot Tribal Ct. June 11, 2007) available at http://tribal-institute.org/opinions/2007.NAMP.0000010.htm (last visited Nov. 25, 2021).

The Tribe's Civil Rights Code provides: "The Tribe shall not . . . deny to any person within its jurisdiction the equal protection of its laws." XX M.P.T.L. ch. 1, § 1(a)(8). This language parallels language contained in the Fourteenth Amendment of the United States Constitution. *See Nevayaktewa v. Hopi Tribe*, No. 97AC000004 (Hopi App. Ct. 1998) (citing the Indian Civil Rights Act language, which also mirrors the U.S. Constitution). Thus, federal precedent may guide the Tribal Court.[61]

The same court, in *Sawyer v. Mashantucket Pequot Tribal Nation*,[62] recognized a workplace sex discrimination claim grounded in the equal protection provision of the Mashantucket Pequot Civil Rights Code.[63] In *Barnes*, which is discussed further in Section C(4), the court found that the plaintiff failed to meet his burden of proving discrimination.[64] In *Sawyer*, the court held that the Civil Rights Code could not be applied retroactively to cover the gender discrimination alleged by the plaintiffs.[65]

b. Mashantucket Pequot Employee Review Code: "Just Cause" and Procedural Protections for Nation Employees

Apart from the protections afforded to employees under the Civil Rights Code, the Mashantucket Pequot Tribal Nation also provides for

---

[61] *Id.* No. CV-GC-2006-153 at ¶ 27.

[62] No. MPTC-CV-2000-135, 3 Mashantucket Rptr. 413 (Mashantucket Pequot Tribal Ct. Nov. 27, 2001), available at http://tribal-institute.org/opinions/2001.NAMP.0000028.htm (last visited Nov. 25, 2021).

[63] *Id.* at ¶¶ 13, 20. The Equal Protection Clause of the United States Constitution likewise supports sex discrimination claims in public sector employment. *See supra* note 6.

[64] *See Barnes*, No. CV-GC-2006-153 at ¶¶ 33-35.

[65] *See Sawyer*, No. MPTC-CV-2000-135 at ¶ 29.

review of employment decisions similar to the process provided by the Navajo Employment Preference Act. Pursuant to the Nation's Employee Review Code, judicial review is available for any termination or suspension of five or more days of an employee of the Nation, its gaming enterprise or any other subdivision, arm, agency, department, or entity of the Nation for an alleged violation of procedures, policies, or a collective bargaining agreement.[66] The code establishes a "Board of Review" that consists of "an impartial panel of employees."[67] This board reviews the disciplinary action in question along with any evidence and testimony presented by the employee and management, and then issues a final decision.[68] To obtain judicial review, either party must file a request for review with the tribal court within thirty days after mailing of the final decision of the board.[69]

Under the Employee Review Code, the role of the court is limited:

> In reviewing an appeal, the court shall determine whether the Board of Review's Final Decision was appropriate by considering whether:
> (1) There was a reasonable basis for the Board of Review's consideration that the Employee did or did not violate the policies and/or procedures established by the Employer for the position held by the Employee;
> (2) There was a reasonable basis for the Board of Review's consideration that the Employee did or did not substantially comply with the policies and/or procedures regarding discipline;
> (3) The Employee was given a description of the offense or conduct that was the basis for the Disciplinary Action and both parties were afforded

---

[66] *See* 8 M.P.T.L. ch.1 §§ 1-13 available at http://www.mptnlaw.com/TribalLaws.htm (last visited Nov. 25, 2021)

[67] *Id.* ch.1, § 1(b).

[68] *Id.*

[69] *Id.* ch.1, § 3(b).

a reasonable opportunity to present and refute evidence regarding the offense or conduct and/or evidence of aggravating or mitigating circumstances relating thereto;

(4) There was a reasonable basis for the Board of Review's decision as to whether the form of discipline was or was not appropriate for the offense of conduct; and

(5) The Board of Review's decision is in violation of tribal law or exceeds the Board's authority under tribal law.[70]

There is no right to a jury trial, and "damages awarded by the tribal court shall be limited to actual damages consisting of ascertainable loss of salary or wages, and/or benefits sustained as a result of a Disciplinary Action."[71] The court may also enter an order reinstating the employee.[72] No other legal or equitable remedies are allowed."[73] The reviewing court must "issue a written reasoned decision supported by references to the record," and either party has the right to appeal to the Mashantucket Pequot Court of Appeals.[74]

While the Employee Review Code states that "[a]n action pursuant to this Law shall be the Employee's exclusive cause of action against the Employer provided that the Employee has first exhausted all administrative remedies," it is clear that employees subject to a collective bargaining agreement may choose a Board of Review or arbitration under tribal law, and it is further clear that employees may choose to bring their claims under the Mashantucket Pequot Civil Rights

---

[70]*Id.* 8 M.P.T.L. ch.1, § 8(f).

[71]*Id.* ch.1, § 9(c).

[72]*Id.*

[73]*Id.* ch.1, § 9(d).

[74]8 M.P.T.L. ch.1, §§ 10(c), 12.

Code for such things as free speech or equal protection violations.[75] Indeed, the Employee Review Code expressly provides that procedural due process claims must be presented solely through the process afforded by the Employee Review Code, but that "other violations of rights enumerated in 20 M.P.T.L., [the] Civil Rights Code . . . shall be pursued under 20 M.P.T.L." against the Tribe.[76]

While the right to due process of law is found in the Mashantucket Pequot Civil Rights Code, the remedy for addressing alleged violations of that civil right in the employment setting is exclusively through the review process provided by the Employee Review Code, and not under the Civil Rights Code. The Employee Review Code states, in pertinent part:

> d. As part of the appeal of the Final Decision, either party may seek review of a violation(s) of procedural due process rights, as that term is defined herein, with respect to the conduct of the Board of Review proceeding; provided the party intending to seek review of a violation of procedural due process rights alleges such a claim(s) in the notice of appeal by stating the following information: (1) date of Disciplinary Action; (2) date of the Board of Review; (3) date of Decision of Board of Review; (4) each and every specific procedural error which the party claims constitutes a violation of procedural due process rights, specifying the date on which such act occurred and who committed such act; and (5) the alleged impact of such violation on the appealing party . . . .
>
> f. As to both parties under this Title, "procedural due process rights" shall mean the parties' rights at

---

[75]*Compare* 8 M.P.T.L. ch.1, § 2(c) (stating that this law provides the exclusive remedy for employee actions against employers) *with* 8 M.P.T.L. § 3(e) (providing for employee suits under 20 M.P.T.L. for other enumerated civil rights violations).

[76]8 M.P.T.L. ch.1, § 3(e).

the Board of Review to a meaningful opportunity to be heard including an opportunity to present witnesses and to question witnesses. Further both parties are entitled to representation by counsel, if desired, retained at their own.[77]

It may make sense to separate the procedural routes for resolving civil rights claims grounded in due process from other claims, like discrimination on the basis of sex, race, or ancestry, grounded in the equal protection clause, for the former typically are remedied through equitable orders, like reinstatement until a proper process is given. The latter may serve as the basis for damages.

As in the case of Navajo law, nothing in the law of the Mashantucket Pequot expressly prohibits (or provides a remedy for) employment discrimination on the basis of disability, sexual orientation, or other classifications protected under the law of other jurisdictions. If the courts of the Mashantucket Pequot construe the Equal Protection Clause of the Tribe's Civil Rights Code in the same manner as federal courts construe the Equal Protection Clause of the Bill of Rights, then

---

[77] 8 M.P.T.L. ch.1, §§ 3(d), (f). This provision is tantamount to establishing that employees of the Mashantucket Pequot Tribal Nation and its gaming enterprise have a "property interest" in their employment and cannot, therefore, be terminated without just cause. *See Johnson v. Mashantucket Pequot Gaming Enter.*, MPCA-EA-97-120, ¶ 21; 27 Indian L. Rptr. 6243 (Mashantucket Pequot Tribal Ct. Apr. 13, 1999), available at http://www.tribal-institute.org/opinions/1999.NAMP.0000013.htm (last visited Nov. 25, 2021); *see also Johnson v. Mashantucket Pequot Gaming Enter.*, MPTC-EA-95-136, ¶ 42; 1 § 115 (Mashantucket Pequot Tribal Ct., Dec. 11, 1995), available at http://tribal-institute.org/opinions/1996.NAMP.0000002.htm (last visited Nov. 25, 2021) (arguing that the precursor to the Employee Review Code, the Mashantucket Pequot Employment Appeal Ordinance, "created and defined an individual entitlement to continued employment that is significant enough to be considered a property right to which [ICRA's] due process protection attaches"); *Johnson v. Mashantucket Pequot Gaming Enter.*, No. MPCA-96-1008, ¶ 76; 1 § 15, (Mashantucket Pequot Tribal Ct., June 11, 1996), available at http://www.tribal-institute.org/opinions/1996.NAMP.0000002.htm (last visited Nov. 25, 2021) (finding that this early ordinance was "replete with indicia of a property interest entitlement to employment").

it will afford strict protection only against employment discrimination on the basis of sex, race, religion, color, and national origin.[78]

3. Mohegan Tribe

a. Protections for Mohegan Government Employees Under ICRA

Courts of the Mohegan Tribe have held that employees may bring actions against the Tribe and its gaming authority "to vindicate rights created by the ICRA."[79] Thus, the protections afforded by the ICRA's equal protection and due process clauses as well as the ICRA protections of free speech and privacy rights (freedom from unreasonable searches and seizures) provide at least injunctive relief to the employees of the Tribe and its gaming authority in ways that are similar to protections afforded to employees of state or federal governments under the analogous provisions of the Bill of Rights.[80]

b. Mohegan Discriminatory Employment Practices Ordinance

The Mohegan Tribe has enacted broad legislation to prohibit most forms of employment discrimination and to provide damages and other remedies in the Mohegan Tribal Court to employees who suffer such discrimination. The Mohegan Discriminatory Employment Practices Ordinance (MDEPO) declares:

---

[78]*But see* Ann E. Tweedy, *Sex Discrimination Under Tribal Law*, 36 WM. MITCHELL L. REV. 392, 407-08 (2010) (it is hard to say whether tribal courts will follow the "federal model of differing levels of scrutiny for different types of classifications").

[79]*Bethel v. Mohegan Tribal Gaming Auth.*, 1 G.D.R. 32 ¶¶ 57-59 (1998)) available at http://www.tribal-institute.org/opinions/1998.NAMG.0000005.htm (last visited Nov. 26, 2021), *rev'd on other grounds*, *Bethel v. Mohegan Tribal Gaming Auth.*, 1 G.D.A.P. (2000).

[80]*See Fountain v. Mohegan Tribal Gaming Authority*, 12 Am. Tribal Law 225 (June 7, 2012) (only injunctive relief available for ICRA claims against the Mohegan Tribe of Connecticut and arms of the Tribe because the Tribe has not waive sovereign immunity from suit for damages).

(a) It shall be an unlawful employment practice for an employer to discriminate, with respect to hiring, discharging, compensation, benefits, demotion, disciplining, suspending, barring, or layoff, on account of an Applicant's or Employee's:

(1) Race, gender, color, national origin, pregnancy or related medical condition, age, ancestry, marital status, sexual orientation, military status or genetic information;

(2) Religion, provided that the religious practice may be reasonably accommodated, when a reasonable accommodation is possible;

(3) Mental or physical disability when reasonable accommodation is available;

(4) Exercise of rights under this Article, the Mohegan Tribal Workers' Compensation Ordinance, the Mohegan Fair Labor Standards Ordinance, the Mohegan Family Medical Leave Ordinance, the Mohegan Labor Relations Ordinance, and the Mohegan Employment Retirement Income Security Ordinance;

(5) Good faith participation in reporting an Employer's violation of a Mohegan Tribal law or regulation to a Mohegan Tribal governmental or regulatory agency; or

(6) Participation, when requested by a Mohegan Tribal governmental or regulatory agency, in an investigation or hearing held by such agency.[81]

The law applies to employment within the "Mohegan Tribe and its governmental entities, authorities, agencies, and instrumentalities including, but not limited to, the Mohegan Tribal Gaming Authority and other tribal commissions, and authorities operating on the Mohe-

---

[81] The Mohegan Tribal Code, Discriminatory Employment Practices Ordinance, § 4-24 available at http://www.municode.com/library/clientCodePage.aspx?clientID=12815 (last visited Nov. 27, 2021).

gan Reservation."[82] It does not trump "any Mohegan Tribal law . . . regarding preferences in employment, including, but not limited to recruiting, hiring, training, and promotions for members of the Mohegan Tribe or other Native Americans."[83] The procedures afforded by the MDEPO create no property interest in employment; the law provides that "[n]othing in this Article is intended to establish a property right in an employee's continued employment."[84]

The MDEPO waives the sovereign immunity of the Tribe and its commissions and agencies, including the Mohegan Tribal Gaming Authority for actions in the Mohegan Court.[85] The statute of limitations is short: any complaint must be commenced within ninety days "after the Applicant or Employee first knew or, through the exercise of reasonable diligence should have known, of the occurrence or event out of which such complaint arises. A complaint that is not timely filed shall be dismissed and no other remedy shall be available."[86]

---

[82]*Id.* § 4-23.

[83]*Id.* § 4-25(a)(3). The definitions section also constrains the scope of protection for age and disability discrimination:

Age means at least forty (40) years of age.

Disability means a mental or physical impairment of which the Employer is aware that substantially impairs one (1) or more of the major life activities of an Applicant or Employee, but shall not include:

(1) Disorders resulting from current illegal use of drugs; or

(2) Compulsive gambling, kleptomania, or pyromania; or

(3) Abuse of alcohol at any time in or upon the employee's workplace or the abuse of alcohol that affects the employee's job conduct or performance; or

(4) Transvestism, transsexualism, pedophilia, exhibitionism, voyeurism, gender identity disorders, or other sexual behavior disorder.

Id. § 4-23.

[84]*Id.* § 4-27(c).

[85]*Id.* § 4-28.

[86]*Id.* §§ 4-27(b), 4-28(a) (sovereign immunity waiver only operates if the 90-day time deadline is met).

The remedies available to prevailing plaintiffs are strictly limited:

> [T]he Court may order the following remedies only:
> (i) One (1) year of lost wages, subject to reduction by any amounts earned or received as unemployment compensation by the Employee in the one-year period following loss or denial of employment;
> (ii) Attorney's fees that shall not exceed one-third (1/3) of the lost wage award; and/or
> (iii) Reinstatement or instatement of the Applicant or Employee, either into the position that is the subject of the litigation or into a comparable position for which the Applicant or Employee is qualified and that is reasonably equivalent in status and compensation as determined by the Court.
>
> . . .
>
> The remedies specifically enumerated within this Section shall be the sole and exclusive remedies for a violation of this Article.[87]

In *Bethel v. Mohegan Tribal Gaming Authority*,[88] an African American employee of the Mohegan Tribal Gaming Authority was transferred to a lower paying job. He brought an action claiming race discrimination and violation of due process under ICRA and the MDEPO. The trial court held that his MDEPO race discrimination claim was barred for failure to comply with the filing deadline and that he could not show a property interest in employment giving rise to due process protection under ICRA.[89] On appeal, the appellate court affirmed the dismissal of the MDEPO race discrimination claim be-

---

[87] *Id.* § 4-27(e).

[88] 1 G.D.R. 32 (1998) available at http://www.tribal-institute.org/opinions/1998.NAMG.0000005.htm (last visited Nov. 26, 2021); *aff'd in part, Bethel v. Mohegan Tribal Gaming Auth.*, 1 G.D.A.P. (2000) available at http://www.tribal-institute.org/opinions/2000.NAMG.0000005.htm (last visited Nov. 26, 2021).

[89] *See Bethel*, ¶¶ 69, 74.

cause it was untimely, but remanded the case on the ICRA due process claim because the plaintiff had been denied a process for redress.[90] It is possible that the plaintiff in *Bethel* could have brought his claim for race discrimination by invoking the equal protection clause of the ICRA, separate and apart from the remedy available under the MDEPO. Such potential claims under ICRA are discussed on the following page.

4. Little River Band of Ottawa Indians

a. Protections for Tribal Government Employees Under the Constitution of the Little River Band of Ottawa Indians

The Constitution of the Little River Band of Ottawa Indians authorizes the Tribal Court to entertain actions against "[t]he Little River Band, its Tribal Council members, Tribal Ogema, and other Tribal officials, acting in their official capacities . . . for declaratory or injunctive relief . . . for the purpose of enforcing rights and duties established by th[e] Constitution and by the ordinances and resolutions of the Tribe."[91] By its plain language, this provision empowers the Tribal Court to order prospective declaratory or injunctive relief to force tribal officers to comply with tribal law, but not a retroactive remedy to individuals who may claim to have suffered a wrong. Employees of the Little River Band of Ottawa Indians have invoked this provision to seek relief from the court for alleged violations of freedom of speech.[92]

---

[90] *See Bethel*, ¶ 72 (citing *Bd. of Regents of State Colls. v. Roth*, 408 U.S. 564, 569-70 (1972)).

[91] Little River Band of Ottawa Indians Constitution, art. XI, § 2(a), available at: https://lrboi-nsn.gov/wp-content/uploads/2019/02/Constitution-2016-Amendments.pdf (last visited Nov. 26, 2021).

[92] *See LaPorte v. Fletcher*, No. 04142AP (Little River Band of Ottawa Indians Tribal Ct. App., Apr. 26, 2005) (available from the Office of the Clerk, Little River Band of Ottawa Indians Tribal Court).

b. Fair Employment Practices Code of the Little River Band of Ottawa Indians

The Fair Employment Practice Code of the Little River Band of Ottawa Indians comprehensively governs all forms of employment discrimination within the jurisdiction of the Band, including discrimination on the basis of race, color, sex (including pregnancy discrimination and sexual harassment), disability, and sexual orientation.[93] The law applies to "any type of organization, including tribal or foreign corporations and partnerships; the Band; any political subdivision, agency, or department of the Band; and any tribally chartered enterprise of the Band doing business on lands within the jurisdiction of the Band and employing any number of employees."[94] It does not, however, trump the provision of tribal or other Native American employment preferences under the law of the Band or under federal law.[95]

While the law provides that actions may be commenced within two years of an event giving rise to a claim, plaintiffs are barred from recovering compensatory or punitive damages or attorney's fees if they do not first file a charge of discrimination with the Band's tribal court and exhaust an administrative procedure designed to encourage early resolution or settlement of claims.[96] Upon the filing of such charge, the tribal court appoints a Fair Employment Practices Investigator (FEPI), a local lawyer with experience in employment law, to investigate the charge and prepare a written report to decide if there is reasonable cause to believe that a violation of the Band's Fair Employment Practices Code has occurred.[97] The law provides, in pertinent part:

---

[93] *See* Little River Band of Ottawa Indians, Fair Employment Practices Code Ordinance No: 05-600-03, § 4.01 available at: https://lrboi-nsn.gov/wp-content/uploads/2015/10/Title-03.pdf (last visited Nov. 26, 2021).

[94] *See id.* § 3.08.

[95] *See. id.* § 5.01.

[96] *See id.* §§ 6.01-6.08.

[97] *See id.* at §§ 6.01-6.03.

(d) If the Report finds reasonable cause to believe that discrimination in violation of this Ordinance has occurred, the FEPI shall convene a meeting of the employer (through a representative with authority to negotiate a settlement if one can be reached) and the complainant within 21 days after mailing the Report and attempt to reach a conciliation agreement. Any such conciliation agreement may include any of the remedies provided by this Article. . . .

. . .

(f) If, within 60 days of the mailing of the Report, the parties fail to enter into a conciliation agreement signed by the complainant and the employer or otherwise resolve the dispute, the FEPI shall issue a "right to sue" letter to the complainant.[98]

This procedure is similar to that used by the EEOC in administering employment discrimination charges brought under Title VII and the ADA.[99]

Tribal court remedies for prevailing plaintiffs against employers may include:

(a)...
1. An order to cease and desist from the unlawful practices specified in the order;
2. An order to employ or reinstate a victim of unlawful employment discrimination, with or without back pay or reasonable front pay if reinstatement is unfeasible;
(b) . . . compensatory damages . . . for future pecuniary losses, emotional pain, suffering, inconvenience, mental anguish, loss of enjoyment of life, and other nonpecuniary losses, provided,

---

[98]*See id*. §§ 6.03(d), (f).

[99]*See* 29 C.F.R. § 1601.1 (2020) (EEOC procedural regulations).

> however, that such compensatory damages shall not include back pay, interest on back pay or any other type of relief authorized elsewhere under this subsection . . . . [and] punitive damages . . . if the complaining party demonstrates that the employer engaged in a discriminatory practice or discriminatory practices with malice or with reckless indifference to the rights of an aggrieved individual protected by this Code.
>
> . . . The total sum of compensatory and punitive damages may not exceed $10,000 for employers with less than 50 employees, $25,000 for employers with between 50 and 99 employees, and $50,000 for employers with 100 or more employees.
>
> . . . [T]he court, in its discretion, may allow the prevailing party reasonable attorneys' fees and costs.[100]

However, plaintiffs may not recover compensatory or punitive damages or attorney's fees if they do not first exhaust the administrative process by filing a charge of discrimination and proceeding through the investigation process.[101]

---

[100] *Id.* §§ 6.05(a)(1)-(2) (b)(1)-(4); 6.07. Damages are limited in the context of disability discrimination: "[w]hen a discriminatory practice involves the provision of a reasonable accommodation, damages may not be awarded when the employer demonstrates good faith efforts, in consultation with the person with the disability who has informed the employer that accommodation is needed, to identify and make a reasonable accommodation that would provide that individual with an equally effective opportunity and would not cause an undue hardship on the operation of the business." *Id.* § 6.05(b)(3).

[101] *See id.* § 6.08.

5. Squaxin Island Tribe

In 2015, the Squaxin Island Tribe enacted a comprehensive Labor and Employment Code.[102] Chapter 12.02 of that code, addressing employment discrimination states, in pertinent part:

> [I]t shall be unlawful employment discrimination, in violation of this code:
>
> A. For any employer to fail or refuse to hire or otherwise discriminate against any applicant for employment because of sex, pregnancy, race, color, national origin, religion, age, sexual orientation, uniformed service, disability, or union affiliation, or because of those reasons, to discharge an employee or discriminate with respect to hire, tenure, promotion, transfer, compensation, terms, conditions or privileges of employment, or any other matter directly or indirectly related to employment; or, in recruiting of individuals for employment or in hiring them, to utilize any employment agency that the employer knows or has reasonable cause to know discriminates against individuals because of their sex, pregnancy, race, color, national origin, religion, age, sexual orientation, uniformed service, disability, or union affiliation; or
>
> B. For an employer to discriminate in any manner against employees because they have opposed a practice that would be a violation of this code or because they have made a charge, testified or assisted in any investigation, proceeding or hearing under this code.[103]

---

[102] Squaxin Island Tribe Labor and Employment Code, Chapters 12.03-12.07 (available at: https://library.municode.com/tribes_and_tribal_nations/squaxin_island_tribe/codes/code_of_ordinances (last visited Nov. 26, 2021).

[103] *Id.* §12.02.010.

The inclusion of protection against discrimination on the bases of uniformed service and union affiliation is broader than most tribal employment discrimination laws. As in every known tribal employment discrimination law, employers may give preference to tribal members and members of other federally recognized Indian tribes without violating the law.[104]

Employees who claim to have suffered employment discrimination under this law may seek remedies by filing a complaint with the clerk of the Squaxin Island Tribal Court no later that 180 days from the alleged violation.[105] Within 30 days of that filing, the claimant and human resources director of the employer at issue must meet and attempt to achieve an early resolution of the claim by mediation.[106] If mediation fails, the case proceeds to a hearing before a committee made up of the human resources directors of other enterprises of the Tribe and its tribal government (but not that of the employing entity of the claimant).[107] The committee may subpoena witnesses and documents and, within ten days after the close of the hearing, issues findings of facts and conclusions of law on whether employment discrimination in violation of the code has occurred.[108] If a violation is found, the committee is required to order "an appropriate remedy," which may include the following:

1. An order to cease and desist from the unlawful practice(s) specified in the order;

2. Where an employee has been wrongfully separated from employment or not properly reinstated to an employment position:

    a. An order to employ or reinstate the employee,

---

[104] *See id.*

[105] *Id.* § 12.07.010(A).

[106] *Id.* § 12.07.020.

[107] *Id.* § 12.07.030(A).

[108] *Id.* § 12.07.040.

       b. An order to restore the employee's back pay and benefits,

       c. In a case where reinstatement would be an appropriate remedy, but it is not feasible, an order of a reasonable amount for front pay; . . .

3. In the case of unlawful disability discrimination, an order to provide reasonable accommodations for an employee's disability; and

4. In a case where the committee is convinced, by a preponderance of evidence, that, as a result of an employer's violation of this code, an employee has suffered emotional or physical pain or injury, the committee may also award damages to the employee not to exceed twenty-five thousand dollars ($25,000.00).[109]

Either party may appeal the committee's decision to the Squaxin Island Tribal Court within 30 days of the committee's decision.

Other tribes have enacted streamlined employment discrimination laws similar to those of the Squaxin Island Tribe with some variations on the protected classifications, enforcement procedures, and remedies.[110]

---

[109] *Id.* § 12.07.040 (D).

[110] *See, e.g.,* Klamath Tribal Code, Title 6, §§ 41.01-41.09; 41.31-41.36 (available at: https://klamathtribalcourts.com/tribal-laws/) (last visited Nov. 26, 2021) (claimant must exhaust grievance procedures with tribal employer before filing complaint; if dispute not resolved, any claim must be filed in the tribal court within 90 days; if claimant prevails, tribal court may issue cease and desist order and/or require reinstatement and back pay (or front pay in lieu of reinstatement); compensatory damages limited to $5,000; and the tribal court "lacks jurisdiction" to provide other remedies); Suquamish Tribal Code, Chapters 18.1.1–18.1.10; 18.4.1-18.4.10 (available at: https://suquamish.nsn.us/home/government/suquamish-tribal-code/) (last visited Nov. 26, 2021) (similar grievance exhaustion requirement; if dispute not resolved, any claim must be filed before an Administrative Law Judge (ALJ) appointed by the Tribal Council within 45 days; the ALJ holds a hearing and if the claimant prevails, may issue cease and desist order, reinstatement and backpay (or front pay in lieu of reinstatement); ALJ "lacks jurisdiction" to order compensatory or punitive damages; ALJ decisions may be appealed to the Suquamish Tribal Court within 10 days of the ALJ's decision).

6. California Tribes with Employment Laws Required by Compact

California-based tribes have entered into compacts with the State of California pursuant to the Indian Gaming Regulatory Act that contain a requirement that each tribe enact an "employment discrimination complaint ordinance" or "Anti-Discrimination and Harassment Policy and Procedures" to provide enforceable remedies for employment discrimination in its gaming facility.[111] The boilerplate language in the compacts provides that the tribe shall:

> Adopt and comply with tribal law that is no less stringent than federal and state laws forbidding harassment, including sexual harassment, in the workplace, forbidding employers from discrimination in connection with the employment of persons to work or working for the Gaming Operation or in the Gaming Facility on the basis of race, color, religion, ancestry, national origin, gender, marital status, medical condition, sexual orientation, age, or disability, gender identity, genetic information, military or veteran status and any other protected groups, [provided that] ... [n]othing herein shall preclude the Tribe from giving a preference in employment to members and

---

[111] *See, e.g., Tribal-State Compact Between the State of California and Table Mountain Rancheria,* § 12.3(f), available at: https://www.gov.ca.gov/wp-content/uploads/2021/08/Table-Mountain-Rancheria-Compact-August-2021.pdf (last visited Nov. 25, 2021): *Tribal-State Compact Between the State of California and the Cahto Tribe of the Laytonville Rancheria,* § 12.3(f), available at: https://www.gov.ca.gov/wp-content/uploads/2021/08/Cahto-Tribe-Compact-August-2021.pdf (last visited Nov. 26, 2021). *See generally Governor Newsom Signs Tribal Compacts,* Office of the Governor, available at: https://www.gov.ca.gov/2021/08/24/governor-newsom-signs-tribal-compacts-august-2021 (last visited Nov. 25, 2021); *Ratified Gaming Compacts,* Office of the Governor, http://www.cgcc.ca.gov/?pageID=compacts (last visited Nov. 26, 2021).

descendants of federally recognized Indian tribes pursuant to a duly adopted tribal ordinance.[112]

The compacts further require the tribe to obtain and keep in effect insurance coverage for damages of up to several millions of dollars for such claims and to waive sovereign immunity from suit up to the coverage limits.[113] Failure on the part of the tribe to enact the required ordinance constitutes a compact violation, giving the state the right sue the tribe in federal court to enforce it.[114] The tribal codes for California tribes complying with this compact provision are not easily found on their official websites.[115]

* * *

As the foregoing discussion makes clear, tribes addressing workplace civil rights issues take a wide variety of approaches. Every tribe is different and will enact laws best suited to its customs and values.

Section C turns to selected substantive issues arising in the provision of remedies for workplace employment discrimination, which a number of tribal courts are beginning to confront. These issues are prevalent when any government provides rights and remedies to guard

---

[112] *See, e.g., Tribal-State Compact Between the State of California and Table Mountain Rancheria*, § 12.3(f); *Tribal-State Compact Between the State of California and the Cahto Tribe of the Laytonville Rancheria*, § 12.3(f), available at: https://www.gov.ca.gov/wp-content/uploads/2021/08/Table-Mountain-Rancheria-Compact-August-2021.pdf (last visited Nov. 25, 2021).

[113] *See Tribal-State Compact Between the State of California and Table Mountain Rancheria*, § 12.3(f)(2)-(3), available at: https://www.gov.ca.gov/wp-content/uploads/2021/08/Table-Mountain-Rancheria-Compact-August-2021.pdf (last visited Nov. 25, 2021).

[114] *Id.* § 12.3(f)(5).

[115] *See, e.g.,* https://www.pechanga-nsn.gov/ (last visited Nov. 26, 2021); https://sanmanuel-nsn.gov/tribal-government/tribal-court (last visited Nov. 26, 21); https://www.aguacaliente.org/tribal-council (last visited Nov. 26, 2021). In 2004, the Pauma-Yuima Band of Mission Indians enacted an Employment Discrimination Regulation to satisfy a similar compact requirement at the time. *See* Pauma Band of Mission Indians Gaming Regulation, Employment Discrimination, Ordinance No. 008 (2006) available at: http://www.narf.org/nill/Codes/paumacode/gaming_reg_008_employment_discrimination.pdf (last visited Nov. 26, 2021).

civil rights in employment. As more tribes develop law in this area, their decisions will add to the jurisprudence of tribal employment law.

C. Civil Rights in the Employment Setting: Selected Substantive Issues

1. Sovereign Immunity Issues and the Scope of Governmental Action Under Tribal Civil Rights Codes

While tribes may adopt constitutional or statutory provisions (including ICRA) that guarantee individuals certain rights *vis-à-vis* the powers of tribal government (i.e., equal protection, due process, freedom of speech, rights to be free from unreasonable searches and seizures), absent an express waiver, sovereign immunity will stand as a barrier to the ability of employees to invoke such provisions to gain relief in tribal courts or other tribal forums.[116] If a tribal court or other

---

[116] Notwithstanding the Supreme Court's statement in *Santa Clara Pueblo v. Martinez* that Congress's enactment of ICRA had "the substantial and intended effect of changing the law which [tribal] forums are obliged to apply," 436 U.S. 49, 65 (1978), some tribal courts have refused to enforce ICRA without a clear waiver of sovereign immunity by the tribal government. *See, e.g., Dawson v. Springer*, No. C02-001, ¶ 11, 13 (Coquille Tr. Ct. June 26, 2003) (dismissing plaintiff's claim because the Tribe has not authorized the court to provide remedies for violations of the ICRA); *Schock v. Mashantucket Pequot Gaming Enter.*, No. MPTC-CV-98-127, ¶ 57; 3 Mashantucket Rptr. 129; 27 Indian L. Rptr. 6225 (Mashantucket Pequot Tribal Ct. Sept. 20, 1999) (stating that "several tribal courts have held that ICRA does not effectuate a general waiver of a tribe's sovereign immunity and that a waiver of tribal sovereign immunity cannot be implied but must be unequivocally expressed") available at: http://www.tribal-institute.org/opinions/1999.NAMP.0000023.htm (last visited Nov. 26, 2021); *Raymond v. Navajo Agric. Prod. Indus.*, No. SC-CV-26-94, ¶¶ 20-21; 7 Nav. R. 142 (Nav. Sup. Ct. 1995) (finding that the ICRA does not explicitly waive the tribe's sovereign immunity) available at: http://www.tribal-institute.org/opinions/1995.NANN.0000013.htm (last visited Nov. 26, 2021); *Johnson v. Navajo Nation*, No. A-CV-16-85, ¶ 42; 14 Indian L. Rptr. 6037, 6040; 5 Nav. R. 192 (Nav. Sup. Ct. 1987) (holding that since ICRA did not waive the tribe's sovereign immunity from suit, the plaintiff's claim is barred by defendant-tribe's sovereign immunity) available at: http://www.tribal- institute.org/opinions/1987.NANN.0000011.htm (last visited Nov. 26, 2021). Others have had no trouble finding that ICRA waives tribal sovereign immunity for enforcement in tribal court. *See, e.g., Oglala Sioux Tribal Personnel Bd. v. Red Shirt*, No. 83-143, 16 Indian L. Rptr. 6052, 6053 (Oglala Siox Tr. Ct. App. Oct. 20, 1983); *Dupree v. Cheyenne River Hous. Auth.*, 16 Indian L. Rptr. 6106, 6108-09 (Cheyenne River Sioux Tr. App. Ct. Aug. 19, 1988); *see generally* Frank Pommersheim,

forum, entertaining a claim under ICRA or a similar tribal law, follows the Supreme Court's conclusion in *Santa Clara Pueblo v. Martinez* — that sovereign immunity does *not* bar actions against tribal officials for prospective relief [117] — then employees who suffer wrongful termination may be able to attain the remedy of reinstatement.[118] The al-

---

Tribal Court Jurisprudence: A Snapshot from the Field, 21 VT. L. REV. 7, 22-23 & n.44 (1996) (collecting cases). One commentator states that "[m]ost Tribal Courts do not find that ICRA waives a Tribe's immunity." Mathew Fletcher, *Tribal Employment Separation: Tribal Law Enigma, Tribal Governance Paradox, and Tribal Court Conundrum*, 38 U. MICH. J.L. REFORM 273, 321-23 & n.202 (2005).

[117] *See Martinez*, 436 U.S. 49, 59 (1978). *See also Garcia v. Akwesasne Hous. Auth.*, 268 F.3d 76, 87-88 (2d Cir. 2001) (recognizing that employee may proceed with civil rights claims against tribal officers).

[118] Under federal constitutional law, reinstatement is considered prospective relief and may be awarded against a state officer under the *Ex Parte Young* doctrine. *See Whalen v. Mass. Trial Court*, 397 F.3d 19, 29 (1st Cir. 2005) (reasoning that reinstatement is prospective relief because it "serves directly to bring an end to a present violation of federal law"); *State Emp. Bargaining Agent Coal. v. Rowland*, 494 F.3d 71, 96 (2d Cir. 2007) (holding that claims for reinstatement satisfy the *Ex Parte Young* doctrine); *Koslow v. Commonwealth of Pa.*, 302 F.3d 161, 179 (3d Cir. 2002) (finding that reinstatement relief is "the type of injunctive, 'forward-looking' relief cognizable under *Ex Parte Young*"); *Coakley v. Welch*, 877 F.2d 304, 307 n.2 (4th Cir. 1989) (discussing reappointment or reinstatement as a form of prospective relief to remedy "ongoing" violations of federal law); *Warnock v. Pecos Cnty.*, 88 F.3d 341, 343 (5th Cir. 1996) ("Plaintiff's claim for prospective relief (reinstatement), however, is not barred by sovereign immunity"); *Carten v. Kent State Univ.*, 282 F.3d 391, 396 (6th Cir. 2002) ("claims for reinstatement are prospective"); *Elliott v. Hinds*, 786 F.2d 298, 302 (7th Cir. 1986) (arguing that the requested relief of reinstatement is prospective and thus unaffected by a sovereign immunity defense); *Murphy v. State of Ark.*, 127 F.3d 750, 754 (8th Cir. 1997); *Doe v. Lawrence Livermore Nat'l Lab.*, 131 F.3d 836, 840-42 (9th Cir. 1997); *Meiners v. Univ. of Kan.*, 359 F.3d 1222, 1232-33 (10th Cir. 2004); *Lassiter v. Ala. A & M Univ.*, 3 F.3d 1482, 1485 (11th Cir. 1993); *Dronenburg v. Zech*, 741 F.2d 1388, 1390 (D.C. Cir. 1984) (noting that claim by military officer against federal government seeking reinstatement was not barred by federal sovereign immunity). *See also State Emp. Bargaining Agent Coal. v. Rowland*, 494 F.3d 71, 97 (2d Cir. 2007) (the "prospective" remedy of reinstatement of an employee who has suffered a constitutional violation may be ordered against a state official under the *Ex Parte Young* doctrine even if the position has been eliminated).

lowance of back pay, however, would likely turn on the scope of any waiver of sovereign immunity.[119]

A somewhat complicated feature of federal civil rights claims, which may affect similar claims against tribal government officials, is the distinction between official capacity suits and individual capacity suits. As discussed in Chapter 4, lawsuits against tribal officials to prevent violations of federal or tribal law proceed under the *Ex Parte Young* doctrine, without the constraints of sovereign immunity.[120] In addition, a lawsuit for damages against tribal employees or officials in their individual capacity may proceed without the constraints of sovereign immunity because the tribe is not the "real party in interest,"[121] but such an individual may invoke "qualified immunity." Under federal law, qualified immunity provides a barrier to liability for such officials "if, at the time they acted, the statutory or constitutional right allegedly violated was not 'clearly established.'"[122] The Supreme Court has said, "[t]he contours of the right must be sufficiently clear that a reasonable official would understand that what he or she did violated that right."[123]

Similar principles may influence tribal law. For instance, in *Navajo Nation v. Crockett*, discussed in Section A, the Navajo Supreme Court made note of the fact that the qualified immunity of Navajo of-

---

[119]Under federal law, a back pay award to an employee who is reinstated after being subjected to wrongful discrimination is a remedy against the government (not against a government official), implicating sovereign immunity. *See Negron-Almeda v. Santiago*, 528 F.3d 15, 26 (1st Cir. 2008) ("It is settled law in the federal courts that back pay as such cannot be awarded against a defendant in his or her individual capacity").

[120]As one court explains:
> *[Ex Parte] Young* treats public officials who violate federal law as renegades, acting *ultra vires*, who therefore may be enjoined without enjoining the state itself. But a suit against a public official as representative of the state (rather than as a renegade) is a suit against the state.

David B. v. McDonald, 156 F.3d 780, 783 (7th Cir. 1998).

[121]*See Lewis v. Clarke,* 137 S. Ct. 1285 (2017).

[122]*Brown v. City of Fort Lauderdale*, 923 F.2d 1474, 1478-79 (11th Cir. 1991).

[123]*Id.* at 1478.

ficials is codified at 1 N.N.C. § 354(f)(4)(B).[124] The Court then described that immunity by reference to federal law standards:

> Individual Navajo Nation officials are entitled to qualified immunity if their conduct does not violate clearly established statutory or constitutional rights of which a reasonable person would have known. *Harlow v. Fitzgerald*, 457 U.S. 813, 818 (1982). For our purposes, constitutional rights are those enumerated in our Bill of Rights.[125]

The court had no occasion to discuss the doctrine further because it concluded that qualified immunity is an affirmative defense, and, in the case before it, that defense had been waived.[126]

Apart from sovereign immunity, issues may arise regarding the scope of the application of tribal constitutional provisions, civil rights codes, or ICRA to particular tribal employers. The Navajo and Mashantucket Pequot civil rights codes constrain the tribes themselves. ICRA, on the other hand, more broadly constrains the "exercis[e of] powers of self-government."[127] Lack of clarity about what acts may or may not be covered by these laws could generate litigation in tribal courts or other tribal forums if not resolved by legislation. For example, one federal court has held that a tribal corporation, chartered under tribal law to operate a tribe's gaming operations under IGRA, does not exercise "powers of self-government" for the purpose of ICRA.[128] Decisions of other courts regarding the nature of tribal gaming under

---

[124] No. SC-CV-14-94, ¶ 35; 7 Nav. R. 237 (Nav. Sup. Ct. 1996) available at: http://www.tribal-institute.org/opinions/1996.NANN.0000006.htm (last visited Nov. 26, 2021).

[125] *Id.* at ¶ 35 (quotations omitted).

[126] *See id.* For further discussion of qualified immunity, *see generally* Matthew L.M. Fletcher, *Tribal Employment Separation: Tribal Law Enigma, Tribal Governance Paradox, and Tribal Court Conundrum*, 38 MICH. J. L. REFORM 273, 324-25 (2005).

[127] *See* 25 U.S.C. § 1302 (2018).

[128] *See Barker v. Menominee Nation Casino*, 897 F. Supp. 389, 395 (E.D. Wis. 1995).

IGRA raise questions about the validity of that conclusion.[129] At least one tribal court has applied ICRA to its tribal gaming operations.[130]

2. Due Process and Government Employment

Tribal civil rights codes and constitutions, like ICRA,[131] likely will contain a "due process clause" similar to that of the Fourteenth Amendment to the United States Constitution,[132] which provides that the government shall not deprive persons of their property without due process of law.[133] In the employment setting, this translates into a rule that, if a governmental employee can show a "property interest" in continued employment, then the governmental employer cannot terminate the employee without providing due process of law.[134]

---

[129] *See Cook v. AVI Casino Enter. Inc.*, 548 F.3d 718, 726 (9th Cir. 2008) (tribal corporation engaged in IGRA gaming is an arm of the tribe and enjoys sovereign immunity of tribe); *Allen v. Gold Country Casino*, 464 F.3d 1044, 1046 (9th Cir. 2006) (tribal gaming facility under IGRA is "not a mere revenue-producing tribal business," but operates, pursuant to IGRA, to directly serve tribal self-governance). An appropriate legal analogy might be found in the body of law that distinguishes state entities that enjoy Eleventh Amendment immunity from those that do not. *See Quern v. Jordan*, 440 U.S. 332, 337 (1979); *Ford Motor Co. v. Dep't of Treasury*, 323 U.S. 459, 464 (1945); *Dugan v. Rank*, 372 U.S. 609, 620-26 (1963); *Metcalf & Eddy Inc. v. Puerto Rico Aqueduct & Sewer Auth.*, 991 F.2d 935, 939 (1st Cir. 1993).

[130] *See Palencia v. Pojoaque Gaming Inc.*, 28 Indian L. Rptr. 6149 (Pueblo of Pojoaque Tribal Ct. 2001).

[131] *See*, 25 U.S.C. §1302(8) (2018).

[132] *See, e.g.*, Navajo Nation, 1 N.N.C. § 3; Mashantucket Pequot, 20 MPTL § 1(8);

[133] *See*, U.S. Const. amend. XIV, § 1. The standards governing the operation of the Due Process Clause of the Fourteenth Amendment *vis-à-vis* state government employment are likewise the same as those operating with respect to the federal government under the Fifth Amendment. *See Bolling v. Sharpe*, 347 U.S. 497 (1954).

[134] *See, e.g., Johnson v. Mashantucket Pequot Gaming Enter.*, No. MPCA-96-1008, 1 MPR 15, ¶ 87; 25 Indian L. Rptr. 6011 (Mashantucket Pequot Tribal Ct. App., June 11, 1996) (holding that an employee of the Mashantucket Pequot Gaming Enterprise has "property interest" in employment); *Hoopa Valley Indian Hous. Auth. v. Gerstner*, No. C-92-035, 3 NICS App. 250, 259; 22 Indian L. Rptr. 6002 (Hoopa Valley Tribal Ct. App., Sept. 27, 1993) (continued employment with the Tribe and its entities "is an important property interest to which due process rights attach"); *Regan v. Finkbonner*,

So-called at-will employees, who have no contract for a given term and who may be discharged with or without cause, generally do not have a property interest in continued employment.[135] Numerous tribes, however, provide that their employees may not be terminated without just cause.[136] When government employees cannot be discharged without just cause, they typically can argue that, under a constitutional or statutory due process clause, they have a protected property interest in their employment and, therefore, are entitled to due process before losing their jobs.[137]

No. NOO-Ci-6/89-0155, 1 NICS App. 82, 84; 21 Indian L. Rptr. 6026 (Nook. Tribal Ct. App., Feb. 15, 1990) (when a tribal employee appeals a termination decision, employer must afford due process in accordance with ICRA).

[135] *See Bd. of Regents v. Roth*, 408 U.S. 564, 578 (1972).

[136] According to one observer, employees of tribal government administrations typically can only be discharged for "just cause," whereas employees of tribe's subordinate economic enterprises typically are "at will." *See generally* Matthew L.M. Fletcher, *Tribal Employment Separation: Tribal Law Enigma, Tribal Governance Paradox, and Tribal Court Conundrum*, 38 MICH. J. L. REFORM 273, 287-288 (2005).

[137] *See Johnson v. Mashantucket Pequot Gaming Enter.*, No. MPCA-96-1008, ¶¶ 68-77; 1 Mash. App. 21; 1 Mashantucket Pequot Rptr. 15; 25 Indian L. Rptr. 6011 (Mashantucket Pequot Tribal Ct. App., June 11, 1996); *Hoopa Valley Indian Hous. Auth. v. Gerstner*, No. C-92-035, 3 NICS App. 250, 259; 22 Indian L. Rptr. 6002 (Hoopa Valley Tribal Ct. App., Sept. 27, 1993); *Bethel v. Mohegan Tribal Gaming Auth.*, No. GDTC-T-98-105, ¶¶ 66, 74; 1 G.D.R. 32 (Mohegan Gaming Disputes Trial Ct., Dec. 14, 1998) available at: http://www.tribal-institute.org/opinions/1998.NAMG. 0000005.htm *rev'd on other grounds*, *Bethel v. Mohegan Tribal Gaming Auth.*, No. GDCA-T-98-500; 1 G.D.A.P. (Mohegan Gaming Disputes Trial Ct. June 15, 2000) available at: http://www.tribal-institute.org/opinions/2000.NAMG.0000005.htm. (last visited Nov. 26, 2021). Under federal constitutional law, the formulation for a government employee's property interest in employment can be generally stated as a legitimate expectation of continued employment under a contract with, or the rules of, a governmental employer, *see, e.g., Cleveland Bd. of Educ. v. Loudermill*, 470 U.S. 532, 538 (1985); *Board of Regents of State colleges v. Roth*, 408 U.S. 564, 577 (1972). *See also Bethel v. Mohegan Tribal Gaming Auth.*, No. GDTC-T-98-105, ¶ 66; 1 G.D.R. 32 (Mohegan Gaming Disputes Trial Ct., Dec. 14, 1998) (tracking federal law standards for "property interest"), *rev'd on other grounds*, *Bethel v. Mohegan Tribal Gaming Auth.*, No. GDCA-T-98-500; 1. G.D.A.P. (Mohegan Gaming Disputes Trial Ct., June 15, 2000).

If a public employee establishes such a property interest in continued employment, due process generally requires the employer to give the employee notice and an opportunity to be fairly heard before the government discharges the employee.[138] This is often referred to as a "pre-deprivation" hearing.[139] It need not be extensive — "something less" than a full evidentiary hearing is required — but to satisfy due process, at least under federal constitutional standards, there should be a further, more extensive post-termination procedure afforded to the employee.[140]

In the view of one scholar of Indian law, Professor Matthew Fletcher, tribes are overly "inundated" with due process claims by employees.[141] Professor Fletcher observes:

> Personnel issues are day-to-day questions that should not occupy the time of tribal leaders who should be prioritizing important questions of tribal governance .... Regardless of the composition of the panel, conflicts of interest arise frequently. Employees, especially if they are Tribal Members or if they have married into the community, will be related in interconnecting ways to many individuals in the community. These individuals will invariably find themselves appointed or elected to an employee review panel. Tribal decision-makers must deal

---

[138] *See, e.g., Cleveland Bd. of Educ. v. Loudermill*, 470 U.S. at 542; *Mullane v. Central Hanover Bank & Trust Co.*, 339 U.S. 306, 313 (1950); *Adams v. Sewell*, 946 F.2d 757, 765-66 (11th Cir. 1991); *Brewer v. Chauvin*, 938 F.2d 860, 862-63 (8th Cir. 1991).

[139] *Cleveland Bd. of Educ. v. Loudermill*, 470 U.S. at 549.

[140] *Id.* at 542. Under the federal due process clause, post-termination hearings may suffice if, within a reasonable time after the adverse job action, employees have the opportunity to present their case to impartial decision makers, including the opportunity to cross-examine adverse witnesses. *See, e.g., D.H. Overmayer Co. v. Rick Co.*, 405 U.S. 174, 185 (1972).

[141] Matthew L. M. Fletcher, *Tribal Employment Separation: Tribal Law Enigma, Tribal Governance Paradox, and Tribal Court Conundrum*, 38 MICH. J. L. REFORM 273, 293 (2005).

with questions as to how distant the relation must be before the panel member may participate.[142]

If the process is not devised carefully, Fletcher warns that hearings may "become painful marathons of emotional, political, and sociological torment."[143] Even more serious, Professor Fletcher questions whether, as a structural matter, tribal governments can respond at all to the due process requirements of tribal government employees who have property interests in their employment:

> In many ways, Tribal government exists to help Tribal Members when they have been wronged. But when the Tribal government is accused of wrongdoing by one of its employees, the legal structure created to ensure due process and to provide a remedy collides with the political structure created to serve the whole of Tribal membership. [When a tribal member complains to the Tribal Council,] the Tribal Council . . . may choose to intervene on behalf of the employee against the interest of the Tribe, even against the interests of the oath they swore to protect the Tribe. . . . [T]he Tribal Council as a political body collides with the Tribal Council as employer. *Without question, personnel questions have the capacity to destroy or seriously undermine Tribal governments.*[144]

To avoid these traps, or for cultural reasons, tribal lawmakers may wish to consider a variety of alternative forums for resolving due process (and even other) public employee claims, including creating a special court for employee claims or a peacemaker-style dispute resolution process.[145] Federal constitutional due process protections, in other

---

[142] *Id.* at 307-08.

[143] *Id.* at 311.

[144] *Id.* at 314-15 (emphasis added).

[145] *Id.* at 335-43.

words, may not necessarily be consistent with the structure of tribal governments or tribal cultural values for resolving disputes.

3. Freedom of Speech and Governmental Employment

Tribal civil rights codes or constitutions, like ICRA,[146] typically provide that the government shall not abridge or interfere with freedom of speech.[147] In the employment setting, this translates into a rule that if governmental employees speak out on a matter of public concern and are discharged for doing so, they may have a claim, at least for reinstatement, because the termination wrongly interfered with the employee's right to freedom of speech.[148]

In *Crockett*, the Supreme Court of the Navajo Nation considered whether employees of the Navajo Agricultural Products Industry (NAPI) engaged in "protected speech" giving rise to a civil rights remedy when they reported to the Navajo Council concerns about mismanagement at NAPI and subsequently lost their jobs. In language worthy of quotation at length, the court eloquently described the Navajo values at issue:

> [S]peech should be delivered with respect and honesty. This requirement arises from the concept of k e', which is the "glue" that creates and binds relationships between people. To avoid disruptions of relationships, Navajo common law mandates that controversies and arguments be resolved by "talking

---

[146] 25 U.S.C. § 1302(1) (2018).

[147] *See, e.g.*, Navajo Nation, 1 N.T.C. § 4; Mashantucket Pequot, 20 MPTL § 1(a)(1); 25 U.S.C. §1302(1).

[148] *See, e.g., Navajo Nation v. Crockett*, No. No. SC-CV-14-94, ¶¶ 38-51; 7 Nav. R. 237, 240-42; 24 Indian L. Rptr. 6027 (Nav. Sup. Ct. 1996) available at: http://www.tribal-institute.org/opinions/1996.NANN.0000006.htm (last visited Nov. 26, 2021); *Barnes v. Mashantucket Pequot Tribal Nation*, No. CV-GC-2006-153; 34 Indian L. Rptr. 6072 (Mashantucket Pequot Tribal Ct., June 11, 2007) available at: http://www.tribal-institute.org/opinions/2007.NAMP.0000010.htm (last visited Nov. 26, 2021) (addressing claim of retaliation for exercise of freedom of speech; applying federal law standards).

things out." This process of "talking things out," call hoozhoojigo, allows each member of the group to cooperate and talk about how to resolve a problem. This requirement places another limitation on speech, which is that a disgruntled person must speak directly with the person's relative about his or her concerns before seeking other avenues of redress with strangers.

In the employment context, relationships are established according to personnel policies, and other instruments. When an employee has a complaint about a supervisor, according to Navajo custom and tradition, he or she should first approach the supervisor and discuss the problem in a respectful manner. Moreover, under the Navajo common law concept of nalyeeh, the employee should not seek to correct the person by summoning the coercive powers of a powerful person or entity, but should seek to correct the wrongful action by "talking things out." . . .

In situations where the complaint alleges employer mismanagement, distinct from internal personnel matters, an employee is entitled to consult others vested with the authority to hear such complaints, such as the organization's own committee, or an oversight of the Navajo Nation Council . . . .

When discussing management concerns with the appropriate oversight committee, an employee must follow certain limitations. The employee must be respectful in his or her approach, and an initial inquiry with management to "talk things out" is encouraged. Second, the speech must involve matters of public concern and fall within the oversight authority of the committee. When an employee gives a statement before an official government committee, he or she speaks in a context that is inherently public in nature . . . .

An employee must comply with these limitations when alleging that he or she was terminated or otherwise mistreated as a result of his or her speech . . . . [T]he employee must [also] show [that] his or her speech was a significant factor or motivation in the adverse employment action.[149]

The court held that that the employees' speech deserved protection, for it involved matters "of public concern."[150] It further held that "NAPI's interest to not disclose demoralizing or disruptive information [was] not an adequate interest to outweigh an individual's right to free speech."[151] Thus, it affirmed the "decision of the district court that the employees' speech was protected."[152]

---

[149] *Navajo Nation v. Crockett*, No. No. SC-CV-14-94, ¶¶ 42-47; 7 Nav. R. 237, 241-42; 24 Indian L. Rptr. 6027 (Nav. Sup. Ct. 1996) available at: http://www.tribal-institute.org/opinions/1996.NANN.0000006.htm (last visited Nov. 26, 2021).

[150] *Id.* at ¶ 51; 7 Nav. R. at 241-42.

[151] *Id.* at ¶ 50; 7 Nav. R. at 242.

[152] *Id.* at ¶ 51; 7 Nav. R. at 241-42. The principles laid down by the Navajo Supreme Court in *Crockett* are not dissimilar to those applied by the United States Supreme Court and federal courts of appeals under federal constitutional principles. See, *e.g.*, *Garcetti v. Ceballos*, 547 U.S. 410, 421 (2006); *Connick v. Myers*, 461 U.S. 138, 146-47 (1983); *Urofsky v. Gilmore*, 216 F.3d 401, 408 (4th Cir. 2000) (en banc); *Koch v. City of Hutchinson*, 847 F.2d 1436, 1445-46 & n.17 (9th Cir. 1988); *Cox v. Dardanelle Pub. Sch. Dist.*, 790 F.2d 668, 672 (8th Cir. 1986); *Knapp v. Whitaker*, 757 F.2d 827, 840 (7th Cir. 1985), *cert. denied,* 474 U.S. 803 (1985); *Marohnic v. Walker*, 800 F.2d 613 (6th Cir. 1986); *Wren v. Spurlock*, 798 F.2d 1313 (10th Cir. 1986), *cert. denied,* 479 U.S. 1085 (1987); *Brasslett v. Cota*, 761 F.2d 827 (1st Cir. 1985); *Czurlanis v. Albanese*, 721 F.2d 98 (3d Cir. 1983). *See also Alaska v. EEOC*, 564 F.3d 1062, 1071-87 (9th Cir. 2009) (O'Scannlain, J., concurring in part and dissenting in part) (discussing examples for line drawing).

In *Barnes v. Mashantucket Pequot Tribal Nation*,[153] the Mashantucket Pequot Tribal Court similarly considered the standards governing public employees' free speech. A former employee of the Mashantucket Pequot Gaming Enterprise (the Enterprise) claimed that he was terminated for exercising his freedom of speech in the context of his requests for review of the Enterprise's decision.[154]

The court looked to federal constitutional law to derive the rule for its decision:

> To prevail on a First Amendment retaliation claim, an employee must establish: "[1] that the speech at issue was protected, [2] that he suffered an adverse employment action, and [3] that there was a causal connection between the protected speech and the adverse employment action." *Blum v. Schlegel*, 18 F.3d 1005, 1010 (2d Cir. 1994). The causal connection must be sufficient to support the inference "that the speech played a substantial part in the employer's adverse employment action." *Ezekwo v. NYC Health & Hosps. Corp.*, 940 F.2d 775, 780-81 (2d Cir. 1991). If a plaintiff establishes these three elements, a defendant may avoid liability by showing "by preponderance of the evidence that it would have reached the same decision as to [the employment action] even in the absence of the protected conduct." *Mount Healthy City Sch. Dist. Bd. of Educ. v. Doyle*, 429 U.S. 274, 287 (1977).[155]

---

[153]No. CV-GC-2006-153; 34 Indian L. Rptr. 6072 (Mashantucket Pequot Tribal Ct., June 11, 2007) available at: http://www.tribal-institute.org/opinions/2007.NAMP.0000010.htm (last visited Nov. 26, 2021).

[154]*Id.* at ¶¶ 11-12.

[155]*Id.* at ¶ 24.

The court had no need to apply these elements, however, because it concluded that Barnes failed to show that his termination was retaliatory.[156]

Given the trend of tribal courts to derive freedom of speech standards for government employees that are similar to those derived from the First Amendment, the vast body of federal constitutional law may at least provide some guidance as tribal law develops.

4. Burden of Proof Issues in Discrimination Cases

Whether a tribe allows employee discrimination claims to proceed against governmental employers by means of an equal protection clause in a constitution or civil rights code, or by means of separate law, proof of causation may present gnarly issues.[157] Most garden-variety employment discrimination claims turn on whether an employee has suffered adverse employment action because of a protected trait (or classification), such as sex, race, color, disability, or age. Thus far, there has been surprisingly little discussion in tribal court decisions about how such discrimination is to be proven.

Barnes v. Mashantucket Pequot Tribal Nation[158] appears to be the first tribal court opinion to address the issue. In that case, an African American invoked the Mashantucket Pequot's Civil Rights Code, claiming not only that his termination violated his free speech rights, but that it also involved gender and race discrimination in violation of

---

[156]*Id.* at ¶¶ 23-25.

[157]It should be noted that, to the extent that a tribe has a tribal employment preference law on the books, the provision of such preferences to tribal members should not constitute a violation of ICRA. *See* Chapter 10 regarding the special status of tribal employment preferences in the law of employment discrimination. Tribes are therefore likely to exclude from any definition of discrimination an employer's differing treatment of Indians from non-Indians (or tribal members from non-tribal members) under a tribal employment preference law or policy. *See, e.g.*, Little River Band of Ottawa Indians, Fair Employment Practices Code ch. 600, tit. 3, § 3.05, available at: https://lrboi-nsn.gov/wp-content/uploads/2015/10/Title-03.pdf (last visited Nov. 26, 2021).

[158]No. CV-GC-2006-153; 34 Indian L. Rptr. 6072 (Mashantucket Pequot Tribal Ct. June 11, 2007) available at: http://www.tribal-institute.org/opinions/2007.NAMP.0000010.htm (last visited Nov. 26, 2021).

that code's equal protection clause. The Mashantucket Pequot Tribal Court derived the burden of proof standard for the latter claim from Supreme Court precedent:

> The United States Supreme Court formulated the standard of review in equal protection cases in *McDonnell Douglas Corp. v. Green*, 411 U.S. 792 (1973). The plaintiff bears the initial burden of "proving by a preponderance of the evidence a prima facie case of discrimination.' *Tex. Dep't of Cmty. Affairs v. Burdine*, 450 U.S. 248, 252-53 (1981). In order to state a prima facie case of discrimination, a plaintiff must demonstrate that (1) he is a member of a protected class; (2) his job performance was satisfactory; (3) he was subjected to an adverse employment action; and (4) the adverse employment action occurred under circumstances giving rise to an inference of discrimination. *McDonnell Douglas*, 411 U.S. at 802. Once a prima facie case is established, the burden shifts to the defendant to rebut the presumption of discrimination by providing a legitimate, non-discriminatory reason for the employment decision. *Burdine*, 450 U.S. at 253-54. If the defendant articulates a legitimate, non-discriminatory reason, the *McDonnell Douglas* framework—and its presumptions and burdens—drops out of the picture. *Reeves v. Sanderson Plumbing Prods., Inc.*, 530 U.S. 133, 142-43 (2000). The plaintiff then must establish that the defendant's articulated reason is a pretext for discrimination.[159]

The *Barnes* court, however, had no occasion to move past the first step in this framework because it found that the plaintiff failed, in the first instance, to establish "a prima facie case of discrimination."[160]

---

[159]*Id.* No. CV-GC-2006-153 at ¶ 28.

[160]*Id.* at ¶ 33.

Again, while any given tribe's law will reflect its unique values and culture, the body of federal employment discrimination law may provide one reference point as tribes develop this area of the law. In *Barnes*, the court simply restated the federal law standards, but had no occasion to apply them in any detail. More elaborate explanation of these standards may prove useful for tribal law practitioners, whether they advocate tracking them or avoiding them.

Under federal law, apart from "hostile work environment" cases, in which employees claim that they have suffered abuse at work, such as offensive jokes, ridicule, or verbal or physical harassment because of a protected trait,[161] most garden-variety employment discrimination cases involve so-called "disparate treatment" in which employees claim that they have suffered an adverse employment decision because of a protected trait (i.e., sex, race, or color) compared to other employees.[162] These cases proceed on one of two tracks (sometimes both): (a) under the so-called "pretext" framework as described in *Barnes*, which leaves the ultimate burden on the employee to prove that the reason given by the employer is a pretext for discrimination[163] or (b) under what has become known as the "mixed motive" framework, in which the burden shifts to the employer to show that it would have taken an employment action regardless of discrimination once an employee shows that discrimination played a role in the adverse employment action.

---

[161] As briefly noted above, so-called hostile work environment cases, including those involving sexual harassment, are a variant of employment discrimination under federal law. *See supra* note 52. *But see* Ann E. Tweedy, *Sex Discrimination Under Tribal Law*, 36 WM. L. REV. 392, 428 (2010) ("[S]ome tribes, contrary to the traditional federal view, consider sexual harassment to be an act perpetrated by one individual against another, rather than an employment rights issue. Such tribes may treat harassment, implicitly or explicitly including sexual harassment, as a civil infraction, a misdemeanor, or even a tort.")

[162] *See Barnes*, No. CV-GC-2006-153 at ¶ 28 (Mashantucket Pequot Tribal Ct., June 11, 2007) available at: http://www.tribal-institute.org/opinions/2007.NAMP.0000010.htm (last visited Nov. 26, 2021) (describing the plaintiff's claim as one involving "disparate treatment").

[163] *Id.* at 28.

As summarized in *Barnes*, under the Supreme Court's formulation in *McDonnell Douglas Corp. v. Green*,[164] employees lacking direct evidence of discriminatory motive, but resting their case on treatment that is different from others, invariably face an explanation from an employer that is nondiscriminatory (*e.g.*, poor performance). Thus, to meet the ultimate burden of proving intentional employment discrimination, such employees must prove that the employer's explanation is false: a pretext, or cover, for discrimination.[165]

The "mixed motive" framework emerged from the Supreme Court's splintered decision in *Price Waterhouse v. Hopkins*,[166] but Congress later clarified it with amendments to Title VII and the ADA to adjust the burdens of proof and remedies.[167] Under this framework, once an employee demonstrates that race, color, religion, sex, or national origin "was a motivating factor" for an adverse employment action (even if other factors played a role), the employer may be subject to a declaratory judgment that it engaged in wrongful discrimination, an injunction prohibiting it from any further discrimination, and payment of the employee's attorney's fees.[168] The employer can prevent the employee from recovering monetary damages only by showing that "it would have taken the same action in the absence of the im-

---

[164] 411 U.S. 792 (1973).

[165] Pursuant to federal law, whether a claim of disparate treatment employment discrimination on the basis of sex, race, color, national origin, or religion proceeds against a government employer under 42 U.S.C. § 1983 and the Equal Protection Clause, or against a private employer under Title VII, the standard for establishing employer liability is the same. *See Salguero v. City of Clovis*, 366 F.3d 1168, 1175 (10th Cir. 2004); *see also Patterson v. County of Oneida*, 375 F.3d 206, 225 (2d Cir. 2004) (discussing similarities and differences between claims brought under Title VII and claims brought under § 1983).

[166] 490 U.S. 228 (1989).

[167] *See Desert Palace, Inc., v. Costa*, 539 U.S. 90 (2003). *See also* Kaighn Smith, Jr., *How Do We Work This? Making Sense of the Liability Standards in Disparate Treatment Employment Discrimination Cases*, 14 MAINE BAR JOURNAL 34 (Jan. 1999) (discussing standards before and after Congress's amendments).

[168] *Desert Palace, Inc., v. Costa*, 539 U.S. at 94-95 (quoting and discussing Congress's amendment to Title VII, 42 U.S.C. § 2000e-2(m)) (citations and quotations omitted).

permissible motivating factor."[169] The differing approaches of the pretext and mixed motive frameworks for establishing an employer's liability for discrimination can be summarized as follows:

Pretext

(a) Employee shows that they were treated differently from others.
(b) Employer gives a reason for the different treatment.
(c) Employee must show that the employer's reason is a pretext for discrimination.

Mixed Motive[170]

(a) Employee shows that a protected trait (*e.g.*, race, color, sex, national origin) was a motivating factor in the adverse employment action. (Employee is entitled to declaratory and injunctive relief and attorney's fees.)
(b) To escape liability for damages, employer must show that it would have taken the same action in the absence of the impermissible motivating factor.

The extent to which these federal law standards influence the operation of tribes' employment discrimination laws remains to be seen. Insofar as individual tribes see fit to enact such laws, they will surely adjust the burdens of proof and remedies consistent with their unique values and culture.

D. Conclusion

Employees within the governmental operations of Indian tribes may well enjoy protections against discrimination on the basis of sex (including sexual harassment), race, national origin, or color by virtue of an equal protection provision of a tribal constitution or through the same provision of the ICRA. Tribes may more explicitly protect

---

[169]*Id.* at 95 (quoting 42 U.S.C. § 2000e-2(m)) (citations and quotations omitted).

[170]This list accounts for Congress's amendment to Title VII, which was intended to clarify the standards and remedies for "mixed motive"cases. *See Desert Palace, Inc.* 539 U.S. at 94.

against such forms of discrimination and provide concrete remedies, as well as protections against other forms of discrimination, such as age, disability, or sexual orientation, by enacting laws to deal specifically with these issues.

Other forms of civil rights, like freedom of speech and due process of law, may also be protected, depending upon the laws and constitutional provisions adopted by a particular tribe or the common law developed by its tribal court.

By expressly recognizing protections against employment discrimination under tribal constitutional or civil rights laws or putting specific employment discrimination laws in place, tribes can give workers a better sense that they will be treated fairly. At the same time, the provision of such remedies under tribal law may prevent those employees from seeking the assistance of federal authorities to impose external legal authority in the tribal setting.

9

DEVELOPING TRIBAL LAW: UNIONS AND COLLECTIVE BARGAINING

A. Introduction

Someday, the Supreme Court will decide whether a federal labor or employment law that is silent about its application to Indian tribes can be applied to them, or whether silence is insufficient and Congress must clearly state its intention if the law is to apply to tribes. The Supreme Court is more likely to take a case when the lower federal circuit courts of appeals are split on an issue. Such a split has emerged when it comes to the application of the National Labor Relations Act (NLRA), which governs unions and collective bargaining.

When Congress excludes states from the coverage of a labor or employment law, as it did in the Occupational Safety and Health Act (OSHA), or treats them differently than private sector employers, as it did in the Fair Labor Standards Act (FLSA), but forgets to address Indian tribes, the case for treating tribes in the same manner as states is forceful because tribes, like states, are sovereign governments.[1] These issues are playing out in cases presenting the question of whether the NLRA — which, like OSHA, excludes states (as well as the federal government) from its coverage but fails to address Indian tribes — applies to Indian tribes. With the emerging split between the federal circuit courts of appeals on the question, tribes under the jurisdiction of those circuit courts protective of tribal sovereignty (or those that have yet to decide the question) can develop a better case to win in the Su-

---

[1] This was the rationale of the National Labor Relations Board for decades when it refused to apply the NLRA to Indian tribes or their reservation enterprises. *See* Chapter 7, Section C. It also undergirds the logic of the U.S. Court of Appeals for the Seventh Circuit in excluding tribal game wardens from coverage of the FLSA. *See Reich v. Great Lakes Indian Fish & Wildlife Comm'n,* 4 F.3d 490, 495 (7th Cir. 1993).

241

preme Court if they enact their own laws to govern unions and collective bargaining. Just as important, they can seek to govern unions and collective bargaining within their public sectors, matters that can have profound effects not only upon labor relations within a tribe's reservation enterprises, but upon the generation and distribution of a tribe's governmental funds.[2] These considerations drive the subject matter of this chapter.

* * *

The 2007 decision of the United States Court of Appeals for the D.C. Circuit in *San Manuel Indian Bingo & Casino v. NLRB*[3] affirmed the National Labor Relations Board's (NLRB) asserted authority to impose the NLRA upon the IGRA gaming operations of an Indian tribe.[4] It did not, however, address whether Indian tribes possess the power to govern unions and collective bargaining within their reservation enterprises, including within their IGRA gaming operations. Nor did it consider what would happen if the application of the NLRA undermined a duly enacted tribal labor law governing such matters.

The 2002 decision of the United States Court of Appeals for the Tenth Circuit in *NLRB v. Pueblo of San Juan*,[5] addressed the latter issue. It held that the right-to-work law of the Pueblo of San Juan (Ohkay Owingeh) exemplified the exercise of inherent sovereign authority and that authority could not be abrogated absent a clear statement of intent by Congress, an intent nowhere found in the NLRA.[6]

---

[2]As discussed in Chapter 7 and further below, the NLRA guarantees the right to strike. Strikes are often prohibited, or substantially curtailed, in the public sector because they can paralyze governments and affect the distribution of limited governmental resources. Tribes are governments and the revenues they generate from their reservation enterprises are essential for providing governmental services to their members. This is one reason why the imposition of the NLRA upon the public sectors of Indian tribes fundamentally thwarts tribal self-determination.

[3]475 F.3d 1306 (D.C. Cir. 2007). For a full discussion of the case, *see* Chapter 7.

[4]*Id.* at 1306.

[5]276 F.3d 1186 (10th Cir. 2002) (en banc). For a full discussion of the case, *see* Chapter 7.

[6]*See id.* at 1194-1200.

In 2015, a divided three-judge panel of the U.S. Court of Appeals for the Sixth Circuit in *NLRB v. Little River Band of Ottawa Indians Tribal Government*[7] upheld a NLRB decision that the Band's labor laws that vary from the NLRA (including a law prohibiting strikes), as applied to the Band's IGRA gaming operations, constituted the unfair labor practices of an "employer" covered by the NLRA. The two-judge majority adopted the Ninth Circuit's *Coeur d'Alene Tribal Farm* framework for determining when "silent" federal laws apply to Indian tribes.[8] The dissenting judge said the case was controlled by *Pueblo of San Juan*: (1) the Band's enactment and implementation of a law governing unions and collective bargaining with its employees within its reservation exemplified the exercise of inherent sovereign authority; (2) that authority cannot be undermined without a clear statement of intent by Congress; (3) Congress failed to provide such a clear statement in the NLRA; and (4) so the tribal law must stand.[9]

Later in 2015, in *Soaring Eagle Casino & Resort v. N.L.R.B.*,[10] a separate three-judge panel of the Sixth Circuit addressed whether a tribe's IGRA gaming operation was an NLRA "employer," subject to an unfair labor practice by the NLRB for restricting union solicitation in a manner that violated the NLRA.[11] The unanimous three-judge panel in that case said that it disagreed with the two judges that issued the majority decision in *Little River Band* and agreed with the judge who dissented, but said that it was compelled by the rule of precedent to follow the majority decision and hold against the Tribe.[12]

Finally, in 2018, in *Pauma v. National Labor Relations Board*,[13] a case with facts similar to *Soaring Eagle Casino,* the U.S. Court of Ap-

---

[7] 788 F.3d 537 (6th Cir. 2015). For a full discussion of the case, *see* Chapter 7.

[8] The *Coeur d'Alene Tribal Farm* framework is discussed in Chapter 3, Section C.

[9] *Id.* at 561-65 (McKeague, J., dissenting).

[10] 791 F.3d 648 (6th Cir. 2015). For a full discussion of the case, *see* Chapter 7.

[11] *See id.* at 653-54.

[12] *See Soaring Eagle Casino & Resort,* 791 F.3d at 661-74.

[13] 888 F.3d 1066, 1071 (9th Cir. 2018). For a full discussion of the case, *see* Chapter 7.

peals for the Ninth Circuit held that a tribe's IGRA gaming operation was an NLRA "employer" subject to an unfair labor practice charge by the NLRB for restricting union solicitation in violation of the NLRA. That three-judge panel refused to overturn the Ninth Circuit's *Coeur d'Alene Tribal Farm* framework.

So there are conflicting rules. On the one hand, the approach of the Tenth Circuit in *Pueblo of San Juan,* requiring a clear statement by Congress in order to interfere with tribal sovereignty, and, on the other hand, the approach of a deeply divided Sixth Circuit and the Ninth Circuit, applying the *Coeur d'Alene Tribal Farm* framework.[14] It is hard to know how the Supreme Court will ultimately resolve this split. In the meantime, as stated at the outset of Part III, there is no reason for Indian tribes to hold back on exercising their inherent sovereign authority to govern reservation labor relations, at least in those parts of the country under the jurisdiction of federal courts adopting the Tenth Circuit's clear statement rule or where the issue is undecided. In fact, enacting such laws could make for a better case when the issue goes to the Supreme Court. This is because the Court has forced Congress to be clear if an abrogation of tribal sovereignty is at stake,[15] and definitions of "employer" that fail to mention Indian tribes, like that in the NLRA, are far from clear.[16]

---

[14] Ironically, four judges in the Sixth Circuit, the dissenting judge in *Little River Band* and the three judges that decided *Soaring Eagle Casino*, are of the view that Indian tribes are *not* "employers" covered by the NLRA, while only two judges, those who wrote the majority decision in *Little River Band*, are of the opposite view. However, the latter's opinion prevails because the *Little River Band* case was decided before *Soaring Eagle Casino.*

[15] *See Iowa Mut. Ins. Co. v. LaPlante,* 480 U.S. 9, 18 (1987); *Santa Clara Pueblo v. Martinez,* 436 U.S. 49, 72 (1978). *See also Michigan v. Bay Mills Indian Cmty.,* 572 U.S. 782, 790 (2014) ("an enduring principle of Indian law" is that "courts will not lightly assume that Congress in fact intends to undermine Indian self-government"; Congress must "unequivocally express" such a purpose); *McGirt v. Oklahoma,* 140 S. Ct. 2452, 2477 (2020) ("this Court has long 'require[d] a clear expression of the intention of Congress' before allowing the tribal sovereignty to be undermined by the application of state or federal law) (citing and quoting *Ex parte Crow Dog,* 109 U.S. 556, 572 (1883)).

[16] The actual abrogation of tribal law should not be necessary to trigger the protections that the Supreme Court has afforded tribal sovereignty; for the mere imposition

Unless the Ninth and Sixth Circuits overrule their adoption of the *Coeur d'Alene Tribal Farm* framework, or the Supreme Court rejects that framework in the meantime, Indian tribes in those circuits (as well as those in the Second and Seventh Circuits, which follow *Coeur d'Alene Tribal Farm*) will have a hard time prevailing if the NLRB challenges their labor laws that vary from the NLRA as applied to their IGRA gaming operations.[17] Similar constraints could confront tribes taking appeals from adverse NLRB decisions to the D.C. Circuit.[18] That does not mean, however, that tribes within the jurisdictions of these federal courts would be precluded from applying their labor laws varying from the NLRA to their other public sector employers, departments and other instrumentalities of tribal government.

---

of a state or federal law upon an Indian tribe, without more, intrudes upon its sovereign prerogatives. *See Merrion v. Jicarilla Apache Tribe,* 455 U.S. 130, 148 (1982) ("even when unexercised, [a tribe's sovereign authority over activities within its lands] is an enduring presence , . . . and will remain intact unless surrendered in unmistakable terms"). *See also Scalia v. Red Lake Nation Fisheries, Inc.,* 982 F.3d 533, 535 (8th Cir. 2020) (holding the tribe's fishery enterprise not "employer" under OSHA even though application of OSHA would not undermine a tribal law). But the actual displacement of an operational tribal law presents a particularly poignant case for protecting tribal sovereignty.

[17] The U.S. Court of Appeals for the Sixth Circuit has jurisdiction over federal appeals arising in Michigan, Ohio, Tennessee, and Kentucky; the Ninth Circuit has jurisdiction over appeals arising in Alaska, Washington, Oregon, California, Arizona, Montana, Nevada, Hawaii, and Guam; the Seventh Circuit has jurisdiction over appeals arising in Illinois, Indiana, and Wisconsin; and the Second Circuit has jurisdiction over appeals arising in New York, Connecticut, and Vermont.

[18] The D.C. Circuit has jurisdiction over appeals of final decisions of federal agencies, like the NLRB, regardless of the location of the alleged violation of the federal law administered by the federal agency involved. Tribes faced with adverse decisions by the NLRB can appeal to the U.S. Court of Appeals for the D.C. Circuit or to the Circuit Court that has jurisdiction over the state within which the tribe is located. In *San Manuel Band,* the D.C. Circuit left open the possibility that if application of the NLRA to an Indian tribe's IGRA gaming operation would significantly undermine tribal sovereignty, the law might not apply. *San Manuel Indian Bingo & Casino v. N.L.R.B.,* 475 F.3d 1306, 1315 (D.C. Cir. 2007). Thus, it is possible that the D.C. Circuit would come out differently if faced with a case like *Little River Band,* where application of the NLRA to a tribe's IGRA gaming operation would displace a tribe's labor law enacted pursuant to its inherent sovereignty.

Tribes outside of the Ninth, Second, Sixth, and Seventh Circuits, particularly those in the Tenth Circuit, following the clear statement rule (as well as in the Eighth Circuit, which does the same) are more likely to prevail if such laws are challenged by the NLRB when applied to their IGRA gaming operations.[19] Further, as in the case of tribes in the Ninth, Second, Sixth and Seventh Circuits, there may be no impediments to the application of such tribal labor laws to other public sector employers.

This chapter looks at how tribes are governing labor relations and at some of the public policy issues involved. The legal framework for tribes to enact laws in this area is reviewed at the outset.

B. Tribal Governance of Labor Relations: Public and Private Sectors

Analytically, tribes may seek to govern labor relations within Indian country in two sectors: (a) employment within the operations and enterprises of tribal government (the public sector), and (b) employment within private enterprises doing business within Indian country (the private sector).[20] In enacting the NLRA, Congress intended to govern private sector labor relations, not those in the public sector (i.e., within the state and federal governments). Indeed, the Act excludes "the United States or any wholly owned Government corporation, or any Federal Reserve Bank, or any State or political subdivision thereof" from the definition of "employer" covered by the NLRA.[21] Again,

---

[19] The U.S. Court of Appeals for the Tenth Circuit has jurisdiction over appeals arising in Oklahoma, Kansas, New Mexico, Colorado, Wyoming, and Utah. The U.S. Court of Appeals for the Eighth Circuit has jurisdiction over appeals arising in Minnesota, North Dakota, South Dakota, Nebraska, Missouri, Iowa, and Arkansas.

[20] The economic enterprises owned and controlled by Indian tribes to generate governmental revenues, including their gaming facilities under IGRA, are not private sector enterprises; they are governmental operations and properly considered part of the public sector. RESTATEMENT OF THE LAW OF AMERICAN INDIANS (Tent. Draft No. 4, April 29, 2020) § 46, cmt. c ("[A]n Indian tribe's operation of a casino pursuant to its inherent authority codified by Congress in . . . [IGRA] . . . is a governmental undertaking for a governmental purpose: to generate revenues to support governmental services.").

[21] 29 U.S.C. § 152 (2) (2018).

Congress failed to address the application of the NLRA to Indian tribes or their enterprises.

As discussed in Chapter 2, tribes have authority to govern relations between themselves and their members, and this extends to labor and employment relations.[22] As also discussed in Chapter 2, under two lines of Supreme Court precedent, tribes also have authority to govern nonmembers who enter the jurisdictions of Indian tribes for economic gain.[23] This is the legal grounding for tribes to govern their labor and employment relations in Indian country. When the employment relationship is with the tribe itself or a tribal agency, commission, or wholly owned instrumentality of the tribe, it is a public sector labor relations setting virtually identical to the public sectors that states govern under state labor laws outside of the NLRA.[24]

Addressing an Indian tribe's authority over private sector labor relations within its jurisdiction, the Tenth Circuit has held that the tribe's regulatory authority exists when there is a relationship "between a member of the tribe and a nonmember individual or entity employing the member within the physical confines of the reservation."[25] The Supreme Court has suggested the same.[26] In *NLRB v. Pueblo of San Juan*, the Tenth Circuit upheld the authority of Ohkay Owingeh to enact and enforce a right-to-work law that prohibits a nonmember employer which employs both tribal members and nonmembers on the reservation from entering into an agreement with a union that would require employees to join the union or pay union dues.[27] The NLRA recognizes the authority of states to enact similar laws to govern the

---

[22]*See* Chapter 2, Section C.

[23]*See id.*

[24]*Compare Public Sector Unions* (cover story), The Economist, Jan. 8-14 (2011), at 9, 21.

[25]*MacArthur v. San Juan Cnty.*, 497 F.3d 1057, 1071-72 (10th Cir. 2007).

[26]*See Plains Commerce Bank v. Long Family Land & Cattle Co. Inc.*, 514 U.S. 316, 334-35 (2008) (referring to tribal regulatory authority over a "business enterprise employing tribal members").

[27]276 F.3d 1186 (10th Cir. 2002) (en banc).

private sector without NLRA preemption, but it is silent about whether tribes may do the same.[28] These cases suggest that tribes have the legal ground for asserting regulatory authority over the labor relations of private employers operating within their territorial jurisdictions.

Whether tribal law governing private sector collective bargaining within Indian country, apart from a right-to-work law, would survive a preemption challenge (that is, an assertion by the NLRB that there is no room for any law, other than the NLRA, to govern such matters) is an unanswered question. A short decision of the D.C. Circuit in 1961 held that the NLRB had jurisdiction over a mining company employing Indians and non-Indians on the Navajo Reservation.[29] Given the NLRA's preemptive force with regard to conflicting state laws, tribal collective bargaining laws seeking to govern private employers, other than right-to-work laws, would likely be preempted.[30]

What follows is an exploration of how Indian tribes have governed unions and collective bargaining before and after the *San Manuel* decision. Apart from the enactment of right-to-work laws, discussed at the outset, the focus is on the public sector.

C. Tribal Laws Governing Unions and Collective Bargaining Before *San Manuel*

Tribal lawmaking in the area of labor relations and collective bargaining before the *San Manuel* decision was mostly limited to the enactment of right-to-work laws and, for tribes in California, a model Tribal Labor Relations Ordinance required by their IGRA gaming compacts with the State. Each is addressed in turn.

---

[28] *See* 29 U.S.C. § 164(b) (2018).

[29] *See Navajo Tribe v. NLRB*, 288 F.2d 162 (D.C. Cir. 1961), *cert. denied*, 366 U.S. 928 (1961). Navajo law now protects "the basic right of Navajo workers to organize, bargain collectively, strike, and peaceably picket to secure their legal rights," but it further provides that "the right to strike and picket does not apply to employees of the Navajo Nation, its agencies, or enterprises." 15 N.N.C. § 606.

[30] *See generally* Vicki J. Limas, *The* Tuscaror*ganization of the Tribal Workforce*, 2008 MICH. ST. L. REV. 467, 481 (2008).

1. Right-to-Work Laws

A typical right-to-work law, like the one sustained in the face of a preemption challenge by the NLRB in *Pueblo of San Juan*, prohibits employers and unions from entering into collective bargaining agreements that would require employees to join a union or pay any dues or other fees to a union as a condition of employment. These kinds of agreements are sometimes known as "union security agreements."

Such agreements give a union that has won an election to represent a bargaining unit of employees the security that it will have a uniform relationship with all members of the unit. This uniform relationship is accomplished either by ensuring that all employees within the unit become paying members of the union, or by requiring those who do not choose to become union members to at least contribute a "fair share" for the services that the union provides. The NLRA and state labor relations laws require a union that is elected to represent a bargaining unit of employees to serve all employees of the unit equally (whether or not they actually become dues-paying members). As such, "union security agreements" may seem reasonable, not only to the elected union, but also to the employer, who may want to ensure workplace equity.[31] On the other hand, a forceful argument can be made that no individual should be required to join a union or pay any amount as a condition of employment if such person did not vote for a union in the first place.[32] The Supreme Court has so held in reference to the public sector labor laws of states.[33]

States and tribes that have enacted right-to-work laws have, in effect, decided as a matter of public policy that the interests of the individual employee should prevail. Those states and tribes that have not enacted such laws, or that have laws making "fair share" a mandatory subject of bargaining have, in effect, decided to place weight on work-

---

[31]*See generally Janus v. Am. Fed'n of State, Cty, & Mun. Emps., Council 31,* 138 S. Ct. 2448, 2488-89 (2018) (Kagan, J., dissenting) (discussing union security agreements in the context of public sector labor relations).

[32]*See id.* at 2460-87 (majority opinion holding that public sector union security agreements violate the First Amendment).

[33]*Id.*

place harmony.[34] As of 2005, twenty-two states had enacted right-to-work laws in some form.[35] Thus, the public policy split across the states on these issues has been fairly even.[36] No formal survey has been done with respect to tribal law differences on this subject.

The ordinance upheld in *Pueblo of San Juan* provides:

> No person shall be required, as a condition of employment or continuation of employment on Pueblo lands, to: (i) resign or refrain from voluntary membership in, voluntary affiliation with, or voluntary financial support of a labor organization; (ii) become or remain a member of a labor organization; (iii) pay dues, fees, assessments or other charges of any kind or amount to a labor

---

[34]So-called fair share provisions of collective bargaining agreements, discussed in Section E(8) below, provide that employees within a bargaining unit represented by a union must pay an amount equivalent to the employee's fair share of union services benefiting the employee. Such provisions may be viewed as promoting workplace harmony by checking what union members may perceive as "free riders": employees in a bargaining unit who get the benefits of union representation without having to pay anything for them. *See generally International Union of the Plumbing and Pipefitting Industry, Local 41 v. NLRB: Closing the Door on Representation Fees in Right to Work States*, 1983 WIS. L. REV. 1231, 1231-33 & n.5 (1983) (explaining issues in private sector context). In 2018, the Supreme Court held that collective bargaining agreements involving states that impose a fair share upon employees within a bargaining unit, whether they choose to join the union or not, violate the First Amendment. *See Janus*, 138 S. Ct. 2448.

[35]*See* Raymond L. Hogler, *The Historical Misconception of Right to Work Laws in the United States: Senator Robert Wagner, Legal Policy, and the Decline of American Unions*, 23 HOFSTRA LAB. & EMP. L.J. 101, 104 (2005).

[36]In 2018, the Supreme Court held that public sector union security agreements requiring all employees represented by a union in a bargaining unit to pay union fees, whether they joined the union or not, violate the First Amendment. *Janus*, 138 S. Ct. at 2478, 2486. This decision does not affect labor relations in the private sector, *see id.* at 2479 n.24, and the NLRA, which governs unions and collective bargaining in that sector, expressly permits such agreements. 29 U.S.C. § 158(a)(3). Indian tribes are not subject to the First Amendment, only to the equivalent provision of the Indian Civil Rights Act, which is not enforceable outside of tribal forums. *See* Chapter 5, Sections A and B.

organization; (iv) pay to any charity or other third party, in lieu of such payments, any amount equivalent to or a pro-rata portion of dues, fees, assessments or other charges regularly required of members of a labor organization; or (v) be recommended, approved, referred, or cleared through a labor organization.[37]

In the wake of *Pueblo of San Juan*, numerous tribes enacted similar right-to-work laws.[38]

2. The Tribal Labor Relations Ordinance in California

Apart from the enactment of an Ohkay Owingeh-style right-to-work law, an initiative for tribal governance of labor relations emerged in California due to the provision in the Indian Gaming Regulatory Act (IGRA) compacts that close to sixty tribes signed with that State in 1999 and have subsequently amended without substantive revision.[39] Language in these compacts requires each tribe to enact a uniform Tribal Labor Relations Ordinance (TLRO).[40] The model TLRO

---

[37]*See NLRB v. Pueblo of San Juan*, 276 F.3d at 1189.

[38]*See, e.g.*, Blue Lake Rancheria, Business Council of the Blue Lake Rancheria Establishing a Right to Work Law for the Rancheria Ordinance No. 03-03, available at: https://www.bluelakerancheria-nsn.gov/wp-content/uploads/2017/07/03-03.pdf (last visited Nov. 29, 2021); Confederated Tribes of Siletz Indians, Right to Work Ordinance, 5.200 available at: https://www.ctsi.nsn.us/wp-content/uploads/2020/12/Right-to-Work-Ordinance-07-24-2008.pdf (last visited Nov. 29, 2021). Other examples of tribes' right-to-work laws are listed in Appendix C.

[39]*See In re Indian Gaming Related Cases*, 331 F.3d 1094 (9th Cir. 2003) (detailing the legal and political processes that led up to these compacts).

[40]*Id.* at 1105-06. *See* California Gaming Control Commission, *Ratified Tribal-State Gaming Compacts (New and Amended)* available at: http://www.cgcc.ca.gov/?pageID=compacts (last visited Nov. 29, 2021). An exemplary compact provision is as follows:
   Sec. 12.10. Labor Relations.
   The Gaming Activities authorized by this Compact may only commence after the Tribe has adopted an ordinance identical to the Tribal Labor Relations Ordinance attached hereto as Appendix C, and the Gaming Activities may only continue as long as the Tribe maintains the ordinance. The Tribe shall provide

"provides limited organizational rights to workers at tribal gaming establishments and related facilities that employ 250 or more employees."[41] The ordinance allows union access to non-work areas during non-work time at the compacting tribes' gaming facilities to solicit employee support, and it imposes the duty of collective bargaining if a union prevails in an election.[42] The TLRO establishes a Tribal Labor Panel to resolve unfair labor practices, which are defined along the same lines as in the NLRA, and to oversee union elections.[43] However, it protects the right of tribes to implement tribal employment preferences.[44] The TLRO provides that unions may strike against the tribes' gaming facilities in the event of bargaining impasses (i.e., when man-

---

written notice to the State that it has adopted the ordinance, along with a copy of the ordinance, on or before the effective date.

Tribal-State Compact Between the State of California and the Dry Creek Rancheria Band of Pomo Indians (Aug. 18, 2018), available at: http://www.cgcc.ca.gov/documents/compacts/amended_compacts/Dry_Creek_Compact_2017.pdf (last visited Nov. 29, 2021).

[41] *In re Indian Gaming Related Cases*, 331 F.3d at 1106.

[42] *See, e.g.*, Hoopa Valley Tribe, Tribal Labor Relations Ordinance, tit. 61 available at: https://www.hoopa-nsn.gov/wp-content/uploads/2015/06/Title61-LaborRelations062000.pdf (last visited Nov. 29, 2021).

[43] The Tribal Labor Panel consists of "ten (10) arbitrators appointed by mutual selection of the parties which panel shall serve all tribes that have adopted this ordinance. The Tribal Labor Panel shall have authority to hire staff and take other actions necessary to conduct elections, determine units, determine scope of negotiations, hold hearings, subpoena witnesses, take testimony, and conduct all other activities needed to fulfill its obligations under this Tribal Labor Relations Ordinance."*Id.*

[44] *Id.* § 9. The TLRO provides:
Section 9: Indian preference explicitly permitted
Nothing herein shall preclude the tribe from giving Indian preference in employment, promotion, seniority, lay-offs or retention to members of any federally recognized Indian tribe or shall in any way affect the tribe's right to follow tribal law, ordinances, personnel policies or the tribe's customs or traditions regarding Indian preference in employment, promotion, seniority, lay-offs or retention. Moreover, in the event of a conflict between tribal law, tribal ordinance or the tribe's customs and traditions regarding Indian preference and this Ordinance, the tribal law, tribal ordinance or the tribe's customs and traditions shall govern.

agement and the union reach a stalemate on a contract provision), but it prohibits "strike-related picketing" on Indian lands.[45] The Ninth Circuit Court of Appeals has upheld the TLRO requirement of the California tribes' compacts in the face of a claim by one tribe that, under IGRA, the State violated its duty to bargain in good faith by demanding its inclusion.[46]

The model TLRO has been criticized as "filled with ambiguity and uncertainty."[47] It could also be criticized as being haphazard. For example, section 13(b)(1) cites to the "American Academy of Arbitrators" as a source for choosing a dispute resolution panel,[48] but there is no organization by that name. It is unclear whether the authors considered how the model TLRO would interact with the NLRA. Thus far, having opened up tribes' IGRA gaming operations to unionization, resulting disputes have sparked the attention of the NLRB, which has been successful in imposing the NLRA upon reservation labor relations, regardless of any differing provisions of the TLRO.[49]

---

[45]*Id.* § 11.

[46]*See In re Gaming Related Cases*, 331 F.3d at 1116.

[47]THE CALIFORNIA TRIBAL LABOR RELATIONS ORDINANCE: OVERVIEW AND ANALYSIS, available at: https://corporate.findlaw.com/litigation-disputes/the-california-tribal-labor-relations-ordinance-overview-and.html (last visited Nov. 29, 2021).

[48]Hoopa Valley Tribe, Tribal Labor Relations Ordinance, tit. 61, section 13(c)(1) available at https://www.hoopa-nsn.gov/wp-content/uploads/2015/06/Title61-LaborRelations062000.pdf (last visited Nov. 29, 2021); *Tribal-State Compact Between the State of California and the Dry Creek Rancheria Band of Pomo Indians* (Aug. 18, 2018) Appendix C, available at: http://www.cgcc.ca.gov/documents/compacts/amended_compacts/Dry_Creek_Compact_2017.pdf (last visited Nov. 29, 2021).

[49]*See Pauma v. Nat'l Lab. Rels. Bd.*, 888 F.3d at 1080 ("We conclude that Casino Pauma's compact with California [requiring the TLRO] does not displace the application of the NLRA to its activities."); *San Manuel Indian Bingo & Casino*, 475 F.3d at 1315. In *San Manuel,* the court did not consider provisions of the TLRO that appear in conflict with the NLRA (like the use of the Tribal Labor Panel, rather than the National Labor Relations Board to resolve disputes and the protection of tribal employment preferences); it stated only that "[t]he total impact on tribal sovereignty at issue here amounts to some unpredictable, but probably modest, effect on tribal revenue and the displacement of legislative and executive authority."

The enforcement provisions of the TLRO have proven problematic. A federal district court held that the 1999 model TLRO's provision for federal court enforcement of an arbitration award, resolving bargaining or other disputes between labor unions and management, did not confer subject matter jurisdiction upon the federal courts.[50] That problematic provision has been changed in the model TLRO amended compacts.[51] The labor relations saga of the Pauma Band includes a failed attempt to force the UNITE HERE International Un-

---

[50] *See Unite Here Int'l Union v. Pala Band of Mission Indians*, 583 F.Supp.2d 1190 (S.D. Cal. 2008). The arbitration enforcement provision of the 1999 TLRO states:
> [E]ither party may seek a motion to compel arbitration or a motion to confirm an arbitration award in Tribal Court, which may be appealed to federal court. If the Tribal Court does not render its decision within 90 days, or in the event there is no Tribal Court, the matter may proceed directly to federal court. In the event the federal court declines jurisdiction, the [Pala Band] agrees to a limited waiver of its sovereign immunity for the sole purpose of compelling arbitration or confirming an arbitration award issued pursuant to the [TLRO] in the appropriate state superior court.

Id. at 1193 (quoting § 13(d) of the TLRO of the Pala Band of Mission Indians) (alterations in original). The first sentence of this provision is strange because federal courts have no jurisdiction to entertain "appeals" from tribal courts. Given the federal court's declination of jurisdiction in *Unite Here*, this provision left enforcement of an arbitration award to the tribal court, unless none existed or a tribal court failed to act "within 90 days," in which case it purported to confer jurisdiction upon "an appropriate state superior court."

[51] The model TLRO now provides:
> Either party may seek a motion to compel arbitration or a motion to confirm or vacate an arbitration award, under this Section 13, in the appropriate state superior court, unless a bilateral contract has been created in accordance with Section 7, in which case either party may proceed in federal court. The Tribe agrees to a limited waiver of its sovereign immunity for the sole purpose of compelling arbitration or confirming or vacating an arbitration award issued pursuant to the Ordinance in the appropriate state superior court or in federal court. The parties are free to put at issue whether or not the arbitration award exceeds the authority of the Tribal Labor Panel.

Tribal-State Compact Between the State of California and the Dry Creek Rancheria Band of Pomo Indians (Aug. 18, 2018) Appendix C §13(e), available at: http://www.cgcc.ca.gov/documents/compacts/amended_compacts/Dry_Creek_Compact_2017.pdf (last visited Nov. 29, 2021).

ion to utilize the TLRO dispute resolution process rather than resort to claims under the NLRA.[52]

D. Tribal Laws Governing Unions and Collective Bargaining After *San Manuel*

As discussed at the outset of this chapter, notwithstanding the NLRB's success in a number of federal circuit courts of appeals (the D.C., Sixth, and Ninth Circuits) to impose the NLRA upon Indian tribes' IGRA gaming operations, only the Supreme Court can ultimately decide whether that is a lawful intrusion upon the sovereign prerogatives of tribal governments. And in at least two federal courts of appeals (the Tenth and the Eighth Circuits), it likely is not. In the face of such uncertainty, many tribes have enacted and implemented their own labor relations and collective bargaining laws, modeled on the public sector labor relations laws of states. The following subsections provides some examples.

1. Mashantucket Pequot Tribal Nation

On October 24, 2007, just over eight months after the D.C. Circuit's decision in *San Manuel*, the NLRB issued a "Decision and Direction of Election" against the Mashantucket Pequot Gaming Enterprise d/b/a Foxwoods Resort Casino, an arm of the Mashantucket Pequot Tribal Nation, established to conduct gaming under IGRA. That decision required Foxwoods to allow an NLRB-administered election to determine whether table game dealers would elect the United Automobile Workers (UAW) to represent them as an exclusive bargaining agent under the terms of the NLRA.[53]

---

[52]*See Pauma Band of Luiseno Mission Indians of the Pauma & Yuima Rsrv. v. Unite Here Int'l Union*, 346 F. Supp. 3d 1365 (S.D. Cal. 2018). *See also Unite Here Int'l Union v. Shingle Springs Band of Miwok Indians*, 2017 WL 2972262 (E.D. Cal. July 12, 2017) (union invoking § 301 of the Labor Management Relations Act (LMRA), 29 U.S.C. § 185, to compel arbitration) *aff'd*, 738 F. App'x 560 (9th Cir. 2018).

[53]*Foxwoods Resort Casino*, No. 34-RC-2230 NLRB (Oct 24, 2007) (Decision and Direction of Election) available at: https://www.nlrb.gov/case/34-RC-002230 (last visited Dec. 2, 2021)

In August 2007, two months before the NLRB election order, the Nation had enacted the Mashantucket Pequot Labor Relations Law.[54] The UAW refused to follow tribal law, the NLRB held the election, and Foxwoods dealers voted in favor of UAW representation.[55]

Foxwoods refused to bargain and challenged the NLRB's jurisdiction, but by a Decision and Order issued in the fall of 2008, the NLRB rejected all of its arguments and ordered Foxwoods to engage in collective bargaining with the UAW.[56] By late 2008, the various litigation briefs of the parties and orders issued by the NLRB amounted to well over 200 pages and covered a vast range of objections, multiple charges of unfair labor practices, and jurisdictional disputes. With appeals pending before the Second Circuit, Foxwoods and the UAW eventually agreed to a litigation standstill while they worked toward entering into a collective bargaining agreement to be governed by the Tribe's newly enacted law.[57]

The Mashantucket Pequot's Labor Relations Law governs labor organizations and collective bargaining in very much the same way as the NLRA, but it prohibits strikes and reserves tribal employment preferences from the subjects of bargaining.[58] The Mashantucket Pequot Employment Rights Law established the MERO, which with regard to labor, functions in much the same way as the NLRB: to oversee union elections and to resolve unfair labor practice charges.[59] Like

---

[54] *See id.* at 9.

[55] *See Foxwoods Resort Casino*, 352 NLRB 771 (2008).

[56] *Id.*

[57] *See* NLRB Press Release: *NLRB General Counsel Meisburg Praises Recent Announcement by Mashantucket Pequot Tribe and UAW to Begin Negotiations for a First Contract* (Nov. 4, 2008), available at: https://www.nlrb.gov/news-publications/news/news-releases (last visited Dec. 2, 2021).

[58] *See* 32, M.P.T.L., the Mashantucket Pequot Labor Relations Law, ch.1 §§ 9(d), 11 (Supp. 20007-2008) available at: http://www.mptnlaw.com/laws/Single/TITLE%2032%20MASHANTUCKET%20PEQUOT%20LABOR%20RELATIONS%20LAW.pdf (last visited Dec. 2, 2021).

[59] *See* 31 M.P.T.L., the Mashantucket Pequot Employment Rights Law.

the labor organization laws of the Eastern Band of Cherokee and Mississippi Choctaw, the Mashantucket Pequot's Labor Relations Law also requires the registration and licensing of unions doing business within the reservation.[60]

On January 30, 2010, Foxwoods Casino Resort announced that it had entered into a collective bargaining agreement with the UAW to govern the employment terms and conditions of 2,500 table game dealers.[61] Foxwoods boasted the first collective bargaining agreement to be entered into pursuant to tribal law.[62] With the consummation of this agreement, jurisdictional and other disputes before the NLRB and the Second Circuit were settled. As of 2021, there were five labor unions operating within the Nation's jurisdiction.

2. Little River Band of Ottawa Indians

The Little River Band of Ottawa Indians has had a comprehensive Fair Employment Practices Code since 2005, covering a wide range of employment matters, from employment discrimination to family medical leave, with specified tribal court remedies.[63] In 2007, the Band enacted Article XVI to the code to, among other things, prohibit strikes against the governmental operations of the Band, including its IGRA gaming operations, and to require unions doing business within the jurisdiction of the Band to be licensed by tribal government.[64] Later amendments to the Band's law in 2008 added more

---

[60] *See* 32 M.P.T.L. §§ 14-15.

[61] Gale Courey Toensing, *Mashantucket-UAW in groundbreaking agreement to negotiate under tribal law*, INDIAN COUNTRY TODAY, (Nov. 7, 2008), available at: https://indiancountrytoday.com/archive/mashantucket-uaw-in-groundbreaking-agreement-to-negotiate-under-tribal-law (last visited Dec. 2, 2021).

[62] *See id.*

[63] *See* Little River Band of Ottawa Indians, Fair Employment Practices Code, Ordinance No: 05-600-03 available at: https://lrboi-nsn.gov/wp-content/uploads/2015/10/Title-03.pdf (last visited Dec. 1, 2021).

[64] *See id.* art. XVI.

comprehensive regulatory provisions to govern labor organizations and collective bargaining within the Band's public employers,[65] including:

- Delineation of procedures for any union election pursuant to a model "election procedures agreement," which must be entered into by the Band's Tribal Council and any union seeking to hold an election campaign;[66]

- Appointment of a neutral election official to oversee any resulting election and to assist in resolving disputes in the event of asserted improprieties during an election campaign;[67]

- Delineation of the requirement of public employers and exclusive bargaining representatives to bargain in good faith;[68]

- The duties of exclusive bargaining representatives with regard to bargaining units;[69]

---

[65] The Band's law applies to "public employers" defined as any "subordinate economic organization, department, commission, agency, or authority of the Band engaged in any Governmental Operation of the Band." The law defines "governmental operations of the Band" as:

> the operations of the Little River Band of Ottawa Indians exercised pursuant to its inherent self-governing authority as a federally recognized Indian tribe or pursuant to its governmental activities expressly recognized or supported by Congress, whether through a subordinate economic organization of the Band or through a department, commission, agency, or authority of the Band, including, but not limited to, (1) the provision of health, housing, education, and other governmental services and programs to its members; (2) the generation of revenue to support the Band's governmental services and programs, including the operation of "Class II" and "Class III" gaming through the Little River Casino Resort; and (3) the exercise and operation of its administrative, regulatory, and police power authorities within the Band's jurisdiction.

Id. § 16.03.

[66] *Id.* §§ 16.09-16.11; 16-26.

[67] *Id.* § 16.03.

[68] *Id.* § 16.12.

- Delineation of unfair labor practices by public employers or labor organizations and the procedures for resolving charges of unfair labor practices, including arbitration and judicial review in the tribal court;[70]

- Methods for resolving bargaining impasses;[71] and

- Provisions for tribal court enforcement of the prohibition against strikes or lock-outs and union licensing requirements, and tribal court jurisdiction over claims arising under collective bargaining agreements.[72]

Because of the 2015 decision of the U.S. Court of Appeals for the Sixth Circuit in *NLRB v. Little River Band of Ottawa Indians Tribal Government*,[73] discussed above, absent the consent of a union operating with the Band's jurisdiction, the provisions of this law that vary from the NLRA (including the prohibition against strikes and the requirement that unions be licensed by the Band) cannot be applied to the Band's IGRA gaming operations. Otherwise, the law is fully operational within the Band's public sector.

3. Other Tribes

In 2015, the Squaxin Island Tribe enacted a comprehensive Labor and Employment Code.[74] The law protects employees from employment discrimination, provides for minimum wages, overtime and family medical leave, and regulates collective bargaining within the Tribe's

---

[69] *Id.* §§ 16.14-16.15.

[70] *Id.* §§ 16.15-16.16.

[71] *Id.* § 16.17.

[72] *Id.* § 16.24.

[73] *Nat'l Lab. Rels. Bd. v. Little River Band of Ottawa Indians Tribal Gov't*, 788 F.3d 537 (6th Cir. 2015).

[74] Available at: https://library.municode.com/tribes_and_tribal_nations/squaxin_island_tribe/codes/code_of_ordinances?nodeId (last visited Dec. 1, 2021).

public sector.[75] The definition of "employer" covered by the law is as follows:

> "Employer" means the Squaxin Island Tribe, any political subdivision, agency, or department of the Tribe, any enterprise, instrumentality, corporation, business association, or other entity owned by the Tribe that is deemed to have the sovereign immunity of the Tribe operating within the territorial jurisdiction of the Tribe and employing any number of individuals. Employment within any such employer is considered to be within the Tribe's "public sector."[76]

Chapter 12.08, "Labor Organizations and Collective Bargaining," introduces the law as follows:

> A. The Squaxin Island Tribal Council finds that the Tribe has inherent sovereign authority to govern economic relations within its jurisdiction, including employment relations between the Tribe and its employees and Tribal Entities and their employees. The economic activities of the Tribe and Tribal Entities generate funds to support the Tribe's governmental services to its citizens and provide critical economic development opportunities for the Tribe and its citizens. Employment relations within the Tribe and Tribal Entities directly affect the health, welfare, and economic security of the Tribe and its citizens because such relations affect the generation and distribution of the Tribe's governmental resources and the economic development of the Tribe.

---

[75]*See id.*

[76]*Id.* §12.01.040(M).

B. Like the state and federal governments, the Tribe has a direct interest in regulating labor relations within governmental agencies and enterprises, known as "public sector labor relations." The labor relations laws of states and of the federal government often prohibit strikes to protect the public interest and provide for alternative procedures to resolve collective bargaining impasses. The Tribe finds that important lessons may be drawn from the state and federal public sector labor relations laws for the design of a law governing labor relations of the employees subject to this code.[77]

The law comprehensively regulates unions and collective bargaining, including the licensing of unions doing business within the Tribe's jurisdiction, and provisions governing union elections, mandatory subjects of bargaining, the resolution of bargaining impasses, and the adjudication of unfair labor practices through mediation, arbitration, and tribal court review.[78]

A number of other tribes have enacted similar comprehensive laws to govern unions and collective bargaining within their public sectors.[79]

---

[77] *Id.*, §12.09.020.

[78] *Id.*, §§ 12.09.030 ("Licensing of labor organizations and business agents; qualifications; fees; term"); 12.09.040 ("Bargaining unit determinations; union election procedures"); 12.09.050 ("Decertification Procedures"); 12.09.060 ("Employees, employers, labor organizations; rights and duties"); 12.09.070 ("Collective bargaining; exceptions") (excepting from mandatory subjects of bargaining laws or policies giving employment preferences to citizens of the Tribe or other Native Americans); 12.09.080 ("Prohibited practices; employer; labor organization"); 12.09.090 ("Procedures for resolving prohibited practices claims"); 12.09.100 ("Procedures for resolving collective bargaining impasses"); 12.09.110 ("Tribal Court Enforcement Authority"); 12.09.120 ("Limited waiver of sovereign immunity").

[79] *See, e.g.,* Jamestown S'Klallam Tribe Tribal Code, Title 3, Chapter 3.03 Labor Organizations and Collective Bargaining, available at: https://jamestowntribe.org/wp-content/uploads/2018/05/Title_03_Labor_Code_9_12_14.pdf (last visited Dec. 1, 2021); Law and Order Code of the Port Gamble S'Klallam Tribe, Title 17, Labor

E. Significant Policy Issues in Tribal Labor Organization Laws

1. Key Decisions Facing Tribes in Enacting Labor Relations Laws

Any tribe engaged in the process of enacting and implementing a law to govern labor relations and collective bargaining must think through a host of public policy matters. The remainder of this chapter discusses a number of these policy choices, including: regulating union solicitation; rules for union elections; defining unfair labor practices and providing for dispute resolution; strikes and lock-outs; developing collective bargaining impasse procedures; regulating picketing and secondary boycotts; and issues related to right-to-work, "free riders," and "fair share" provisions.

There is no set model; tribes may weigh their policy choices differently. Importantly, as discussed in the introduction to this chapter, until the Supreme Court resolves the question of whether the NLRA applies to Indian tribes (or their wholly owned economic enterprises, like their IGRA gaming facilities), any tribe contemplating the enactment of such laws must consider whether its location within the jurisdiction of a particular federal circuit court of appeals presents a risk that the NLRB could succeed in challenging the law if it varies from the NLRA and applies to the tribe's gaming operations. Given the current array of decisions discussed in the introduction, Indian tribes in the Tenth and Eighth Circuits are on the low side of that risk; those in the Ninth, Second, Sixth, and Seventh Circuits may be on the high side; and those within the jurisdictions of the other "undecided" feder-

---

Organizations and Collective Bargaining, available at: https://www.pgst.nsn.us/images/law-and-order/Title-27.pdf (last visited Dec. 1, 2021); Pokagon Band of Potawatomi Indians Labor Organizations and Collective Bargaining Code, available at https://www.pokagonband-nsn.gov/sites/default/files/assets/department/government/form/2012/labor-organizations-and-collective-bargaining-code-824-621.pdf (last visited Dec. 1, 2021); Mohegan Tribe of Indians of Connecticut Code of Ordinances, Chapter 4, Employment, Article XI, Labor Relations, available at https://library.municode.com/tribes_and_tribal_nations/mohegan_tribe/codes/code_of_laws?nodeId (last visited Dec. 1, 2021).

al circuit courts of appeals are in the middle.[80] Such risks could be averted altogether, of course, if a union consents to the application of a given tribal law. Further, tribes with laws governing unions and collective bargaining in the Ninth, Second, Sixth, and Seventh Circuits may have the opportunity to invoke the exhaustion doctrine discussed in Chapter 3 to resolve unfair labor practices within forums they have set up for that purpose, and to stay or dismiss parallel unfair labor charges before the NLRB.[81]

2. Union Solicitation

Any tribe facing union organizing efforts will first confront the issue of what restrictions it can or should place upon union solicitation. Should unions soliciting tribal government employees be required to comply with tribal law restrictions? What if the union is simply calling employees at home, off-reservation? Should any union engaged in such activity within the territorial jurisdiction of the tribe be required to have a license issued by tribal authorities?[82]

---

[80]*See supra* at 242-246 (discussion of developing caselaw across the federal circuit courts of appeals as yet unresolved by the Supreme Court).

[81]*See* NLRB, Office of General Counsel, Advice Memorandum, *Little River Band of Ottawa Indians d/b/a Little River Casino Resort*, Cases GR-7-CA-52446 and GR-7-52449, available at: https://www.nlrb.gov/search/all/52446?dt[0]=Advice%20Response%20Memo (last visited Dec. 4, 2021) (describing tribal exhaustion argument for resolving unfair labor practice charge under tribal law).

[82]In *Montana v. United States,* 450 U.S. 544 (1981), the Supreme Court made clear that Indian tribes retain inherent sovereign authority to "regulate, *through . . . licensing . . .,* the activities of nonmembers who enter consensual relationships with the tribe or its members." *Id.* at 566 (emphasis added). When Indian tribes employ nonmembers within their reservation enterprises and unions act as agents for those employees, there exists a "consensual relationship" triggering this licensing authority; for an employment relationship is a contractual relationship.

A number of tribes require unions and their agents to be licensed by tribal authorities in order to engage in any form of business activity, including the solicitation of employees for union membership within the tribe's territorial jurisdiction. *See, e.g.,* Squaxin Island Tribe Labor and Employment Code, *supra* note 74, § 12.09.030; Jamestown S'Klallam Tribe Labor Code, *supra* note 79, § 3.03.04; Port Gamble S'Klallam Tribe, Labor Organizations and Collective Bargaining Code, *supra* note 79 § 27.01.05; Pokagon Band of Potawatomi Indians Labor Organizations and Collective Bargaining Code, *supra* note 79, §§ 12.1 – 12.3.

Stated at the most general level, under the NLRA, an employer's union solicitation rules must allow unions the same type of access to employees that is allowed for other entities seeking access to employees.[83] For example, if vendors or others are allowed to solicit employees during non-work hours within a tribe's IGRA gaming facility, the NLRB would require that a union have the same opportunity. Even if an employer prohibits any on-site solicitation, if such employer addresses employees on-site during non-work hours about its views about union representation, its failure to provide the union the same kind of access could be deemed an unfair labor practice under the NLRA.[84] Further, the NLRA protects the right of workers to engage in union solicitation activities in non-work areas during non-work times even if the employer has a policy banning co-worker solicitation altogether (i.e., a policy prohibiting all forms of solicitation, including such things as the sale of Girl Scout cookies).

Good arguments can be made that once a union engages in business on tribal land, including the solicitation of the tribe's employees to join the union, it is subject to the tribe's inherent authority to regulate those activities.[85] Assuming a tribe decides not to prohibit union activity involving its employees altogether, whether it makes sense for a tribe to mirror the NLRA in promulgating tribal law to govern the terms and conditions for union solicitation turns on a host of issues, including:

- The tribe's public policy reasons for restricting union solicitation;
- Whether there are good reasons to vary from the NLRA with regard to such restrictions; and

---

[83]*See generally* THE DEVELOPING LABOR LAW 107-115 (John E. Higgins, Jr. et al eds., 5th ed. 2006); WILLIAM B. GOULD IV, A PRIMER ON AMERICAN LABOR LAW 71-80 (4th ed. 2004).

[84]*See* 29 U.S.C. §§ 157-58 (2018).

[85]*See* Chapter 2, Section C.

- Litigation risks associated with the case law, if any, of the federal circuit court of appeals where the tribe is located.[86]

3. Elections

Under the NLRA, the NLRB can order an election upon a showing by a union that it has the support of thirty percent or more of employees within a bargaining unit of an employer.[87] A bargaining unit is defined as a unit of employees who have the same or substantially similar interests concerning wages, hours, and working conditions (those matters that are the subjects of collective bargaining under the NLRA).[88] There are methods and procedures under the NLRA and under public sector labor relations laws for addressing disputes over appropriate bargaining units. Such disputes are typically resolved during the initial NLRB proceeding to determine the validity of a union petition seeking to have a representation election.[89] Once a petition showing that the number of supporters is equal to or greater than thirty percent, a secret ballot election is then scheduled.[90]

Once an election is ordered, there are a host of rules governing election campaigns, under states' public sector labor laws, tribes' public sector labor laws, and under the NLRA. The rules regarding union access to employer premises typically are similar to union solicitation rules. Stated at the most general level, they encourage equal access by employers and union-supporting employees to employees within a

---

[86]*See supra* at 242-246 (discussion of developing caselaw across the federal circuit courts of appeals as yet unresolved by the Supreme Court). As discussed above, *Soaring Eagle Casino & Resort v. N.L.R.B.,* 791 F.3d 648 (6th Cir. 2015) and *Pauma v. Nat'l Lab. Rels. Bd.,* 888 F.3d 1066 (9th Cir. 2018) both involved the interference with union solicitation efforts by employees in a manner that violated the NLRA.

[87]*See* NLRB, *Conduct Elections,* https://www.nlrb.gov/about-nlrb/what-we-do/conduct-elections (last visited Dec. 4, 2021) (describing NLRB election petition process).

[88]29 U.S.C. § 159 (2018).

[89]*See, e.g.,* 29 U.S.C. § 159(b) (2018).

[90]29 U.S.C. § 159(c)(1) (2018).

bargaining unit.[91] There are also numerous rules governing what employers and unions can or cannot say or do to coerce employees join their side of the debate.[92] Violations of these rules can trigger unfair labor practice charges and related sanctions against employers or unions.[93] There are likewise detailed NLRB rules governing the conduct of elections and sanctions for violations of those rules.[94] State public sector laws and tribal laws similarly address union election procedures.

For the same reasons that Indian tribes have inherent sovereign authority to regulate the union solicitation of their employees, they have the same authority to regulate union election processes involving their employees on tribal lands.[95] A union seeking an election to serve as the bargaining agent for tribal employees within a tribe's jurisdiction could agree to follow tribal law (if one exists) or, if in the jurisdiction of a federal court of appeals that has applied the NLRA to Indian tribes (or one that has not decided the issue),[96] seek a NLRA-regulated election.

4. Employee Rights, Union and Employer Duties, Unfair Labor Practices, and Dispute Resolutions

As discussed in Chapter 2, Indian tribes have inherent authority to govern their employment relations with their tribal members and nontribal members. Their authority over the latter, including unions that represent tribal employees, stems from the sovereign authority of tribes to exclude nontribal members from tribal lands and to condition

---

[91]*See generally* THE DEVELOPING LABOR LAW 104-34 (John E. Higgins, Jr. et al., eds., 5th ed. 2006).

[92]*Id*. at 136-84.

[93]*See id*.

[94]*See id*. at 471-537.

[95]The tribal laws governing unions and collective bargaining described in Section D and set out in note 79, exemplify a variety of approaches to union election procedures.

[96]*See supra* at 242-246 (discussion of developing case law across the federal circuit courts of appeals as yet unresolved by the Supreme Court).

their economic activities on tribal lands while they remain.[97] If a union is elected by a bargaining unit of employees within a tribal government employer, the tribe will have a separate basis for regulating the union. Under the Supreme Court's decision in *United States v. Montana*, also discussed in Chapter 2,[98] tribes have inherent sovereign authority to regulate the consensual employment relationship between nonmember employees and the tribe or its enterprises on tribal lands. Unions, acting as agents for these employees in that consensual relationship, would be subject to the same tribal authority.

For tribes that do not prohibit unions altogether, any tribal law governing collective bargaining would need to delineate, at a minimum, the following: (a) the rights of public employees to organize for the purpose of collective bargaining through an exclusive representative freely chosen by them, (b) the duties of a union, once elected, to serve as the exclusive representative of such employees, (c) the duties of employers with regard to the rights of public employees and their exclusive representatives, and (d) processes for resolving unfair labor practices, or a union or employer's failure to bargain in good faith. Under the NLRA and state and tribal public sector labor laws, these rights and duties include the following:

a. Employee Rights

- To organize, form, or join a labor organization for the purpose of collective bargaining;

- To negotiate or bargain collectively with employers through freely elected exclusive bargaining representatives; and

- To refuse to join or participate in the activities of labor organizations.

---

[97] See Chapter 2, Section C.

[98] *See id.*

b. **Union Duties, Violations of Which May Be Unfair Labor Practices**

- To fairly represent all employees within the bargaining unit, whether or not they decide to join the union, and whether or not they pay some portion of the costs of the services performed by the union;
- To bargain in good faith with management in developing a collective bargaining agreement covering the bargaining unit;
- Not to interfere with the delineated rights of employees; and
- Not to discriminate against an employee because of the employee's membership or nonmembership in a union.

c. **Employer Duties, Violations of Which May Be Unfair Labor Practices**

- To bargain in good faith with exclusive bargaining representatives in developing a collective bargaining agreement covering a bargaining unit;
- Not to interfere with the delineated rights of employees; and
- Not to encourage or discourage union membership.

The scope of a union and employer's "duty to bargain in good faith" may be separately defined to establish the mandatory subjects of bargaining – generally defined to include wages, hours, and terms and conditions of employment. Items that might be excepted from that duty, consistent with most public sector labor laws, might include: (a) matters that would conflict with tribal law (in the same manner that state public sector laws prohibit bargaining over matters that would conflict with state law), and (b) so-called management prerogatives like decisions to hire, lay off, or recall employees, or to reorganize duties within the workplace.

Under the NLRA and most state and tribal public sector labor relations laws, a body or board (the NRLB, in the case of the NLRA) is vested with the authority to address and resolve unfair labor practice charges. Such charges can emerge out of any alleged violation of the delineated rights of public employees and duties of elected unions or employers. Mediators or arbitration panels may be suited to resolve these issues, or they may be directed to a labor commission or agency, like the NLRB. Further provisions may be made for full or limited judicial review.[99]

5. Strikes and Lock-Outs

The NLRA guarantees employees in the private sector the right to strike, and any interference with that right can trigger an unfair labor practice charge.[100] In contrast, strikes against governments and their instrumentalities in the public sector are often expressly prohibited and may be subject to criminal sanctions.[101] Indeed, as a matter of common law in the absence of legislation establishing the right, there is no right to strike against a government or its operations in any form.[102] Tribes that prohibit strikes in their public sectors in the same manner as many states and the federal government have grounds to defend such a prohibition as a legitimate exercise of tribal sovereignty. As discussed in Chapter 2, this derives from the inherent authority of tribes to govern

---

[99]The tribal laws governing unions and collective bargaining described in Section D and set out in note 79, exemplify the delineation of the rights and duties of employees, unions, and employers; unfair labor practices; and forums for resolving unfair labor practices.

[100]29 U.S.C. § 157; § 159(c)(1)(A)(3) (2018).

[101]*See, e.g., United Fed'n of Postal Clerks v. Blount*, 325 F. Supp. 879, 882 (D.D.C. 1971); *City of San Diego v. American Fed'n of State Cnty. & Mun. Emp.*, 87 Cal. Rptr. 258, 260 (Cal. Ct. App. 1970); *Bd. of Educ. Twp. of Middletown v. Middletown Twp. Educ Ass'n*, 800 A.2d 286, 288-89 (N.J. Super. Ct. Ch. Div. 2001).

[102]*See generally* James Duff, Jr., Annotation, *Labor Law: Right of Public Employees to Strike or Engage in Work Stoppage*, 37 A.L.R.3d 1147, 1152 (1971 & Supp. 2007).

individuals and entities who enter tribal lands for economic gain, as well as those who enter into consensual relations with the tribe or its enterprises.[103] Given the state of flux in the federal courts of appeals and the lack of a Supreme Court ruling on whether the NLRA can be applied to Indian tribes, whether these seemingly strong arguments will ultimately prevail is uncertain. They have not prevailed in the Sixth Circuit, at least when applied to a tribe's IGRA gaming operations, but they have a good chance of prevailing across the public sectors of Indian tribes in the Tenth and Eighth Circuits.[104]

One reason that the NLRA guarantees employees the right to strike in the private sector is that the right to strike constitutes the most effective bargaining tool available to employees in seeking to resolve an impasse in the process of collective bargaining.[105] A counterpart tool in the employer's arsenal is the right to "lock out" employees during a bargaining impasse to prevent them from working.[106] The threat of strikes and lock-outs may be strategically used by unions and management to achieve leverage in the negotiating process. Thus, public sector labor laws that prohibit strikes by public employees also prohibit lock-outs by public employers.[107] This prevents public employers from having an unfair advantage during collective bargaining negotiations. It follows that, if tribes enact laws prohibiting strikes in the public sector, they should also consider prohibiting lock-outs.

---

[103] *See* Chapter 2, Section B.

[104] *See supra* at 242-246 (discussion of developing caselaw across the federal circuit courts of appeals as yet unresolved by the Supreme Court).

[105] *See generally* THE DEVELOPING LABOR LAW 1572-73 (John E. Higgins, Jr. et al. eds., 5th ed. 2006).

[106] *See generally id.* at 1650-51 (discussing lock-out found by the Supreme Court not to violate NLRA in *American Ship Bldg. Co. v. NLRB*, 380 U.S. 300 (1965)).

[107] *See, e.g.*, Squaxin Island Tribe, Labor and Employment Code, *supra* note 74, §§ 12.09.060(A)(7), 12.09.080(A)(1); Jamestown S'Klallam Tribe Labor Code, *supra* note 79, §§ 3.03.08 (F), 3.03.09(A)(1); Pokagon Band of Potawatomi Indians, Labor Organizations and Collective Bargaining Code, *supra* note 79, §§ 4-5; IOWA CODE ANN. § 20.10(2)(h) (West 2021) (as amended by 2010 Iowa Legis. Serv. 2485 (West)); OHIO REV. CODE ANN. § 4117.11(A)(7) (West 2021).

6. Collective Bargaining Impasse Procedures

If employee strikes and the equivalent employer lock-outs are prohibited, then arguably, the most effective means of bringing the parties to closure in the bargaining process are lost. Public sector labor laws, therefore, typically provide alternative processes to resolve collective bargaining impasses. These processes range in form from a mediation requirement to full-fledged formal and binding arbitration. The legislative decision about which method should be required raises important public policy choices about the best resolution method. These include whether there should there be only one method (*e.g.*, mediation or binding arbitration), or a series of steps (*e.g.*, mediation or fact finding with recommendations if the impasse is not resolved, to be followed by binding arbitration if the impasse is not resolved by mediation or fact finding)[108] that the parties are required to follow if early resolution is not achieved. Should decisions be made by a single fact finder or arbitrator or by a panel?[109]

A further complicating issue for tribal lawmakers is the extent to which they should be involved in approving the resolution of any particular bargaining impasse (or any final collective bargaining agreement, for that matter).[110] One reason that strikes are prohibited in the

---

[108]*Compare* Squaxin Island Tribe, Labor and Employment Code, *supra* note 74, §§ 12.09.100 (mediation followed by arbitration and limited tribal court review); Jamestown S'Klallam Tribe Labor Code, *supra* note 79, § 3.03.11 (same); Little River Band of Ottawa Indians Fair Employment Practices Code, *supra* note 63 § 16.16 (mediation followed by fact finding followed by binding arbitration); DEL. CODE ANN. TIT. 19, §§ 1314-1315 (West 2021) (mediation followed by binding arbitration); IOWA CODE ANN. §§ 20.20, 20.22 (West 2021) (mediation followed by binding arbitration); N.H. REV. STAT. ANN. § 273-A:12 (2021) (mediation followed by fact finding; if agreement is not reached, the recommendation goes to the legislature; if recommendation still not accepted, the parties start over); N.J. STAT. ANN. § 34:13A-7 (West 2021) (three-person arbitration panel may issue arbitration decision if agreed to by the parties).

[109]*Compare* Squaxin Island Tribe, Labor and Employment Code, *supra* note 74, § 12.09.100 (C)(1) (single arbitrator); Jamestown S'Klallam Tribe Labor Code, *supra* note 79, § 3.03.11(C)(1) (same); CONN. GEN. STAT. ANN. § 5-276a (b)-(d) (West 2021) (parties may proceed to mediation before single mediator, followed by arbitration before single arbitrator).

[110]*Compare* CONN. GEN. STAT. ANN. § 5-276a (e)(6) (West 2021) (arbitration award binding upon parties "unless rejected by the legislature"), § 5-278 (addressing appro-

public sector is that they have a direct effect upon the resources of governments.[111] Tribes, like states, set their budgets in accordance with their expected revenues and costs. Taking a tribe's IGRA gaming facility as an example, a strike against such a facility, implemented to leverage higher wages for employees in a bargaining unit, could put a strain upon the affected tribe's revenues and decisions about how to allocate the resources of tribal government. Resolution of the bargaining impasse about wages through mediation, fact finding, or arbitration could have the same effect upon public finances. If there is no check by the tribal government on such impasse resolutions, important *governmental* issues may be left to decision makers who are not part of that government. Thus, there may be good reasons for a tribal law to establish that arbitration decisions resolving impasses over economic terms within a collective bargaining agreement (*e.g.*, wages and insurance) are not binding upon the parties absent oversight by tribal government.[112]

7. Picketing

Picketing by employees and union representatives in Indian country presents tricky legal problems. Tribes have inherent authority to exclude nonmembers from tribal lands and to put conditions on their

---

priations by legislature necessary to meet obligations of collective bargaining agreement); 19 DEL. CODE ANN. TIT. § 1315(h) (West 2021) (arbitrator results may be contingent "upon appropriation by the General Assembly"); 43 PA. STAT. ANN. § 1101.805 (WEST 2021) ("decisions of the arbitrators which would require legislative enactment to be effective shall be considered advisory only").

[111] *See generally* James Duff, Jr., Annotation, *Labor Law: Right of Public Employees to Strike or Engage in Work Stoppage*, 37 A.L.R.3d 1147, 1151-52 & n.14 (1971 & Supp. 2007) (citing cases); Richard Doherty, *Review: The Politics of Public Sector Unionism*, 81 YALE L.J. 758, 767 (1972) ("[S]trikes have the potential of altering our system of public benefit conferral").

[112] For examples of tribal laws allocating to elected tribal representatives final decisions to resolve bargaining impasses concerning matters affecting government finances, *see* Squaxin Island Tribe, Labor and Employment Code, *supra* note 74, § 12.09.100(H) ("Limited Review by Tribal Council of Economic Terms Recommended by Arbitrator Upon Rejection by Employer"); Jamestown S'Klallam Tribe Labor Code, *supra* note 79, § 3.03.11(H) (same).

presence while on tribal lands.[113] This is particularly true when the nonmembers have consensual employment relationships with the tribe or its members.[114] A union that operates on tribal land as an agent for employees employed by the tribe should fall squarely within a tribe's regulatory authority under the *Montana* standards.[115] Thus, tribes have good grounds to assert authority to regulate picketing activity on tribal land, whether by tribal member employees, nonmember employees, or union representatives licensed under tribal law.

NLRA rules governing employee picketing rights are complex, but generally authorize off-duty employees to engage in peaceful picketing in non-work areas such as parking lots, so long as such activity does not interfere with the employer's business operations.[116] In contrast, the public sector labor laws of a number of states prohibit picketing at the residences of, or places of employment of, public officials who may be in a position to affect decisions on the state's labor relations.[117] Likewise, some states prohibit efforts by employees or union representatives to communicate during collective bargaining negotiations with any public officials other than those designated to represent the public employer at the negotiating table.[118] A number of tribes similarly restrict or prohibit picketing within their territorial jurisdictions[119] and outlaw union pressures on tribal government elections.[120]

---

113 *See* Chapter 2, Sections B and C.

114 *See* Chapter 2, Section C(1).

115 *See Montana v. United States*, 450 U.S. 544, 565-66 (1981).

116 *See, e.g., Tri-County Med. Ctr.*, 222 NLRB 1089 (1976); *Santa Fe Hotel Inc.*, 331 NLRB 723 (2000).

117 *See* Benjamin Aaron, *Unfair Labor Practices and the Right to Strike in the Public Sector*, 38 STAN. L. REV. 1097, 1102 n.36 (1986) (citing to Illinois, Iowa, Minnesota, Pennsylvania, and Vermont).

118 *Id*. at 1102 n. 44 (citing to Oregon law).

119 *See* Squaxin Island Tribe, Labor and Employment Code, *supra* note 74, § 12.09.080 (B)(7) (prohibiting attempts to influence any tribal elections); Jamestown S'Klallam Tribe Labor Code, *supra* note 79, § 3.03.09 (B)(7) (same).

How these tribal laws would fare if challenged by the NLRB as unfair labor practices of an "employer" turns upon the particular federal circuit court of appeals within which the tribe is located.[121]

8. "Right to Work," "Free Riders," and "Fair Share"

As discussed earlier in this chapter, so-called right-to-work laws have been enacted by states and tribes to guarantee that employees within a bargaining unit that is represented by a union need not join the union as a condition of employment or pay any fees to cover the cost of the union's services. These laws typically govern private sector employment, and the NLRA specifically provides that states may enact laws in this area notwithstanding the NLRA's otherwise preemptive sweep over the regulation of collective bargaining and labor relations in the private sector.[122] As noted earlier, there are differing public policy views as to the value of such a law.[123]

Consider a hypothetical situation. Suppose a tribe enacts a public sector labor relations law, and a union is elected to represent a bargaining unit of public employees. It is self-evident that workplace stability will be best served if the elected union is required to represent every member of the bargaining unit. Indeed, the very purpose of *collective* bargaining would be defeated if individual employees of a bargaining unit went their own way in dealing with the employer. Employees in the unit who did not vote for the union may, however, decide not to join the union for a variety of reasons. These employees, even if not union members, will still benefit from the union's services in negotiating an agreement covering the terms and conditions of employment for the collective whole. If they do not pay for such services, they may

---

[120]*See* Squaxin Island Tribe, Labor and Employment Code, *supra* note 74, § 12.09.08C (B)(8) (prohibiting picketing within the territorial jurisdiction of the tribe); Jamestown S'Klallam Tribe Labor Code, *supra* note 79, § 3.03.09 (B)(8).

[121]*See supra* at 242-246 (discussion of developing case law across the federal circuit courts of appeals as yet unresolved by the Supreme Court).

[122]*See* 29 U.S.C. § 164(b) (2018).

[123]*See supra* at 249-251.

be vulnerable to the label of "free riders."[124] Such potential disharmony might be viewed as a necessary cost to preserve the principle that no one should be forced to join an organization or to pay for something that they do not choose on their own.

On the other hand, arguments can be made that no one should receive the benefits of union services for free. Indeed, tribes may consider it important for workplace morale and stability to prevent anyone from suffering the "free rider" label. As a result, they may want to design a public sector labor laws that allow collective bargaining over fair share contributions from employees within a bargaining unit who decide not to join the union to cover the essential benefits they receive from the union representation. Such contributions are not membership dues; rather, they represent a reasonable value for services provided by the labor union, which will typically be less than full membership dues.[125] Tribal laws governing unions and collective bargaining could make such a provision a permissive or mandatory subject of bargaining. Tribes could enact "right-to-work" laws to ensure that employees within a bargaining unit are not compelled to join a union and, at the same time, require unions and tribal employers to bargain over provisions for fair share contributions from members of a bargaining unit who do not join the union.[126]

In *Janus v. Am. Fed'n of State, Cty., & Mun. Emps., Council 31*,[127] the Supreme Court held that within the public sector, collective bargaining agreements that include agency shop agreements (requiring all employees in a bargaining unit to become union members) and fair share

---

[124]*See generally International Union of the Plumbing and Pipefitting Industry, Local 41 v. NLRB: Closing the Door on Representation Fees in Right to Work States*, 1983 WIS. L. REV. 1231, 1233, & n.10 (1983).

[125]*See generally International Union of the Plumbing and Pipefitting Industry, Local 41 v. NLRB: Closing the Door on Representation Fees in Right to Work States*, 1983 WIS. L. REV. 1231, 1232, 1246 (1983) (discussing "fair share" fees as "representation fees").

[126]*See, e.g.,* Little River Band of Ottawa Indians Fair Employment Practices Code, *supra* note 63 §§ 16.05 (right to work law, entitled "Freedom of Choice Guaranteed"), 16.12 ("Fair Share Provisions for Nonmember Public Employees; De-Authorization of Fair Share Provisions; Payroll Deductions").

[127]138 S. Ct. 2448 (2018).

agreements violated the First Amendment because the state (the party to these public sector labor agreements) was effectively forcing employees to engage in speech (the activities of a union) that they did not necessarily agree with.[128] Indian tribes are not subject to the First Amendment, but it is possible that a tribal court empowered to enforce the Indian Civil Rights Act (ICRA) could find *Janus* persuasive in construing ICRA's provision that prohibits tribes from "abridging the freedom of speech" and strike down a such agreements within a tribe's public sector.[129] But tribal courts are not bound by *Janus* and could side with the dissenting Supreme Court justices in that case, which would uphold these agreements so long as they do not compel employees to fund a union's political and ideological activities.[130]

Time will tell how this these myriad considerations play out for any given tribe in the long run, but working through them when the time is ripe to govern labor unions and collective bargaining is the very business of exercising sovereignty.

F. Conclusion

Tribes have opportunities to enact laws governing unions and collective bargaining within Indian country in much the same way that states govern their own public sector labor relations. How tribes enact and implement such laws not only affects fundamental employment relations and the allocation of resources derived from tribal lands, but poses significant risks and opportunities for the development of the law.

As stated at the outset, the Supreme Court will someday take a case to resolve the conflicting approaches to tribal sovereignty that arise when the NLRB seeks to impose the NLRA upon public sector employment relations in Indian country. This decision will be significant because it will determine whether Congress must be explicit if it is to impose its labor and employment laws upon tribes. If silence won't do, Congress will have to do the hard work — to decide, for example,

---

[128]*See id.* at 2478, 2486.

[129]ICRA is discussed in some detail in Chapter 5, Section B.

[130]*See Janus,* 138 S. Ct. at 2487-99 (Kagan, J., dissenting).

whether tribes should be excluded from certain laws, like OSHA and the NLRA, in the same manner as states.

As tribes grapple with whether and how to enact laws governing unions and collective bargaining in Indian country, they should be cognizant that what they do on the ground could end up as the facts for a case in the Supreme Court.

10

DEVELOPING TRIBAL LAW: NATIVE AMERICAN EMPLOYMENT PREFERENCES IN TRANSITION

A. Introduction

One of the earliest codified forms of tribal sovereign authority over employment relations in Indian country took the form of laws requiring on-reservation employers to hire tribal members or other Native Americans before others. Indeed, federal laws conferring preferential treatment to Indians for employment opportunities with federal agencies operating within Indian country have been on the books for more than a century.[1] Today, tribal laws requiring employers to give preferences to tribal members and other Native Americans in training, hiring, and retention in the workplace are common.[2] Appendix C lists numerous employment preference laws adopted by various Indian tribes.[3]

---

[1] *See Morton v. Mancari*, 417 U.S. 535, 541 (1974) (discussing the long history of such laws). For over 150 years, Congress has ensured that federal agencies involved in Indian affairs give employment preferences to tribal members. *Id.* at 541-43 (citing 25 U.S.C. §§ 44-47, 274, 472). It has also exempted private businesses operating "on or near" Indian reservations from employment discrimination lawsuits when such businesses provide employment preference to Indians living on or near reservations. *See* 42 U.S.C. § 2000e-2(i) (2018).

[2] As used herein, the term "tribal member employment preference" or "tribal affiliation employment preference" refers to preferences accorded to members of a specific tribe, while "Indian (or Native American) preference" refers to preferences given to all Indians regardless of membership in a particular tribe.

[3] Tribes' employment preference laws vary widely. A number of tribes have adopted a model Tribal Employment Rights Ordinance, and set up commissions to oversee and enforce the ordinance. *See, e.g.*, Hoopa Valley Indian Tribe, Tribal Employment Rights Ordinance, tit. 13, available at: https://www.hoopa-nsn.gov/wp-content/

Tribes enact and enforce these laws pursuant to their inherent sovereign authority over their reservations and members.[4] Such laws can be viewed as reflecting the right of any national government to hire its own citizens before hiring noncitizens visiting from other countries.[5] Nevertheless, as is so often the case in federal Indian law, the established history of this exercise of sovereign authority provides no security for the future exercise of sovereign authority. Thus, it is fitting to close this book with a chapter that explores the roots of the earliest formal means of tribal employment regulation in Indian country, while pointing to some challenges to that authority on the horizon.

B. The Legal Basis for Indian Employment Preference Laws

1. *Morton v. Mancari*: "An employment criterion reasonably designed to further the cause of Indian self-government"

The most important case addressing Indian employment preferences is the Supreme Court's decision in *Morton v. Mancari*.[6] In that

---

uploads/2018/03/Title-13_TERO-Ordinance01052018153037_1.pdf; (last visited Dec. 8, 2021); Mohegan Tribe of Indians Code, Tribal Employment Rights, ch.4, art. 5, available at: https://library.municode.com/tribes_and_tribal_nations/mohegan_tribe/codes/code_of_laws?nodeId=PTIIMOTRINCO_CH4EM_ARTVTREMRI (last visited Dec. 8, 2021); Mashantucket Pequot Tribal Laws, Tribal and Native American Preference Law, tit. 33, available at: http://www.mptnlaw.com/laws/Single/TITLE%2033%20MASHANTUCKET%20PEQUOT%20TRIBAL%20AND%20NATIVE%20AMERICAN%20PREFERENCE%20LAW.pdf (last visited Dec. 8, 2021); Oglala Sioux Law & Order Code, ch. 18, available at: https://narf.org/nill/codes/oglala_sioux/chapter18-tero.html (last visited Dec. 8, 2021); White Mountain Apache Labor Code, ch. 1, available at: https://thorpe.law.ou.edu/archives/apache/labor.html#c1 (last visited Dec. 8, 2021).

[4]*See, e.g., FMC v. Shoshone-Bannock Tribes*, 905 F.2d 1311 (9th Cir. 1990) (tribe has jurisdiction to enforce Indian employment preference law against non-Indian employer on fee land within reservation). *See also Wardle v. Ute Indian Tribe*, 623 F.2d 670 (10th Cir. 1980); *Stroud v. Seminole Tribe of Florida*, 606 F. Supp. 678 (S.D. Fla 1985).

[5]*See Mancari*, 417 U.S. at 553-54; *Krueth v. Indep. Sch. Dist. 38*, 496 N.W.2d 829, 836 (Minn. Ct. App. 1993).

[6]417 U.S. 535 (1974).

case, the Court described such preferences as "an employment criterion reasonably designed to further the cause of Indian self-government."[7] *Mancari*'s recognition of the link between such employment preferences and tribal sovereignty is the legal cornerstone supporting such preferences.

Mancari involved a challenge by non-Indian employees to the implementation of Native American preferences within the Bureau of Indian Affairs (BIA). Those preferences had been mandated by Section 12 of the Indian Reorganization Act of 1934 (IRA).[8] The non-Indian employees claimed that, by enacting Section 11 of the Equal Employment Opportunity Act of 1972 (EEOA),[9] Congress implicitly repealed the IRA's Indian employment preferences. When the BIA sought to implement policies giving promotion preferences to Indians, non-Indian employees filed suit, claiming that the policies violated the EEOA and the Fifth Amendment's prohibition against race discrimination grounded the Equal Protection Clause.[10]

The Supreme Court first held that Section 11 of the EEOA did not repeal the IRA's Indian employment preference provision. The Court found that these preferences reflected "the longstanding federal policy of providing a unique legal status to Indians in matters concerning tribal or 'on or near' reservation employment."[11] The Court noted that Congress exempted Indian tribes and, in certain circumstances, non-Indian employers on or near reservations, from the employment discrimination provisions of Title VII of the Civil Rights Act of 1964 (Title VII)[12] in recognition of the "unique legal status of tribal and res-

---

[7] *Id.* at 554.

[8] 25 U.S.C. § 5116 (2018). The IRA is discussed in Chapter 1.

[9] 42 U.S.C. § 2000e-16(a) (2018).

[10] *See Mancari*, 417 U.S. at 540-41.

[11] *Id.* at 548.

[12] 42 U.S.C. § 2000e-2(i) (2018).

ervation-based activities" and in furtherance of tribal self-government.[13]

With regard to the non-Indians' Fifth Amendment challenge, the Court held that the BIA's employment preferences for Indians over non-Indians was not "racial discrimination":

> Rather, it is an employment criterion reasonably designed to further the cause of Indian self-government and to make the BIA more responsive to the needs of its constituent groups. It is directed to participation by the governed in the governing agency.[14]

In this manner, the Court established that the BIA's Indian preference policy was rationally related to political affiliation in furtherance of Congress's goal of promoting tribal self-government. Thus, the policy was not subject to Fifth Amendment "strict scrutiny" review on the ground that it treated employees differently because of race, but rather to a lower level of review, which was much more deferential. The fundamental principle of *Mancari* has been well summarized by one court as follows:

> American Indians who belong to a recognized tribe or sovereign entity are a race and, unlike white, black and yellow, are also part of a bona fide political class. Other races are not designated as independent political entities. A preference given to American Indians, although falling heavily on those individuals affected, is neither new nor startling in

---

[13]*Mancari*, 417 U.S. at 546.

[14]*Id.* at 553-54. *Accord Mullenberg v. United States*, 857 F.2d 770, 772 (Fed. Cir. 1988); *Krueth v. Indep. Sch. Dist. 38*, 496 N.W.2d 829, 836 (Minn. Ct. App. 1993). *See also AFL-CIO v. United States*, 104 F.Supp.2d 58 (D.D.C. 2000) (rejecting request for preliminary injunction to prevent U.S. Air Force from granting maintenance contract to wholly-owned subsidiary of Alaska Native Corporation in accordance with statute allowing contracting preference for firms owned 51 percent or more by Native Americans).

view of the policy that while race, color, and creed cannot be the basis for discrimination, membership in a political entity can be.[15]

2. The Inherent Authority of Tribes to Enact Indian or Tribal Member Employment Preference Laws

Mancari involved a challenge to an Indian employment preference law enacted by Congress. Many Indian tribes, however, have enacted their own laws, requiring employers operating within the territorial jurisdiction of the tribe to give preference to Indians in general and/or their own tribal members in relation to training, hiring, promoting, and retaining employees.[16] Federal courts addressing challenges to these laws have held that tribes have inherent authority to enact and enforce such laws against non-Indian employers within their jurisdictions.

In *FMC v. Shoshone-Bannock Tribes*,[17] the Ninth Circuit addressed the authority of the Tribes to enact and enforce their Indian employment preference laws. FMC — a non-Indian employer — manufactured phosphorus at its plant located on land that it owned in fee within the exterior boundaries of the reservation.[18] It obtained all of the phosphorus shale for this operation through mining leases with the Tribes and their members on reservation lands.[19] Applying *Montana*'s "consensual relationship" test,[20] the Ninth Circuit held that the Tribes had authority to enforce their Indian employment preference laws

---

[15] *Krueth v. Indep. Sch. Dist. 38*, 496 N.W.2d 829, 836 (Minn. Ct. App. 1993).

[16] *See supra* note 3.

[17] 905 F.2d 1311 (9th Cir. 1990).

[18] *See FMC*, 905 F.2d at 1312.

[19] *See id.*

[20] *See United States v. Montana*, 450 U.S. 544, 557 (1981). *Montana*'s consensual relationship test is discussed in Chapter 2.

against FMC.[21] By actively engaging in commerce with the Tribes, the court concluded, FMC "subjected itself to the civil jurisdiction of the Tribes" with respect to enforcement of the Tribes' Indian employment preference law.[22] The decisions of other federal courts support the inherent authority of Indian tribes to enforce Indian preference laws against non-Indian businesses within their jurisdictions.[23]

---

[21] *FMC*, 905 F.2d at 1314-15. In reaching its decision, the Ninth Circuit relied on two of its earlier decisions: one, in which it held that a tribe could enforce its health regulations against a non-Indian owner of a grocery store on fee land inside the reservation because of the commercial nexus between that business and the tribe and its members, and the other, in which it held that a tribe could enforce its property repossession laws against a non-Indian car dealer that conducted business with the tribe within the reservation. *See id.* at 1314-15 (citing *Cardin v. De La Cruz*, 671 F.2d 363 (9th Cir. 1982) and *Babbitt Ford, Inc. v. Navajo Indian Tribe*, 710 F.2d 587 (9th Cir. 1983)).

[22] *FMC*, 905 F.2d at 1315.

[23] *See generally NLRB v. Pueblo of San Juan*, 276 F.3d 1166 (10th Cir. 2002) (en banc) (confirming inherent authority of tribes to govern employment relations of non-Indian employers within reservation); *Duncan Energy Co. v. Three Affiliated Tribes of Fort Berthold Reservation*, 27 F.3d 1294 (8th Cir. 1994) (reversing federal district court decision holding that tribe lacked authority to impose employment preference laws and other laws on non-Indian oil company operating on fee lands within reservation; requiring exhaustion of tribal court remedies). *See also Arizona Public Service Co. v. Office of Navajo Labor Relations*, No. A-CV-08-87; 6 Nav. R. 246; 17 Indian L. Rptr. 6105, 6109-10 (Nav. Sup. Ct. 1990) (discussing, in detail, inherent power of tribes to regulate employment relations and civil rights issues concerning non-Indian reservation employer).

The question of whether the Navajo Nation may waive, by contract, its sovereign authority to require on-reservation employers to follow Navajo employment preferences has come up in a number of cases. *See Salt River Project Agricultural Improvement and Power Dist. v. Lee*, 2009 WL 89570 (D. Ariz. 2009) (whether Nation waived requirements of Navajo Preference in Employment Act in lease subject to dispute resolution by the Secretary of Interior under terms of lease). *Compare Arizona Public Service Co.*, No. A-CV-08-87; 6 Nav. R. 246; 17 Indian L. Rptr. 6105 (upholding application of NPEA to non-Indian employer on reservation) *with Arizona Public Service Co. v. Aspaas*, 77 F.3d 1128, 1135 (9th Cir. 1995) (assuming Nation had authority to impose NPEA upon non-Indian reservation employer, but concluding that the Nation waived that authority in its lease); *Salt River Project Agr. Imp. And Power Dist. v. Lee*, 2010 WL 4977621 (D. Ariz.) (dismissing non-Indian employer's action to enjoin Navajo officers from asserting NPEA authority because Nation was indispensable party).

The Ninth Circuit's decision in *State of Montana Department of Transportation v. King*,[24] provides an example of the limits of such authority. In *King*, the court held that the inherent authority of the Fort Belknap Indian Community did not allow that Tribe to impose its employment preference law upon the State of Montana when state crews were engaged in a highway construction project on state-owned land crossing the reservation.[25] The Ninth Circuit held that, because the land was owned by the State and neither of the *Montana* standards (discussed in Chapter 2) applied, the Tribe lacked authority to enforce its employment preference laws against the State.[26] In contrast, the Navajo Supreme Court has made clear that a state entity operating on the Navajo Reservation (not on state-owned land) is subject to the Navajo Preference in Employment Act,[27] and the Ninth Circuit has essentially confirmed the same.[28]

C. Tribal Member Preference Versus Indian Preference: Contradictions and Controversy

Tribes may decide to enact laws granting employment preference to their own members rather than to members of Indian tribes generally. Such tribal employment preferences seem readily justifiable: these laws ensure that the economic benefits derived from a tribe's

---

[24] 191 F.3d 1108 (9th Cir. 1999).

[25] *Id.* at 1114.

[26] *Id.* at 1113.

[27] *See Cedar Unified Sch. Dist. v. Navajo Nation Labor Comm'n*, No. SC-CV-53-06, slip op., No. SC-CV-54-06 (Nav. Sup. Ct. 2007) available at: http://tribal-institute.org/opinions/2007.NANN.0000018.htm (last visited Dec. 8, 2021).

[28] *See Window Rock Unified School District v. Reeves*, 861 F.3d 894 (9th Cir. 2017) (for purposes of applying the tribal exhaustion doctrine, discussed in Chapter 3, it is at least "plausible" that Navajo Nation Labor Commission would have authority to adjudicate employee NPEA claims against school district run by state within Navajo reservation).

lands inure to the benefit of its citizens.²⁹ Nevertheless, some federal laws only provide for "Indian" employment preferences on or near Indian reservations, seemingly blind to the importance of tribal member preferences for individual Indian tribes within their reservations. Further, lengthy legal battles have arisen on the Navajo reservation about whether private employers that give employment preferences to Navajo citizens over other Indians in accordance with Navajo law or the terms of a lease with the Nation engage in "national origin" discrimination, a form of discrimination that is illegal under Title VII.³⁰

1. Inconsistent Federal Statutes and Regulations

There are inconsistencies across federal statutes and regulations addressing tribal member employment preferences and Indian employment preferences. Some federal laws protect the authority of tribes to require tribal member employment preferences. Others require Indian employment preferences and place a check on the ability of tribes to enforce tribal member employment preference laws within their jurisdictions.

The Indian Self-Determination and Education Assistance Act (ISDEAA) of 1975,³¹ through which Congress provides funding for a wide range of tribal governmental projects, accommodates tribal member employment preferences. Under ISDEAA, the BIA may contract with tribes to provide funding for governmental services under so-called Public Law 638 contracts. Most of these contracts benefit

---

²⁹*See EEOC v. Peabody Western Coal Co.*, 773 F.3d 977, 988-89 (9th Cir. 2014). States, of course, would be barred by the Constitution from requiring employers to give preferences to the residents of their states over residents of other states, but Indian tribes are not states and the constitutional provisions that constrain states do not apply to tribes. *Cotton Petroleum Corp. v. New Mexico*, 490 U.S. 163, 192 (1989) (Article I, § 8, cl. 3 of the Constitution "no more admits of treating Indian tribes as States than of treating foreign nations as States."); *see also Santa Clara Pueblo v. Martinez*, 436 U.S 49, 55-56 (1978).

³⁰*See Peabody Western Coal Co.*, 773 F.3d 977; *Dawavendewa v. Salt River Project Agricultural Improvement & Power District* 154 F.3d 1117 (9th Cir. 1998). These legal battles are discussed in Subsection 2, below.

³¹25 U.S.C. §§ 5301-5310 (2018). ISDEEA is discussed in Chapter 1.

specific tribes, and, in that setting, Congress mandates that "the tribal employment or contract preference laws adopted by such tribe shall govern with respect to the administration of the contract."[32] Thus, if a given tribe has enacted a law providing for tribal member employment preferences, that law controls.

In contrast, Department of the Interior regulations governing federal contractors working on or near Indian reservations and receiving federal financing expressly prohibit tribal member employment preferences, but allow preferences if granted to all Indians.[33] Department of Labor regulations governing federal contractors engaged in work "on or near Indian reservations" likewise prohibit tribal member preferences, while allowing Indian preferences,[34] as do Department of Transportation regulations governing federal highway projects.[35]

For employment settings that are not within a single tribe's territorial jurisdiction, that is, "near" reservations, the logic of requiring employers to give preferences to all Indians may make sense. As the EEOC has observed:

> [I]n some parts of the country, employers are situated near the reservations of more than one tribe or more than one tribe may share the same reservation. The potential inequities resulting from according a preference based on tribal affiliation are

---

[32] 25 U.S.C. § 5307(c) (2018). *See also* 25 U.S.C. § 5324(c) (2018) (exempting Public Law 638 contracts from federal procurement contract requirements, including Executive Order 11246, which requires equal employment opportunity provisions); 48 C.F.R. § 1426.7005(a) (2020) (contracting officer may add to the funding contract "specific Indian preference requirements of the Tribe on whose reservation the work is to be performed").

[33] 48 C.F.R. §§ 1452.226-70, 1452.226-71 (2020).

[34] 41 C.F.R. § 60-1.5(a)(7) (2020).

[35] 23 C.F.R. § 635.117(d) (2020).

most clearly evident when these circumstances are contemplated.[36]

For employment settings within a single tribe's territorial jurisdiction, however, there should be little controversy about that tribe's sovereign authority to require employers to follow a tribal employment preference law, and it would seem simple enough for federal regulations to honor that exercise of tribal sovereignty in like manner to ISDEEA. But controversies abound.

2. Challenges to Tribal Member Preferences: Do They Constitute Unlawful Discrimination on the Basis of "National Origin"?

Title VII exempts private employers "on or near" Indian reservations from liability for employment discrimination "with respect to any publicly announced employment practice of such business or enterprise under which a preferential treatment is given to any individual because he is an Indian living on or near a reservation."[37] Since 1988, the EEOC, which is charged with the administration of most federal employment discrimination laws, has interpreted this provision to protect against liability for employment discrimination only if preferences are given to all Indians, but not if they are given only to tribal members.[38] This does not answer the question, in the first instance, of whether a private employer can be liable for national origin discrimination under

---

[36]*See Policy Statement on Indian Preference Under Title VII*, Fair Empl. Prac. (BNA) 405:6647, 6653 (May 16, 1988), available at: https://www.eeoc.gov/laws/guidance/policy-statement-indian-preference-under-title-vii (last visited Dec. 8, 2021).

[37]42 U.S.C. § 2000e-2(i) (2018).

[38]The EEOC's policy statement states that the "extension of an employment preference on the basis of tribal affiliation is in conflict with and violates"the "on or near reservation"exemption of Title VII. *See Policy Statement on Indian Preference Under Title VII*, Fair Empl. Prac. (BNA) 405:6647, 6653 (May 16, 1988), available at: https://www.eeoc.gov/laws/guidance/policy-statement-indian-preference-under-title-vii (last visited Dec. 8, 2021). Since Indian tribes are expressly excluded from the provisions of Title VII, the policy has no effect upon tribal member preferences imposed by a tribe with respect to its own employment practices.

Title VII for complying with a requirement in a tribal law or a lease that it give employment preferences to that tribe's members over other Indians.[39]

It took two decades for a federal court of appeals with jurisdiction over the great bulk of federally recognized Indian tribes, the Ninth Circuit, to finally conclude that a coal mining company operating on the Navajo Reservation is not liable for national origin discrimination under Title VII for giving employment preferences to Navajo tribal members over other Indians in compliance with the terms of a lease between the company and the Navajo Nation. A case has yet to reach the Supreme Court on this question. Thus, uncertainties remain, and there are ongoing challenges to the underpinning of this conclusion, the *Mancari* decision. So it is worth recounting the history of legal developments in this area to understand the setting for the future.

* * *

In the mid-1990s, Harold Dawavendewa, a member of the Hopi Tribe, was denied employment by the Salt River Project Agricultural Improvement and Power District (SRP), an Arizona corporation operating on the Navajo reservation, when SRP passed him over to hire a Navajo tribal member.[40] SRP made its employment decision by following the Navajo Nation's law requiring reservation employers to provide employment preferences to qualified Navajo tribal members.[41] The Navajo Nation's lease with SRP required the same preference.

---

[39] *See E.E.O.C. v. Peabody W. Coal Co.,* 773 F.3d at 984–85.

[40] *Dawavendewa v. Salt River Project Agricultural Improvement & Power District,* 154 F.3d 1117 (9th Cir. 1998).

[41] Section 604 of the Navajo Preference in Employment Act, 15 N.N.C. §§ 601-19, states as follows:
   § 604. Navajo employment preference
   A. All employers doing business within the territorial jurisdiction [or near the boundaries] of the Navajo Nation, or engaged in any contract with the Navajo Nation, shall:
   1. Give preference in employment to Navajos ...
15 N.N.C. § 604.

Dawavendewa sued SRP in federal court for national origin discrimination in violation of Title VII.[42]

SRP sought dismissal, claiming that it did not engage in national origin discrimination because the Navajo Nation's law requiring tribal member preferences constituted the political affiliation preferences of a sovereign. The federal district court did not reach that specific question. It simply held that Title VII exempted private employers from any liability under Title VII when they follow such employment preferences.[43]

The Ninth Circuit reversed. It did not reach the merits of the discrimination allegations; it simply held that the case could go forward. The court found that "differential employment treatment [by a private company on an Indian reservation] based on tribal affiliation is actionable as 'national origin' discrimination under Title VII."[44] It further said that Title VII's liability exemption for private employers giving preferential treatment "to any individual because he is an Indian living on or near a reservation" did not protect SRP from liability for awarding preference to a member of one tribe over a member of another tribe.[45] It also rejected SRP's argument that the Navajo Nation's employment preference law furthered tribal self-government in accord with the spirit of *Mancari*.[46]

---

[42] *See Dawavendewa*, 154 F.3d 1117.

[43] *Dawavendewa*, 154 F.3d at 1119 ("The district court ... held that Title VII exempts tribal preference policies, and therefore found it unnecessary to decide whether discrimination on the basis of tribal membership constitutes national origin discrimination under Title VII.").

[44] *Id*. at 1120.

[45] *Id*. at 1121-22 (quoting 42 U.S.C. § 2000e-2(i)).

[46] *Id* at 1121-23 ("Preferential employment of Navajo Indians on a privately owned facility, while certainly helpful to the tribe's employment problems," the court said "has little to do with increasing the tribe's capacity for self-governance"). The court made note of an intractable contradiction that would develop if the Navajo Nation had contracted with SRP pursuant to the ISDEAA. In that setting, a national origin discrimination claim against SRP under Title VII would clash with the mandate of the ISDEAA that SRP provide tribal affiliation employment preferences to Navajo

Four years later, the case returned to the Ninth Circuit. This time, the court held that dismissal was proper because the Navajo Nation, whose law was under attack, was an "indispensable party" to the action but could not be joined as a party because of sovereign immunity.[47] As an absent party, the Navajo Nation would not be bound by the judgment, and if Dawavendewa won, SRP would find itself "between the proverbial rock and a hard place—comply with the injunction prohibiting the hiring preference policy or comply with the lease requiring it."[48] But the court also said that if the EEOC were to join in the action and bring suit against both SRP and the Navajo Nation on behalf of Dawavendewa, the case could proceed because the Navajo Nation could not claim sovereign immunity with respect to actions by the EEOC, an agency of the United States.[49]

Three years later, the EEOC stepped into the fray in another case arising on the Navajo reservation, *EEOC v. Peabody Western Coal Co.*[50] Peabody Western Coal Company (Peabody) has had longstanding leases with the Navajo Nation for coal mining on the Navajo reservation, which require the same Navajo tribal employment preferences at issue in *Dawavendewa* and track the identical requirement under the Navajo Nation's law.[51] The leases were approved by the Department of the

---

tribal members pursuant to Navajo law. *See id.* at 1124 n.15. *See also supra* note 29, referencing ISDEAA requirement.

[47]*Dawavendewa v. Salt River Project Agric. Improvement & Power Dist.*, 276 F.3d 1150 (9th Cir. 2002). Chapter 4 discusses the doctrine of tribal sovereign immunity.

[48]*Id.* at 1156.

[49]*See id.* at 1162-63.

[50]400 F.3d 774 (9th Cir. 2005).

[51]The Navajo Nation has a longstanding and widespread practice of enforcing tribal member preference standards. As the Arizona federal district court explained:
> Since 1985 a Navajo Nation tribal ordinance has required employers doing business on the Navajo Nation reservation to give employment preference to Navajo members. As a result, employment preference provisions are standard terms in leases within the Navajo Nation's jurisdiction. According to the Nation, as of 2005, there were 326 current or recently expired business leases on tribal lands that contain similar employment preference provisions for Navajo job applicants, and all of these leases have been approved by the DOI's Bureau

Interior.⁵² The EEOC sued Peabody on behalf of Indians who were not Navajo citizens, claiming that Peabody engaged in national origin employment discrimination in violation of Title VII.⁵³

Drawing upon the lessons of *Dawavendewa*, Peabody moved to dismiss on the ground that the Navajo Nation was an indispensable party that could not be joined in the action. The EEOC and Peabody agreed that the Navajo Nation needed to be joined because the outcome could undermine the authority of its law and the effectiveness of its leases.⁵⁴ They differed, however, on whether the Nation could be brought in as a party. Because the EEOC was the plaintiff, Peabody could not argue that the Navajo Nation's sovereign immunity prevented it from being joined (as was the case in *Dawavendewa*) because sovereign immunity is no defense to suits brought by the United States or its agencies. Instead, Peabody argued that the Nation could not be joined because the EEOC had brought suit under Title VII, and Congress expressly excluded tribes from the employment discrimination laws of Title VII.⁵⁵ The federal district court agreed with Peabody, but the Ninth Circuit reversed and held that so long as the EEOC did not seek affirmative relief from the Navajo Nation, it could join the Nation as a defendant notwithstanding its exclusion from Title VII.⁵⁶ Thus, the case moved forward with EEOC suing the Navajo Nation along with Peabody.

---

of Indian Affairs. The Nation has entered into at least two lease agreements that require the lessee to maintain a tribal employment preference, but only to the extent the preference is not in derogation of federal law.
Equal Emp. Opportunity Comm'n v. Peabody W. Coal Co., No. 2:01-CV-01050 JWS, 2012 WL 5034276, at *2 (D. Ariz. Oct. 18, 2012) (footnotes omitted), *aff'd sub nom. E.E.O.C. v. Peabody W. Coal Co.*, 773 F.3d 977 (9th Cir. 2014).

⁵²*See EEOC v. Peabody Western Coal Co.*, No. CV 01-01050-PHX-MHM, 2006 WL 2816603, at *5 (D. Ariz. Sep. 30, 2006).

⁵³42 U.S.C. § 2000e-2(a)(1) (2018).

⁵⁴*See E.E.O.C. v. Peabody Coal Co.*, 214 F.R.D. 549, 557 (D. Ariz. 2002), *rev'd and remanded sub nom. E.E.O.C. v. Peabody W. Coal Co.*, 400 F.3d 774 (9th Cir. 2005).

⁵⁵42 U.S.C. § 2000e(b) (2018).

⁵⁶*Peabody Western Coal Co.*, 400 F.3d at 780-83.

After additional proceedings, the EEOC also joined the Secretary of the Interior as a party because the Department of the Interior had approved the leases with the tribal employment preference requirement.[57] So the EEOC ended up on one side of the case against Peabody for national origin discrimination, but also against the Secretary of the Interior, defending the lease terms, and the Navajo Nation, defending its employment preference law as well as the lease terms.[58]

In finally reaching the merits of the case in 2014, the Ninth Circuit held the Peabody could not be held liable for national origin discrimination by following the tribal employment preference requirements of its Interior-approved leases with the Navajo Nation.[59] It first reasoned that tribal affiliation is a political classification, not based on "national origin" as such, and that in *Mancari,* the Supreme Court characterized the BIA's Indian employment preference in the same manner, albeit to provide "a general Indian hiring preference rather than a tribe-specific preference."[60] The Ninth Circuit then relied heavily on "the policy considerations that undergird *Mancari,*" the furtherance of tribal self-governance. It pointed out that the leases in question were approved by the Secretary of the Interior pursuant to the Indian Mineral Leasing Act of 1938 (IMLA), a fundamental purpose of which is to empower tribal governments to maximize economic returns for their citizens with respect to mining operations on tribal lands in harmony with the self-governance goals of the Indian Reorganization Act of 1934 (IRA).[61]

Focusing solely on the leases, and not upon the Navajo Nation's employment preference law, the Ninth Circuit summarized:

---

[57]*See EEOC v. Peabody Western Coal Co.*, 610 F.3d 1070, 1081 (9th Cir. 2010).

[58]*See EEOC v. Peabody Western Coal Co.,* 773 F.3d at 980-82.

[59]*See id.* at 986-89.

[60]*Id.* at 987.

[61]The IRA and the IMLA are described in Chapter 1 as emblematic of the shift in federal Indian policy away from a goal of "assimilating"tribes to one of promoting tribal self-government and self-determination.

A key purpose of the IRA was the advancement of tribal self-government. The IMLA aimed to foster tribal self-determination by giving Indians a greater say in the use and disposition of resources found on Indian lands. Where the exploitation of mineral resources on a particular tribe's reservation is concerned, the federal government's responsibility necessarily runs to that tribe, not to all Indians.

We therefore have no difficulty concluding that the tribal hiring preferences here are based on a political classification within the meaning of *Mancari*. Peabody accords preference in hiring to members of the Navajo Nation, pursuant to the terms of Interior-approved leases. Interior viewed those preferential hiring provisions as useful in ensuring that the economic benefits flowing from the "most important resource" on the Navajo reservation accrued to the tribe and its members.[62]

Having concluded that the tribal affiliation preference required by the leases involved a political classification in accord with *Mancari*, the Ninth Circuit then examined "whether Title VII's specific prohibition on national origin discrimination extends to . . . differential treatment based on tribal affiliation, the political classification at issue here" and concluded that it did not.[63]

This came down to a question of Congress's intent in Title VII: whether it intended national origin discrimination to encompass the Navajo employment preference at issue. The court reasoned:

Interior's approval of mineral leases containing tribal hiring preferences is a well-established practice that long predates the enactment of Title VII. Tribal hiring preferences were, and are,

---

[62]*Id.* at 988 (quotations, alterations, and citation omitted).

[63]*Id.* at 988-89.

intended to further the policy goals embodied in the IRA and the IMLA. Nothing indicates that Congress viewed Title VII as a recalibration of its policy toward tribal communities that had been articulated in its prior legislation. Nor is there any suggestion that Congress viewed Title VII as a specific disapproval of Interior's longstanding and settled practice of approving tribal hiring preferences in mineral leases.[64]

Thus, on the specific facts presented by the Navajo tribal employment preference set forth in the Interior-approved leases, the Ninth Circuit held that Peabody's actions in hiring Navajo tribal citizens before other Indians did not constitute national origin discrimination in violation of Title VII.

One might ask how the Ninth Circuit arrived at this conclusion in *Peabody Western Coal* when, sixteen years earlier, in *Dawavendewa*, it held that SRP could be sued for national origin discrimination for complying with the Navajo Nation's tribal employment preference law and leases tracking it. First, in *Dawavendewa*, the Ninth Circuit only addressed whether Mr. Dawavendewa stated a claim, not whether he would win on the merits of his claim. In *Peabody Western Coal*, the Ninth Circuit explained, "we declined to consider whether . . . the federal policy favoring tribal self-governance, the Navajo Preference in Employment Act, or any other legal defense justified SRP's hiring preference."[65] Second, in *Peabody Western Coal,* the Ninth Circuit narrowed its decision to the specific facts presented and focused heavily upon the furtherance of Congress's goals under the IMLA and IRA that stood behind the Interior Department's approval of the leases in question.

One might also ask why tribal self-government is any less at stake when the Navajo Nation exercises its inherent sovereign authority to enact and implement a law requiring employers operating within its

---

[64]*Id.* at 989.

[65]*Peabody Western Coal,* 773 F.3d at 986 (emphasis and alterations in original eliminated).

reservation (whether tribal or non-tribal) to give employment preferences to Navajo citizens than when the Nation enters into a lease with a non-tribal company, approved by the Secretary of Interior, that requires such an employment preference? Recall that in *Dawavendewa*, the Ninth Circuit rejected SRP's argument that the Nation's law implicated tribal self-government in the spirit of *Mancari*.[66] This seems at odds with the Ninth Circuit's treatment of the subject in *FMC* described above[67] and the general consensus across the federal courts, in accord with well-established Supreme Court cases, that tribes enact and enforce such laws as an exercise of their inherent sovereign authority, the very right of self-government.[68] In any event, as it stands, the *Peabody Western Coal* decision appears limited to its facts, and it cogently weaves a logic to construe Congress's intent in Title VII not to upset existing federal practices consistent with its longstanding commitment to tribal self-government reflected in the IMLA and IRA.

* * *

For advocates of tribal sovereignty, the laws of any given tribe requiring employers within their jurisdictional territories, like Peabody and SRP on the Navajo Reservation, to hire qualified tribal citizens before non-tribal citizens, comports with Congress's commitment to tribal self-government and should not place these employers in jeopardy for national origin discrimination under Title VII. Yet the Ninth Circuit's decision in *Peabody Western Coal* does not go that far because it is limited to a situation where the preference appears in leases approved by the Secretary of Interior in accord with federal laws that would clash with Title VII were the preference construed as national origin discrimination. It remains to be seen whether a federal court will reach the same outcome if only a tribal law requiring the preference is at issue, not a Department of Interior approved lease.

In addition, if Congress and its agencies were to earnestly follow modern federal policy of enhancing tribal self-government, tribal affiliation employment preferences should be able to operate in accord

---

[66]*See supra* note 46.

[67]*See supra* text accompanying notes 17-23.

[68]*See* Chapter 2, Section C. *See also supra* at 279-280.

with the laws of a given tribe for federally funded projects within the territorial jurisdiction of the tribe. The problem is starkly revealed by the Ninth Circuit's comment in the second *Dawavendewa* appeal, that had the Navajo Nation contracted with SRP under ISDEAA, Title VII liability for SRP would be in direct conflict with ISDEAA.[69] This is because, as explained above, ISDEAA requires tribal contractors operating under Public Law 638 contracts to comply with the employment preference laws of the tribe, including tribal member preferences.[70]

One obvious solution would be for Congress to amend Title VII's liability exemption for employers that give "preferential treatment . . . to any individual because he is an Indian living on or near a reservation"[71] to establish that the exemption also extends to employers located within the jurisdiction of an Indian tribe, who give preferential treatment to members of the tribe. Without that amendment, lengthy litigation, like the *Dawavendewa* and *Peabody Western Coal Co* cases, may be on the horizon.

D. Conclusion: Challenges Past and Present

The challenges to Indian employment preferences presented in *Mancari*, on the one hand, and those to tribal member preferences in *Dawavendewa* and *Peabody Western Coal Co.*, on the other, show the two basic contexts in which attacks have been made upon employment preferences on the bases of "Indian" status and tribal member status. *Mancari* involved a direct challenge to a congressional enactment to provide advantages to individuals because of their status as Indians. *Dawavendewa* and *Peabody Western Coal Co.*, however, involved indirect challenges to a tribal member employment preference law, taking the form of federal employment discrimination lawsuits against private employers who followed tribal law and lease requirements.[72]

---

[69]*See Dawavendewa*, 154 F.3d at 1124 n.15.

[70]*See* 25 U.S.C. § 5307(c) (2018).

[71]42 U.S.C. § 2000e-2(i) (2018).

[72]*See also Malabed v. North Slope Borough*, 335 F.3d 864 (9th Cir. 2003) (Borough's Indian employment preference code was held to violate the Alaska Constitution's

In *United States v. Antelope*,[73] the Supreme Court said that the key to its holding in *Mancari* — that the IRA's Indian employment preferences did not constitute "racial" preferences in violation of the Equal Protection Clause of the Fifth Amendment — was the Court's view that such preferences involved Congress's "[legislation] rooted in the unique status of Indians as a separate people with their own political institutions."[74] Indeed, "[c]lassifications expressly singling out Indian tribes as subjects of legislation," the Court said, "are expressly provided for in the Constitution."[75] They are also linked to the trust responsibility of the federal government to Indian tribes, and "[a]s long as the special treatment can be tied rationally to the fulfillment of Congress's unique obligation toward the Indians, such legislative judgments will not be disturbed."[76] From these pronouncements, it reasonably follows that that Congress's acts protecting tribal member employment preferences (as in the case of the ISDEAA) or promoting Indian employment preferences generally must be upheld in the face of challenges on the basis of national origin or race discrimination so long as they are related to the "governance of once-sovereign political communities."[77]

Again, tribal member employment preferences are enacted by Indian tribes pursuant to their inherent sovereign authority over their members and their reservations. They therefore reflect the direct exercise of government authority by Indian tribes as "sovereign political communities." While enacted by tribes and not by Congress, they are

---

Equal Protection Clause; Congress's exemption of Indian employment preferences from the employment discrimination provisions of Title VII did not preempt application of the state constitutional bar to the Borough's code).

[73] 430 U. S. 641, 646 (1977).

[74] *United States v. Antelope*, 430 U. S. 641, 646 (1977) (citing *Mancari*, 417 U.S. at 553 n.24) (emphasis added) (quotation marks omitted). *See also Williams v. Babbitt*, 115 F.3d 657, 665 (9th Cir. 1997) (*Mancari* involved "preferences or disabilities directly promoting Indian interests in self-government").

[75] *Antelope*, 430 U.S. at 645 & n.6 (citing U.S. CONST. art. I, § 8).

[76] *Mancari*, 417 U.S. at 555.

[77] *Antelope*, 430 U. S. at 646.

certainly "rooted in the unique status of Indians as a separate people with their own political institutions."[78] Nevertheless, like so many other issues in the field of federal Indian law, whether tribal member employment preferences, or even Indian employment preferences under *Mancari*, will survive ongoing attacks from a variety of sources remains to be seen.[79]

---

[78] *See id.*

[79] *See generally* Matthew L.M. Fletcher, *Politics, Indian Law, and the Constitution*, 108 CAL. L. REV. 495, 500–02 (2020) (observing that "conservative Supreme Court Justices have signaled that they are willing to reconsider the political classification doctrine" of *Mancari*, and Supreme Court review of the splintered decision of the U.S. Court of Appeals for the Fifth Circuit in *Brackeen v. Haaland*, 994 F.3d 249 (5th Cir. 2021), addressing the constitutionality of the Indian Child Welfare Act, may give them a chance to do so); Michael Doran, *The Equal-Protection Challenge to Federal Indian Law*, 6 U. PA. J.L. & PUB. AFF. 1, 8 (2020) ("[T]he prospect of the Supreme Court taking a hard look at the equal-protection status of federal Indian law seems stronger now than at any time since *Mancari* and the cases decided in its immediate wake."); Gregory Smith, Caroline Mayhew, *Apocalypse Now: The Unrelenting Assault on* Morton v. Mancari, FED. LAW., April 2013, at 47 (canvasing well-organized challenges to *Mancari*.)

11

CONCLUSION

The law strives for fairness, but federal Indian law is caught in a paradox; the process of colonization is fundamentally unfair and attempts to justify it are, therefore, fraught. The result is messy doctrinal inconsistencies. Indeed, the Supreme Court itself admitted that the logic for the first "discovering" European nation in America to take title to Indigenous lands, grounded in presumed Christian superiority over Indigenous peoples, was shaky.[1]

The sub-area of federal Indian law explored in this book, that pertaining to labor and employment relations in Indian country, reflects the same paradox in a pointed way. The central, reoccurring problem throughout is that Congress forgot to mention Indian tribes in a host of labor and employment statutes, leaving the federal courts to grapple with what to do in the face of such silence. Indian tribes are governments, and when one government (the United States or a state) imposes its laws upon another (an Indian tribe), there is an intrusion upon the latter's dignity as a sovereign.[2] The intrusion is real even when the tribe has not yet enacted a law governing the same area, but it is all the worse when the external, imposed law displaces a tribal law governing the same area in accord with the tribe's own unique values and norms. Worse still is if Congress clearly intended the particular law (like the NLRA or OSHA) not to apply to sovereign governments, but simply forgot to mention Indian tribes.

As tribes continue to expand their economies, they will generate more employment opportunities within their territories. Federal agencies like the Equal Employment Opportunities Commission, the

---

[1] *See Worcester v. State of Ga.*, 31 U.S. 515, 517 (1832).

[2] *See Iowa Mut. Ins. Co. v. LaPlante,* 480 U.S. 9, 18 (1987); *Williams v. Lee,* 358 U.S. 217, 220–221 (1959).

National Labor Relations Board, and the Department of Labor show no signs of retreating from their efforts to regulate employment in Indian country through the various laws they administer.[3] Congress's failure to address Indian tribes in those laws will not deter them. But the *central question* for the future of labor and employment law in Indian country remains: what rule will determine whether a federal labor or employment law that is silent about its application to Indian tribes may be imposed upon tribes? Will it be the rule of the Tenth and Eighth Circuits: that Congressional silence will not do and that courts must identify a clear statement from Congress before they will condone such intrusions upon the sovereign dignity of Indian tribes? Will it be the rule of the Ninth, Second, and Sixth Circuits: that courts should presume that such "silent" laws apply to tribes unless they would abrogate an express treaty right or interfere with "exclusive rights of self-governance in purely intramural matters"? Or will it be something else?[4]

Congress can be accused of being remiss in not correcting its deafening silence,[5] but it shows no inclination to do so.[6] This means that it will be up to the Supreme Court to decide which rule prevails. And when that case is decided, it could have a profound impact upon the entire field of federal Indian law. For it will likely address the fundamental roles of Congress and the Court with respect to Indian affairs in this country.

The Supreme Court recently held that, absent a clear directive from Congress, it would not second-guess the promise of a treaty between the United States and the Muscogee (Creek) Nation, setting

---

[3] *See* Chapter 3, Section C.

[4] These various approaches are discussed in Chapter 3, Section C, and for the various federal laws in question in Chapters 5 through 7.

[5] See Kaighn Smith Jr., *When Congress Forgets: Breaking Through Congress's Failure to Mention Indian Tribes in Federal Employment Laws,* FED. LAW. March/April 2021, at 8.

[6] *See* discussion of the Tribal Labor Sovereignty Act, discussed in the conclusion to Chapter 7; Noam Scheiber, *Senate Bill to Curtail Labor Rights on Tribal Land Falls Short,* N.Y. Times, April 16, 2018.

aside land for the Nation in present-day Oklahoma, notwithstanding encroachments upon those lands by nonmembers and the state's presumption of authority therein for years on end.[7] Justice Gorsuch, writing for the Court, said it was not up to the Court to engage in the messy business of "nullifying the promises made in the name of the United States."[8] He wrote:

> That would be at odds with the Constitution, which entrusts Congress with the authority to regulate commerce with Native Americans , . . . Art. I, § 8.
> [The] courts have no proper role in the adjustment of reservation borders. Mustering the broad social consensus required to pass new legislation is a deliberately hard business under our Constitution. . . [S]aving the political branches the embarrassment of disestablishing a reservation is not one of our constitutionally assigned prerogatives. Only Congress can divest a reservation of its land and diminish its boundaries.[9]

The Court has suggested that the same principles apply for the abrogation or infringement of inherent tribal sovereignty,[10] but it has yet to face the precise issue of whether Congress must clearly state its intention to impose a federal labor or employment law upon an Indian tribe before the Court will allow it. The lower federal courts have been split on the issue for over thirty-five years, and that split has only

---

[7]*McGirt v. Oklahoma*, 140 S. Ct. 2452 (2020).

[8]*Id.* at 2462.

[9]*Id.* (quotations, alterations and citations omitted).

[10]*Id.* at 2477 (the Court has required "a clear expression of the intention of Congress" before abrogating inherent tribal sovereignty by allowing "the state or federal government [to] try Indians for conduct on their lands") (quoting *Ex parte Crow Dog*, 109 U.S. 556, 572 (1883)); *Michigan v. Bay Mills Indian Cmty.*, 572 U.S. 782, 790 (2014) ("an enduring principle of Indian law [is that] [a]lthough Congress has plenary authority over tribes, courts will not lightly assume that Congress in fact intends to undermine Indian self-government").

deepened in the eleven years since the first edition of this book. So it appears to be just a matter of time before the Court reaches the issue.

In this unstable legal environment, the type of labor or employment case that reaches the Supreme Court could well determine the outcome of this central question for all tribes. If the application of a federal labor or employment law would clearly infringe upon the exercise of a tribe's sovereign authority — as exhibited, for instance, through a tribe's enactment, implementation, and enforcement of tribal law — the Supreme Court may more readily pause before holding that the federal law applies. On the other hand, if there is no governing tribal law and, therefore, a void to fill, the Court may be more inclined to allow the federal law in question to "fill the gap." In other words, the very act of exercising tribal authority over labor and employment relations could stave off the imposition of external authority. These may be matters of optics, but they important ones.

The great French observer of American democracy, Alex de Tocqueville, wrote in the nineteenth century:

> The conduct of the United States Americans toward the natives was inspired by the most chaste affection for legal formalities.
>
> . . .
>
> The Spaniards, by unparalleled atrocities which brand them with indelible shame, did not succeed in exterminating the Indian race and could not even prevent them from sharing their rights; the United States Americans have attained both these results with wonderful ease, quietly, legally, and philanthropically. . . . It is impossible to destroy men with more respect for the laws of humanity.[11]

Having completed his survey of federal Indian law in the twentieth century, Felix Cohen made his famous observation the year he passed away:

---

[11] TOCQUEVILLE, DEMOCRACY IN AMERICA (1848) (Doubleday Edition 1969) at 339.

> ... like the miner's canary, the Indian marks the shift from fresh air to poison gas in our political atmosphere; and our treatment of Indians, even more than our treatment of other minorities, reflects the rise and fall in our democratic faith. . . .[12]

Notwithstanding Tocqueville's view, Indian tribes have survived in America. That survival turns on the sustainability of their authority as sovereign nations. When a case reaches the Supreme Court to resolve the above-highlighted "central question," it will be an important moment for federal Indian law, and Felix Cohen's canary will be taking it all in.

---

[12] Felix S. Cohen, *The Erosion of Indian Rights,* 62 YALE L.J. 348, 390 (1953).

APPENDIX A

VARIABLES AFFECTING THE GOVERNANCE OF LABOR AND EMPLOYMENT RELATIONS IN INDIAN COUNTRY

EMPLOYMENT RELATIONS ON INDIAN TRIBE'S RESERVATION OR TRUST LANDS (NOT FEE LAND)

A. NONMEMBER EMPLOYER, EMPLOYING TRIBAL MEMBERS AND NONMEMBERS

1. **Tribal Authority**

Basis for Indian tribe's authority over the nonmember employer:

- Nonmember extracting economic value from reservation or trust lands subject to authority of tribe to exclude the nonmember and to condition the nonmember's activity while remaining on the tribe's land.[1]

- Nonmember who extracts economic value from reservation or trust lands, and enters into contract or lease with the tribe for that purpose, has a "consensual relationship" with the tribe, which is subject to regulation by the tribe, including the regulation of employment relations, so long as the regulation has a "nexus" to the consensual relationship.[2]

---

[1] *See Merrion v. Jicarilla Apache Tribe,* 455 U.S. 130, 144 (1982); *Williams v. Lee,* 358 U.S. 217 (1959); *Arizona Public Service Co.,* 17 Indian L.Rptr. 6105, 6109-10 (Nav. Sup. Ct. 1990); *Smith v. Salish Kootenai College,* 434 F.3d 1127, 1139 (9th Cir. 2006) (en banc); *NLRB v. Pueblo of San Juan,* 276 F.3d 1186, 1192-93 (10th Cir. 2002) (en banc);

[2] *See Montana v. United States,* 450 U.S. 544, 565-66 (1981).

- Nonmember enterprise employing tribal members has a "consensual relationship" with tribal members subject to regulation by the tribe.³

Basis for Indian tribe's authority over nonmember employees:

- Nonmember employees deriving economic value from activity on reservation or trust lands (in potential competition with tribal members) are subject to authority of tribe to exclude them and to condition their activity while remaining on the tribe's land.⁴

- Regulation may be warranted if necessary to protect the tribe's political integrity and/or the health and welfare of the tribal community.⁵

Basis for Indian tribe's authority over tribal member employees:

- Indian tribes have inherent authority to regulate the activities of their own members within reservations or trust lands.⁶

2. **State Authority (not considering outcomes under Public Law 280)**

- State authority is preempted as a matter of federal law if assertion of state authority is incompatible with federal goals for tribal self-government reflected in congressional enactments.⁷

---

³*See Plains Commerce Bank v. Long Family & Cattle Co., Inc.*, 128 S. Ct. 2709, 2723 (2008); *Manygoats v. Atkinson Trading Co. Inc.*, No. SC-CV-62-2000, ¶¶ 35-41, at 5 (Nav. Sup. Ct. Aug. 12, 2003); *MacArthur v. San Juan County*, 497 F.3d 1057, 1071 -72 (10th Cir. 2007).

⁴*See Merrion v. Jicarilla Apache Tribe*, 455 U.S. at 144.

⁵*See Montana v. United States*, 450 U.S. at 565-66; *Manygoats v. Atkinson Trading Co., Inc.*, No. SC-CV-62-2000, ¶¶ 43-44 at 5 (Nav. Sup. Ct. Aug. 12, 2003); *Rodriguez v Wong*, 82 P.3d 263, 266-67 (Wash. Ct. App. 2004).

⁶*See Santa Clara Pueblo v. Martinez*, 436 U.S. 49, 55-56 (1978); *Williams v. Lee*, 358 U.S. 217.

- State lacks jurisdiction if asserted authority would infringe upon "the right of reservation Indians to make their own laws and be ruled by them."[8]
    - For state adjudicatory authority, party alignment could matter:
        - No state jurisdiction if nonmember suing tribal member[9]
        - Potential concurrent state and tribe jurisdiction if tribal member suing nonmember.[10]

3. **Federal Authority**

Basis for federal agency authority over nonmember employer:

- If nothing on the face of the federal law restricts the application of the law to the nonmember employer, and such application does not conflict with other federal law, federal authority may be permitted.[11]
- Potential for concurrent federal and tribal authority.[12]

---

[7]*See White Mountain Apache Tribe v. Bracker*, 448 U.S. 136, 142 (1980). *See also New Mexico v. Mescalero Apache Tribe*, 462 U.S. 324, 332-33 (1983).

[8]*Williams v. Lee*, 358 U.S. at 220.

[9]*See Williams v. Lee*, 358 U.S. 217.

[10]*See Smith v. Salish Kootenai College*, 434 F.3d at 1140 n.6.

[11]*See EEOC v. Peabody Western Coal Co.*, 610 F.3d 1070 (9th Cir. 2010); *Dawavendewa v. Salt River Project Agric. Improvement & Power Dist.*, 154 F.3d 1117 (9th Cir. 1998). *See also Navajo Tribe v. NLRB*, 288 F.2d 162 (D.C. Cir. 1961), *cert. denied*, 366 U.S. 928 (1961).

[12]*See Reich v. Mashantucket Sand & Gravel*, 95 F.3d 174, 181 (2d Cir. 1996).

B. Tribe or Tribe's Subordinate Economic Organization, Employing Tribal Members and Nonmembers

1. Tribal Authority

Basis for Indian tribe's authority over (a) itself or its subordinate economic organization (as employer), and (b) tribal member employees:

- Indian tribes have inherent authority to regulate themselves and their members within reservations or trust lands.[13]

Basis for tribe's authority over nonmember employees:

- Nonmember employee on reservation or trust lands for economic gain subject to authority of tribe to exclude the nonmember and to condition the nonmember's activity while remaining on the tribe's land.[14]

- Nonmember employee of tribe or tribal government enterprise is in a "consensual relationship" with the tribe; tribe has the right to regulate that consensual relationship.[15]

2. State Authority

- State courts lack jurisdiction to enforce state law against the tribe or its subordinate economic organization unless sovereign immunity waived by the tribe or by Congress.[16]

---

[13]*See Santa Clara Pueblo v. Martinez,* 436 U.S. at 55-56; *Williams v. Lee,* 358 U.S. 217.

[14]*See Merrion v. Jicarilla Apache Tribe,* 455 U.S. at 144.

[15]*See Montana v. United States,* 450 U.S. at 565-66; *MacArthur v. San Juan County,* 497 F.3d at 1071-72.

[16]*Kiowa Tribe of Okla. v. Mfg. Tech's., Inc.,* 523 U.S. 751 (1998); *Okla. Tax Comm'n v Citizen Band Potawatomi Indian Tribe of Okla.,* 498 U.S. 505, 510 (1991).

- State regulation may be preempted as a matter of federal law if it is incompatible with federal goals for tribal self-government reflected in congressional enactments.[17]
- State lacks jurisdiction if asserted authority would infringe upon "the right of reservation Indians to make their own laws and be ruled by them."[18]

3. Federal Authority

- If nothing on the face of the federal law addresses application of the law to the tribe or its subordinate economic enterprise, then federal authority may turn on the rule applicable in the federal court of appeals with jurisdiction to decide the issue:
  - In some federal courts of appeals: whether application of the law would infringe upon the inherent or treaty-protected sovereignty of the tribe.[19]
  - In other federal courts of appeals: whether application of the law would undermine an express treaty right or rights of tribal self-governance of "purely intramural matters," or there is evidence that Congress intended the law not to apply to the tribe.[20]
    - If federal authority operates, potential for concurrent federal and tribal authority.[21]

---

[17]*See White Mountain Apache Tribe v. Bracker*, 448 U.S. at 142.

[18]*Williams v. Lee*, 358 U.S. at 220.

[19]*See EEOC v. Fond du Lac Heavy Equip. & Constr. Co., Inc.*, 986 F.2d 246, 249 (8th Cir. 1993); *EEOC v. Cherokee Nation*, 871 F.2d 937, 939 (10th Cir. 1989); *Donovan v. Navajo Forest Prods. Inds.*, 692 F.2d 709, 712 (10th Cir. 1982).

[20]*See Donovan v. Coeur d'Alene Tribal Farm*, 751 F.2d 1113 (9th Cir. 1985); *Reich v. Mashantucket Sand & Gravel*, 95 F.3d 174 (2d Cir. 1996).

[21]*See Reich v. Mashantucket Sand & Gravel*, 95 F.3d at 181.

C. Enterprise Owned and Operated by Tribal Member (As Sole Proprietor or Corporation formed under Tribal Law), Employing Tribal Member and Nonmember Employees

1. Tribal Authority

Basis for Indian tribe's authority over tribal member enterprise (as employer), and tribal member employees:

- Indian tribes have inherent authority to regulate their members within reservations or trust lands.[22]

Basis for tribe's authority over nonmember employees of tribal member enterprise (as employer):

- Nonmember employee on reservation or trust lands for economic gain subject to authority of tribe to exclude the nonmember and to condition the nonmember's activity while remaining on the tribe's land.[23]

- Nonmember employee of tribal member enterprise may be considered to have a "consensual relationship" with a tribal member; tribe has the right to regulate that consensual relationship.[24]

2. State Authority (not considering outcomes under Public Law 280)

- State regulation may be preempted as a matter of federal law if it is incompatible with federal goals for tribal self-government reflected in congressional enactments.[25]

---

[22]*See Donovan v. Coeur d'Alene Tribal Farm,* 751 F.2d at 1115-16.

[23]*See Marrion v. Jicarilla Apache Tribe,* 455 U.S. at 144.

[24]*See Montana v. United States,* 450 U.S. at 565-66; *MacArthur v. San Juan County,* 97 F.3d at 1071-72.

[25]*See White Mountain Apache Tribe v. Bracker,* 448 U.S. at 142.

- State lacks jurisdiction if asserted authority would infringe upon "the right of reservation Indians to make their own laws and be ruled by them."[26]
  - For state adjudicatory authority, party alignment could matter:
    - No state jurisdiction if nonmember suing tribal member[27]
    - Potential concurrent state and tribe jurisdiction if tribal member suing nonmember.[28]

3. **Federal Authority**

- In some jurisdictions, if assertion of federal authority would undermine authority of tribe to govern itself and its members, and Congress is not clear about application of the federal law to the employment relationship at issue, doubts about whether the federal law may apply to undermine tribal authority may be resolved in favor of preserving tribal authority from infringement.[29]
- In other jurisdictions, if Congress is not clear about application of the federal law to the employment relationship at issue, the law is presumed to apply unless it would undermine an express treaty right or tribal self-governance of "purely intramural

---

[26]*Williams v. Lee*, 358 U.S. at 220.

[27]*See Williams v. Lee*, 358 U.S. 217.

[28]*See Smith v. Salish Kootenai College*, 434 F.3d at 1140 n.6.

[29]*See Reich v. Great Lakes Indian Fish & Wildlife Comm'n*, 4 F.3d 490, 494-96 (7th Cir. 1993); *EEOC v. Fond du Lac Heavy Equip. and Constr. Co., Inc.*, 986 F.2d at 249. *See also Solis v. Matheson*, 563 F.3d 425, 433-34 (9th Cir. 2009) (no undermining of tribal regulatory authority at issue).

matters," or there is evidence that Congress intended the law not to apply in the situation presented.[30]

- If federal authority operates, potential for concurrent federal and tribal authority.[31]

EMPLOYMENT RELATIONS ON FEE LAND WITHIN EXTERIOR BOUNDARIES OF AN INDIAN RESERVATION

A. NONMEMBER ENTERPRISE OWNING FEE LAND AND EMPLOYING TRIBAL MEMBERS AND NONMEMBERS

1. Tribal Authority

Basis for Indian tribe's authority over the nonmember employer:

- Nonmember enterprise employing tribal members has a "consensual relationship" with tribal members subject to regulation by tribe.[32]

Basis for Indian tribe's authority over nonmember employees:

- Regulation may be warranted if necessary to protect the tribe's political integrity and/or the health and welfare of the tribal community.[33]

---

[30]*See Reich v. Mashantucket Sand & Gravel,* 95 F.3d at 181; *Donovan v. Coeur d'Alene Tribal Farm,* 751 F.2d at 1115.

[31]*See Reich v. Mashantucket Sand & Gravel,* 95 F.3d at 181.

[32]*See Plains Commerce Bank v. Long Family & Cattle Co., Inc.,* 128 S. Ct. at 2723; *Manygoats v. Atkinson Trading Co., Inc.,* No. SC-CV-62-2000, ¶¶ 35-41, at 5 (Nav. Sup. Ct. Aug. 12, 2003); *MacArthur v. San Juan County,* 497 F.3d at 1071-72.

[33]*See Montana v. United States,* 450 U.S. at 565-66; *Manygoats v. Atkinson Trading Co., Inc.,* No. SC-CV-62-2000,) ¶¶ 43-44 at 5; *Rodriguez v. Wong,* 82 P.3d at 266-267.

2. **State Authority (not considering outcomes under Public Law 280)**

- State regulatory authority may be preempted as a matter of federal law if assertion of state authority is incompatible with federal goals for tribal self-government reflected in congressional enactments.[34]

- State lacks jurisdiction if asserted authority would infringe upon "the right of reservation Indians to make their own laws and be ruled by them."[35]

3. **Federal Authority**

Basis for federal agency authority over nonmember employer:

- If nothing on the face of the federal law restricts the application of the law to the nonmember employer, and such application does not conflict with other federal law, federal authority may be permitted.[36]

- Potential for concurrent federal and tribal authority.[37]

B. **INDIAN TRIBE OR AN ARM OF THE TRIBE OWNING FEE LAND AND EMPLOYING TRIBAL MEMBERS AND NONMEMBERS**

1. **Tribal Authority**

Basis for Indian tribe's authority over (a) itself or its subordinate economic organization (as employer), and (b) tribal member employees:

---

[34]*See White Mountain Apache Tribe v. Bracker*, 448 U.S. at 142.

[35]*Williams v. Lee*, 358 U.S. at 220.

[36]*See EEOC v. Peabody Western Coal Co.*, 610 F.3d 1070; *Dawavendewa v. Salt River Project Agric. Improvement & Power Dist.*, 154 F.3d 1117. *See also Navajo Tribe v. NLRB*, 288 F.2d 162.

[37]*See Reich v. Mashantucket Sand & Gravel*, 95 F.3d at 181.

- Indian tribes have inherent authority to regulate themselves and their members within reservations or trust lands.[38]

Basis for tribe's authority over nonmember employees:

- Nonmember employee of tribe or tribal government enterprise is in a "consensual relationship" with the tribe; tribe has authority to regulate that consensual relationship.[39]

2. **State Authority**

- State courts lack jurisdiction to enforce state law against the tribe or its subordinate economic organization unless sovereign immunity waived by the tribe or by Congress.[40]

- State regulatory authority may be preempted as a matter of federal law if assertion of state authority is incompatible with federal goals for tribal self-government reflected in congressional enactments.[41]

- State lacks jurisdiction if asserted authority would infringe upon "the right of reservation Indians to make their own laws and be ruled by them."[42]

3. **Federal Authority**

- If nothing on the face of the federal law addresses application of the law to the tribe or its subordinate economic enterprise, then federal authority may turn on the rule applicable in the federal court of appeals with jurisdiction to decide the issue:

---

[38]*Santa Clara Pueblo v. Martinez,* 436 U.S. at 55-56; *Williams v. Lee,* 358 U.S. 217.

[39]*See Montana v. United States,* 450 U.S. at 565-66; *MacArthur v. San Juan County,* 497 F.3d at 1071-72.

[40]*Kiowa Tribe of Okla. v. Mfg. Tech's., Inc.,* 523 U.S. 751; *Okla. Tax Comm'n v. Citizen Band Potawatomi Indian Tribe of Okla.,* 498 U.S. at 510.

[41]*See White Mountain Apache Tribe v. Bracker,* 448 U.S. at 142.

[42]*Williams v. Lee,* 358 U.S. at 220.

- o In some federal courts of appeals: whether application of the law would infringe upon the inherent or treaty-protected sovereignty of the tribe.[43]

- o In other federal circuit courts: whether application of the law would undermine an express treaty right or rights of tribal self-governance of "purely intramural matters," or there is evidence that Congress intended the law not to apply to the tribe.[44]

- If federal authority operates, potential for concurrent federal and tribal authority.[45]

C. TRIBAL MEMBER OR TRIBAL MEMBER ENTERPRISE (AS SOLE PROPRIETOR OR CORPORATION FORMED UNDER TRIBAL LAW) OWNING FEE LAND AND EMPLOYING TRIBAL MEMBERS AND NONMEMBERS

1. Tribal Authority

Basis for Indian tribe's authority over tribal member enterprise (as employer), and tribal member employees:

- Indian tribes have inherent authority to regulate their members within reservations or trust lands.[46]

---

[43]*See EEOC v. Fond du Lac Heavy Equip. & Constr. Co., Inc.,* 986 F.2d at 249; *EEOC v. Cherokee Nation,* 871 F.2d at 939; *Donovan v. Navajo Forest Prods. Inds.,* 692 F.2d 709 at 712.

[44]*See Coeur d'Alene Tribal Farm,* 751 F.2d 1113; *Reich v. Mashantucket Sand & Gravel,* 95 F.3d 174.

[45]*See Reich v. Mashantucket Sand & Gravel,* 95 F.3d at 181.

[46]*See Santa Clara Pueblo v. Martinez,* 436 U.S. at 55-56; *Williams v. Lee,* 358 U.S. 217.

Basis for tribe's authority over nonmember employees of tribal member enterprise (as employer):

- Nonmember employee of tribal member enterprise may be considered to have a "consensual relationship" with a tribal member; tribe has the right to regulate that consensual relationship.[47]

2. **State Authority (not considering outcomes under Public Law 280)**

- State regulatory authority may be preempted as a matter of federal law if assertion of state authority is incompatible with federal goals for tribal self-government reflected in congressional enactments.[48]

- State lacks jurisdiction if asserted authority would infringe upon "the right of reservation Indians to make their own laws and be ruled by them."[49]

    o For state adjudicatory authority, party alignment could matter:

    ▪ No state jurisdiction if nonmember suing tribal member.[50]

    ▪ Potential concurrent state and tribe jurisdiction if tribal member suing nonmember.[51]

---

[47] *See Montana v. United States,* 450 U.S. at 565-66; *MacArthur v. San Juan County,* 497 F.3d at 1071-72.

[48] *See White Mountain Apache Tribe v. Bracker,* 448 U.S. at 142.

[49] *Williams v. Lee,* 358 U.S. at 220.

[50] *See Williams v. Lee,* 358 U.S. 217.

[51] *See Smith v. Salish Kootenai College,* 434 F.3d at 1140 n.6.

3. **Federal Authority**

- In some jurisdictions, if assertion of federal authority would undermine authority of tribe to govern itself and its members, and Congress is not clear about application of the federal law to the employment relationship at issue, doubts about whether the federal law may apply to undermine tribal authority may be resolved in favor of preserving tribal authority from infringement.[52]

- In other jurisdictions, if Congress is not clear about application of the federal law to the employment relationship at issue, the law applies unless it would undermine an express treaty right or tribal self-governance of "purely intramural matters," or there is evidence that Congress intended the law not to apply in the situation presented.[53]

- If federal authority operates, potential for concurrent federal and tribal authority.[54]

---

[52]*See Reich v. Great Lakes Indian Fish & Wildlife Comm'n,* 4 F.3d at 494-96; *EEOC v. Fond du Lac Heavy Equip. and Constr. Co., Inc.,* 986 F.2d at 249. *See also Solis v. Matheson,* 563 F.3d at 433-34 (no undermining of tribal regulatory authority at issue).

[53]*See Reich v. Mashantucket Sand & Gravel,* 95 F.3d at 181; *Donovan v. Coeur d'Alene Tribal Farm,* 751 F.2d at 1115.

[54]*See Reich v. Mashantucket Sand & Gravel,* 95 F.3d at 181.

APPENDIX B

FEDERAL LABOR AND EMPLOYMENT LAWS OF GENERAL APPLICATION

LAW/APPLICATION TO INDIAN TRIBES	PURPOSE	ENFORCEMENT	REMEDY
Title VII of the Civil Rights Act of 1964 (Title VII) Indian tribes excluded.	Prohibits employment discrimination on the basis of race, color, sex, national origin, and religion.	By (1) the Equal Employment Opportunity Commission (EEOC) or (2) employees by court actions after first exhausting EEOC process.	If the EEOC does not resolve the dispute, a court may grant remedies for violations of the law. Remedies may include hiring, reinstatement, back pay, injunctive relief, compensatory and punitive damages (for intentional discrimination), and attorney's fees.
Americans with Disabilities Act (ADA) Indian tribes excluded.	Prohibits discrimination against individuals with disabilities.	Same as Title VII.	Same as Title VII.
Age Discrimination in Employment Act (ADEA) Indian tribes not addressed.	Prohibits employment discrimination based on age.	Same as Title VII.	Same as Title VII, except that, in cases of willful age discrimination, courts may grant up to twice the injured party's damages as punitive damages.

LAW/APPLICATION TO INDIAN TRIBES	PURPOSE	ENFORCEMENT	REMEDY
Family and Medical Leave Act (FMLA) Indian tribes not addressed.	Prohibits discharging or adversely affecting employment terms for employee on unpaid leave for up to 12 weeks for the birth or care of a child; the placement of a child for adoption or foster care; the care of a child, spouse, or parent with a serious health condition; or the employee's own serious health condition.	By (1) Department of Labor (DOL) or (2) individual employee action in court. Unlike Title VII, employees need not exhaust the DOL process before commencing a court action.	A court may grant remedies for violations of the law, including reinstatement, back pay, recovery of lost benefits, and attorney's fees. Employees may also recover damages up to double the actual damages (lost wages, benefits, and other compensation).
Whistleblower Protection Laws Indian tribes not addressed.	These laws prohibit employers from discharging or adversely affecting the terms or conditions of employment for an employee who reports what the employee reasonably believes to be a violation of law.	The enforcement mechanism varies. Employees can usually proceed to court.	A court may grant remedies for violations of whistleblower protection laws, including back pay, reinstatement, restoration of benefits and seniority rights, injunctive relief, and compensatory damages.

LAW/APPLICATION TO INDIAN TRIBES	PURPOSE	ENFORCEMENT	REMEDY
Fair Labor Standards Act (FLSA) Indian tribes not addressed.	Establishes minimum wage, overtime pay, recordkeeping, and child labor standards for employees.	By (1) DOL or (2) individual employee action in court. Unlike Title VII, employees need not exhaust the DOL process before commencing a court action.	Employers who willfully or repeatedly violate the minimum wage or overtime pay requirements are subject to a civil penalty of up to $1,000 for each such violation. Remedies to employees are twice the amount of the wages owed, plus attorney's fees and court costs.
Occupational Safety and Health Act (OSHA) Indian tribes not addressed.	Protects employees' health and safety while on the job.	The Occupational Safety and Health Administration sets standards and conducts investigations to enforce the Act. Individuals may not file suit in court for OSHA violations.	The Act provides that an employer who willfully violates the Act may be assessed a civil penalty of not more than $70,000 but not less than $5,000 for each violation.
Employee Retirement Income Security Act (ERISA) Indian tribes addressed in 2006 amendment.	Establishes minimum standards for many employee benefit plans to ensure that they are managed in a fair and financially sound manner.	By (1) the Department of Labor's Employee Benefits Security Administration (EBSA), which, together with the Internal Revenue Service (IRS), has the statutory and regulatory authority to ensure that workers receive the promised benefits; or (2) individual employee actions in court.	The Department of Labor has authority to bring a civil action to correct violations of the law and impose criminal penalties on any person who willfully violates ERISA. EBSA has authority under ERISA Section 502(c)(2) to assess civil penalties for reporting violations.

APPENDIX C

LABOR AND EMPLOYMENT LAWS OF INDIAN TRIBES

Benefits: Family/Medical Leave, Insurance and Retirement

BLACKFEET NATION, *Tribal Employment Rights Ordinance and Safety Enforcement Act of 2010*, § 6-101 – "Family Medical Leave Protection Act" (2010), available at: https://www.btero.com/.

CONFEDERATED TRIBES OF SILETZ INDIANS, SILETZ TRIBAL CODE § 2.846 – "Employee Leave Policy" (2018), available at: http://www.ctsi.nsn.us/uploads/downloads/Ordinances/Personnel%20Manual%202-21-2018.pdf.

CROW LAW & ORDER CODE, *Workforce Protection Act*, § 17.10.1.1 – "Family, Medical, and Cultural Leave" (2009), available at: http://www.ctlb.org/wp-content/uploads/2015/09/CLB-09-01-WorkForce-Protection-ActWPA.pdf.

EASTERN BAND OF CHEROKEE INDIANS CHEROKEE CODE, § 95-50 – "Leave for Parent Involvement in Schools" (2018), available at: https://library.municode.com/nc/cherokee_indians_eastern_band/codes/code_of_ordinances.

FORT BELKNAP COMMUNITY COUNCIL, *Personnel Policies Manual*, § 600 – "Employee Benefits" (1996), available at: https://ftbelknap.org/forms%2Fdocuments.

GRAND TRAVERSE BAND OF OTTAWA & CHIPPEWA INDIANS TRIBAL CODE, 5 GTBC § 701 *et seq.* – "Tribal Member/Employee Medical Insurance Coverage" (2009), available at: https://www.narf.org/nill/codes/grand_traverse/Title_5.pdf.

Ho-Chunk Nation Code, 6 HCC 5, *Employment Rights Act*, Ch. 4 – "Employee Benefits" (2017), available at: http://www.hochunknation.com/Laws/Title6-Personnel EmploymentandLabor/6HCC5%20ERA%20UPDATED.pdf.

Jamestown S'Klallam Tribal Code, Ch. 3.06 – "Tribal Family Medical Leave Protection" (2014), available at: http://www.jamestowntribe.org/govdocs/Tribal_Code/Title_03_Labor_Code_9_12_14.pdf.

Karuk Tribe, *Tribal Employment Rights Ordinance and Workforce Protection Act* § 5 – "Family Medical Leave Act" (2015) available at: http://www.karuk.us/images/docs/tero/TERO_Ordinance_06-08-15.pdf.

Little River Band of Ottawa Indians, Ch. 600, Tit. 03, Art. 8 – "Family Medical Leave Protection" (2017) available at: https://lrboi-nsn.gov/wp-content/uploads/2015/10/Title-03.pdf.

Lummi Nation Code of Laws, *Employers Liability Code*, Tit. 31 (2008) (incorporates Title 51 Of Wash. Rev. Code by reference), available at: https://www.narf.org/nill/codes/lummi/31Employers.pdf.

Mashantucket Pequot Tribal Laws, 15 M.P.T.L. ch. 1 § 1 *et seq.* – "Administration and Claims Review of Tribally Sponsored Employee Benefit Plans Under ERISA" (2003) available at: http://www.mptnlaw.com/laws/Single/TITLE%2015%20TRIBALLY%20SPONSORED%20EMPLOYEE%20BENEFIT%20PLANS%20(TERISA).pdf.

Mille Lacs Band Statutes Annotated, 6 MLBSA § 1133 – "Allowable Fringe Benefits" (2014), available at: http://www.millelacsband.com/content/3-government/17-statutes-policies/title-6-government-employees1.pdf.

THE MOHEGAN TRIBE OF INDIANS OF CONNECTICUT CODE OF ORDINANCES, § 4.251 *et seq.* – "Employee Retirement Income Security" (2008), available at: https://library.municode.com/tribes_and_tribal_nations/mohegan_tribe/codes/code_of_laws?nodeId=PTIIMOTRINCO_CH4EM_ARTVIIIEMREINSE.

THE MOHEGAN TRIBE OF INDIANS OF CONNECTICUT CODE OF ORDINANCES, § 4.286 *et seq.* – "Family Medical Leave" (2008) available at: https://library.municode.com/tribes_and_tribal_nations/mohegan_tribe/codes/code_of_laws?nodeId=PTIIMOTRINCO_CH4EM_ARTIXFAMELE.

NOTTAWASEPPI HURON BAND OF THE POTAWATOMI TRIBAL CODE, § 5.2-21 – "Family Medical Leave Protection" (2017), available at: https://ecode360.com/NO3539.

OGLALA SIOUX LAW AND ORDER CODE, Ch. 17, Pt. II.F.1 – "Employment Benefits" (2002), available at: https://www.narf.org/nill/codes/oglala_sioux/chapter17-personnel1.html.

PUEBLO OF ISLETA, Res. No. 2016-377, *Family & Medical Leave Ordinance* (2016), available at: http://isletapueblo.com/uploads/3/4/3/9/34393135/poifmlaord-sept012016-082417.pdf.

SAGINAW CHIPPEWA TRIBAL LAW, Ord. 29, *Tribal Member Employee Benefit Ordinance* (2015), available at: http://www.sagchip.org/tribalcourt/ordinance/Ordinance%2029%20Tribal%20Member%20Benefit%20070815.pdf.

SALT RIVER PIMA-MARICOPA INDIAN COMMUNITY CODE OF ORDINANCES, Ch.23, Art IV –"Retirement/Benefit Compliance and Advisory Committee" (2012), available at: https://www.srpmic-nsn.gov/government/ordinances/files/Chapter23.pdf.

SAUK-SUIATTLE INDIAN TRIBE, Res. 11/31/12, *Native Employment Works Program (NEW) Applications, Policies, and Procedures* (2012), available at: http://www.sauk-suiattle.com/Documents/ NEW%20Program%20Policies,%20Procedures%20and%20forms.pdf.

SEMINOLE NATION OF OKLAHOMA CODE, Tit. 11 § 715 – "Family Medical Leave" (2016), available at: http://sno-nsn.gov/Government/ GeneralCouncil/CodeofLaws/Seminole%20Nation%20Code% 20PDFs%202017%20June%20Update.pdf.

SQUAXIN ISLAND TRIBAL CODE, Ch. 12.03 – "Family Medical Leave Protection" (2015), available at: https://library.municode.com/ wa/squaxin_island_tribe/codes/code_of_ordinances?nodeId=TIT12L AEMCO_CH12.03FAMELEPR.

SUQUAMISH TRIBAL CODE, Ch. 18.2 – "Family Medical Leave" (2016), available at: https://suquamish.nsn.us/wp-content/uploads/2016/11/ Chapter-18.2.pdf.

TULALIP TRIBAL CODES, Ch. 9.30 – "Qualified Medical Leave" (2014), available at: http://www.codepublishing.com/WA/Tulalip/.

Conduct, Discipline, and Grievance Procedure

CONFEDERATED TRIBES OF SILETZ INDIANS, SILETZ TRIBAL CODE § 2.854 – "Disciplinary Action" (2018), available at: http://www.ctsi.nsn.us/uploads/downloads/Ordinances/Personnel%20 Manual%202-21-2018.pdf.

CONFEDERATED TRIBES OF SILETZ INDIANS, SILETZ TRIBAL CODE § 2.877 – "Drug-Free Workplace Policy" (2018), available at: http://www.ctsi.nsn.us/uploads/downloads/Ordinances/Personnel%20 Manual%202-21-2018.pdf.

CHEHALIS TRIBAL CODE § 6.45.010 – "Background Character Investigations" (2016), available at:
http://www.codepublishing.com/WA/ChehalisTribe/#!/chehalistribe06/ChehalisTribe0645.html#6.45.

THE CONFEDERATED TRIBES OF THE GRAND RONDE COMMUNITY OF OREGON, Ch.307 - *Employment Action Review Ordinance* (2014), available at:
https://weblink.grandronde.org/weblink/0/doc/37810/Page1.aspx.

EASTERN BAND OF CHEROKEE INDIANS CHEROKEE CODE § 96-2 – "Code of Ethics" (2018), available at:
https://library.municode.com/nc/cherokee_indians_eastern_band/codes/code_of_ordinances.

EASTERN BAND OF CHEROKEE INDIANS CHEROKEE CODE § 95-60. – "Criminal History Checks Required" (2018) available at:
https://library.municode.com/nc/cherokee_indians_eastern_band/codes/code_of_ordinances

ELK VALLEY RANCHERIA, Ord. No. 2001-04, Tit. 16 Ch. 3 – "Background Investigations/Dissemination of Criminal Background Information" (2002), available at: https://www.narf.org/nill/codes/elkvalleycode/elkvallclets.html#ch3.

FOND DU LAC BAND OF LAKE SUPERIOR CHIPPEWA, Ord. #13/94 – *Character Investigations and Employment Prohibitions for Employees Whose Positions Involve Contact With or Control Over Children* (1994), available at: http://www.fdlrez.com/government/ords/13-94CharInvestigations_v2.pdf.

FORT BELKNAP COMMUNITY COUNCIL, *Personnel Policies Manual*, § 500 – "Evaluation/Discipline" (1996), available at:
https://ftbelknap.org/forms%2Fdocuments.

GRAND TRAVERSE BAND OF OTTAWA & CHIPPEWA INDIANS TRIBAL CODE, 5 GTBC § 501 – "Criminal Background Investigations of Tribal Employees" (2009), available at: https://www.narf.org/nill/codes/grand_traverse/Title_5.pdf.

GRAND TRAVERSE BAND OF OTTAWA & CHIPPEWA INDIANS TRIBAL CODE, 5 GTBC § 601 *et seq.* – "GTB Code of Ethics" (2009), available at: https://www.narf.org/nill/codes/grand_traverse/Title_5.pdf.

GRAND TRAVERSE BAND OF OTTAWA & CHIPPEWA INDIANS TRIBAL CODE, 18 GTBC § 1401 *et seq.* – "Drug and Alcohol Testing" (2009), available at: https://www.narf.org/nill/codes/grand_traverse/Title_18.pdf.

HO-CHUNK NATION CODE, 6 HCCA 5, *Employment Rights Act*, Ch. 5 – "Work Rules and Employee Conduct, Discipline, and Administrative Review" (2017), available at: http://www.ho-chunknation.com/Laws/Title6-PersonnelEmploymentandLabor/6HCC5%20ERA%20UPDATED.pdf.

HO-CHUNK NATION CODE, 6 HCCA 5, *Employment Rights Act*, Ch. 7 – "Drug, Alcohol, and Controlled Substance Policy" (2017), available at: http://www.ho-chunknation.com/Laws/Title6-PersonnelEmploymentandLabor/6HCC5%20ERA%20UPDATED.pdf.

HOOPA VALLEY TRIBAL LAW & ORDER CODE, Tit. 30A – "Employment Background Check Policy" (2013), available at: https://www.hoopa-nsn.gov/wp-content/uploads/2015/07/Title30A-EmploymentBackgroundCheckPolicy.pdf.

HOOPA VALLEY TRIBAL LAW & ORDER CODE, Tit. 30 – "Personnel Policies and Procedures" (2013), available at: https://www.hoopa-nsn.gov/wp-content/uploads/2015/07/Title30-PersonnelPoliciesAndProcedures-13FEB2013.pdf.

KARUK TRIBE, *Tribal Employment Rights Ordinance and Workforce Protection Act* § 7 – "Complaints and Enforcement" (2015), available at: http://www.karuk.us/images/docs/tero/TERO_Ordinance_06-08-15.pdf.

LITTLE RIVER BAND OF OTTAWA INDIANS, Ch. R600, Part 1 – "Government Operations Personnel Manual" (2006), available at: http://lrboi-nsn.gov/images/docs/council/docs/regulations/chapter-r600/Chapter%20R600.pdf.

MASHANTUCKET PEQUOT TRIBAL LAWS, 8 M.P.T.L. ch. 1 § 3 – "Filing an Appeal from a Final Decision" (2018), available at: http://www.mptnlaw.com/laws/Single/TITLE%208%20EMPLOYMENT.pdf.

MASHANTUCKET PEQUOT TRIBAL LAWS, 37 M.P.T.L. ch. 1 § 1 *et seq.* – "Mashantucket Pequot Tribal Whistleblower Law" (2010), available at: http://www.mptnlaw.com/laws/Single/TITLE%2037%20MASHANTUCKET%20PEQUOT%20TRIBAL%20WHISTLEBLOWER%20LAW.pdf.

MENOMINEE INDIAN TRIBE OF WISCONSIN CODES, Ch. 170, Art. II – "Policies and Procedures" (2014), available at: https://www.ecode360.com/12185444.

MILLE LACS BAND STATUTES ANNOTATED, 6 MLBSA § 1151 – "Ethics Code" (2014) available at: http://www.millelacsband.com/content/3-government/17-statutes-policies/title-6-government-employees1.pdf.

MUSCOGEE (CREEK) NATION CODE ANNOTATED, Tit. 37, § 3-501 – "Employee Protection" (2010), available at: http://www.creeksupremecourt.com/wp-content/uploads/title37.pdf.

OGLALA SIOUX LAW AND ORDER CODE, Ch. 17, Pt. II.D.1 – "Work Standards" (2002), available at: https://www.narf.org/nill/codes/oglala_sioux/chapter17-personnel1.html.

OSAGE NATION CODE, Tit. 15 § 9-101 – "Whistleblower Protection" (2008), available at: https://www.osagenation-nsn.gov/who-we-are/congress-legislative-branch/legislation.

OSAGE NATION CODE, Tit. 15 § 14-101 – "Due Process in Termination of Employment" (2012), available at: https://www.osagenation-nsn.gov/who-we-are/congress-legislative-branch/legislation.

OSAGE NATION CODE, Tit. 19 § 6-101 – "Drug Testing" (2015), available at: https://www.osagenation-nsn.gov/who-we-are/congress-legislative-branch/legislation.

POKAGON BAND OF POTAWATOMI, *Wdetanmowen in Service Code* (2017), available at: http://www.pokagonband-nsn.gov/sites/default/files/assets/group/2017/wdetanmoweninservicepolicycurrentfebruary142017-5161.pdf.

PUEBLO OF ISLETA, *Employee Grievance Review Procedures* (2014), available at: http://isletapueblo.com/uploads/3/4/3/9/34393135/employeegrievancereviewprocedures-addies-rev01102014.01-web092517_.pdf.

PUEBLO OF POJOAQUE LAW & ORDER CODE, Subpart S, S-1 – "Employee Drug Testing Policy and Procedures for Employees of the Pueblo of Pojoaque Tribal Government" (2016), available at: http://pojoaque.org/wp-content/uploads/2016/03/2016-Law-Order-Code-Official.pdf.

SAMISH INDIAN NATION, SAMISH TRIBAL CODE § 2.500 – "Personnel Policies and Procedures Ordinance" (1999) [NILL classification No. 008279/1999 c1].

San Manuel Tribal Code, SMTC Ch. 36 – "San Manuel Gaming Operation Employment Claims Act" (2017), available at: https://www.sanmanuel-nsn.gov/Tribal-Government/Tribal-Court.

Seminole Nation of Oklahoma, Tit. 11, Ch. 8 – "Work Rules, Employee Conduct, Discipline, and Administrative Review" (2016), available at: http://sno-nsn.gov/Government/GeneralCouncil/CodeofLaws/Seminole%20Nation%20Code%20PDFs%202017%20June%20Update.pdf.

Seminole Nation of Oklahoma, Tit. 11, Ch. 4 – "Human Resources" (2016), available at: http://sno-nsn.gov/Government/GeneralCouncil/CodeofLaws/Seminole%20Nation%20Code%20PDFs%202017%20June%20Update.pdf.

Shingle Springs Band of Miwok Indians, *Human Resources Policy Manual* (2017), available at: http://www.shinglespringsrancheria.com/ssr/wp-content/uploads/documents/policies/HR%20Policy%20Manual.pdf

Snoqualmie Tribal Code, STC 5.5 – "Hiring Policies and Procedures" (2002), available at: http://www.snoqualmietribe.us/sites/default/files/hiring_polices_and_procedures.5.5.codified.pdf.

Standing Rock Sioux Tribal Code of Justice, Tit. 18 Ch. 3 – "Disciplinary Action and Employee Grievances" (2016), available at: https://www.narf.org/nill/codes/standingrocksioux/index.html.

Standing Rock Sioux Tribal Code of Justice, Tit. 27 Ch. 2 – "Employee Code of Ethics" (2016), available at: https://www.narf.org/nill/codes/standingrocksioux/index.html.

Stockbridge-Munsee Tribal Law, § 53.4 – "Employee Appeals to Tribal Court" (2012), available at: http://www.mohican.com/mt-content/uploads/2015/11/ch-53-employee-rights_563a76dd130c0.pdf.

Tulalip Tribal Codes, Ch. 9.35 – "Drug and Alcohol Free Workplace" (2014), available at: http://www.codepublishing.com/WA/Tulalip/.

WAGANAKISING ODAWA TRIBAL CODE OF LAW, WOTCL 14.401 *et seq.* – "Whistle Blower Protection" (2018), available at: http://www.ltbbodawa-nsn.gov/TribalCode.pdf.

WAMPANOAG TRIBAL CODE, Trib. Ord. No. 97-03, *Criminal Background Checks* (2000) [NILL classification No. 008648/2000].

WINNEBAGO TRIBAL CODE, WTC 7-1101 – "Winnebago Drug-Free Workplace" (2012), available at: http://www.winnebagotribe.com/images/joomlart/corporate/tribe/court/tribalcode/2016-WTN-TITLE-7-Health-Safety-Welfare.pdf.pdf.

WINNEBAGO TRIBAL CODE, WTC 7-1801 – "Whistleblower Protection" (2012), available at: http://www.winnebagotribe.com/images/joomlart/corporate/tribe/court/tribalcode/2016-WTN-TITLE-7-Health-Safety-Welfare.pdf.pdf.

Discrimination & Harassment

BLACKFEET NATION, *Tribal Employment Rights Ordinance and Safety Enforcement Act of 2010*, § 4-101 – "Equal Opportunity Employment Act" (2010), available at: https://www.btero.com/.

BLUE LAKE RANCHERIA, BLR Ord. 03-01 – "Employment Non-Discrimination Ordinance" (2003), available at: http://www.bluelakerancheria-nsn.gov/BLR_Employment_Non-Discrimination_Ordinance_03-01.pdf.

CHEYENNE AND ARAPAHO TRIBES OF OKLAHOMA, LAW AND ORDER CODE, Ord. No. 6147001, § 3 – "An Ordinance Establishing Cheyenne-Arapaho Tribal Employment Rights" (1988), available at: https://www.narf.org/nill/codes/cheyaracode/employment.html.

CROW LAW & ORDER CODE, *Workforce Protection Act*, § 17.8.1.1 – "Prohibition of Employment Discrimination" (2009), available at: http://www.ctlb.org/wp-content/uploads/2015/09/CLB-09-01-WorkForce-Protection-ActWPA.pdf.

ELK VALLEY RANCHERIA, Ord. No. 01-02, § 17.04.060 – "Impermissible Consideration of Race, Color, Religion, Gender, National Origin,

Sexual Orientation, Age, Disability, or Medical Condition" (2002), available at: https://www.narf.org/nill/codes/elkvalleycode/elkvallemprts.html#ch4.

KARUK TRIBE, *Tribal Employment Rights Ordinance and Workforce Protection Act* § 4 – "Fair Employment" (2015), available at: http://www.karuk.us/images/docs/tero/TERO_Ordinance_06-08-15.pdf.

LITTLE RIVER BAND OF OTTAWA INDIANS, Ch. 600, Tit. 03, Art. 4 – "Unlawful Employment Discrimination" (2017) available at: https://lrboi-nsn.gov/wp-content/uploads/2015/10/Title-03.pdf.

MASHANTUCKET PEQUOT TRIBAL LAWS, 32 M.P.T.L. ch.1 § 6(a)(3) – "Prohibited Practices" (2008), available at: http://www.mptnlaw.com/laws/Single/TITLE%2032%20MASHANTUCKET%20PEQUOT%20LABOR%20RELATIONS%20LAW.pdf.

MILLE LACS BAND STATUTES ANNOTATED, 18 MLBSA § 425 – "Prohibited Discrimination" (2014), available at: http://www.millelacsband.com/content/3-government/17-statutes-policies/mltitle18compractices-revised-5-5-14.pdf.

THE MOHEGAN TRIBE OF INDIANS OF CONNECTICUT CODE OF ORDINANCES, § 4.21 *et seq.* – "Discriminatory Employment Practices" (2008), available at: https://library.municode.com/tribes_and_tribal_nations/mohegan_tribe/codes/code_of_laws?nodeId=PTIIMOTRINCO_CH4EM_ARTIIDIEMPR.

MUSCOGEE (CREEK) NATION CODE ANNOTATED, Tit. 37, § 3-902 – "Prohibition of Sex, Race, Age, or Disability Discrimination" (2010), available at: http://www.creeksupremecourt.com/wp-content/uploads/title37.pdf.

NAVAJO NATION BILL OF RIGHTS, 1 N.N.C., § 3 – "Denial or Abridgement of Rights on Basis of Sex; Equal Protection and Due Process of Navajo Nation Law" (1980), available at: http://www.navajocourts.org/Harmonization/NavBillRights.htm.

NOTTAWASEPPI HURON BAND OF THE POTAWATOMI TRIBAL CODE, § 5.2-5 – "Unlawful Employment Discrimination Prohibited; General Rule" (2017), available at: https://ecode360.com/NO3539.

OGLALA SIOUX LAW AND ORDER CODE, Ch. 17, Pt. II.B.1 – "Equal Employment Opportunities – Nondiscrimination" (2002), available at: https://www.narf.org/nill/codes/oglala_sioux/chapter17-personnel1.html.

PAUMA BAND OF LUISENO MISSION INDIANS, Gaming Ord. Reg. 008 – "Employment Discrimination" (2006), available at: https://www.narf.org/nill/codes/paumacode/gaming_reg_008_employment_discrimination.pdf.

POARCH BAND OF CREEKS CODE OF ORDINANCES, § 33-4-3 – "Prohibited Bases of Discrimination" (2016), available at: https://library.municode.com/tribes_and_tribal_nations/poarch_band_of_creek_indians/codes/code_of_ordinances?nodeId=TIT33TREMRI_CHIVFAEM.

PRAIRIE ISLAND INDIAN COMMUNITY, Ord. No. 94-8-16-1, *Equal Employment and Indian Preference Ordinance* (1994), available at: http://prairieisland.org/wp-content/uploads/2018/05/Equal-Employment-and-Indian-Preference-Ordinance.pdf.

SAC & FOX TRIBE OF THE MISSISSIPPI IN IOWA CODE § 9-1206(f) – "Unlawful Employment Practices" (2007), available at: https://www.meskwaki.org/government/tribal-constitution-codes-bylaws/.

SQUAXIN ISLAND TRIBAL CODE, Ch. 12.03 – "Family Medical Leave Protection" (2015), available at: https://library.municode.com/wa/squaxin_island_tribe/codes/code_of_ordinances?nodeId=TIT12LAEMCO_CH12.03FAMELEPR.

STOCKBRIDGE-MUNSEE TRIBAL LAW, § 53.3(B) – "Guaranteed Employee Rights" (2012), available at: http://www.mohican.com/mt-content/uploads/2015/11/ch-53-employee-rights_563a76dd130c0.pdf.

SUQUAMISH TRIBAL CODE, Ch. 18.1 – "Employment Discrimination" (2016), available at: https://suquamish.nsn.us/wp-content/uploads/2016/11/Chapter-18.1.pdf.

SWINOMISH TRIBAL CODE, 14-01.125 – "Discrimination Prohibited" (2017), available at: http://www.swinomish.org/media/4680/1401_tero.pdf.

SYCUAN BAND OF THE KUMEYAAY NATION, *Employment Discrimination Complaint Ordinance* (2015), available at: https://www.sycuan.com/wp-content/uploads/2016/01/employment-discrimination-complaint-ordinance.pdf.

Occupational Safety and Health

BLACKFEET NATION, *Tribal Employment Rights Ordinance and Safety Enforcement Act of 2010*, § 7-101 – "Occupational Safety and Health Act" (2010), available at: https://www.btero.com/.

CHOCTAW NATION CODE, *Worker's Injury Code* (2015), available at: https://www.choctawnation.com/sites/default/files/2015/09/16/workersinjurycode_original.pdf.

CONFEDERATED TRIBES OF SILETZ INDIANS, SILETZ TRIBAL CODE § 2.886 – "Safety" (2018), available at: http://www.ctsi.nsn.us/uploads/downloads/Ordinances/Personnel%20Manual%202-21-2018.pdf.

CHEHALIS TRIBAL CODE § 11.10.010 *et seq.* – "Construction Safety" (2018), available at: http://www.codepublishing.com/WA/ChehalisTribe/#!/chehalistribe11/ChehalisTribe1110.html#11.10.

DRY CREEK RANCHERIA BAND OF POMO INDIANS, GOVERNMENT CODE, Tit. 12, § 7 – "Promulgation of Building and Safety Regulations" (2013), available at: http://drycreekrancheria.com/wp-content/uploads/2013/08/12-Building-and-Safety-Code-FINAL1.pdf.

Ho-Chunk Nation Code, 6 HCCA 8, *Occupational Safety and Health Program Act of 2002* (2004), available at: http://www.ho-chunknation.com/Laws/Title6-PersonnelEmploymentandLabor/6HCC8%20Occupational%20Safety%20and%20Health%20Program%20Act%20of%202002%2006.08.04.pdf.

Jamestown S'Klallam Tribe Tribal Code, Ch. 28.07 – "Injury Prevention, Occupational Safety and Personal Protective Equipment" (2012), available at: http://www.jamestowntribe.org/govdocs/Tribal_Code/Title_28_%20Public_Health_and_Safety_Code_%206_6_12.pdf.

Law and Order Code of the Kalispel Tribe of Indians, § 23-1.01 – "Workers Protection Code" (2017), available at: https://www.kalispeltribe.com/government/tribal-court/law-order-code.

Little River Band of Ottawa Indians, Ch. 600, Tit. 03, Art. 9 – "Occupational Health and Safety Standards" (2017) available at: https://lrboi-nsn.gov/wp-content/uploads/2015/10/Title-03.pdf.

Mashantucket Pequot Tribal Laws, 34 M.P.T.L. § 1 – "Tribal Occupational Safety and Health Law" (2008), available at: http://www.mptnlaw.com/laws/Single/TITLE%2034%20TRIBAL%20OCCUPATIONAL%20SAFETY%20AND%20HEALTH%20LAW%20(TOSHA).pdf.

Mille Lacs Band Statutes Annotated, 18 MLBSA § 439 – "Duties of Employers and Employees" (2014), available at: http://www.millelacsband.com/content/3-government/17-statutes-policies/mltitle18compractices-revised-5-5-14.pdf.

The Mohegan Tribe of Indians of Connecticut Code of Ordinances, § 4.311 *et seq.* – "Occupational Safety and Health" (2008) available at: https://library.municode.com/tribes_and_tribal_nations/mohegan_tribe/codes/code_of_laws?nodeId=PTIIMOTRINCO_CH4EM_ARTXOCSAHE.

NAVAJO NATION CODE, 15 N.N.C. § 1401 – "Navajo Nation Occupational Safety and Health Act" (2014), available at: http://www.navajonationcouncil.org/Navajo%20Nation%20Codes/V0 030.pdf.

NEZ PERCE TRIBAL CODE, § 9-5-1 – "Tribal Occupational Safety and Health Administration" (2017), available at: http://nezperce.org/~code/pdf%20convert%20files/2018-04-17%20Nez%20Perce%20Tribal%20Code.pdf.

NOTTAWASEPPI HURON BAND OF THE POTAWATOMI TRIBAL CODE, § 5.2-39 – "Occupational Health and Safety Standards" (2017), available at: https://ecode360.com/NO3539.

ONEIDA CODE OF LAWS, 2 O.C. 303 – "Oneida Safety Law - YuthinikulálΛ KayanlΛhsla" (2018), available at: https://oneida-nsn.gov/dl-file.php?file=2016/02/Chapter-303.-Safety-BC-09-22-99-A.pdf.

PONCA TRIBE OF NEBRASKA LAW AND ORDER CODE, Tit. VII – "Occupational Injury Ordinance" (2016), available at: https://www.poncatribe-ne.org/wp-content/uploads/2016/10/law_codetitle_v7_160520.pdf.

POTAWATOMI LAW AND ORDER CODE, § 20-5-1 – "Tribal Occupational Injury Code" (2017), available at: http://www.codepublishing.com/KS/Potawatomi/#!/potawatomi20/Potawatomi2005.html#20-5.

Prevailing Wage

BISHOP PAIUTE TRIBAL ORDINANCES, Ord. No. T2001-02, *Bishop Paiute Tribal Prevailing Wage Ordinance* (2003), available at: http://www.bishoppaiutetribe.com/assets/ordinances/Tribal%20Prevailing%20Wage.pdf.

CONFEDERATED TRIBES OF THE COOS, LOWER UMPQUA AND SIUSLAW INDIANS TRIBAL CODE, § 9-8-2 – "Tribally Determined Prevailing Wage Rates" (2012), available at: https://ctclusi.org/assets/57f6d614c9e22c160b00000b.pdf.

THE CONFEDERATED TRIBES OF THE GRAND RONDE COMMUNITY OF OREGON, Trib. Res. No. 109-06, *Tribal Prevailing Wage Ordinance* (2006), available at: https://weblink.grandronde.org/weblink/0/doc/9255/Page1.aspx

HOOPA VALLEY TRIBAL LAW & ORDER CODE, Tit. 66 – "Prevailing Wage Ordinance" (2002), available at: https://www.hoopa-nsn.gov/wp-content/uploads/2015/06/Title66-PrevailingWage030702.pdf.

JAMESTOWN S'KLALLAM TRIBE TRIBAL CODE, Ch. 3.05 – "Prevailing Wage" (2014), available at: http://www.jamestowntribe.org/govdocs/Tribal_Code/Title_03_Labor_Code_9_12_14.pdf.

NISQUALLY TRIBAL CODE, § 26.07 – "Nisqually Prevailing Wage Ordinance" (2013), available at: http://www.nisqually-nsn.gov/files/8514/0615/4752/Title_26_-_Labor_and_Employment.pdf.

PUYALLUP TRIBAL CODE, § 3.36.040 – "Establishment of Tribal Prevailing Wage" (2010), available at: http://www.codepublishing.com/WA/PuyallupTribe/html/PuyallupTribe03/PuyallupTribe0336.html#3.36

QUINAULT TRIBAL CODE OF LAWS, Tit. 82 – "Prevailing Wages" (2008) [NILL classification No. 008188/2008].

RINCON TRIBAL CODE, § 5.400 – "Rincon Prevailing Wage Ordinance" (2013), available at: https://www.rincontribe.org/tribal-law.

SAULT STE. MARIE TRIBE OF CHIPPEWA INDIANS TRIBAL CODE, Ch. 97 – "Prevailing Wage Ordinance" (2002), available at: https://www.saulttribe.com/government/tribal-code.

STOCKBRIDGE-MUNSEE TRIBAL LAW, § 55-A.1 – "Prevailing Wage Ordinance" (2002), available at: http://www.mohican.com/mt-content/uploads/2015/11/ch-55a-prevailing-wage.pdf.

TOHONO O'ODHAM CODE, Tit. 13 Ch. 2 – "Prevailing Wages" (2008), available at: http://www.tolc-nsn.org/docs/Title13ch2.pdf.

Unions and Collective Bargaining (Right-to-Work Laws)

ABSENTEE-SHAWNEE TRIBE, *Right To Work Code*, § 2 – "Right to Work" (2010), available at: https://www.narf.org/nill/codes/absentee-shawnee/righttw.html.

BISHOP PAIUTE TRIBAL ORDINANCES, Ord. No. T99-01, *Tribal Labor Relations Ordinance* (1999), available at: http://www.bishoppaiutetribe.com/assets/ordinances/Tribal%20Labor%20Relations.pdf.

BLACKFEET NATION, *Tribal Employment Rights Ordinance and Safety Enforcement Act of 2010*, § 9-101 – "Freedom to Work without Joining a Labor Union Act" (2010), available at: https://www.btero.com/.

BLUE LAKE RANCHERIA, BLR Ord. 03-03 – "Establishing a Right to Work Law for the Rancheria" (2003), available at: http://www.bluelakerancheria-nsn.gov/BLR_Right_To_Work_Ordinance_03-03.pdf.

CHEROKEE NATION CODE ANNOTATED, Tit. 40, Ch. 4 § 401 – "Union Agreements" (2015), available at: http://www.cherokee.org/Portals/AttorneyGeneral/Users/213/13/213/Word%20Searchable%20Full%20Code.pdf?ver=2015-10-22-083614-130.

CONFEDERATED TRIBES OF SILETZ INDIANS, SILETZ TRIBAL CODE § 5.200 – "Right to Work Ordinance" (2008), available at: http://www.ctsi.nsn.us/uploads/downloads/Ordinances/Right%20to%20Work%20Ordinance%2007-24-08.pdf

CHEHALIS TRIBAL CODE § 2.15.060 – "Freedom of Choice Guaranteed" (2018), available at: http://www.codepublishing.com/WA/ChehalisTribe/#!/chehalistribe02/ChehalisTribe0215.html#2.15.060.

THE CONFEDERATED TRIBES OF THE GRAND RONDE COMMUNITY OF OREGON, Trib. Res. No. 174-08, *Right to Work Ordinance* (2006), available at: https://weblink.grandronde.org/weblink/0/doc/18017/Page1.aspx.

CONFEDERATED TRIBES OF THE UMATILLA INDIAN RESERVATION, *Right To Work Code* (2009), available at: http://ctuir.org/right-work-code.

COQUILLE INDIAN TRIBAL CODE, § 240.202 – "Labor Organization and Strikes" (2008), available at: http://www.coquilletribe.org/?page_id=1326.

CROW LAW & ORDER CODE, *Workforce Protection Act*, § 17.7.2.1 – "Right to Work Act - Unions" (2009), available at: http://www.ctlb.org/wp-content/uploads/2015/09/CLB-09-01-WorkForce-Protection-ActWPA.pdf.

EASTERN BAND OF CHEROKEE INDIANS CHEROKEE CODE, Ch. 95, Art III – "Labor Organizations" (2018), available at: https://library.municode.com/nc/cherokee_indians_eastern_band/codes/code_of_ordinances.

EASTERN BAND OF CHEROKEE INDIANS, *Cherokee Code*, Ch. 95, Art. IV – "Tribal Employers Prohibited From Entering Into Collective Bargaining Contracts With Labor Unions, Trade Unions, or Labor Organizations" (2018) available at: https://library.municode.com/nc/cherokee_indians_eastern_band/codes/code_of_ordinances.

ELK VALLEY RANCHERIA, Ord. No. 01-02, § 17.04.020 – "Labor Organization Practices" (2002), available at: https://www.narf.org/nill/codes/elkvalleycode/elkvallemprts.html#ch4.

FOND DU LAC BAND OF LAKE SUPERIOR CHIPPEWA, Ord. #03/07 – *Prohibiting Compulsory Membership in a Labor Organization as a Condition of Employment on the Fond du Lac Reservation* (2007), available at: http://www.fdlrez.com/government/ords/03-07aord.pdf.

FOREST COUNTY POTAWATOMI CODE OF LAWS, Ch. 1-9 – "Right to Work Ordinance" (2015), available at: https://www.fcpotawatomi.com/wp-content/uploads/2014/12/Chapter-1-9-Right-to-Work-05.09.15.pdf.

FORT BELKNAP COMMUNITY COUNCIL, *TERO Ordinance*, § 15(A) – "Union Benefits and Fees" (2004), available at: https://ftbelknap.org/forms%2Fdocuments.

REVISED LAW AND ORDER CODE OF THE FORT MCDOWELL YAVAPAI NATION, ARIZONA, § 2-477 – "Right to Work Ordinance" (2004), available at: https://www.narf.org/nill/codes/fort_mcdowell/index.html.

GRAND TRAVERSE BAND OF OTTAWA & CHIPPEWA INDIANS, 5 GTBC § 801 – "Labor Relations" (2009), available at: https://www.narf.org/nill/codes/grand_traverse/Title_5.pdf

HOOPA VALLEY TRIBAL LAW & ORDER CODE, Tit. 61 – "Labor Relations Ordinance" (2000), available at: https://www.hoopa-nsn.gov/wp-content/uploads/2015/06/Title61-LaborRelations062000.pdf.

JAMESTOWN S'KLALLAM TRIBE TRIBAL CODE, Ch. 3.03 – "Labor Organizations and Collective Bargaining" (2014), available at: http://www.jamestowntribe.org/govdocs/Tribal_Code/Title_03_Labor_Code_9_12_14.pdf

KARUK TRIBE, *Tribal Employment Rights Ordinance and Workforce Protection Act* § 6 – "Right to Work and Union Membership" (2015) available at: http://www.karuk.us/images/docs/tero/TERO_Ordinance_06-08-15.pdf.

LAC DU FLAMBEAU TRIBAL CODE, Ch. 47 – "Labor Ordinance" (1995) (incorporates Title 29 U.S.C. by reference), available at: https://www.ldftribe.com/uploads/files/Court-Ordinances/CHAP47%20Labor%20Ordinance.pdf.

LOS COYOTES BAND OF CAHUILLA AND CUPENO INDIANS, *Tribal Labor Relations Ordinance* (2005), [NILL classification No. 007790/2005 d1].

MASHANTUCKET PEQUOT TRIBAL LAWS, 32 M.P.T.L. ch.1 § 5 – "Rights and Duties of Tribal Employers, Tribal Employees, and Labor Organizations" (2008), available at: http://www.mptnlaw.com/laws/Single/TITLE%2032%20MASHANTUCKET%20PEQUOT%20LABOR%20RELATIONS%20LAW.pdf.

Mashantucket Pequot Tribal Laws, 28 M.P.T.L. § 3 – "Right to Work" (2008), available at: http://www.mptnlaw.com/laws/Single/TITLE%2028%20RIGHT%20TO%20WORK%20LAW.pdf.

Mille Lacs Band Statutes Annotated, 18 MLBSA § 603 – "Right to Work" (2014), available at: http://www.millelacsband.com/content/3-government/17-statutes-policies/mltitle18compractices-revised-5-5-14.pdf.

Mississippi Band of Choctaw Indians Tribal Code, § 30-1-6 – "Freedom of Choice and Recognition of Indian Preference Rights Guaranteed" (2016), available at: http://www.choctaw.org/government/tribal_code/TITLE%2030%20LABOR%20ORGANIZATIONS.pdf

The Mohegan Tribe of Indians of Connecticut Code of Ordinances, § 4.408 – "Collective Bargaining; Exceptions" (2008) available at: https://library.municode.com/tribes_and_tribal_nations/mohegan_tribe/codes/code_of_laws?nodeId=PTIIMOTRINCO_CH4EM_ARTXILARE_S4-408COBAEX

The Mohegan Tribe of Indians of Connecticut Code of Ordinances, § 4.412 – "Right to Work" (2008) available at: https://library.municode.com/tribes_and_tribal_nations/mohegan_tribe/codes/code_of_laws?nodeId=PTIIMOTRINCO_CH4EM_ARTVIRIWO.

Muckleshoot Tribal Code of Laws, Tab N, Ord. No. 07-386, *To Enact an Ordinance Concerning Labor Organizations* (2012), [Nill classification No. 007918/2012].

Nisqually Tribal Code, § 26.04 – "Union Agreements With Tribal Enterprises" (2013), available at: http://www.nisqually-nsn.gov/files/8514/0615/4752/Title_26_-_Labor_and_Employment.pdf.

Nottawaseppi Huron Band of the Potawatomi Tribal Code, § 5.3-13 – "Unfair Labor Practices" (2017), available at: https://ecode360.com/NO3539.

Pascua Yaqui Tribal Code, 8 PYTC § 3-5-80 – "Prohibition of Agreements Denying Employment Because of Nonmembership in Labor Organization" (2017), available at: http://www.pascuayaqui-nsn.gov/_static_pages/tribalcodes/docs/8_PYTC/3-5_Right_To_Work.pdf.

Poarch Band of Creeks Code of Ordinances, § 33-7-2 – "Agreement or Combination to Deny Right to Work on Account of Membership or Non-membership in Labor Union, etc., Prohibited" (2016), available at: https://library.municode.com/tribes_and_tribal_nations/poarch_band_of_creek_indians/codes/code_of_ordinances?nodeId=TIT33TREMRI_CHVIIRIWO_S33-7-2AGCODERIWOACMENMBLAUNETPR.

Pokagon Band of Potawatomi, *Labor Organization and Collective Bargaining Code* (2017), available at: http://www.pokagonband-nsn.gov/sites/default/files/assets/department/government/form/2012/labor-organizations-and-collective-bargaining-code-824-621.pdf.

Port Gamble S'Klallam Tribe Law and Order Code, Tit. 27 – "Labor Organizations and Collective Bargaining" (2011), available at: https://www.pgst.nsn.us/images/law-and-order/Title-27.pdf.

Potawatomi Law and Order Code, § 22-3-1 "Labor Organizations Are Prohibited." (2017), available at: http://www.codepublishing.com/KS/Potawatomi/#!/potawatomi22/Potawatomi2203.html#22-3.

Prairie Island Indian Community, *Tribal Right to Work Ordinance*, available at: http://prairieisland.org/wp-content/themes/tempera-child/docs/Tribal%20Right%20to%20Work%20Ordinance.pdf

Pueblo of Isleta, Res. No. 2016-375, *Labor Relations Ordinance* (2016), available at: http://isletapueblo.com/uploads/3/4/3/9/34393135/poilaborrelationsord-sept012016-web082417.pdf.

Pueblo of Laguna Code, § 13-2-1 – "Union Organizing Activities" (2018), available at: https://library.municode.com/nm/pueblo_of_laguna/codes/tribal_code?nodeId=TITXIIIBU_CH2UNORAC

Pueblo of Pojoaque Law & Order Code, Subpart S, S-3 – "Labor Organization Ordinance" (2016), available at: http://pojoaque.org/wp-content/uploads/2016/03/2016-Law-Order-Code-Official.pdf. Salt River Pima-Maricopa Indian Community Code of Ordinances, Ch.23, Art II –"Right to Work" (2012), available at: https://www.srpmic-nsn.gov/government/ordinances/files/Chapter23.pdf.

Squaxin Island Tribal Code, Ch. 12.09 – "Labor Organizations and Collective Bargaining" (2015), available at: https://library.municode.com/wa/squaxin_island_tribe/codes/code_of_ordinances?nodeId=TIT12LAEMCO_CH12.05EMWAHO.

Swinomish Tribal Code, 14-03.080 – "Freedom of Choice Guaranteed" (2017), available at: http://www.swinomish.org/media/14642/1403_labororg.pdf.

Tulalip Tribal Codes, Ch. 9.20 – "Right to Work" (2014), available at: http://www.codepublishing.com/WA/Tulalip/.

Waganakising Odawa Tribal Code of Law, WOTCL 14.201 *et seq.* – "Management and Labor Relations" (2018), available at: http://www.ltbbodawa-nsn.gov/TribalCode.pdf.

Yurok Tribal Code, Tit. 5, Div. II, Ch. 5.60 – "Labor Relations" (2015), available at: https://yurok.tribal.codes/YTC/5.60

Workers' Compensation and Unemployment

Bad River Band of Lake Superior Tribe of Chippewa Indians Tribal Court Code, § 1100 – "Worker's Compensation" (2018), available at: http://www.badriver-nsn.gov/legislative/tribal-court-code.

BISHOP PAIUTE TRIBAL ORDINANCES, Ord. No. 2-8-16, *Tribal Worker's Compensation Ordinance for the Bishop Paiute Casino* (2016), available at: http://www.bishoppaiutetribe.com/assets/ordinances/WorkmansCompOrdPPC.pdf.

BLUE LAKE RANCHERIA, BLR Ord. 02-03 – "Worker's Compensation Ordinance Amended" (2003), available at: http://www.bluelakerancheria-nsn.gov/BLR_Workers'_Compensation_Ordinance_Amended_02-03.pdf.

CHEROKEE NATION CODE ANNOTATED, Tit. 85, Ch. 1 § 1 – "Worker's Compensation" (2015), available at: http://www.cherokee.org/Portals/AttorneyGeneral/Users/213/13/213/Word%20Searchable%20Full%20Code.pdf?ver=2015-10-22-083614-130.

COEUR D'ALENE TRIBAL CODE, Ch. 59 – "Tribal Workers Compensation Claims Act" (2012) [NILL Classification No. 007260/2012].

CONFEDERATED TRIBES OF SILETZ INDIANS, SILETZ TRIBAL CODE § 5.500 – "Siletz Workers' Compensation Claims Ordinance" (2008), available at: http://www.ctsi.nsn.us/uploads/downloads/Ordinances/Siletz%20Workers%20Compensation%20Claims%20Ordinance%2008-19-10.pdf.

COLVILLE TRIBAL LAW AND ORDER CODE, § 6-15-1 – "Worker's Compensation Claims Act" (2011), available at: https://www.cct-cbc.com/current-code/.

CONFEDERATED TRIBES OF THE COOS, LOWER UMPQUA AND SIUSLAW INDIANS TRIBAL CODE, § 9-7-1 – "Worker's Compensation" (2012), available at: https://ctclusi.org/assets/57f6d612c9e22c160b000009.pdf

THE CONFEDERATED TRIBES OF THE GRAND RONDE COMMUNITY OF OREGON, Trib. Res. No. 155-10, *Worker's Compensation Ordinance* (2006), available at: https://weblink.grandronde.org/weblink/0/doc/21928/Page1.aspx.

CONFEDERATED TRIBES OF THE UMATILLA INDIAN RESERVATION, *Worker's Benefit Code* (2012), available at: http://ctuir.org/workers-benefit-code.

DRY CREEK RANCHERIA BAND OF POMO INDIANS, GOVERNMENT CODE, Tit. 12, § 10 – "Workers Compensation Requirements" (2013), available at: http://drycreekrancheria.com/wp-content/uploads/2013/08/12-Building-and-Safety-Code-FINAL1.pdf.

ELK VALLEY RANCHERIA, Ord. No. 2002-04 – "Worker's Compensation Ordinance" (2002), available at: https://www.narf.org/nill/codes/elkvalleycode/elkvallwkcomp.html.

FOND DU LAC BAND OF LAKE SUPERIOR CHIPPEWA, Ord. #05/15 – *Workers' Compensation Appeals* (2015), available at: http://www.fdlrez.com/government/ords/05-15WorkersCompensationAppeals2015.11.18.pdf.

HO-CHUNK NATION CODE, 6 HCCA 5, *Employment Rights Act*, Ch. 8 – "Worker's Compensation Plan" (2017), available at: http://www.ho-chunknation.com/Laws/Title6-PersonnelEmploymentandLabor/6HCC5%20ERA%20UPDATED.pdf.

HOOPA VALLEY TRIBAL LAW & ORDER CODE, Tit. 46 – "Workers Compensation Ordinance" (2000), available at: https://www.hoopa-nsn.gov/wp-content/uploads/2015/06/Title46-WorkersComp072000.pdf.

HOOPA VALLEY TRIBAL LAW & ORDER CODE, Tit. 23 – "Unemployment and Disability Insurance Ordinance" (2005), available at: https://www.hoopa-nsn.gov/wp-content/uploads/2015/06/Title23-UIDisability122085.pdf.

HOPLAND TRIBAL CODE, § 6-1.10 – "Worker's Compensation Ordinance" (2017), available at: http://www.hoplandtribe.com/sites/default/files/2017-05/Hopland%20Tribal%20Code.pdf.

Jamestown S'Klallam Tribe, *Tribal Code*, Title 8 – "Worker's Compensation Claims Code" (2016), available at: http://www.jamestowntribe.org/govdocs/Tribal_Code/Title_08_Workers_Compensation_Claims_2_4_16.pdf.

Jamul Indian Village of California, Ord. No. 2016-33, *Casino Worker's Compensation Ordinance* (2016), available at: http://www.jamulindianvillage.com/tribal-law/.

Lac du Flambeau Tribal Code, Ch. 93 – "Workers Compensation" (2014), available at: https://www.ldftribe.com/uploads/files/Court-Ordinances/CHAP93-Workers-Compensation.pdf.

Mashantucket Pequot Tribal Laws, 13 M.P.T.L. § 5 – "Notice of Availability of Compensation; Regulations. Employer-sponsored Plan for Medical Care and Treatment" (2006), available at: http://www.mptnlaw.com/laws/Single/TITLE%2013%20WORKERS%20COMPENSATION%20CODE.pdf.

Mescalero Apache Tribal Code, Ch. 34 – "Worker's Compensation" (2016), available at: https://mescaleroapachetribe.com/wp-content/uploads/Tribal-Code-FINAL-092716-for-tabbing-372018.pdf

The Mohegan Tribe of Indians of Connecticut Code of Ordinances, § 4.191 – "Employer Liability" (2008) available at: https://library.municode.com/tribes_and_tribal_nations/mohegan_tribe/codes/code_of_laws?nodeId=PTIIMOTRINCO_CH4EM_ARTVIIWOCO_DIV1GEPR.

Muscogee (Creek) Nation Code Annotated, Tit. 48 – "Worker's Compensation Vtotkv Setemfeketv" (2005), available at: http://www.creeksupremecourt.com/wp-content/uploads/title48.pdf.

Navajo Nation Code, 15 N.N.C. § 1001 – "Worker's Compensation Act" (2014), available at: http://www.navajonationcouncil.org/Navajo%20Nation%20Codes/V0030.pdf.

NEZ PERCE TRIBAL CODE, § 11-1-1 – "Workers Compensation Code" (2017), available at: http://nezperce.org/~code/pdf%20convert%20files/2018-04-17%20Nez%20Perce%20Tribal%20Code.pdf.

ONEIDA INDIAN NATION, Ord. O-15-1, *Worker's Compensation Ordinance* (2015), available at: http://www.theoneidanation.com/codesandordinances/ordinances/Workers_Compensation_Ordinance_(Amended).pdf.

ONEIDA CODE OF LAWS, 2 O.C. 203 – "Oneida Worker's Compensation Law - LatiyótΛshe KayanlΛhsla" (2018), available at: https://oneida-nsn.gov/dl-file.php?file=2016/02/Chapter-203-Workers-Compensation-BC-06-25-14-B.pdf.

OSAGE NATION CODE, Tit. 19 § 4-101 – "Osage Nation Workers' Compensation Act" (2012), available at: https://www.osagenation-nsn.gov/who-we-are/congress-legislative-branch/legislation.

POARCH BAND OF CREEKS CODE OF ORDINANCES, § 35-1-1 *et seq.* – "Worker's Compensation" (2016), available at: https://library.municode.com/tribes_and_tribal_nations/poarch_band_of_creek_indians/codes/code_of_ordinances?nodeId=TIT35WOCO_CHIGEPR_S35-1-1TI.

PRAIRIE ISLAND INDIAN COMMUNITY, *Worker's Compensation Ordinance* (1996), available at: http://prairieisland.org/wp-content/themes/tempera-child/docs/Workers%20Compensation%20Ordinance.pdf.

PUYALLUP TRIBAL CODE, Ch. 14.04 – "Worker's Compensation Ordinance" (2010), available at: http://www.codepublishing.com/WA/PuyallupTribe/html/PuyallupTribe14/PuyallupTribe1404.html#14.04.

QUINAULT TRIBAL CODE OF LAWS, Tit. 96 – "Workers Compensation" (2008) [NILL classification No. 008188/2008].

RED CLIFF BAND OF LAKE SUPERIOR CHIPPEWA INDIANS TRIBAL CODE, Ch. 36 – "Worker's Compensation" (2017), available at: http://redcliff-nsn.gov/Government/TribalChapters/Chapter36.pdf.

RED LAKE TRIBAL CODE, Tit. 14, Ch. 1600 – "Tribal Worker's Compensation Plan" (2000) [NILL Classification No. 008200/2000].

REVISED LAW AND ORDER CODE OF THE FORT MCDOWELL YAVAPAI NATION, ARIZONA, § 2-525 – "Worker's Compensation" (2004), available at: https://www.narf.org/nill/codes/fort_mcdowell/index.html.

SAGINAW CHIPPEWA TRIBAL LAW, Ord. 23, *Worker's Compensation Ordinance* (2014), available at: http://www.sagchip.org/tribalcourt/ordinance/Ordinance%2023%20Workers%20Compensation%20122214.pdf.

SALT RIVER PIMA-MARICOPA INDIAN COMMUNITY CODE OF ORDINANCES, Ch.23, Art III –"Workers' Compensation" (2012), available at: https://www.srpmic-nsn.gov/government/ordinances/files/Chapter23.pdf.

SAN MANUEL TRIBAL CODE, SMTC Ch. 21 – "San Manuel Gaming Enterprise Workers' Compensation Act" (2017), available at: https://www.sanmanuel-nsn.gov/Tribal-Government/Tribal-Court.

SAULT STE. MARIE TRIBE OF CHIPPEWA INDIANS TRIBAL CODE, Ch. 45 – "Worker's Compensation Code" (2018), available at: https://www.saulttribe.com/government/tribal-code.

SNOQUALMIE TRIBAL CODE, STC 5.2 – "Workers Compensation Claims" (2008), available at: http://www.snoqualmietribe.us/sites/default/files/workers_comp._act.5.2.codified.2.27.12.pdf.

SOUTHERN UTE TRIBAL CODE, Tit. 24 – "Worker's Compensation Code" (2017) [NILL Classification No. 008428/2010].

STOCKBRIDGE-MUNSEE TRIBAL LAW, § 52.1 – "Workers Compensation" (2015), available at: http://www.mohican.com/mt-content/uploads/2015/11/ch-52_563a76c3bf051.pdf.

SUSANVILLE INDIAN RANCHERIA, Ord. No. 2005-02, *Worker's Compensation Ordinance for Employees of the Tribe* (2005), available at: https://www.narf.org/nill/codes/susanville/Workers__Compensation_Ordinance__2005-002_.pdf.

SWINOMISH TRIBAL CODE, 14-02.010 – "Worker's Compensation Code" (2017), available at: http://www.swinomish.org/media/4683/1402workerscomp.pdf.

THREE AFFILIATED TRIBES OF THE FORT BERTHOLD RESERVATION TRIBAL ORDINANCES, Ch. 27.2 – "Worker's Compensation" (2004) [NILL Classification No. 008529/2004 v1 d1].

TULALIP TRIBAL CODES, Ch. 9.15 – "Workers' Compensation" (2014), available at: http://www.codepublishing.com/WA/Tulalip/.

WAGANAKISING ODAWA TRIBAL CODE OF LAW, WOTCL 14.1001 *et seq*. – "Worker's Compensation Statute" (2018), available at: http://www.ltbbodawa-nsn.gov/TribalCode.pdf.

WASHOE TRIBE OF NEVADA AND CALIFORNIA LAW & ORDER CODE, Tit. 38 – "Worker's Compensation Code" (2015), available at: https://www.washoetribe.us/contents/images/documents/LawAndOrderCode/Title_38_Workers_Compensation.pdf.

WHITE MOUNTAIN APACHE LABOR CODE, Ch. 3 – "Unemployment Benefits" (2010), available at: http://www.wmat.nsn.us/Legal/Labor%20Code%20-%2009.01.2010.pdf.

WHITE MOUNTAIN APACHE LABOR CODE, Ch. 4 – "Workers Compensation" (2010), available at: http://www.wmat.nsn.us/Legal/Labor%20Code%20-%2009.01.2010.pdf.

WINNEBAGO TRIBAL CODE, WTC 7-1201 – "Winnebago Worker's Compensation" (2012), available at: http://www.winnebagotribe.com/images/joomlart/corporate/tribe/court/tribalcode/2016-WTN-TITLE-7-Health-Safety-Welfare.pdf.pdf.

YUROK TRIBAL CODE, Tit. 5, Div. II, Ch. 5.65 – "Workers' Compensation for Casino Employees" (2016), available at: https://yurok.tribal.codes/YTC/5.65.

Wage & Hour Laws

BLACKFEET NATION, *Tribal Employment Rights Ordinance and Safety Enforcement Act of 2010*, § 5-101 – "Minimum Wage" (2010), available at: https://www.btero.com/.

CHEROKEE NATION CODE ANNOTATED, Tit. 40, Ch. 9 § 901 – "Minimum Wage" (2015), available at: http://www.cherokee.org/Portals/AttorneyGeneral/Users/213/13/213/Word%20Searchable%20Full%20Code.pdf?ver=2015-10-22-083614-130.

CONFEDERATED TRIBES OF THE UMATILLA INDIAN RESERVATION, *Tribal Employment Rights Office Code,* § 2.03 – "Tribal Minimum or Prevailing Wage" (2017), available at: http://ctuir.org/tribal-employment-rights-office-code.

CROW LAW & ORDER CODE, *Workforce Protection Act*, § 17.9.1.1 – "Employee Wage and Hour" (2009), available at: http://www.ctlb.org/wp-content/uploads/2015/09/CLB-09-01-WorkForce-Protection-ActWPA.pdf.

EASTERN BAND OF CHEROKEE INDIANS CHEROKEE CODE, § 95-1. – "Minimum Wage Scale" (2000), available at: https://library.municode.com/nc/cherokee_indians_eastern_band/codes/code_of_ordinances.

GRAND TRAVERSE BAND OF OTTAWA & CHIPPEWA INDIANS, 18 GTBC § 1501 *et seq.* – "Labor Standards" (2009), available at: https://www.narf.org/nill/codes/grand_traverse/Title_18.pdf.

JAMESTOWN S'KLALLAM TRIBE TRIBAL CODE, Ch. 3.02 – "Fair Labor Standards" (2014), available at: http://www.jamestowntribe.org/govdocs/Tribal_Code/Title_03_Labor_Code_9_12_14.pdf.

LITTLE RIVER BAND OF OTTAWA INDIANS, Ch. 600, Tit. 03, Art. 10 – "Employee Wages and Hours" (2017) available at: https://lrboi-nsn.gov/wp-content/uploads/2015/10/Title-03.pdf.

MILLE LACS BAND STATUTES ANNOTATED, 18 MLBSA § 431 – "Minimum Wage" (2014), available at: http://www.millelacsband.com/content/3-government/17-statutes-policies/mltitle18compractices-revised-5-5-14.pdf.

MILLE LACS BAND STATUTES ANNOTATED, 18 MLBSA § 506 – "Overtime" (2014), available at: http://www.millelacsband.com/content/3-government/17-statutes-policies/mltitle18compractices-revised-5-5-14.pdf.

THE MOHEGAN TRIBE OF INDIANS OF CONNECTICUT CODE OF ORDINANCES, § 4.75 – "Minimum Wage" (2008), available at: https://library.municode.com/tribes_and_tribal_nations/mohegan_tribe/codes/code_of_laws?nodeId=PTIIMOTRINCO_CH4EM_ARTIVFALAST_S4-75CHLAPR.

MUSCOGEE (CREEK) NATION CODE ANNOTATED, Tit. 37, § 3-901 – "Establishment of Minimum Wage Rates" (2010), available at: http://www.creeksupremecourt.com/wp-content/uploads/title37.pdf.

NOTTAWASEPPI HURON BAND OF THE POTAWATOMI TRIBAL CODE, § 5.2-5 – "Employee Wages and Hours" (2017), available at: https://ecode360.com/NO3539.

OSAGE NATION CODE, Tit. 19 § 2-101 – "Osage Fair Minimum Wage Act" (2011), available at: https://www.osagenation-nsn.gov/who-we-are/congress-legislative-branch/legislation.

PUEBLO OF ISLETA, Res. No. 2016-376, *Fair Labor Standards Ordinance* (2016), available at: http://isletapueblo.com/uploads/3/4/3/9/34393135/poifairlaborstandardsordsept012016-web082417.pdf.

PUYALLUP TRIBAL CODE, § 3.24.530 – "Fair Labor Standards Act Incorporated Herein" (2010), available at: http://www.codepublishing.com/WA/PuyallupTribe/html/PuyallupTribe03/PuyallupTribe0324.html#3.24.

Seminole Nation of Oklahoma Code, Tit. 11 § 601 – "Salary/Wage" (2016), available at: http://sno-nsn.gov/Government/GeneralCouncil/CodeofLaws/Seminole%20Nation%20Code%20PDFs%202017%20June%20Update.pdf.

Squaxin Island Tribal Code, Ch. 12.05 – "Employee Wages and Hours" (2015), available at: https://library.municode.com/wa/squaxin_island_tribe/codes/code_of_ordinances?nodeId=TIT12LAEMCO_CH12.09LAORCOBA.

Stockbridge-Munsee Tribal Law, § 55.4 – "Pay" (1997), available at: http://www.mohican.com/mt-content/uploads/2015/11/ch-55-fair-labor-standards.pdf.

Suquamish Tribal Code, Ch. 18.3 – "Employee Wages and Hours" (2016), available at: https://suquamish.nsn.us/wp-content/uploads/2016/11/Chapter-18.3.pdf.

Waganakising Odawa Tribal Code of Law, WOTCL 14.113 – "Employee Wages and Hours" (2018), available at: http://www.ltbbodawa-nsn.gov/TribalCode.pdf.

White Mountain Apache Labor Code, Ch. 2 – "Minimum Wage" (2010), available at: http://www.wmat.nsn.us/Legal/Labor%20Code%20-%2009.01.2010.pdf.

Miscellaneous

Absentee-Shawnee Tribe, *Governmental Tort Claims Act*, § 16 – "Constitutional or Statutory Rights, Privileges or Immunities – Violation by Employee-Defending-Indemnification-Right of Recovery-Punitive or Exemplary Damages" (2010), available at: https://www.narf.org/nill/codes/absentee-shawnee/gtca.html.

Blackfeet Nation, *Tribal Employment Rights Ordinance and Safety Enforcement Act of 2010*, § 8-101 – "Immigrant Worker Control Act" (2010), available at: https://www.btero.com/.

Laws of the Confederated Salish & Kootenai Tribes Codified, CSKT Cod. § 4-1-504 – "Indemnification" (2013), available at: http://www.csktribes.org/judicial/cskt-laws-codified.

Colville Tribal Law and Order Code, § 6-6-11 – "Penalties for Employees" (1981) (penalties for unauthorized disclosure of Tribal information to researchers), available at: https://www.cct-cbc.com/current-code/.

Confederated Tribes of the Coos, Lower Umpqua and Siuslaw Indians Tribal Code, § 9-2-1 – "Tribal Employees Records Confidentiality" (2002), available at: https://ctclusi.org/assets/57f6d60ac9e22c160b000001.pdf

Eastern Band of Cherokee Indians Cherokee Code, Ch. 95 Art. 7 – "Foreign Workers" (2018), available at: https://library.municode.com/nc/cherokee_indians_eastern_band/codes/code_of_ordinances.

Elk Valley Rancheria, Ord. No. 99-32 – "An Ordinance Limiting the Liability of Tribal Officials, Officers and Employees" (1999), available at: https://www.narf.org/nill/codes/elkvalleycode/elkvalord99-32.html.

Hopland Tribal Code, § 1-8.30 – "Immunity of Elected Officers, Tribal Officials and Tribal Employees Ordinance" (2017), available at: http://www.hoplandtribe.com/sites/default/files/2017-05/Hopland%20Tribal%20Code.pdf.

Mashantucket Pequot Tribal Laws, 17 M.P.T.L. ch. 1 § 29 – "Unsuitable Persons Prohibited from Having Financial Interest in Permit Businesses; Employment of Minors" (2008), available at: http://www.mptnlaw.com/laws/Single/TITLE%2017%20LIQUOR%20CONTROL%20CODE.pdf.

The Mohegan Tribe of Indians of Connecticut Code of Ordinances, § 4.51 *et seq.* – "Indemnification of Public Officers and Employees" (2008), available at: https://library.municode.com/tribes_and_tribal_nations/mohegan_tribe/codes/code_of_laws?nodeId=PTIIMOTRINCO_CH4EM_ARTIIIINPUOFEM.

The Mohegan Tribe of Indians of Connecticut Code of Ordinances, § 4.78 – "Child Labor Provisions" (2008), available at: https://library.municode.com/tribes_and_tribal_nations/mohegan_tribe/codes/code_of_laws?nodeId=PTIIMOTRINCO_CH4EM_ARTIVFALAST_S4-78CHLAPR.

Navajo Nation Code, 15 N.N.C. § 801 – "Adherence to Child Labor Laws of States" (2014), available at: http://www.navajonationcouncil.org/Navajo%20Nation%20Codes/V0030.pdf.

Oglala Sioux Law and Order Code, Ch. 17, Pt. II.C.1 – "Veteran Preference" (2002), available at: https://www.narf.org/nill/codes/oglala_sioux/chapter17-personnel1.html.

Oneida Code of Laws, 2 O.C. 207 – "Layoff Policy" (2018), available at: https://oneida-nsn.gov/dl-file.php?file=2016/02/Chapter-207-Layoff-Policy-BC-09-23-98-D.pdf.

Oneida Code of Laws, 2 O.C. 223 – "Workplace Violence" (2018), available at: https://oneida-nsn.gov/dl-file.php?file=2018/06/Chapter-223-Workplace-Violence-BC-06-28-17-E.pdf.

Redding Rancheria Ordinances, Art. 3 Ch. 1 – "Claims and Actions Against Tribal Entities and Tribal Officers and Employees" (1998), available at: https://www.narf.org/nill/codes/redding/reddclaims.html.

Sac & Fox Tribe of the Mississippi in Iowa Code § 9-1206(d) – "Unlawful Employment Practices" (2007), available at: https://www.meskwaki.org/government/tribal-constitution-codes-bylaws/.

Law and Order Code of The Spokane Tribe of Indians, § 24-7.04 – "Employment of Minors" (2001) [NILL Classification No. 008435/2001].

Stockbridge-Munsee Tribal Law, § 55.10 – "Child Labor" (1997), available at: http://www.mohican.com/mt-content/uploads/2015/11/ch-55-fair-labor-standards.pdf.

Native American Employment Preference[1]

Absentee-Shawnee Tribe, *Employment Rights Act*, § 108 – "Indian Preference in Employment" (2010), available at: https://www.narf.org/nill/codes/absentee-shawnee/employment_rights.html.

Bad River Band of Lake Superior Tribe of Chippewa Indians Tribal Court Code, § 900 – "Hiring Ordinance" (2018), available at: http://www.badriver-nsn.gov/legislative/tribal-court-code.

Bishop Paiute Tribal Ordinances, Ord. No. T92-01, *Tribal Employment Rights Ordinance* (2012), available at: http://www.bishoppaiutetribe.com/assets/ordinances/TribalEmploymentRightsOrdinance.pdf.

Blackfeet Nation, *Tribal Employment Rights Ordinance and Safety Enforcement Act of 2010*, § 3-101 – "Indian Preference in Employment" (2010), available at: https://www.btero.com/.

Central Council of the Tlingit & Haida Tribal Statutes, § 03.01.016 – "Employment Preference" (2014), available at: http://www.ccthita.org/government/legislative/GoverningDocs/TITLE%2003%20Development%20Operation%20of%20Tribal%20Enterprise.pdf.

---

[1] This list is a general cross-section of Tribal Employment Rights (TERO) laws across Indian Country, and should provide practitioners examples of wide-ranging approaches to establishing and administering TERO offices and codes. This list is not exhaustive of all existing TERO ordinances.

CHEROKEE NATION CODE ANNOTATED, Tit. 40, Ch. 3 § 304 – "Indian Preference in Contracting and Subcontracting" (2015), available at: http://www.cherokee.org/Portals/AttorneyGeneral/Users/213/13/213/Word%20Searchable%20Full%20Code.pdf?ver=2015-10-22-083614-130.

CHEYENNE AND ARAPAHO TRIBES OF OKLAHOMA, LAW AND ORDER CODE, Ord. No. 6147001, § 3 – "An Ordinance Establishing Cheyenne-Arapaho Tribal Employment Rights" (1988), available at: https://www.narf.org/nill/codes/cheyaracode/employment.html.

CHEYENNE RIVER SIOUX TRIBE, Ord. 42-A, *Tribal Employment Rights Ordinance* (1987) [NILL Classification No. 1419].

CHICKASAW CODE, § 2-510.01 – "Discrimination Prohibited; Employment Preference" (2011) available at: https://code.chickasaw.net/Title-02.aspx.

COEUR D'ALENE TRIBAL CODE, Ch. 41 – "Tribal Employment Rights" (2012) [NILL Classification No. 007260/2012].

COLORADO RIVER INDIAN TRIBES, CRIT LABOR CODE, § 1-307 – "Indian Preference" (2011), available at: http://www.crit-nsn.gov/crit_contents/ordinances/LaborCodeAmendments_100810.pdf.

CHEHALIS TRIBAL CODE § 2.15.010 – "Tribal Employment Preference" (2018), available at: http://www.codepublishing.com/WA/ChehalisTribe/#!/chehalistribe02/ChehalisTribe0215.html#2.15.010

COLVILLE TRIBAL LAW AND ORDER CODE, § 10-3-1 – "Indian Preference In Contracting" (2014), available at: https://www.cct-cbc.com/current-code/.

THE CONFEDERATED TRIBES OF THE GRAND RONDE COMMUNITY OF OREGON, Ch. 604, *Tribal Employment Rights Ordinance* (2016), available at: https://weblink.grandronde.org/weblink/0/doc/70212/Page1.aspx.

CONFEDERATED TRIBES OF THE UMATILLA INDIAN RESERVATION, *Tribal Employment Rights Office Code* (2017), available at: http://ctuir.org/tribal-employment-rights-office-code.

CROW CREEK SIOUX TRIBE LAW AND ORDER CODE, § 17-1-1 – "Tribal Employment and Contracting Rights Ordinance" (1997) [NILL Classification No. 007372/1997 d3].

DRY CREEK RANCHERIA BAND OF POMO INDIANS, GOVERNMENT CODE, Tit. 9, § 4 – "Employment Requirements" (2013), available at: http://drycreekrancheria.com/wp-content/uploads/2013/08/9-DCR-TERO-original1.pdf.

EASTERN BAND OF CHEROKEE INDIANS, CHEROKEE CODE § 95-13 – "Indian Preference In Employment" (2018), available at: https://library.municode.com/nc/cherokee_indians_eastern_band/codes/code_of_ordinances.

FOND DU LAC BAND OF LAKE SUPERIOR CHIPPEWA, Ord. #12/94, *Workers' Compensation Appeals* (1994), available at: http://www.fdlrez.com/government/ords/12-94TERO2017.09.12.pdf.

FORT BELKNAP COMMUNITY COUNCIL, *TERO Ordinance*, § 3(A)(1) – "Employment Preference" (2004), available at: https://ftbelknap.org/forms%2Fdocuments.

FORT PECK TRIBES COMPREHENSIVE CODE OF JUSTICE, Tit. 13, Ch. 2 – "Tribal Employment Rights Office" (2018), available at: https://fptc.org/comprehensive-code-of-justice-ccoj/.

FORT PECK TRIBES COMPREHENSIVE CODE OF JUSTICE, 13 CCOJ § 401 – "Indian Employment Preference" (2018), available at: https://fptc.org/comprehensive-code-of-justice-ccoj/.

HOOPA VALLEY TRIBAL LAW & ORDER CODE, Tit. 13 – "Employment Rights Ordinance" (2012), available at: https://www.hoopa-nsn.gov/wp-content/uploads/2018/03/Title-13_TERO-Ordinance01052018153037_1.pdf.

JICARILLA APACHE NATION CODE, Tit. 23 – "Indian Preference Contracting and Employment Ordinance" (2010) [NILL Classification No. 007633/2010 d1 v1].

KARUK TRIBE, *Tribal Employment Rights Ordinance and Workforce Protection Act* § 2 – "Administration of TERO Ordinance" (2015), available at: http://www.karuk.us/images/docs/tero/TERO_Ordinance_06-08-15.pdf.

KIOWA TRIBE, *Tribal Employment Rights Office Act of 2018* (2018), available at: https://www.kiowatribe.org/legislative.html.

LAC DU FLAMBEAU TRIBAL CODE, Ch. 45 – "Employment Rights Ordinance" (1986), available at: https://www.ldftribe.com/uploads/files/Court-Ordinances/CHAP45%20Tribal%20Employment%20Rights%20Ordinance.pdf.

LAW AND ORDER CODE OF THE CHIPPEWA CREE INDIANS OF THE ROCKY BOY'S RESERVATION, Trib. Ord. 2-86, *Tribal Employment Rights Commission* (1986), available at: http://indianlaw.mt.gov/cc/codes.

LAWS OF THE CONFEDERATED SALISH & KOOTENAI TRIBES CODIFIED, CSKT Cod. § 4-1-504 – "Indemnification" (2013), available at: http://www.csktribes.org/judicial/cskt-laws-codified.

LEECH LAKE BAND OF OJIBWE, *Tribal Employment Rights Ordinance* (2018), available at: http://www.llojibwe.org/court/tcCodes/tc_title17_TERO.pdf

MASHANTUCKET PEQUOT TRIBAL LAWS, 31 M.P.T.L. § 1 – "Establishment of Mashantucket Employment Rights Office" (2008), available at: http://www.mptnlaw.com/laws/Single/TITLE%2031%20MASHANTUCKET%20EMPLOYMENT%20RIGHTS%20LAW%20(MERO).pdf.

MASHANTUCKET PEQUOT TRIBAL LAWS, 33 M.P.T.L. ch. 1 § 5 – "Preference in Employment" (2008), available at: http://www.mptnlaw.com/laws/Single/TITLE%2028%20RIGHT%20TO%20WORK%20LAW.pdf.

MENOMINEE INDIAN TRIBE OF WISCONSIN CODES, Ch. 170 Art. I – "Employment Preference" (2014), available at: https://www.ecode360.com/11987740.

MILLE LACS BAND STATUTES ANNOTATED, 18 MLBSA § 410 – "Indian Preference in Employment" (2014), available at: http://www.millelacsband.com/content/3-government/17-statutes-policies/mltitle18compractices-revised-5-5-14.pdf.

THE MOHEGAN TRIBE OF INDIANS OF CONNECTICUT CODE OF ORDINANCES, § 4.10 – "Native American Contractor Preference and Certification" (2008), available at: https://library.municode.com/tribes_and_tribal_nations/mohegan_tribe/codes/code_of_laws?nodeId=PTII MOTRINCO_CH4EM_ARTVTREMRI_S4-106NAAMCOPRCE.

MUSCOGEE (CREEK) NATION CODE ANNOTATED, Tit. 37, § 3-203 – "Preference" (2010), available at: http://www.creeksupremecourt.com/wp-content/uploads/title37.pdf.

NAVAJO NATION CODE, 15 N.N.C. § 601 – "Navajo Preference in Employment Act" (2014), available at: http://www.navajonationcouncil.org/Navajo%20Nation%20Codes/V0030.pdf.

NEZ PERCE TRIBAL CODE, § 9-2-1 – "Employment Preference Requirements" (2017), available at: http://nezperce.org/~code/pdf%20convert%20files/2018-04-17%20Nez%20Perce%20Tribal%20Code.pdf.

NISQUALLY TRIBAL CODE, § 42.01 – "Tribal Employment Rights Ordinance" (2013), available at: http://www.nisqually-nsn.gov/files/5014/3637/0366/Title_42_-_Employment_Rights.pdf.

NOTTAWASEPPI HURON BAND OF THE POTAWATOMI TRIBAL CODE, § 5.1-5 – "Indian Preference in Employment; General" (2017), available at: https://ecode360.com/NO3539.

OGLALA SIOUX LAW AND ORDER CODE, Ch. 17, Pt. II.C.1 – "Indian Preference" (2002), available at: https://www.narf.org/nill/codes/oglala_sioux/chapter17-personnel1.html

OMAHA TRIBAL CODE, Tit. 27 § 27-3-1 – "Establishment and Purpose of Commission" (2013), available at: http://omaha-nsn.gov/wp-content/uploads/2013/08/Title-27-Tribal-Employment-Rights.pdf.

ORDINANCES OF THE FALLON PAIUTE-SHOSHONE TRIBE, *Tribal Employment Rights Ordinance*, § 3 – "Indian Preference in Employment" (2018), available at: http://www.fpst.org/tero-program/.

OSAGE NATION CODE, Tit. 19 § 1-104(A) – "Actions Required for Osage Employment Preference" (2014), available at: https://www.osagenation-nsn.gov/who-we-are/congress-legislative-branch/legislation.

PASCUA YAQUI TRIBAL CODE, 8 PYTC § 3-1-10 – "Indian Preference Employment and Training Policy" (2017), available at: http://www.pascuayaqui-nsn.gov/_static_pages/tribalcodes/docs/8_PYTC/3-1_Employment_FINAL.pdf.

POARCH BAND OF CREEKS CODE OF ORDINANCES, § 33-3-3 – "Employment by the Tribe" (2016), available at: https://library.municode.com/tribes_and_tribal_nations/poarch_band_of_creek_indians/codes/code_of_ordinances?nodeId=TIT33TREMRI_CHIIIINPR_S33-3-3EMTR.

PRAIRIE ISLAND INDIAN COMMUNITY, Ord. No. 94-8-16-1, *Equal Employment and Indian Preference Ordinance* (1994), available at: http://prairieisland.org/wp-content/uploads/2018/05/Equal-Employment-and-Indian-Preference-Ordinance.pdf.

PUEBLO OF ACOMA, Res. No. TC-AUG-08-16-Vic, Tribal Employment Rights Office Ordinance (2016), available at: http://dlfelipe.wixsite.com/tero/about.

Pueblo of Laguna Code, § 8-3-1 – "Indian Preference Code" (2018), available at: https://library.municode.com/nm/pueblo_of_laguna/codes/tribal_code?nodeId=TITVIIIHOLATE_CH3INPRCO.

Pueblo of Pojoaque Law & Order Code, Subpart S, S-4 – "Tribal Employment Rights Office Ordinance" (2016), available at: http://pojoaque.org/wp-content/uploads/2016/03/2016-Law-Order-Code-Official.pdf.

Puyallup Tribal Code, § 3.24.030 – "Indian Preference In Employment" (2010), available at: http://www.codepublishing.com/WA/PuyallupTribe/html/PuyallupTribe03/PuyallupTribe0324.html#3.24

Quinault Tribal Code of Laws, Tit. 97 – "Tribal Employment Rights" (2008) [NILL classification No. 008188/2008].

Sac & Fox Tribe of the Mississippi in Iowa Code § 9-1204 – "Indian Preference" (2007), available at: https://www.meskwaki.org/government/tribal-constitution-codes-bylaws/.

Saint Regis Mohawk Tribe, TCR 2016-82, *Resolution of the Saint Regis Mohawk Tribe to Adopt Native American Preference Policy* (2016), available at: https://www.srmt-nsn.gov/_uploads/site_files/20161025083616.pdf.

Sauk-Suiattle Indian Tribe, Ord. No. 11-10-07, *Indian Preference* (2011), available at: http://www.sauk-suiattle.com/Documents/RES%206711%20Indian%20Preference%20Ordinance.pdf.

Sault Ste. Marie Tribe of Chippewa Indians Tribal Code, Ch. 13 – "Affirmative Action Plan" (1995), available at: https://www.saulttribe.com/government/tribal-code.

Seminole Nation of Oklahoma Code, Tit. 11A § 108 – "Indian Preference in Employment" (2016), available at: http://snonsn.gov/Government/GeneralCouncil/CodeofLaws/Seminole%20Nation%20Code%20PDFs%202017%20June%20Update.pdf.

SHOSHONE-PAIUTE TRIBES OF THE DUCK VALLEY RESERVATION, 2004-SPO-02, *Tribal Employment Rights Ordinance* (2004), available at: https://shopaitribes.org/sptero/.

SISSETON-WAHPETON OYATE CODE OF LAWS, § 59-03-01 – "Indian Preference in Employment" (2003), available at: https://www.narf.org/nill/codes/sisseton_wahpeton/Chapter59.pdf.

SNOQUALMIE TRIBAL CODE, STC 5.1 – "Tribal Employment Rights" (2001), available at: http://www.snoqualmietribe.us/sites/default/files/tero.5.1.codified.pdf.

SOUTHERN UTE TRIBAL CODE, Tit. 17 – "Tribal Employment Rights Code" (2017) [NILL Classification No. 008428/2010].

SPIRIT LAKE LAW AND ORDER CODE, § 15-4-101 – "Indian Preference Required" (1999), available at: http://www.spiritlakenation.com/data/upfiles/media/Title_15_Employment_Rights.pdf.

STANDING ROCK SIOUX TRIBAL CODE OF JUSTICE, Tit. 30 Ch. 2 – "Indian Preference In Employment" (2016), available at: https://www.narf.org/nill/codes/standingrocksioux/index.html.

STOCKBRIDGE-MUNSEE TRIBAL LAW, § 54.1 – "Employment Preference Policy Ordinance" (2004), available at: http://www.mohican.com/mt-content/uploads/2015/11/ch-54-employee-preference-policy_563a76f980227.pdf.

SWINOMISH TRIBAL CODE, 14-01.120 – "Employment Preference to be Given" (2017), available at: http://www.swinomish.org/media/4680/1401_tero.pdf.

THREE AFFILIATED TRIBES OF THE FORT BERTHOLD RESERVATION TRIBAL ORDINANCES, Ch. 26 – "Tribal Employment Rights Office Ordinance" (2004) [NILL Classification No. 008529/2004 v1 d1].

TOHONO O'ODHAM CODE, Tit. 13 Ch. 1 – "Tribal Employment Rights" (2014), available at: http://www.tolc-nsn.org/docs/Title13ch1.pdf.

Torres Martinez Desert Cahuilla Indians, Ord. No. TMORD-001-97, *Tribal Employment Rights Ordinance of the Torres Martinez Desert Cahuilla Indians* (2013), available at: http://www.torresmartinez.org/Departments/TERO.aspx.

Tulalip Tribal Codes, Ch. 9.05 – "TERO Code" (2014), available at: http://www.codepublishing.com/WA/Tulalip/.

Turtle Mountain Band of Chippewa Indians Tribal Codes, Tit. 32 – "Tribal Employment Rights Ordinance" (2013), available at: http://www.tmbci.org/data/upfiles/files/TITLE32-TERO-ordinance-updated-aug-20131.pdf.

Ute Mountain Ute Tribe, Res. No. 3101 – "Establishing Tribal Employment Rights Office" (1988) [NILL Classification No. 008627/1988].

Waganakising Odawa Tribal Code of Law, WOTCL 14.109 – "Indian Preference in Hiring, Employment, and Training" (2018), available at: http://www.ltbbodawa-nsn.gov/TribalCode.pdf.

White Mountain Apache Labor Code, Ch. 1 § 1.4 – "Employment Requirements" (2010), available at: http://www.wmat.nsn.us/Legal/Labor%20Code%20-%2009.01.2010.pdf.

Yakama Nation Revised Law and Order Codes, Tit. LXXI – "Tribal Employment Rights Ordinance" (2009) [NILL Classification No. B3137].

Yavapai-Apache Nation Tribal Code, Tit. 22 – "Tribal Employment Rights Office Code" (2013), available at: http://www.yavapai-apache.org/wp-content/uploads/2017/04/Title-22-Tribal-Employment-Rights-Office-Code.pdf.

Yurok Tribal Code, Tit. 5, Div. I, Ch. 5.20 – "Indian Preference in Employment" (2014), available at: https://yurok.tribal.codes/YTC/5.20

INDEX

Affordable Care Act
See United States Affordable Care Act

Age Discrimination Act of 1975
See United States Age Discrimination Act.

Age Discrimination in Employment Act
See United States Age Discrimination in Employment Act.

Americans with Disabilities Act
See United States Americans with Disabilities Act.

At Will Employment
Generally, 227
Contrast with just cause, 227-228

Burden of Proof for Employment Discrimination
Generally, 234
Federal law standards, 230-238
Mixed motive framework, 237
Pretext framework, 237
Prima facie case, 235

California
Gaming compacts with Indian tribes and model employment discrimination law, 220-222
Gaming compacts with Indian tribes and model Tribal Labor Relations Ordinance, 251-255

Civil Rights Act of 1964
See Title VII of the United States Civil Right Act.

Cohen, Felix
Generally, 6-8
Contrast with Dillon Myer, 7
Indian law treatise, 6
Indian Reorganization Act and, 6

Collective Bargaining
See also Jamestown S'Klallam Tribe, Little River Band of Ottawa Indians, Lock-Outs, Mashantucket Pequot Tribal Nation, Mohegan Tribe of Connecticut, National Labor Relations Act, Ohkay Owingeh, Pokagon Band of Pottawatomi Indians, Port Gamble S'Klallam Tribe, Squaxin Island Tribe, Strikes.
Employee rights, 266-268
Employer duties, 268
Foxwoods Casino Resort and agreement under tribal law, 256-257
Impasse procedures in public sector, 270-272
Labor organization duties, 267-268
Laws governing (public and private sectors), 246-248
Picketing, 272-276
Tribal law governing, generally, 248-261
Unfair labor practices and laws governing, 266-269

Due Process
See also Indian Civil Rights Act.
Tribal government employment and, 226-230

Employee Retirement Income Security Act
See United States Employee Retirement Income Security Act.

367

Employment Discrimination
See Burden of Proof for Employment Discrimination, Federal Civil Rights Acts (42 U.S.C. §§ 1981, 1983, 1985), California, Indian Civil Rights Act, Klamath Tribes, Little River Band of Ottawa Indians, Mashantucket Pequot Tribal Nation, Mohegan Tribe of Connecticut, Navajo Nation, Squaxin Island Tribe, Title VII of the Civil Rights Act, Tribal Employment Law, United States Age Discrimination in Employment Act, United States Constitution, and United States Family Medical Leave Act.

Employment Preferences
See Native American Employment Preferences, Tribal Employment Preferences.

Equal Employment Opportunity Commission
See United States Equal Employment Opportunity Commission.

Equal Protection
See Indian Civil Rights Act, United States Constitution.

Exhaustion Doctrine
Generally, 64-68
Application as marker for tribal authority, 69
Arising in employment cases, 69-78

Fair Labor Standards Act
See United States Fair Labor Standards Act.

Family Medical Leave Act
See United States Family Medical Leave Act.

Federal Authority in Indian Country
Conflicting rules when Congress fails to address, 52-63
Congressional silence and application of labor and employment laws to tribes, 52-63, 183-186, 241-246
Exhaustion doctrine and federal courts generally, 64-68
Exhaustion doctrine and labor and employment disputes, 69-78
Sovereign immunity and, 48, 81
Standard for whether tribal law is preempted by federal law, 173-175
Tuscarora dictum, 50-51, 53, 56-57, 61, 174

Federal Civil Rights Acts (42 U.S.C. §§ 1981, 1983, 1985)
Application to Indian tribes and tribal enterprises, 116-121

Federal Indian Policy
Allotment, 3,
Assimilation, 3
Future and, 14-18
Indian New Deal, 4-6
"Indian Problem," 1
Removal, 2
Reservation, 2
Self-Determination, 8-14
Termination, 7-8

Federal Labor and Employment Laws of General Application
See also Fair Labor Standards Act, United States Age Discrimination in Employment Act, United States Employee Retirement Income Security Act, United States Family Medical Leave Act, United States Occupational Safety and Health Act.
Defined, 49, 52,
D.C. Circuit approach to applying to Indian tribes and tribal enterprises, 61-62

Eighth Circuit approach to applying to Indian tribes and tribal enterprises, 58-59
Ninth Circuit approach to applying to Indian tribes and tribal enterprises, 52-55
Second Circuit approach to applying to Indian tribes and tribal enterprises, 55
Seventh Circuit approach to applying to Indian tribes and tribal enterprises, 59-61
Sixth Circuit approach to applying to Indian tribes and tribal enterprises, 55
Tenth Circuit approach to applying to Indian tribes and tribal enterprises, 56-57

Freedom of Speech
See also Mashantucket Pequot Tribal Nation, and Navajo Nation.
Tribal government employment and, 199, 213, 230--234

Indian Civil Rights Act
Generally, 110-111
Due Process, 111, 188, 226-230
Employment rights, 111, 188-189
Equal protection, 111, 189
Freedom of speech, 111, 188, 230-234
Lack of federal court enforcement, 111-112, 189
Mohegan Tribe courts and, 209
Navajo Nation courts and, 194
Search and seizure, 111
Sovereign immunity, 88, 112
Tribal court enforcement, 114-115

Indian Country
Defined, 21

Indian Employment Preferences:
See Native American Employment Preferences, Tribal Employment Preferences.

Indian Gaming
California gaming compacts and model employment discrimination law, 220-221
California gaming compacts and model Tribal Labor Relations Ordinance, 251-255
Employment from, 13
Inherent sovereignty and, 44
Tribal revenues from, 13

Indian Reorganization Act
Generally, 4-5
Corporation charters and sovereign immunity, 99

Indian Self-Determination and Education Assistance Act
Generally, 10-11

Indispensable Party
Dismissal of employment lawsuit when Indian tribe cannot be joined, 291

Jamestown S'Klallam Tribe
Family medical leave law, 186
Unions and collective bargaining law, 261, 272
Wages law, 186

Klamath Tribes
Employment discrimination law, 193
Family medical leave law, 186
Wages law, 186

Labor Organizations
See also Jamestown S'Klallam Tribe, Little River Band of Ottawa Indians, Lock-Outs, Mashantucket Pequot Nation, Mohegan Tribe of Conneciticut, National Labor Relations Act, Pokagon Band of Pottawatomi Indians, Port Gamble S'Klallam Tribe, Squaxin Island Tribe, and Strikes.

Elections of and laws related to, 265-266
Employee rights relative to, 266-267
Laws governing (public and private sectors), 157, 26-248
Licensing under tribal law, 257, 261
Solicitation of employees by and laws related to, 263-264
Tribal law governing, generally, 255-261

Little River Band of Ottawa Indians
Actions against tribal officials under constitution, 213
Fair Employment Practices Code (procedures, remedies), 214-216
Fair Employment Practices Investigator, 214
Law governing labor organizations and collective bargaining, 257-259

Lock-Outs by Employers
See also Strikes
Public sector prohibition when strikes prohibited, 269

Mashantucket Pequot Tribal Nation
Civil Rights Code (procedures, remedies), 202
Due process rights and remedies for employees, 208
Employee Review Code, 205
Freedom of speech, lawsuit by employee, 234
Labor Relations Law, 255-259

Mohegan Tribe of Connecticut
Courts and Indian Civil Rights Act enforcement, 209
Employment discrimination law, 209-213
Unions and collective bargaining law, 262

National Labor Relations Act
Generally, 157
Application to Indian gaming, *Pauma Band of Luiseno Mission Indians* decision, 178-179
Application to Indian gaming, *San Manuel Indian Bingo* decision, 167-172
Application to Indian gaming, *Soaring Eagle Casino Resort* decision, 177-178
Application to Indian tribes and tribal enterprises in general, 158, 161-167
Application to non-governmental employers in Indian country, 248
Not preempting tribal law, *Pueblo San Juan* decision, 173
Preempting tribal law, *Little River Band of Ottawa Indian Tribal Government* decision, 175-176
Treaty rights barrier to application of, *Winstar World Casino decision*, 179-180

National Labor Relations Board
Generally, 157
Assertion of authority over Indian gaming, 167-170, 175-180
Early views on application of NLRA to Indian tribes, 158, 161-167
Position in *Pueblo of San Juan* case, 173
Proceedings against private employers in Indian country, 248
San Manuel Indian Bingo decision, 167-170

Native American Employment Preferences
Bureau of Indian Affairs implementation not race discrimination, 282
Compared to tribal member employment preferences, 279
Defined, 279, 285-286
History of, 279

Inherent tribal sovereignty and, 283-285
Morton v. Mancari decision, 280-283
Political, not racial classification, 282
Political, not nation-origin classification, 293
Private employer exempt from federal discrimination lawsuit for following US approved lease requiring tribal member preference, 295

Native American Housing Assistance and Self-Determination Act
Employment discrimination regulations, 130-132

Navajo Nation
Bill of Rights, 194-199
Freedom of speech and Navajo values, 230-231
Freedom of speech, lawsuit by employee, 198, 230-232
"Just cause" protection for employees, 200-202
Labor Commission, 200
Office of Navajo Labor Relations, 200
Preference in Employment Act, generally, 200-202
Sexual harassment and employment, 197
Sovereign Immunity Act, 195
Sovereign immunity waivers for civil rights claims and insurance coverage, 196

Ohkay Owingeh
Right to Work Law, 247, 250

Occupational Safety and Health Act
See United States Occupational Safety and Health Act.

Official Immunity
See Tribal Sovereign Immunity.

Picketing
See Collective Bargaining.

Port Gamble S'Klallam Tribe
Unions and collective bargaining law, 261-262

Pokagon Band of Pottawatomi Indians
Unions and collective bargaining law, 262

Preemption
See National Labor Relations Act, State Authority in Indian Country.

Public Law 638 Contracts
Antidiscrimination provisions, 130

Rehabilitation Act of 1973
See Section 504 of the United States Rehabilitation Act.

Right-to-Work Laws
Defined, 249
"Fair share" issues and, 274
Ohkay Owingeh law, 173, 247, 250-251
Policy debates about, 275

Secondary Boycotts
See Collective Bargaining.

Section 504 of the United States Rehabilitation Act
Generally, 129-130
Tribal sovereign immunity and, 129

Sovereign Immunity
See Tribal Sovereign Immunity

Squaxin Island Tribe
Employment discrimination law, 193, 217-219
Family medical leave law, 186

Unions and collective bargaining law, 261-262, 272
Wages law, 186

State Authority in Indian Country
Generally, 40-41
Infringement barrier and employment disputes, 45-48
Infringement barrier, generally, 41-43
Overlap of infringement and preemption tests, 45
Preemption barrier, generally, 43-45

Strikes
See also Lock-Outs.
Prohibition of against governments, 269-270
Relationship to employer lock-outs, 269-270
Tribal laws prohibiting, 256, 257, 259, 269, 270

Suquamish Tribe
Employment discrimination law, 193
Family medical leave law, 186
Wages law, 186

Title VII of the United States Civil Rights Act
Generally, 122
Exclusion of Indian tribes, cases, 123-126
Exclusion of Indian tribes generally, 122
Exemption for employers following Native American employment preferences, 289-297
Private employers subject to suit for following tribal member employment preferences, 290

Tribal Employment Rights Ordinances
Generally, 279, 283-285
History and purpose related to Native American employment preferences, 279

Tribal Labor and Employment Laws
See also, Jamestown S'Klallam Tribe, Klamath Tribes, Little River Band of Ottawa Indians, Mashantucket Pequot Tribal Nation, Mohegan Tribe of Connecticut, Pokagon Band of Pottawatomi Indians, Port Gamble S'Klallam Tribe, Squaxin Island Tribe, Suquamish Tribe, Tribal Employment Rights Ordinances.
Generally, 183-186
Legal bases for assertion of authority, 27-37
Importance for workforce stability, 183, 187, 191
Importance for protecting tribal sovereignty, 78, 106, 108, 187-188, 304
Tailored to unique values, 221

Tribal Labor Relations Ordinance
Amended California gaming compacts and revisions to same, 254
California gaming compacts with Indian tribes and model ordinance, 251-254

Tribal Member Employment Preferences
Compared to Native American employment preferences, 279, 285-286
Defined, 279
Equal Employment Opportunity Commission policy position, 288
Federal contractors prohibited from following, 287
Inherent tribal sovereignty and, 283-284
Private employers vulnerable to national origin discrimination lawsuits for following, 288-284
Supported by Indian Self Determination and Education Assistance Act, 286-287

Tribes as indispensable parties to lawsuits challenging, 291

Tribal Sovereignty
Affirmative and defensive, compared, 19, 39
Basis for adjudicatory authority, 36
Basis for labor and employment regulation, 27-37
Basis for tribal member and Native American employment preferences, 283
Congress and, 22-25
Exhaustion doctrine and, 64
Federal interference with, 48-51
Inherent attributes of, 22-27
Montana standards and, 32
Protection against infringement by application of federal law, 48-52
Rules against diminishment, 39-63
Sovereign immunity compared, 39
State interference with, 40-48

Tribal Sovereign Immunity
Generally, 82-85
Arising in employment cases, 87, 89-90, 93-97, 101
As jurisdictional barrier to courts, 82-83
Indian Reorganization Act corporations, 99
Individual capacity and, 86-87
Lawsuits against tribes by federal agencies and, 107, 135
Qualified immunity, 224-225
Tribal enterprises, 90-97
Tribal officials and the *Ex Parte Young* doctrine, 88-90
Tribal officials, generally, 85
Tribal sovereignty compared, 39
Uniformed Services Employment and Reemployment Rights Act and, 155
Waivers and "sue and be sued" clauses, 99-101
Waivers and forum selection clauses, 104-105

Waivers and Indian Civil Rights Act, 114-115, 222-223
Waivers by contract, 98
Waivers, generally, 97-98

Unfair Labor Practices
See Collective Bargaining.

Uniformed Services Employment and Reemployment Rights Act
No waiver of tribal sovereign immunity, 155

Unions
See Labor Organizations.

United States Affordable Care Act
Application to Indian tribes and tribal enterprises, 154

United States Age Discrimination Act
Generally, 129
No waiver of tribal sovereign immuunity, 129-130

United States Age Discrimination in Employment Act
Generally, 121, 126-127
Application to Indian tribes and tribal enterprises, 127-129

United States Americans with Disabilities Act
Generally, 116, 121
Exclusion of Indian tribes, cases, 116, 124, 126
Exclusion of Indian tribes generally, 123

United States Constitution
Employment lawsuits brought under, 223
Equal Protection Clause and lawsuits brought by government employees, 189-190

Fifth Amendment and Native American Employment Preferences, 282

Indian tribes not subject to Bill of Rights and Fourteenth Amendment, 189

Qualified immunity for violations by government officials, 224-225

United States Department of Labor
Suits against Indian tribes and tribal enterprises, 52-55, 59

United States Employee Retirement Income Security Act
Generally, 145
Amendment of and application to Indian tribes and tribal enterprises, 149-154
Pre-amendment application to Indian tribes and tribal enterprises, 147-149

United States Equal Employment Opportunities Commission
Lawsuits against private employers following tribal member employment preferences, 291-296
Suits against Indian tribes and tribal enterprises, 58, 124, 126-128
Policy position on Title VII of the Civil Rights Act and tribal member employment preferences, 288

United States Fair Labor Standards Act
Application to Indian tribes and tribal enterprises, 59, 140-144

United States Family Medical Leave Act
Application to Indian tribes and tribal enterprises, 144-145

United States Occupational Safety and Health Act
Application to Indian tribes and tribal enterprises, 52-54, 56, 136-140,

KAIGHN SMITH, JR., is Of Counsel with Drummond Woodsum. He has been representing Native nations and their enterprises across the country in the federal, state, and tribal courts and before federal administrative agencies for over 25 years. He has garnered a national reputation for his committed advocacy for tribal sovereignty. Based on peer reviews, *Chambers USA* awarded him its highest national ranking for his Native American Law practice, listing him among the top practitioners in the United States. He regularly teaches federal Indian law, most recently at the University of Michigan Law School and Cornell Law School, where he served the Distinguished Practitioner in Residence Fellowship. From 2012 to 2021, he was an Associate Reporter in drafting the *Restatement (Third) of the Law of American Indians*. He published the first edition of *Labor and Employment Law in Indian Country* in 2011.